CONSERVATIVE PARTY GENERAL ELECTION MANIFESTOS 1900–1997

CONSERVATIVE PARTY GENERAL ELECTION MANIFESTOS 1900–1997

Edited by Iain Dale

With an introduction by Alistair B. Cooke

London and New York

First published 2000
by Routledge
2 Park Square, Milton Park, Abingdon, Oxon, OX14 4RN

and Politico's Publishing
8 Artillery Row, Westminster, London SW1P 1RZ

Simultaneously published in the USA and Canada
by Routledge
711 Third Avenue, New York, NY 10017

Routledge is an imprint of the Taylor & Francis Group

First issued in paperback 2013

Transferred to Digital Printing 2008

Typeset in Times by RefineCatch Limited, Bungay, Suffolk

British Library Cataloguing in Publication Data
A catalogue record for this book is available from the British Library

Library of Congress Cataloging in Publication Data
British political party manifestos, 1900–1997 / edited by Iain Dale.
p. cm.
Contents: v. 1. Conservative Party general election manifestos / with an introduction by Alistair B. Cooke – v. 2. Labour Party general election manifestos / with an introduction by Dennis Kavanagh – v. 3. Liberal Party general election manifestos / with an introduction by Duncan Brack.
1. Political parties – Great Britain – Platforms – History – 20th century. 2. Great Britain – Politics and government – 20th century.
I. Dale, Iain.
JN1121.B78 1999
324.241′009′04 – dc21 99–25226
CIP

ISBN13: 978-0-415-20589-4 (hbk)

ISBN13: 978-0-415-85291-3 (pbk)

CONTENTS

CONSERVATIVE MANIFESTOS 1900–1997

In compiling and co-publishing this series of twentieth-century General Election manifestos I am conscious that I owe a great debt to F. W. S. Craig, the doyen of political reference book compilers. Before his untimely death in 1989 Fred Craig had published three separate collections of manifestos, the latest containing all manifestos published between 1959 and 1987. As we enter the new millennium it seems appropriate to continue Craig's work by publishing a three volume series containing all the General Election Manifestos of the three main political parties published during the twentieth century.

It should be noted that the publication of an official party manifesto is a relatively new invention. At the beginning of the century the Party's manifesto normally consisted of a statement of policy issued by the Leader of the Party in his election address to his own constituents. Nowadays it is not quite so simple. Manifestos go through umpteen drafts and are carefully worded to appeal to the maximum number of electors. The pictures selected often tell the voter more than the words.

Since 1950 the various political parties have often issued separate manifestos for Wales and Scotland. Space considerations prevent their reproduction here.

The manifestos in this collection are reproduced verbatim in their original style. There are naturally changes to the textual layout, particularly for latter-day manifestos where the use of pictures is more commonplace.

I would like to thank the Conservative Party for their co-operation in this project and all those Conservative supporters who have been involved in drafting their manifestos down the years. This book is for them.

Iain Dale
Politico's Publishing
London, 1999

THE CONSERVATIVE PARTY AND ITS MANIFESTOS

A personal view

Alistair B. Cooke

General election manifestos are the best-known documents produced by the British political parties, but they have never secured a place in the affections of the British electors for whom they are devised. Few people read manifestos: fewer still applaud them, even in the abbreviated versions which the modern Conservative Party has distributed widely in the (vain) hope of combating indifference (printing them in vast quantities with a blithe disregard for expense). Those who do take manifestos seriously – the leader-writers and the political analysts – are often inclined to be disrespectful: the leading academic assessment of the 1992 election, for example, concluded that the parties' manifestos had 'rarely made less impact'.[1]

That verdict was peculiarly harsh in view of the immense care with which the Tory manifesto had been prepared by John Major's key advisers, despite the fact that the work had been made more difficult for them by a prominent figure at Central Office, the Director of the Conservative Research Department (a once-great institution), who tried late in the day to tamper with the text.[2]

Not even harmony among the experts, however, can ensure that manifestos are invested with grandeur and nobility of expression. They often tend to resemble the speeches delivered by the Queen at the start of each Session of Parliament in that they fail to harness the English language to powerful effect.

There have been a number of notable exceptions (some manifestos indeed have been very well crafted), but the most recent Conservative general election manifesto in 1997 had so few literary pretensions that it could easily have been mistaken for an extremely long internal party briefing document (some 30,000 words in all), poorly executed and overburdened with fact, into which a number of pledges and promises for the future – the things that ought to stand out prominently in any manifesto – had been rather hastily and casually bundled. The overall impression it conveys is one of extreme incoherence.[3]

1997 represented the nadir of the Tory manifesto (as well as of Conservatism itself). The party had come far – indeed much too far – since its first venture in this area, the Tamworth Manifesto of 1834, which Tories still recall, even if they have forgotten all its successors. Through the Tamworth Manifesto, Sir Robert Peel provided a lucid explanation of the manner in which Conservatives would conduct themselves in the new political world created by the 1832 Reform Act. No one reading this comparatively short document could fail to understand how the party intended to approach the chief issues of the time, to which the Manifesto confined itself. Anyone who tries to read the 1997 manifesto is likely to recoil from the surfeit of information on a vast range of issues from job creation to roll on/roll off ferries, and from mental health to the Countryside Stewardship Scheme. It also took the Conservative Party to the literary depths where New Labour has always been happy to reside.

In one sense the 1997 manifesto is plainly untypical. It displays and records with cruel clarity the crippling weaknesses of a particular government: its ill-discipline, its internal confusion and its lack of firm convictions. At the same time, however, the 1997 manifesto exemplifies, in a particularly stark form, the difficulties which always tend to occur when a manifesto is being prepared and which are probably incapable of being resolved with absolute success. Every political issue under the sun has its advocates who clamour for the inclusion of their cause in the manifesto: and Conservative leaders less pliant than John Major have been unwilling to brandish the great Tamworth Manifesto and draw a firm line between questions of overwhelming national significance with which a manifesto should certainly be concerned and other, secondary matters that might usefully be excluded from it. Edward Heath, whom no one has ever accused of being pliant, was a particularly serious offender in admitting issues of the second rank, as the 1966 manifesto shows.

It may be that the inexorable demands of modern British politics simply make it impossible to establish a firm dividing line that would enable the party to produce a really taut, brief manifesto that recaptures exactly the spirit of Tamworth. There will after all always be persistent people who want to know where the Conservative Party stands on roll on/roll off ferries or the Countryside Stewardship Scheme. When brevity was seriously practised in the early part of the century, all it indicated was that the party was not treating its manifestos at all seriously. The best modern manifestos, however, are directly in the Tamworth tradition in that they do not allow their central ideas and proposals to be overwhelmed by a welter of detail. The manifestos of 1950 and 1987, though very different in content, are conspicuous examples of the modern Tamworth.

The excess of political causes seeking inclusion in the modern manifesto is accompanied by an excess of contributors whose submissions do not respond readily to attempts to weave them together seamlessly and impose a uniform (and high) standard upon them. Many fine writers have been called to this task (including Chris Patten and Ferdinand Mount, the current editor of the *Times Literary Supplement*): but none has regarded it as enjoyable and all have found success hard to achieve. Even Churchill had to accept the limitations under which manifesto writers inevitably labour when he intervened in the final stages of the drafting of the 1950 manifesto. He felt that extensive changes were necessary. In the words of Rab Butler, 'he let the whole weight of his mind fall upon the paragraphs prepared, shredding to bits discrepancies or ellipsis'.

But no brilliant Churchillian draft took their place. Conscious of the extreme difficulty of recasting the text himself, he sent Butler off to 'produce a completely revised version without style'.[4] For Churchill of all people to call for a manifesto 'without style' there must indeed exist formidable obstacles to the achievement of powerful and sustained eloquence. However, the really vital requirement is not eloquence but a rather different quality identified by Iain Macleod: 'the unique and exasperating art of presenting the major themes of contemporary politics whilst several voices obtrude several dozen variations of "We must say something about white fish"'.[5] It is essential not to give way unduly to those voices if a manifesto is to emerge in coherent form. Otherwise it becomes no more than a political laundry list – a collection of disparate items assembled without any clear organising principle (of which the 1997 manifesto is the perfect example).

These problems emerged swiftly when the party broke with its nineteenth- and early twentieth-century practice of simply leaving the leader to decide what should be published at the start of a campaign (which invariably up to 1918 meant very little indeed), and whether it should take the form of a personal address or a party document. Lord Salisbury in 1900 thought it sufficient simply to ask for a large majority in order to 'investigate and remove the defects of our military system' exposed by the Boer War, adding as an aside: "to the difficulties which will occupy a future Government China will furnish an abundant contribution' about which he could say nothing because 'the fact that we are acting with other Powers forbids me from entering without reserve upon questions of Chinese policy'.[6] This was certainly no laundry list, but, revealing so little about Tory policy, it was hardly a very satisfactory basis on which to seek a term of Tory government.

Salisbury's immediate successors were scarcely more forthcoming. Balfour in 1906 was entirely silent about Tory policy over which the party was split from top to bottom, and concentrated on predicting difficulties for his opponents which in the event failed to materialise.

The Conservative Party has Neville Chamberlain to thank (though it never acknowledges any of the services he rendered) for providing it with something infinitely more substantial with which to counter the explicit promises of both parties of the left (rising Socialists and declining Liberals) after the First World War. It was Chamberlain who extracted a range of carefully considered and distinctive proposals from the party policy secretariat set up very reluctantly in 1924 by the then leader, Stanley Baldwin, whose interest in policy work was never exactly intense. As a result, in the election that year the party possessed the means, for the first time in its history, of producing a manifesto that contained a reasonably full and coherent political programme (as distinct from a coherent set of basic principles of the kind Peel had provided at Tamworth), even though it was published in the form of a personal election address by the leader, as were subsequent manifestos up to 1945. There was a marked emphasis on social reform which subsequent manifestos were to enlarge still further with regular Disraelian incantations, making 'One Nation' the most wearisomely familiar slogan in the Tory vocabulary. (It is hard not to feel some relief that New Labour has now filched it.)

1924's ground-breaking achievement could be repeated with comparatively little difficulty after 1929 when the party revived its short-lived policy secretariat as a permanent Conservative Research Department under Chamberlain's control. Though a number of very odd, and very lazy, people were to work in the Research Department over the years (some of them appointed with my help), it provided the party with an extraordinarily productive factory for the manufacture of policy documents and briefing material of every kind. With a few exceptions like Enoch Powell, political geniuses with a fund of original ideas did not come to reside there, but by and large its members proved remarkably adept at plundering the products of right-wing thought (though

Hayek aroused no serious interest there until the 1980s) to provide an intellectual backdrop to the practical political activities in which they were engaged.

After the Second World War the Research Department was stuffed with facts, figures, intelligence and shrewdness which enabled the finest of its Directors, David Clarke (1945–50), to give its work real authority, reflected in a series of policy documents which culminated in the 1950 manifesto 'This is the Road'. Churchill may not have been its greatest admirer: but then, like Baldwin in this one respect, he never understood the need for the party to engage in serious policy work at all. Political victories, in his view, were the result of outstanding personal courage and leadership deployed in the national interest: in other words of the qualities which he so signally possessed. 'It was largely in spite of Churchill rather than because of him that the party achieved its remarkable come-back from the 1945 catastrophe.'[7] Though no one would admit it, some of the credit belonged to Neville Chamberlain who invented the modern Tory manifesto and, through his political heir Rab Butler (who in private constantly extolled Chamberlain's virtues), provided the party with a policy supremo who relished the task of working for post-war recovery.

Not the least of the reasons why Butler enjoyed it was that he had at his disposal a successful Chamberlainite organisation, the Conservative Research Department, to fashion the policies on which recovery could be based (not so very different from Chamberlain's in some respects) and express them in effective words in the 1950 manifesto.

Butler's Research Department was the chief repository of the principles which shaped post-war Conservatism: and until those principles were themselves fundamentally recast in the late 1970s it remained the party manifesto's natural custodian. Under successive post-war Conservative governments its leading members would prepare drafts which ministers were then asked to expand by providing details of their future plans; often it turned out that they did not have much to offer.

In May 1959, for example, Macmillan asked all his ministers to give the Research Department information about the action they intended to take in the five years from 1960 ('I am much taken with the idea of a Five-Year Plan,' said Macmillan), but the results were so meagre that those responsible for the manifesto were relieved to discover that an obscure committee had recently produced a policy on leisure which could be put into the manifesto to make it seem more positive, even though there was considerable doubt as to whether the party ought to have such a policy at all.[8]

The appearance of such matters in a manifesto did not trouble Edward Heath when he became party leader. To him it was a case of the more, the merrier. He shrank from the contemplation of political ideas, and gloried in the accumulation of detail. It was natural therefore that his first election manifesto in 1966 should take the form of a political laundry list. Its title, 'Action Not Words', indicated an indifference even to the manner in which its long list of specific commitments was expressed: and the manifesto was indeed singularly deficient in literary merit.

Iain Macleod subsequently criticised it on the grounds that it 'contained 131 specific promises. This was far too much to put across to the electorate, and the net result was that everybody thought we had no policy'. Even Alec Douglas-Home, not a man with a marked penchant for political philosophy, asked 'if "ideas" ought not to be brought into it'.[9]

When in 1970 Heath did produce a manifesto that contained some ideas – radical economic ideas – on which precise commitments to free market policies were based, they turned out unfortunately to be ideas in which he did not actually believe at all with disastrous consequences both for him personally and for the country as a whole.

By contrast, Mrs Thatcher began cautiously: her first manifesto in 1979 was no resounding declaration of Thatcherism. It had its odd features: fishing occupied almost as much space as law and order. In 1983 and 1987, however, she ensured that her manifestos embodied decisive and bold policies that gave unambiguous expression to the free market principles which she had by then clearly defined. The Tamworth Manifesto with its clear declaration of personal convictions was very much in her mind.[10] Where Heath had loved detail, she worked (through endless drafts) to produce manifestos with 'a limited number of radical and striking measures, rather than irritating little clutches of minor ones'.[11] She was in no doubt at all that her last manifesto in 1987 measured up to the highest standards:

> The manifesto was the best ever produced by the Conservative Party. This was not just because it contained far-reaching proposals to reform education, housing, local government finance, trade unions and for more privatization and lower taxes. It was also because the manifesto projected a vision and then arranged the policies in a clear and logical way around it.[12]

Ten years later the vision had been lost. The 'little clutches' of minor measures which had rightly caused her such irritation had returned to infest a Conservative manifesto once again.

It is easy to be impolite about manifestos. Most people are. No one knows the extent to which they affect the outcome of an election. They are difficult to produce. The difficulties, however, only become overwhelming when a party lacks clarity of purpose. That is the chief lesson to be learnt from these Conservative manifestos. But they also contain a second important lesson. They confound the assumption, so beloved of younger writers about the Conservative Party ('the Andrew Roberts school of thought'), that there exists within the party an overwhelming predisposition in favour of economic freedom which naturally takes priority over all else, but which Rab Butler and his contemporaries flagrantly disregarded after 1945, destroying true Conservatism until Mrs Thatcher recreated it. These manifestos show that Disraelian social reform, the protection of property and the maintenance of the authority of the state have all been as prominent amongst the concerns of the Tory Party as economic freedom.

Biographical note

Alistair B. Cooke OBE was Deputy Director of the Conservative Research Department from 1985 to 1997, and Director of the Conservative Political Centre from 1988 to 1997. During that time he edited some 300 pamphlets for the Conservative Party, along with six volumes of its comprehensive record of policy, *The Campaign Guide*, and collections of Margaret Thatcher's and John Major's speeches. He also assisted with the preparation of the 1987 and 1992 general election manifestos.

He is the editor of a collection of essays, 'The Conservative Party: Seven Historical Studies, 1680 to the 1990s' (1997).

Alistair Cooke is now General Secretary of the Independent Schools Council, where his chief task is to safeguard the interests of 1,300 independent schools under the New Labour government.

Notes

1 Quoted in Anthony Seldon, *Major: A Political Life* (Phoenix paperback edition, 1998), p. 285.
2 The tale is told in Sarah Hogg and Jonathan Hill, *Too Close to Call: Power and Politics – John Major in No. 10* (Little, Brown and Company, 1995), pp. 175–82. So meticulous were the preparations that changes to the text to the manifesto continued to be supplied as I sat, in uncongenial company, throughout the whole of one night during the final stages of proof-reading.
3 A small declaration of personal interest needs to be made at this point. The 1997 manifesto was the only one in which I played no part whatsoever during my ten years as the editor of the Party's principal publications (1987–97). That made no significant difference to the content, since my involvement in earlier manifestos had been limited largely to matters of style, lucidity and factual accuracy. But in those areas there was plenty of scope for improvement in the 1997 manifesto which, for example, promised safer ferry services 'through higher standards of survivability'!
4 Quoted in John Ramsden, *The Making of Conservative Party Policy: The Conservative Research Department since 1929* (Longman, 1980), p. 147.
5 Quoted in John Barnes and Richard Cockett, 'The Making of Party Policy', in Anthony Seldon and Stuart Ball (eds), *Conservative Century: The Conservative Party since 1900* (Oxford University Press, 1994), p. 357.
6 See the 1900 Conservative Manifesto below.
7 John Ramsden, *An Appetite for Power: A History of the Conservative Party since 1830* (HarperCollins, 1998), p. 316.
8 Ramsden, *The Making of Conservative Party Policy*, pp. 203–5.
9 Ramsden, *An Appetite for Power*, p. 394
10 Margaret Thatcher, *The Downing Street Years* (HarperCollins, 1993), p. 281.
11 Ibid., p. 570.
12 Ibid., p. 572.

CONSERVATIVE PARTY GENERAL ELECTION MANIFESTO 1900

The manifesto of the Marquess of Salisbury

Date of Election	September 28–October 24
Party Leader	Marquess of Salisbury
Candidates	579
MPs	402
Votes	1,797,444
% of vote	51.1%

On the eve of the dissolution I take the liberty of recalling to your minds the considerations which, in my judgement, should weigh with you in the exercise of your rights as voters during the next few weeks.

The one object you should have in view is to bring about, to the utmost of your power, by the exercise of your vote, the result you desire to attain. This counsel seems a truism; but it is nevertheless tolerably evident that, if the elections fail to produce a Parliament fitted to deal with the emergency of the time, it can only be because the truism is neglected.

In the forecast of competent prophets we are threatened with many abstentions. These abstentions will be due to one of two causes. Either the candidate whom the voter prefers upon broad issues of policy differs from him as to some subordinate question on which he has set his heart, or the voter is convinced that his friend will succeed without his troubling himself to give a vote.

It is obvious that if these causes of abstention operate in a sufficient number of instances they will imperil a considerable number of seats; and no man can know how many of his fellow-electors are disposed, by imitating it, to give to his conduct its natural result.

If they are many the majority of the winning party will be reduced; and it will be so far crippled in carrying out the policy on which the nation has decided. Whose purpose will this result have served?

It is certainly not the result the abstaining voter desires. He will not be one whit nearer his ideals in respect to various sectional objects in regard to which independent electoral combinations have been proposed. On the fate of these questions the election that is pending will have left no trace; and the abstention of the abstaining elector will have been without effect. But on the broad questions of policy the electors abstaining from whatever cause, whether from resentment on a subordinate question or from indolent over-confidence, will have a formidable influence. They will have contributed within the limits of their ability to weaken the Parliamentary force of the Unionist party, and of the Unionist Government to whom power may be entrusted.

The gravest questions must be dealt with. The Imperial Power over the territories of the two South African Republics, which, as events have proved, was unwisely relinquished, must be rebuilt upon durable foundations.

In due time those territories will doubtless enjoy the benignant colonial policy which this country has pursued for half a century, and whose brilliant fruit may be discerned in the affection that so many of our colonies have displayed to the mother country during the recent war.

How long an interval must elapse before the full position of a British colony can be attained by these South African territories will naturally depend on the disposition and conduct of the inhabitants. But we cannot expect to secure the steady submission of those whom we have overcome in the field, unless they see that the Government of the Queen has so much Parliamentary strength that there is no hope of driving it from its policy by persistent resistance or agitation. All the recent troubles of South Africa have come from a shift of Parliamentary opinion at a crucial moment.

The brilliant success of Lord Roberts and his Army must not blind us to the fact that the war has disclosed imperfections in our own armour of defence which, but for it, might have remained unnoticed. It will be among the most urgent duties of Parliament and the Government, now that peace is apparently restored, to investigate and remove the defects our military system in the light of scientific progress and the experience of other Powers. But for such a task a Government will need strong Parliamentary support. Some may think, though I should not agree with them, that the task might be as effectively performed by our opponents, if they possessed an adequate majority and a party organisation capable of sustaining the burden of government. But it certainly could not be discharged by a nearly divided House of Commons and a Ministry depending upon a broken party.

To the difficulties which will occupy a future Government China will furnish an abundant contribution. We have fully shared with other Powers the calamities by which the disturbances in that Empire have been commenced; and we are probably more interested than any other nation in the preservation of the treaty rights which protect our commerce. The fact that we are acting with other Powers forbids me from entering without reserve upon questions of Chinese policy. But in maintaining our own rights, and joining in the efforts of our allies to restore and secure tranquillity, we shall be approaching a task of which it is difficult to overrate the complexity.

I earnestly trust that the electors, in confiding the solution of this and the other problems I have mentioned to the party which is victorious at the polls, will remember that, unless the party is armed with a strong majority in the House of Commons, it will lack the authority at home and abroad which is essential to the performance of its task.

CONSERVATIVE PARTY GENERAL ELECTION MANIFESTO 1906

Mr A. J. Balfour's election address

Date of Election	January 12–February 7
Party Leader	Arthur Balfour
Candidates	574
MPs	157
Votes	2,451,454
% of vote	43.6%

The party with which I am connected, and the Government of which I was a member, after being in power for ten years, have been replaced by the late Opposition. The task the constituencies have now to perform is to choose between them. It should not be a difficult one. So far as we are concerned your information is ample; our legislation, our foreign policy, our Colonial policy, are before you, and they are such as need cause neither shame in us nor regret in you. The same principles on which we have based our actions in the past will serve as their foundation in the future, and in the future as in the past they will promote peace among nations, closer union between different portions of the Empire, and social legislation at home which is not likely to be less beneficient to the community because it is mindful of individual rights.

Your information about the new Government and its supporters is no doubt more limited. You know them chiefly as critics, and it must be owned that their criticism has been singularly unscrupulous – as in the case of Chinese labour – and sometimes singularly perverse – as in the case of the Prime Minister's famous attack on the humanity of our Army. But, after all, we are not restricted in our survey to the performances of his Majesty's present advisers while they were in Opposition. Some of the most distinguished of them have held office before, and as they boast an unrepentant fidelity to the views which they entertained in 1892, we must anticipate a return to the policy they then attempted, but were fortunately too feeble to accomplish. There are many things still obscure in the long catalogue of revolutionary changes advocated by the new Ministers, but some things are plain enough – Home Rule, disestablishment, the destruction of voluntary schools, and the spoliation of the licence-holder have lost none of their ancient charm in the eyes of Radical law-makers, and to the troupe of old acquaintances is now added a procession of shadowy suggestions respecting which we hardly yet know enough to say whether they are dangerous or merely useless.

On one subject only does change, nay, even to hint of change, seem to them abhorrent. With a light heart the Radical leaders are prepared to destroy the Union, to uproot an ancient Church, to banish denominational religion, or even all religion, from the elementary schools. But one thing is sacred, and that is the fiscal practice of this country. The conditions of international trade may alter, the relation of Britain to other industrial communities may be utterly transformed, her Colonies may press for closer commercial union with the mother country – it matters not at all. The fiscal creed of the new Radical is that what was good 60 years ago must not only be good now, but must for ever be incapable of improvement. I take a more conservative view. I believe in the wisdom of adapting our policy, in fiscal matters as in all matters, to the changing conditions of a changing world, and 1 hold that the time has come when such adapting is urgently required. Should you return the Unionist party to power, it is to the reform of our fiscal system that its attention ought first to be directed – a task worthy of the efforts of a great party.

To the foreign policy of the new Government we might seem justified in looking with more satisfaction than to its legislative projects, for apparently it is designed to be a continuation of our own. But, confident as I am of the capacity and patriotism of Sir Edward Grey, I doubt the successor his imitation. A foreign policy which is to be pacific, honourable, and consistent, requires not merely a Foreign Minister of ability, but a Foreign Minister who has two conditions in his favour. The first is a strong defensive naval and military force, without which diplomacy in time of serious stress degenerates either into bluff, or into appeals for mercy, or into a haggle over blackmail. Whether this condition will be fulfilled some recent utterances of the Prime Minister leave me in anxious doubt. But there is a second and not less important condition of success which the new Foreign Secretary cannot hope to secure, and that is the support of a united Cabinet dependent on a United Party. On their legislation the Ministers may have come to some working agreement – time will show – but no agreement on the unforeseen problems of international statesmanship is possible among men who will look at them when they arise from such different points of view as those of the "Little Englander" and the "Liberal Imperialists". But the differences in the Cabinet, serious as in this connexion they cannot fail to be, are nothing compared with the differences which divide the confederation of parties on which the Cabinet depends. In Imperial matters the gulf which divides, say, Mr Perks from Mr Redmond is immeasurable; no formula can conceal it, no compromise can bridge it; and if the new Government survive the general election, and if during their term of office this country becomes involved in international difficulties, the Foreign Secretary may find himself labouring under conditions which are favourable neither to his own fame nor his country's welfare.

Such, in brief outline, are the public grounds on which I venture to recommend my candidature to your favourable consideration. Other grounds there are – ancient friendship, mutual confidence, long habits of loyal co-operation – to which I might make appeal; but if the personal side of the question is to be touched at all, I have, perhaps no right to do more than ask whether, during the 20 years in which you have extended to me an ungrudging support, I have not done political service which may make me not unworthy of your continued confidence.

CONSERVATIVE PARTY GENERAL ELECTION MANIFESTO JANUARY 1910

Mr A. J. Balfour's election address

Date of Election	January 14–February 9
Party Leader	Arthur Balfour
Candidates	600
MPs	273
Votes	3,127,887
% of vote	46.9%

It is understood that Parliament will be dissolved early in 1910; and I shall then solicit the renewal of the confidence which you bestowed on me in such generous measure nearly four years ago. The immediate occasion of the dissolution is the resolution of the House of Lords that the country shall be consulted upon the Budget proposals of 1909. The Budget, therefore, is the subject primarily before the constituencies, and it might have been supposed that the alternative methods of raising the money necessary to meet the obligations of the Treasury would have been the topic most deeply interesting to Government. For motives not difficult to conjecture this does not seem to be the case. It is not the merits of the Budget about which they are concerned; it is that those merits should be submitted to the judgement of the people and (bitterest of all) submitted at the instance of the Upper House. There may be good reasons for their irritation; but assuredly they are not reasons drawn either from the letter or the spirit of the British Constitution; nor are they based on those more general principles of government common to representative institutions in the best types of modern democracy.

The claim of the Government, stripped of the bad history and bad law with which it is obscured, is simplicity itself. They hold that the House of Commons, no matter how elected, or when elected, no matter what its relation to public opinion at the moment, is to be the uncontrolled master of the fortunes of every class in the community; and that to the community itself no appeal, even in the extremest cases, is to be allowed to lie. The question, be it noted, is not whether the Second Chamber may originate money Bills, for that has never been raised; nor whether they may amend money Bills, for that has not been raised; nor raised are three

1 May there not be occasions on which an appeal to the people on matters of finance is necessary?
2 Is not this one of them?

3 If these questions be answered in the affirmative, does any other machinery exist for securing such an appeal than that which has been set in motion by the House of Lords?

In the United States of America it is a fundamental principle of the Constitution that no kind of property shall be prejudiced by special taxation. That Constitution is not easily changed; and before a measure like the British Budget could be legally attempted the consent must be obtained of a two-thirds majority in both Houses, nor could any such measure become law without a national mandate from a still stronger majority of the country.

If we suggest the impossible, and imagine these constitutional safeguards withdrawn, would the American taxpayer even then be reduced to the precarious position of his British brother. Far from it. Special taxation might, indeed, be imposed by the House of Representatives, but it could be rejected by the Senate, it could be vetoed by the President.

I do not ask that the British citizen should enjoy the same security for his property as the citizen of the United States. I am not so immoderate. I only ask that if his property be subjected to exceptional taxation, by the caprice of a Minister and his majority, he should not be deprived of the only methods known to our Constitution by which an appeal to his fellow-countrymen may possibly be secured.

The truth of the matter is that the present attack on the House of Lords is but the culmination of a long-drawn conspiracy. The Government came into office, not to work the Constitution of the country, but to destroy it. They desire what is in effect a single Chamber Legislature. The Second Chamber may be permitted to survive, partly to reassure that amiable and influential class which cares not how much realities are changed so long as names remain the same; partly to correct the legislative slips of the Lower House which, under our existing system, are numerous, and I believe inevitable. But they desire that for all important purposes the Constitution of Britain shall be as definitely a single Chamber Constitution as the Constitution of Guatemala. For this end they have continuously laboured. It is this policy which represents the solitary thread of consistency connecting the wayward legislative projects of the last four years.

I have watched with interest the progress of this conspiracy. Its results must so far have disappointed the conspirators. On no single occasion when Bills have been rejected by the Upper House or abandoned in the Lower on the alleged grounds that they had been mutilated by the Lords, has the rising tide of the Ministerial unpopularity shown the slightest pause or check. Then came the Budget; and with it the opportunity of manoeuvring the House of Lords into the position of either abandoning its functions as a Second Chamber or of taking action which might give new life and hope to the contrivers of the single Chamber plot.

The scheme was ingenious. I do not think it is proving successful. The people of this country are not insulted by having their opinion asked on the Budget, nor do they think that the House of Lords has gone beyond their duty in asking for it. And they are surely right. For the single Chamber system is not consistent with the democratic working of representative Government in complex and developing communities. The representative Assembly is no doubt the primary organ of the popular will, and it possesses powers in this country which it certainly does not possess either in the Republic of America or in the Republic of France. It determines without appeal the political complexion of the Government. It controls all the Estimates. In initiates all the taxes. In legislation it is the dominating partner. The Ministers who direct, and sometimes tyrannize over, its deliberations, are nevertheless its creatures; and while no vote of the House of Lords could reduce the salary of an Under Secretary by a shilling, the most powerful Cabinet must bow to the House of Commons.

These are great powers; in some respects they are, I believe, without example. But they do not satisfy the single Chamber conspirators. And why? Because they wish the House of Commons to be independent, not merely of the Peers, but of the people.

Nor would there be grave objection to this if there was any security that the action of the elected embodied on all great and far-reaching issues the deliberate will of the electors. But there is not and cannot be any such security. It is only by a transparent convention that we can, for example, assume that a House of Commons returned on the cry of Chinese slavery represents the mind of the nation on the question of Socialism. And the convention, which is convenient and in many respects even necessary, becomes not merely absurd, but perilous, when it is applied to questions of fundamental importance, which have been but imperfectly discussed, which are perhaps but imperfectly understood, which deeply affect individual rights and social well-being.

In such cases there should be an appeal from the people's representatives to the people themselves; and no machinery, however imperfect, for securing this end should be abandoned until a better has been devised.

In any case the single Chamber system is impossible. And it is as impossible in the region of finance as in any other. If finance meant in 1909 what it used to mean in earlier days, the question would be unimportant. But directly the need for money is used by a Government as an excuse for adopting the first instalment of a Socialist Budget, for treating property not according to its amount, but according to its origin, and for the vindictive attack on political opponents, then the people have a right to be consulted; and that right could never have been exercised had the Peers not used on behalf of the people the powers entrusted to them by the Constitution.

If you ask me whether this constitutional machinery could not be improved, either by some change in the composition of the House of Lords, or by the institution of a Referendum, I am certainly not going even to suggest a negative reply. The House of Lords as at present constituted contains, I suppose, more men of first-class eminence in the business of law, of arms, of literature, of science, and of finance, more men who have held great administrative posts overseas, more men in daily touch with local business than does the House of Commons. Its debates on great occasions (for reasons in no way derogatory to the Chamber in which I hope to spend all the working days of my political life) are on a more even level of excellence. Nor would it, I think, be wise to turn it into a second and rival House of Commons and make it completely elective. But this does not mean that, even for its comparatively subordinate, though all-important, constitutional functions, it cannot be improved. Nor is any such opinion held by its most distinguished members.

But schemes of reform, however desirable, are but remotely connected with the present issue. It is not so much the privileges of the Lords which are threatened by the single Chamber plot, as the rights of the people. It is in their interests that the plot must be defeated.

On the Budget itself I have already said so much elsewhere, that I need say little now. I am interested in it chiefly as it affects security, and through security the prosperity of the country and the employment of its people. For here it touches the problems, or rather groups of problems, which lie at the very heart and centre of social well-being.

I say groups of problems because unemployment is not a single disease, nor can it be dealt with by a single remedy. It is as complex in its causes as it is tragic in its results. A man may be unemployable through inherited defects of body or mind, through evil training and surroundings, through illness, accident, or age, through the slow deterioration which too often creeps over those who have wasted hope and courage, not in the endeavour to do something, but in the baffled search for something to do.

Again, a man though employable may be unemployed, either because he and some willing employer do not get into touch, or because there is no demand for the kind of work he is qualified to perform.

This brief statement is, of course, incomplete; but even as it stands it shows how complicated is the social problem before us. It has long been evident that it cannot be solved through the machinery of the existing Poor Law. Since the Commission appointed by the late Government have reported, it has become plain that the Poor Law machinery cannot even aid in its solution. For every member of that Commission, Unionist and Radical, official and unofficial, Individualist and Socialist, agreed, after exhaustive inquiries, that the machinery of the Poor Law must be 'scrapped'.

The task thus imposed upon us must be faced. But it is difficult, and in some respects perilous. The sentimentalist and the doctrinaire, the man who thinks that other people's misfortunes are part of an appointed order requiring on his part the exercise of no virtue but resignation; the enthusiast who is prepared to tax two men out of employment in order to compensate one man for being unemployed – all these represent types of criticism which in an unfavourable hour, may prove formidable to the best considered schemes. In truth, this great and pressing reform requires caution as well as courage. If we succeed, the amount of suffering which may be cured or prevented is beyond computation. If we fail (but I think we shall not), we may end by increasing the very ills we desire to remedy.

It is important, however, to observe that State-organised methods of dealing with destitution, either by way of prevention or cure, can do little directly to promote the market demand for labour. They may add to the labour supply – as by turning the unemployable into the employable. They may render the supply more available – as by the establishment of labour exchanges. They may increase the number of workmen seeking for employers, but they will not increase the numbers of employers seeking for workmen. Yet, surely, this is at least as important an object as is the other. If the wise and humane treatment of those who cannot support themselves belong to social pathology, the encouragement of enterprise belongs to social hygiene. And how from this point of view do the fiscal policies compare of Government and Opposition?

The Budget, now waiting the sentence of the people, seems designed of set purpose to make every man who has invested his money in this country consider how he can remove it, and every man who is hesitating where to invest it, determine to invest it abroad. The super-tax frightens some, the new death duties cripple others, and worse than all, the origin of the proposals and the principles on which they have been defended, show clearly how thin is the dividing line which separates the policy of the Government from that of the avowed Socialists.

Such is, and must be, the effect of the Budget and Budget speeches on the mind of the investor. Very different are the results I anticipate from Tariff Reform.

There are those who regard it as a paradox to say that Tariff Reform will stimulate home industry. It seems to me a truism. Only by Tariff Reform can you hope to retain colonial preference; only by Tariff Reform can you hope to modify commercial treaties in your favour. Only by Tariff Reform can you secure from unfair competition the home producer in the home market. It will do him no injury in neutral markets, it may give him valuable aid in protected markets. Is it credible, then, that it will not keep capital here that would otherwise go abroad? Is it credible that, if it does, the demand for labour will not increase?

On other aspects of Tariff Reform I will here say nothing. The very fact that it is the first 'plank' in the Unionist programme has prevented it ever receiving less than its due need of attention, whether from friends or foes.

But some observation on land I must make; for on the subject of land no absurdity in argument, and no folly in legislation, seems wholly ruled out of court.

The Government began their career by loudly proclaiming the doctrine known as 'Back to the land'. It might have been supposed, in these circumstances, that they would have done their best to make the position of the small cultivator as attractive as possible. Not at all. The life of the small cultivator living solely on his holding is often a hard one – harder often than that of the agricultural labourer. He is not within easy reach of the urban amusements which attract so many, and in our climate the risks of weather can neither be forgotten nor escaped. These are disadvantages. But there is one great advantage which his urban brother rarely possesses to the same degree – the advantage of ownership. The hope of this may bring him to the land. The enjoyment of it may keep him there. But it is just this that the Government in their wisdom refuse to give him. They have some vague idea that private ownership in land is a thing to be discouraged. They do not, I gather, think it criminal, like Henry George. They do not argue, like the land nationalists, that since 'the earth is the Lord's' therefore its rents should go to the Chancellor of the Exchequer. But they do apparently think ownership a little discreditable except in the case of the Irish farmer. To make him a proprietor, British credit may, indeed, be lavishly employed. But a different policy is good enough for Britain. Here the possession of land is treated almost as an abuse. Those who indulge in it shall be made to pay: and nothing shall be done to increase their number.

This being, so far as I can make out, their view, they insist that the small holders should be tenants and (in England at least) tenants of a public body. Now there is not a farmer of sense in the whole of Great Britain who would not rather be a tenant of Mr Lloyd George's favourite duke than of any public authority from Caithness to Cornwall. Their whole way of looking at the problem is illogical and absurd. If it be desirable that money should be spent on the land with slight hopes of profit, property in land should not be talked of as an abuse. If it be desirable that small cultivators should give long hours of toil to the development of their holdings, the reward of possession should be within their reach.

In this address I am compelled to restrict myself to broad constitutional issues and certain great social and financial problems. I am thus perforce constrained to be silent about the Navy, but this is of the less importance, as I have spoken more than once in the City upon this great theme since the perilous position of the country first became evident earlier in the year. The situation remains grave and the future is anxious. I do not think the public will readily forget or forgive the lamentable negligence which so dangerously encouraged the very rivalry in shipbuilding which they have so often and, I doubt not, so sincerely deplored.

Here, then, I close what is not and cannot be more than an indication of certain important portions of the policy which I trust our party will pursue. To maintain the Empire, the Union and the Constitution, these are among the traditional obligations of the party which gain rather than lose in force as time goes on. But we have more to do than merely to preserve what we have received. The world moves, new conditions arise, problems of Empire, problems of trade, problems of national finance, problems of national defence, problems of social amelioration meet us in forms not dreamed of a few years since. They must be solved each in its own appropriate way. But, diverse as they are, it will, I think, be found that no substantial advance can be made towards the solution of any one of them, till a change of Government takes place, and a party is returned to office prepared to press through to the utmost of its powers the policy of Tariff Reform.

CONSERVATIVE PARTY GENERAL ELECTION MANIFESTO DECEMBER 1910

Mr A. J. Balfour's election address

Date of Election	December 2–December 19
Party Leader	Arthur Balfour
Candidates	550
MPs	272
Votes	2,420,566
% of vote	46.3%

In less than a year since the last General Election the Government has resolved again to appeal to the country. They have selected the season at which the register least accurately represents the constituencies, and which is most inconvenient to trade; and have done so without the excuse of a Parliamentary defeat in either House, and with no visible breach in the strange coalition of parties which keeps them in office.

It is in these circumstances that I ask you for the third time to honour me with your suffrages. I have little to add to the detailed statement of my views, which I sent to every elector for the City of London last December. Now, as then, Tariff Reform, National Defence, the wider extension of freehold ownership, Poor Law and other social reforms, are vital parts of the programme, to which the party with which I am connected stands pledged. Now, as then, we are resolved that the party of revolution shall not, under the thin disguise of an attack on the Upper House, impair the liberties of the people. Our principles on this last subject are plain, and we share them with all the great men who have helped to develop our Constitution, or have been concerned in framing free institutions for self-governing communities beyond the limits of these islands. Nor would the Ministry, even in the Parliament now drawing to a close, have obtained serious support for their destructive policy were it not forced upon them by their Socialist and Nationalist allies. It is because both Nationalists and Socialists are aware that their darling projects are not in harmony with the considered will of the people that they press for the abolition of the only Constitutional safeguard which at critical moments will enable that will to prevail.

Behind the Single Chamber conspiracy lurk Socialism and Home Rule. The alternative scheme of Reform which we desire to see adopted has, in spite of the Government, now been brought to the notice of the country. It is true that a full Parliamentary discussion of it has been made impossible by the date selected for the Dissolution. It is also true that in consequence the constituencies have not enjoyed that assistance in judging of its merits which they had a right to demand. Yet I cannot doubt that if they fairly survey the constructive programme which the Unionist Party offers them – fiscal, social, Imperial, and Constitutional – they will feel that on these lines, and on these lines only, is ordered progress possible.

THE COALITION GENERAL ELECTION MANIFESTO 1918

The manifesto of Mr Lloyd George and Mr Bonar Law

Date of Election	Saturday 14 December
Party Leader	Andrew Bonar Law
Candidates	374 Coalition Conservatives, 37 Conservatives
MPs	335 Coalition Conservatives, 23 Conservatives
Votes	3,504,198 Coalition Conservatives, 370,375 Conservatives
% of vote	32.6% Coalition Conservatives, 3.4% Conservatives

The Coalition Government, supported by the strenuous and united labours of the whole nation, has now accomplished the gravest portion of its task. Our enemies have been defeated in the field, their armies are broken, and their Governments are overturned. Thanks to the patient valour of the hosts of freedom, the knell of military autocracy has sounded forever in the Continent of Europe. Other tasks directly arising out of the war now await our nation, and can only be surmounted by the good sense, the patriotism, and the forbearance of our people. The unity of the nation which has been the great secret of our strength in war must not be relaxed if the many anxious problems which the war has bequeathed to us are to be handled with the insight, courage, and promptitude which the times demand.

As a preliminary to the solution of these problems it is essential that a fresh Parliament should be summoned, possessed of the authority which a General Election alone can give it, to make the peace of Europe and to deal with the difficult transitional period which will follow the cessation of hostilities. Indeed, the present Parliament has long outstayed its appointed term, and meanwhile millions of new voters, including for the first time representatives of the womanhood of the country, have been added to the electorate. It is right that the Government, upon whom it devolves in conjunction with our Dominions and our allies to settle the political future of Europe, should be supported by the confidence of the vast body of newly enfranchised citizens.

We appeal, then, to every section of the electorate, without distinction of party, to support the Coalition Government in the execution of a policy devised in the interests of no particular class or section, but, so far as our light serves us, for the furtherance of the general good. Our first task must be to conclude a just and lasting peace, and so to establish the foundations of a new Europe that occasion for further wars may be for ever averted. The brilliant and conclusive triumph of the Allied Armies will, we hope, render it possible to reduce the burden of our armaments and to release by successive and progressive stages the labour and capital of the Empire for the arts of peace. To avert a repetition of the horrors of war, which are aggravated by the onward march of science, it will be the earnest endeavour of the Coalition Government to promote the formation of a League of Nations, which may serve not only to ensure society against the calamitous results of militarism but to further a fruitful mutual understanding between the associated peoples. Never have the men and women of our race played so great and commanding a part in the affairs of the whole world as during the tempests and trials of this great war, and never has the British name been so widely honoured.

The care of the soldiers and sailors, officers and men, whose heroism has won for us this great deliverance, and who return to civil life, is a primary obligation of patriotism, and the Government will endeavour to assist such members of the armed forces of the Crown as may desire to avail themselves of facilities for special industrial training and to return to civil life under conditions worthy of their services to the country. Plans have been prepared, and will be put into execution as soon as the new Parliament assembles, whereby it will be the duty of public authorities and, if necessary, of the State itself to acquire land on simple and economical basis for men who have served in the war, either for cottages with gardens, allotments, or small holdings as the applicants may desire and be suited for, with grants provided to assist in training and initial equipment. In addition to this, we intend to secure and to promote the further development and cultivation of allotments and small holdings generally so far as may be required in the public interest.

Increased production must necessarily be the basis of all schemes for the improvement the conditions of the people. The war has revealed the extent to which the resources of the country have been dissipated and depressed by lack of organisation or by wasteful organisation. It has been demonstrated that the land of the country, if properly cultivated and used, could have yielded food and other products of the soil to a much larger extent. It must be among the first tasks of the new Government to repair this error, which added so much to our difficulties in our struggles against the submarines of the enemy.

The war has given a fresh impetus to agriculture. This must not be allowed to expire. Scientific farming must be promoted, and the Government regard the maintenance of a satisfactory agricultural wage, the improvement of village life, and the development of rural industries as essential parts of an agricultural policy. Arrangements have been made whereby extensive afforestation and reclamation schemes may be entered upon without delay. A systematic improvement in the transport facilities of the agricultural areas must form an essential part of every scheme for the development of the resources of the soil, and the Government are preparing plans with a view to increasing these facilities on a large scale.

The principal concern of every Government is and must be the condition of the great mass of the people who live by manual toil. The steadfast spirit of our workers, displayed on all the wide field of action opened out by the war – in the trenches, on the ocean, in the air, in field, mine, and factory – has left an imperishable mark on the heart and conscience of the nation. One of the first tasks of the Government will be to deal on broad and comprehensive lines with the housing of the people, which during the war has fallen so sadly into arrears, and upon which the well-being of the nation so largely depends. Larger opportunities for education, improved material conditions, and the prevention of degrading standards of employment; a proper adaptation to peace conditions of the experience which during the war we have gained in regard to the traffic in drink – these are among the conditions of social harmony which we shall earnestly endeavour to promote. It will be the fundamental object of the Coalition to promote the unity and development of our Empire and of the nations of which it is composed, to preserve for them the position and influence and authority which they have gained by their sacrifices and efforts in the cause of human liberty and progress, and to bring into being such conditions of living for the inhabitants of the British Isles as will secure plenty and opportunity to all.

Until the country has returned to normal industrial conditions it would be premature to prescribe a fiscal policy intended for permanence. We must endeavour to reduce the war debt in such a manner as may inflict the least injury to industry and credit. The country will need all the food, all the raw materials, and all the credit which it can obtain, and fresh taxes ought not to be imposed on food or upon the raw materials of our industry. At the same time a preference will be given to our Colonies upon existing duties and upon any duties which, for our own purpose, may be subsequently imposed. One of the lessons which has been most clearly taught us by the war is the danger to the nation of being dependent upon other countries for vital supplies on which the life of the nation may depend. It is the intention therefore of the Government to preserve and maintain where necessary these key industries in the way which experience and examination may prove to be best adapted for the purpose. If production is to be maintained at the highest limit at home, security must be given against the unfair competition to which our industries may be subjected by the dumping of goods produced abroad and sold on our market below the actual cost of production. The military institutions of the country must necessarily be dependent upon the needs of the Empire and the prospective requirements of any League for the preservation of peace to which this country may hereafter be a party. Meanwhile it will be the aim of the Government to carry through the inevitable reductions in our military and naval establishments with the least possible suffering to individuals and to the best advantage of industry and trade.

Active measures will be needed to secure employment for the workers of the country. Industry will rightly claim to be liberated at the earliest possible moment from Government control. By the development and control in the best interests of the State of the economical production of power and light, of the railways and the means of communication, by the improvement of the Consular Service, and by the establishment of regular machinery for consultation with representative trade and industrial organisations on matters affecting their interest and prosperity, output will be increased, new markets opened out, and great economies effected in industrial production.

It will be the duty of the new Government to remove all existing inequalities of the law as between men and women.

It has been recognised by all parties that reform is urgently required in the constitution of the House of Lords, and it will be one of the objects of the Government to create a Second Chamber which will be based upon direct contact with the people, and will therefore be representative enough adequately to perform its functions.

The people of this country are not unmindful of the conspicuous services rendered by the Princes and people of India to the common cause of civilisation during the war. The Cabinet has already defined in unmistakable language the goal of British policy in India to be the development of responsible government by gradual stages. To the general terms of that declaration we adhere and propose to give effect.

Ireland is unhappily rent by contending forces, and the main body of Irish opinion has seldom been more inflamed or less disposed to compromise than it is at the present moment. So long as the Irish question remains unsettled there can be no political peace either in the United Kingdom or in the Empire, and we regard it as one of the first obligations of British statesmanship to explore all practical paths towards the settlement of this grave and difficult question on the basis of self-government. But there are two paths which are closed – the one leading to a complete severance of Ireland from the British Empire, and the other to the forcible submission of the six counties of Ulster to a Home Rule Parliament against their will. In imposing these two limitations we are only acting in accordance with the declared views of all English political leaders.

It is a source of pride to be of this age, and to be members of this nation. In the whole course of the world's history no generation has been compelled to face sacrifices such as we have steadfastly endured, or perils such as we have victoriously confronted. Well and truly have rich and poor, castle and cottage, stood the ordeal of fire. Right earnestly do we trust that the united temper, the quiet fortitude, the high and resolute patriotism of our nation may be long preserved into the golden times of peace.

CONSERVATIVE PARTY GENERAL ELECTION MANIFESTO 1922

Mr Bonar Law's election address

Date of Election	Wednesday 15 November
Party Leader	Andrew Bonar Law
Candidates	483
MPs	345
Votes	5,500,382
% of vote	38.2%

His Majesty has been graciously pleased to appoint me First Minister of the Crown. I appeal to you to renew your confidence in myself as your representative, and to give your support to the new Government of which I am the head. The crisis which has arisen so suddenly has made it absolutely necessary that an immediate appeal should be made to the people, and in consequence it has been impossible to have an examination with my colleagues into the many questions with which we have to deal. Of necessity, therefore, the outlines of policy which I now submit to you cannot be as definite and precise as in other circumstances would have been possible.

The crying need of the nation at this moment – a need which in my judgement far exceeds any other – is that we should have tranquillity and stability both at home and abroad so that free scope should be given to the initiative and enterprise of our citizens, for it is in that way far more than by any action of the Government that we can hope to recover from the economic and social results of the war.

With this in view I think it is of the utmost importance that we should return as quickly as possible, and as completely as possible, to the normal procedure which existed before the war. In pursuance of this aim I am satisfied that the time has now come when a change should be made in the machinery of the central Government. Some of the work which has hitherto been done by the Cabinet Secretariat is essential and must be continued, but we intend to bring that body in its present form to an end, and I am certain that the necessary work can be continued, and the invaluable services of the present Secretary retained, in connection with the Treasury, which in the past has always been the central department of Government. As an illustration of the changes which we contemplate, instructions have been already given to transfer to the Foreign Office the machinery of the League of Nations, and in the same way to arrange, as regards any future International Conferences, that even where it is necessary that I as Prime Minister should be present, the machinery of the Conferences and the preliminary work in connection with them will be performed not by the Cabinet Secretariat but by the Foreign Office itself.

At the present moment the first foreign interest not alone of Great Britain and of the British Empire, but of the world, is the re-establishment of peace. In all our foreign relations we intend to pursue an even course, loyally fulfilling the obligations we have undertaken, but resolutely determined not to extend our commitments, and should reasonable occasion arise to curtail them. It was by wholehearted co-operation, often under great difficulty, and with great differences of opinion, that we won the war. It is only by the same frank and full co-operation, conducted in the same spirit, with France and our other great Allies, that we can hope to solve the difficult problems with which we are now confronted. It is my confident hope that under the well-tried guidance of the Secretary of State for Foreign Affairs the negotiations for the settlement of the Near Eastern crisis will result in a true and lasting peace, conducing both to the political tranquillity of the Near and Middle East, with which so many of our Imperial interests are bound up, and to the personal security and happiness of the inhabitants of all races and creeds in the regions which have been the scene of so much disturbance and suffering.

During the war the feeling supreme in the minds of men and women throughout the world was that a similar calamity should never again be allowed to fall upon mankind. It was to meet this feeling that the League of Nations was instituted, and it will be our earnest aim to give it wholehearted and practical support. The maintenance of our friendship and good understanding with the United States, based not on any formal alliance but on community of inherited ideals as well as on recent comradeship in arms, must always be a principal aim of British policy. Above all, we mean, in all matters affecting the external policy or security of the Empire, to act in close and continuous consultation with the Governments of the Dominions and of India in order to ensure that our policy shall keep fully in view both the interests and sentiments of our fellow subjects overseas, and at all times have behind it the moral support of the whole British Commonwealth.

Our first task, if returned to power, will be the ratification of the Irish Treaty. We are prepared to take our part in making good that Treaty, both in the letter and in the spirit, and to co-operate with the Irish Government in the new relationship within the Empire which the Treaty will have created. We are equally pledged to safeguard the freedom of choice and the security of the Parliament and Government of Northern Ireland. We earnestly hope that further progress will be made in dealing with the anarchy in the South, and that both in the North and in the South it will be realised that the prosperity of Ireland as a whole can only be achieved by good will between the Governments and peoples of the two portions of that country. The position of the innocent victims of recent disturbances is a matter of the gravest concern to the people of this country, and it will be the duty of the Government to keep in the closest touch with the Government of the Irish Free State on this matter, so that just claims for compensation may have sympathetic consideration.

We desire to promote the quiet and orderly development of India under the constitution which was conferred on her by the Act of 1919. The co-operation of all classes and sections is essential to the progress and prosperity of India, and, if this be secured, we can look forward with confidence to an industrial development which will add to her resources and give increased stability to her economic structure.

At home our chief preoccupation at this time is the state of trade and employment. The immediate problem of unemployment this winter will call for emergency measures.

Plans for dealing with the situation have already been considered by the late Government. They will be examined afresh by us with a view of seeing whether any improvements are possible, and the necessary steps will then be taken with the least avoidable delay. Such remedies, however, can only be palliatives, and the real recovery will not come except from the revival of trade and industry. To secure this result, the first essential is to reduce expenditure to the lowest attainable level in the hope that the taxpayer may find some relief from the burden of taxation which not only presses so heavily upon individuals, but is the greatest clog upon the wheels of national industry.

Every Candidate, in every constituency, will, as I do, make retrenchment an essential part of his programme. All that I can possibly say, knowing how great are the difficulties, is that we should do our best to secure it. It will also be our endeavour in any way in our power to help trade, and the method of doing this, which seems to me most helpful, is the development of trade within the Empire itself. The markets, which for the time at least, as a consequence of the war, we have lost in Europe, can best be replaced by further development of trade with overseas countries, and especially of trade within the British Empire. We propose, therefore, immediately to consult the Governments of the self-governing Dominions and, if they approve, to summon, as early as possible, an Economic Conference with the view of finding in what way by mutual co-operation we can best develop the vast trade of which, in my opinion, the resources of the Empire admit.

There is one branch of industry to which I must specially refer. As a consequence of the war, agriculture, the greatest of our national industries, is in a most serious condition, and demands the practical sympathy of the Government. It is not easy to specify the exact method by which that sympathy can be shown, but we shall immediately examine the whole problem afresh in the hope of making proposals which will assist the agricultural community to overcome the difficulties that now confront them.

There are many measures of legislative and administrative importance which, in themselves, would be desirable, and which, in other circumstances, I should have recommended to the immediate attention of the electorate. But I do not feel that they can, at this moment, claim precedence over the nation's first need, which is, in every walk of life, to get on with its own work with the minimum of interference at home and of disturbance abroad.

CONSERVATIVE PARTY GENERAL ELECTION MANIFESTO 1923

Mr Stanley Baldwin's election address

Date of Election	Thursday 6 December
Party Leader	Stanley Baldwin
Candidates	540
MPs	258
Votes	5,538,824
% of vote	38.1%

In submitting myself to you for re-election, I propose frankly to put before you the present situation as I see it, and the measures which in the opinion of myself and my colleagues are necessary adequately to deal with it.

1 The unemployment and under-employment which our working people and our great national industries are now facing for the fourth winter in succession, on a scale unparalleled in our history, have created a problem which calls urgently for a solution. Their indefinite continuance threatens to impair permanently the trained skill and the independent spirit of our workers, to disorganise the whole fabric of industry and credit, and, by eating away the sources of revenue, to undermine the very foundations of our national and municipal life.

2 In large measure this state of affairs is due to the political and economic disorganisation of Europe consequent on the Great War. In accordance with the policy affirmed by the Imperial Conference we shall continue to devote every effort through the League of Nations and by every other practical means, to the restoration of a true peace in Europe. But that at the best must take time. A year ago Mr Bonar Law could still hope that a more settled condition of affairs was in prospect, and that with it trade might enjoy a substantial and steady revival, even in the absence of any modification of fiscal policy, of the ultimate necessity of which he himself was always convinced. Since the occupation of the Ruhr it has become evident that we are confronted by a situation which, even if it does not become worse, is not likely to be normal for years to come.

3 The disorganisation and poverty of Europe, accompanied by broken exchanges and by higher tariffs all the world over, have directly and indirectly narrowed the whole field of our foreign trade. In our own home market the bounty given to the importation of foreign goods by depreciated currencies, and by the reduced standard of living in many European countries, has exposed us to a competition which

is essentially unfair and is paralysing enterprise and initiative. It is under such conditions that we have to find work for a population which, largely owing to the cessation during the war period of the normal flow of migration to the Dominions, has in the last census period increased by over a million and three quarter souls.

4 No Government with any sense of responsibility could continue to sit with tied hands watching the unequal struggle of our industries or content itself with palliatives which, valuable as they are to mitigate the hardship to individuals, must inevitably add to the burden of rates and taxes and thereby still further weaken our whole economic structure. Drastic measures have become necessary for dealing with present conditions as long as they continue.

5 The present Government hold themselves pledged by Mr Bonar Law not to make any fundamental change in the fiscal system of the country without consulting the electorate. Convinced, as I am, that only by such a change can a remedy be found, and that no partial measures such as the extension of the Safeguarding of Industries Act, can meet the situation, I am in honour bound to ask the people to release us from this pledge without further prejudicing the situation by any delay. That is the reason, and the only reason, which has made this election necessary.

6 What we propose to do for the assistance of employment in industry, if the nation approves, is to impose duties on imported manufactured goods, with the following objects: –

i to raise revenue by methods less unfair to our own home production which at present bears the whole burden of local and national taxation, including the cost of relieving unemployment;
ii to give special assistance to industries which are suffering under unfair foreign competition;
iii to utilise these duties in order to negotiate for a reduction of foreign tariffs in those directions which would most benefit our export trade;
iv to give substantial preference to the Empire on the whole range of our duties with a view to promoting the continued extension of the principle of mutual preference which has already done so much for the expansion of our trade, and the development, in co-operation with the other Governments of the Empire, of the boundless resources of our common heritage.

7 Such a policy will defend our industries during the present emergency and will enable us, as more normal conditions return, to work effectively to secure a greater measure of real Free Trade both within the Empire and with foreign countries. Trade which is subject to the arbitrary interference of every foreign tariff, and at the mercy of every disturbance arising from the distractions of Europe, is in no sense free, and is certainly not fair to our own people.

8 It is not our intention, in any circumstances, to impose any duties on wheat, flour, oats, meat (including bacon and ham), cheese, butter or eggs.

9 While assisting the manufacturing industries of the country we propose also to give a direct measure of support to agriculture. Agriculture is not only, in itself, the greatest and most important of our national industries, but is of especial value as

supplying the most stable and essentially complementary home market for our manufactures.

10 We propose to afford this assistance by a bounty of £1 an acre on all holdings of arable land exceeding one acre. The main object of that bounty is to maintain employment on the land and so keep up the wages of agricultural labour. In order to make sure of this we shall decline to pay the bounty to any employer who pays less than 30/- a week to an able-bodied labourer.

11 The exclusion from any import duties of the essential foodstuffs which I have mentioned, as well as of raw materials, undoubtedly imposes a certain limitation upon the fullest extension of Imperial Preference. But even the preferences agreed to at the recent Economic Conference within our existing fiscal system, have been acknowledged as of the greatest value by the Dominion representatives, and our present proposals will offer a much wider field, the value of which will be progressively enhanced by the increasing range and variety of Empire production.

12 Moreover in the field of Empire development, as well as in that of home agriculture, we are not confined to the assistance furnished by duties. We have already given an earnest of our desire to promote a better distribution of the population of the Empire through the Empire Settlement Act, and at the Economic Conference we have undertaken to co-operate effectively with the Government of any part of the Empire in schemes of economic development. More especially do we intend to devote our attention to the development of cotton growing within the Empire, in order to keep down the cost of a raw material essential to our greatest exporting industry.

13 These measures constitute a single comprehensive and inter-dependent policy. Without additional revenue we cannot assist agriculture at home, but the income derived from the tariff will provide for this and leave us with means which can be devoted to cotton growing and other development in the Empire, and to the reduction of the duties on tea and sugar which fall so directly upon the working class household.

14 For the present emergency, and pending the introduction of our more extended proposals, we are making, and shall continue to make, every effort to increase the volume of work for our people. The Government are spending very large sums on every measure of emergency relief that can help in this direction. Further, the local Authorities of all kinds throughout the country, and great individual enterprises, such as the railways, with the assistance of the Government, or on its invitation, are co-operating wholeheartedly in the national endeavour to increase the volume of employment. This great combined effort of the Government, of the Local Authorities, and of individual enterprises, represents an expenditure of no less than £100 millions sterling.

15 The position of shipbuilding, one of the hardest hit of all our industries, is peculiar. It can only recover as shipping revives with the development of Empire and foreign trade which we believe will follow from our measures. We propose in the meantime to give it special assistance by accelerating the programme of light cruiser construction which will in any case become necessary in the near future. We

are informed by our Naval advisers that some light cruisers will be required during the next few years in replacement of the County class, as well as a variety of smaller and auxiliary craft, and we intend that a substantial proportion of these shall be laid down as soon as the designs are ready and Parliamentary sanction secured.

16 The solution of the unemployment problem is the key to every necessary social reform. But I should like to repeat my conviction that we should aim at the reorganisation of our various schemes of insurance against old age, ill-health and unemployment. More particularly should we devote our attention to investigating the possibilities of getting rid of the inconsistencies and the discouragement of thrift at present associated with the working of the Old Age Pensions Act. The encouragement of thrift and independence must be the underlying principle of all our social reforms.

CONSERVATIVE PARTY GENERAL ELECTION MANIFESTO 1924

Mr Stanley Baldwin's election address

Date of Election	Wednesday 29 October
Party Leader	Stanley Baldwin
Candidates	552
MPs	419
Votes	8,039,598
% of vote	48.3%

The Socialist minority Government have forced a rush election upon the country not upon any great issue of principle, such as was submitted to you a year ago, but on the plea that it was incompatible with their dignity to tolerate any inquiry into their conduct in connection with the withdrawal of the Campbell prosecution.

The Campbell case

The admissions already extorted from Ministers in Parliament are sufficient to convince any reasonable person that it was as a result of undue political pressure that the Attorney-General withdrew a prosecution instituted on the grave charge of inciting the troops to sedition and mutiny. The refusal to allow any inquiry inevitably suggests that the result of such investigation would only have been to emphasise the conclusion that the course of justice had been deflected by partisan considerations and to increase the public anxiety.

The Russian Treaty

There are, however, other considerations which may well have influenced the Government in their decision to precipitate an election. Under pressure from the same extremist section which reversed the considered action of the Attorney-General in the Campbell case – and, indeed, at the same moment – the Government, going back upon its own better judgement and upon the assurances given by the Prime Minister in Parliament, hurriedly patched up a makeshift Treaty with the Soviets which they now realise to be no less indefensible and no less incapable of standing close scrutiny. Under that Treaty the rightful claims of British subjects are whittled down to an undefined extent, and Parliament is to be asked to commit itself in the eyes of Russia and of the world, to the principle of guaranteeing that the British taxpayer shall repay a Bolshevik loan, if the Bolsheviks, in accordance with their principles and their practice, should fail to repay that loan.

Unemployment

By dissolving Parliament the Government are, no doubt, also hoping to obscure their utter failure to deal with unemployment, or to make good the boast that they possessed the only positive remedy for that most serious of all the problems of the day. The unemployment situation is as grave, if not graver, than it was a year ago, and more than justifies the warning I then gave of the necessity of looking ahead. Ever since the economic policy of the present Government, as distinguished from the measures initiated by ourselves and carried on by our successors, has had time to take effect, unemployment has steadily increased. At the end of September the unemployment figure was 180,000 higher than at the end of June, and is, I fear, still rising. In this disquieting situation the Government have no remedy whatsoever to propose, beyond mere palliatives or an increase of doles.

The folly committed by the Government of choosing such a time in order to abolish the McKenna duties and Part 2 of the Safeguarding of Industries Act, under which certain industries were rapidly expanding and giving increasing employment, and the even greater folly of wrecking the hopes of the rapid expansion of Imperial trade which would have followed on the adoption of the proposals of the Imperial Economic Conference, are now only too clearly evident.

Safeguarding of industry

The Unionist Party would be unfaithful to its principles and to its duty if it did not treat the task of grappling with the unemployment of our people and with the serious condition of industry as a primary obligation. While a general tariff is no part of our programme, we are determined to safeguard the employment and standard of living of our people in any efficient industry in which they are imperilled by unfair foreign competition, by applying the principle of the Safeguarding of Industries Act or by analogous measures. Without such provision the carrying out of the policy embodied in the Dawes Report, in itself desirable as calculated to secure German reparations and to restore stable economic conditions in Europe, might only prove disastrous to ourselves.

Economy

The burden of taxation weighs heavily upon industry and trade, diminishes real wages, and in a variety of ways adds to the cost of living. To assist in relieving the community of this burden, the most rigid economy in administration is essential.

Juvenile unemployment

Pending the restoration of trade, our duty will be to continue to take all the special relief measures in our power to ease the situation. More particularly do I feel that the grave problem of juvenile unemployment requires fuller and more careful consideration than it has received from the present Government.

Imperial preference

The best hope of industrial revival lies, however, in my opinion, in the development of the resources and trade of the British Empire. The policy of encouraging mutual trade in the Empire by measures of Imperial Preference, and of using our finance to promote Empire Development and Empire Settlement, is one to which we adhere, and which we shall steadily keep to the front.

Imperial unity

To strengthen and develop the Empire by every possible means is, indeed, the first and dominant item in our policy, believing, as we do, that only through the fullest co-operation of the partner states of the British Commonwealth can the common peace, security and prosperity of each and all of us be assured.

We favour the progressive grant of constitutional liberties in every part of the Empire where the capacity and loyalty of the people will make such measures a benefit to themselves and a strength to the Empire. But we are no less determined to maintain the authority and the unity of the Empire against factious and misguided agitation wherever it may assert itself.

Imperial foreign policy

The same principles must underly our policy in relation to the outside world. The foreign policy of this country must be such as will commend itself to the Dominions and must be carried on in closest consultation with their Governments. We stand for the maintenance of the most friendly relations with our Allies, for the re-establishment of a settled state of affairs in Europe and for co-operation in all matters admitting common action with the United States of America. The support and strengthening of the League of Nations on practical fines should, in our opinion, continue to be a cardinal principle of British foreign policy, subject always to the overriding consideration that we cannot enter into any commitments involving issues of peace and war without the concurrence of the Dominions which would inevitably be affected by them.

Imperial defence

The maintenance of our security at sea, on land and in the air is one of the first duties of any Government, and the Unionist Party, if returned to power, will have to examine afresh the position in which the defences of the Empire have been left by the present Administration. While in favour of any practical proposals for a general limitation of armaments, we shall have to scrutinise carefully in conjunction with the Dominions, the far-reaching commitments and implications of the scheme recently put forward at Geneva.

Agriculture

I regard it as vital that the great basic industry of agriculture should be not merely preserved, but restored to a more prosperous condition as an essential balancing element in the economic and social life of the country. For a permanent solution of the agricultural problem, a common agreement between all parties is desirable; and the Unionist Party, if returned to power, will summon a representative Conference in the hope of arriving at an agreed policy by which the arable acreage may be maintained and regular employment and adequate wages secured to the agricultural worker. The Act for the regulation of wages, passed in the last session of Parliament, will be maintained. Unionists can justly claim to have been instrumental in passing this Act in a form more generally acceptable to all agriculturists.

- We shall continue to agricultural ratepayers the relief already given during our previous tenure of office.
- We shall support the provision of agricultural credits for all forms of efficient, co-operative enterprise.
- The interests of the Fishing Industry will not be neglected, and with that object in view the provision of further and extended credit facilities in this direction will be the subject of enquiry.
- We shall promote the provision of small and cottage holdings by affording facilities for occupation and ownership, and will encourage the allotment movement with reasonable security for holders.
- We shall seek to make available on easy terms to all cultivators the results of the latest agricultural scientific research.
- We shall take all practical steps to ensure that imported foreign foodstuffs should be sold as such.
- The further development of the sugar beet industry and rural industries generally will receive particular consideration.
- Afforestation and land drainage will be developed and improved rural transport promoted.
- We are opposed to land nationalisation, the taxation of land values, and all schemes of spoliation.

In short, the purpose of our Party is to protect agriculturists from Socialistic and bureaucratic tyranny, and to secure for them the just reward due to all investment in the soil, whether it be of money, muscle, or brains.

Cost of foodstuffs

The problem of the cost of foodstuffs is one which demands careful investigation by a Royal Commission. The importance of any feasible reduction in those costs in its effects, both directly upon the cost of living, and indirectly upon our industrial position, is obvious.

Housing

Next to the problem of unemployment, the gravest of our domestic problems still is the housing problem. The Unionist Act of 1923, under which no less than 161,441 houses have been authorised by the Ministry of Health, has demonstrated that it will produce all the houses for which labour and materials are available with present methods of construction, and the best tribute to its success is that the present Government by the first section of their own Housing Act have prolonged its operation unchanged until the year 1939.

Something more, however, is required if the rate of building is to be materially increased, and houses are to be produced capable of being let at a rent approaching that which can be afforded by the poorer classes. This end can only be achieved by the employment of new materials and new methods of construction. The Unionist Party, which was the first to recognise the importance of this aspect of the problem, will, if returned to power, do everything possible to foster and develop the various experiments which are now being carried out in these directions, and will not hesitate, if it be necessary, to lend financial aid to bring them to early fruition, recognising that, in this way, and in this way alone, can the provision of the housing accommodation so sorely needed be secured in a reasonable time.

Slum improvement

The Unionist Party is, moreover, determined that side by side with the provision of new houses, the improvement of the slums shall be taken in hand. The conditions in large cities are such that new houses can only be built at a considerable distance from the factories and other places of business at which the occupants work. For many of them, migration into the suburbs would be difficult, if not impossible, on account of the expense and time that would be taken up in travelling to and from their work. It is, therefore, urgently necessary that without waiting until the whole population is re-housed, the standard of existing houses should be made to approximate more nearly to modern ideas, and as soon as the present shortage of accommodation has been sufficiently eased, steps will be taken to carry out this reform.

Insurance for old age and widows' pensions

Soon after the resignation of the late Government in the early part of the year, I appointed a Committee to investigate a comprehensive scheme of Insurance to cover both Old Age and Widows' Pensions. The three principal defects in the present Old Age Pension scheme are:

First: That it involves an investigation into the means of the applicant.

Second: That the pension is reduced where the means exceed a certain annual sum, even though those means result from his own thrift; and

Third: That the pension itself is inadequate in amount.

Most of the proposals for Widows' Pensions also include investigation and supervision of a kind that would be a constant source of irritation and annoyance to the widow. The Committee have come to the conclusion that the only way of avoiding such investigation is, whilst conserving the present rights of old age pensioners, to supplement them by a contributory scheme which would enable the contributor to receive his old age pension at an earlier age and of a substantially larger amount. In the same system, provision should be made for the widow with dependent children to receive her pension as a right, for which payment had been made, instead of a dole or a charity. Accordingly, they have caused exhaustive actuarial investigation to be made, and although their labours are not yet completed, they are satisfied that it will be possible to frame a workable scheme. It will be the task of a Unionist Government, returned with an adequate majority, to complete the details of the scheme, and to carry it into operation as soon as practicable.

Education

Believing that the object of any Education Policy should be the welfare of the child rather than the forwarding of some plan of educational progress, based on social theories, and keeping in mind that our immediate aim should be to develop our existing national system on practical lines, and to link up elementary education more closely with the various forms of advanced study, so that no child which can profit thereby shall be debarred from doing so by reason of the inability of the parents to pay fees, we are in favour of the carrying out of agreed schemes as between local Education Authorities and the Board of Education which shall ensure, among other matters:

1 A Progressive Reduction in the size of classes.
2 The improvement, or when necessary, the replacement of insanitary schools.
3 The development of Central Schools and other forms of education above the Elementary School stage, with an adequate supply in the number of Secondary School places, and a corresponding increase in the number of scholarships and free places, applicable to all advanced courses.
4 The maintenance, by agreement between Local Education Authorities and the Teachers, of such scales of salaries as will secure efficient teachers and attract the best men and women to the profession. Such scales, when they have been accepted by Local Education Authorities, to be obligatory.
5 The systematic promotion of schemes of adult education under the Local Education Authorities and the further development of all kinds of technical education.
6 The maintenance of the rights of parents to have their children brought up in the religion to which they are attached.

Women and children

In addition to such questions as Housing and Widows' Pensions, there are certain other reforms affecting women and children that I desire to see carried out. The Probationary system for dealing with offenders should be developed; a Bill to amend and consolidate the Factory and Workshop Acts should be passed; children born out of wedlock whose parents have subsequently married should be legitimised, the law relating to separation and maintenance orders should be amended; equal rights should be ensured to women in the guardianship of children; adoption should be legalised, the number of women police should be increased, and the penalties for criminal assaults against women and children made adequate to the offence.

Ex-service men

The Unionist Party will not cease to safeguard and further the interest of those who sacrificed so much for their country in the Great War, or that of their dependants. The proposals of the present Government for carrying out the recommendations of the Southborough Committee with regard to the position of Temporary ex-Service Civil Servants will be carefully examined, if we are returned to power, and our conclusions will be presented to Parliament before any action is taken to put them into effect.

A broad and national policy

In conclusion, I would appeal to you to help to secure for the country, in this difficult and anxious time, a strong and stable Government, based on an independent majority in Parliament, resolved to maintain the existing constitutional and economic liberties under which Britain has grown great and prosperous, and empowered to solve on practical and commonsense lines the urgent industrial and social problems of the day. The experiment of a minority Government has proved a short-lived failure. But it has afforded sufficient indication of what would be the character of a Socialist Government dependent, not upon other Parties, but upon the extremist section of its own majority, to make it imperative upon all who wish to see the restoration of prosperity and social peace, to unite their efforts in averting such a possibility. The only way in which that can be achieved lies in the return of a solid Unionist majority. I appeal, therefore, to all men and women who desire stable Government to support the broad and national policy that I have outlined and to ensure the return of a House of Commons that will have the will and power to carry it into effect.

CONSERVATIVE PARTY GENERAL ELECTION MANIFESTO 1929

Mr Stanley Baldwin's election address

Date of Election	Thursday 30 May
Party Leader	Stanley Baldwin
Candidates	590
MPs	260
Votes	8,656,473
% of vote	38.2%

Four and a half years ago, you returned me to Parliament and to Office as the leader of a great majority. Today it is my duty to lay before you the record of the Conservative and Unionist Government and its policy for the future; and to ask at your hands a renewal of your confidence. The Conservative Government has had to face difficulties and dangers at home and abroad which could not have been foreseen at the last Election. In spite of all obstacles, we have fulfilled the pledges given in 1924, to an extent which no Government has equalled, and as a result of our administration the Empire is more firmly united, the prestige of the country stands higher, the prosperity and welfare of our people is greater than ever before in our history. In submitting myself to the electorate, I make no spectacular promises for a sudden transformation of our social or industrial conditions, but I am resolved to maintain and consolidate the advance already made, to bring to fruition the schemes on which we are engaged, and to carry still further the solid work of reconstruction on which depend the unity of the Empire and the peace and well-being of its people.

The Empire

The Imperial Conference of 1926 will remain a memorable landmark in the constitutional development of the British Empire. The policy of any British Government of the future must be based on the principle then laid down: that the unity of the British Commonwealth is to be maintained by unfettered co-operation between its partner members, who enjoy an equal freedom under the Crown. This principle has consistently inspired and shaped our policy. In foreign affairs, in defence, in trade and in migration, we have worked and shall work to promote unity of aim and every form of helpful co-operation with the Dominions.

Imperial preference

Among these forms of co-operation none is of greater importance than the policy of Imperial Preference. That policy we have consistently and successfully pursued from the first moment of our entry into office. Reversing the unwise action of our predecessors, we at once honoured all the undertakings given at the Imperial Economic Conference of 1923, partly by the preferential remission of existing duties, and partly by the establishment of the Empire Marketing Board. The preferences to which we then gave effect have since been stabilised and extended with excellent results. In sugar, tobacco, silk, coffee, cocoa, dried fruits, and wine, there has been a great expansion of Empire production. The Empire Marketing Board has proved its value as a new agency of Imperial co-operation in many ways, and not least by its encouragement of scientific research both in Britain and in the Dominions and Colonies. Throughout the Empire, our policy has met with an appreciative response. The Empire today is by far our best market, buying nearly as much of our manufactures as all foreign countries together. Our opponents both liberal and Socialist, have, by their action in 1924, and by their declarations since, shown their determined hostility to the whole idea of Imperial Preference. We, on the contrary, have demonstrated its great possibilities, and, subject to my pledge not to impose any protective taxation on food, we shall continue to promote it as an essential part of our policy of Imperial development.

Colonial development

In working out a policy of Imperial development, we have a special duty towards the vast colonial territories for which the British nation is responsible. That duty was defined at the end of last century by Joseph Chamberlain, when he declared that these territories should be treated as the undeveloped estates of the British Empire to be developed by British capital and British enterprise. Such a task is frequently beyond the unaided resources of the Colony concerned, for trade and population will follow rather than precede the opening up of the country. For this purpose transport must be improved and production must be stimulated by scientific research, but capital expended upon these subjects may often bring in no return for several years.

We propose, therefore, to extend and expedite the policy already pursued in Africa and elsewhere, which in the past 4½ years has resulted in so great an expansion in the Colonial market for British produce. A Colonial Development Fund will be created which will assist Colonial Governments in financing approved projects of development.

While thus fulfilling our responsibilities towards the native populations and towards those of our own race who have linked their fortunes with them, we regard the employment of British capital to finance British enterprise as likely to prove a more fruitful investment for this country than speculative loans or guarantees to a foreign Government which has squandered its own resources in a futile war against capitalism, and which has hitherto shown neither a friendly disposition to us nor any readiness to recognise past obligations.

Trade and employment

This policy of Empire development forms part of a comprehensive programme directed to stimulate trade and to create permanent employment. The following are the main features in that programme.

Safeguarding

First, we are pressing steadily on with our policy of helping special industries. The country has watched with keen interest the progress and effect of safeguarding. Few people are interested in catchwords; they want to judge by practical results. The results of the duties which have been imposed are already apparent. Not only has employment been improved in every one of the safeguarded industries, but coal, steel, engineering, building, transport and other industries have profited by orders received and work created. The employment thus given directly and indirectly has put thousands of men in work, has increased their purchasing power, and has thus benefited the distributive trades. In many cases prices have been reduced because costs of production have fallen with increased output. Exports over the whole range of dutiable articles have materially increased; efficiency has been encouraged; new capital has been introduced; new factories have been built and existing factories have been extended. This experience has convinced many people of the wisdom of our policy. Our opponents have consistently obstructed it and are committed to its reversal, a step which must throw thousands out of work. We, on the other hand, are determined to continue it. We pledged ourselves at the last Election that there should be no protective taxation of food and that there should be no general tariff. We have kept that pledge and we renew it. But, subject to that pledge, we intend that no manufacturing industry, large or small, shall be debarred from presenting its case for a safeguarding duty to an impartial tribunal, which will judge each case on its merits and make recommendations accordingly.

Rating relief

One of the main purposes of safeguarding duties, as of Empire development is to stimulate the export trade.

No greater stimulus could, however, be given in this direction than the great scheme of Rating Relief which we have carried through in the face of persistent opposition from our political opponents, and which we are now putting into force. By relieving the whole of productive industry from three-fourths of the burden of rates we have not only swept away an unjust form of taxation but have greatly increased the competitive power of our national industries. This is no temporary or sporadic encouragement. It is on the contrary a continuing benefit, which will add about £27 millions every year to the resources of industry. This unprecedented measure of relief operates universally. The assistance is greatest where the need is greatest; but it is no mere subsidy to the depressed industries. It is an essential feature of the scheme that it should also encourage the prosperous industries on which we rely to create new employment, and the distributive trades will benefit by the increased purchasing power of the wage earners.

Railway freights

One important part of the Rating Reform Scheme has already been brought into operation – the reduction of railway freights. By this means the heavy basic industries have been granted reductions of freights amounting in all to more than £3 millions a year, while agriculture is benefited by similar relief amounting to over £750,000. Already this reduction is having marked effect on the recovery of these industries.

The basic industries and the railways

Here we approach the central problem of our national trade. The heavy basic industries of Britain – the coal, iron and steel group – depend upon the railways. Their traffics can only be carried along the steel track. They employ a fifth of our insured wage earners, contain more than a quarter of the whole number of the unemployed and constitute with cotton and woollens two-thirds of our export trade. It is to this point especially that help must be directed if unemployment is to be swiftly and effectually reduced to normal. The rating relief scheme and particularly the reduction of railway freights and dock dues is designed to afford a special measure of assistance to these industries and to agriculture. The remission of the railway passenger duty in the Budget has enabled the railways to undertake a programme of capital expenditure amounting to £6.5 millions, which will assist to modernise and develop the means of transport, and will facilitate the use of heavier rolling stock. In our view the basic trades of Britain which have to depend on the railways as their principal means of transport ought to have at their disposal facilities at least equal to any transportation system in any part of the world. The Government will take such further steps as may seem to them necessary to assist the railways, and the industries concerned, to achieve this end.

Road development

While we attach special importance to railway development we realise the part which our great highways must play in a national transportation system.

The last five years have seen the building and improvement of roads upon the greatest scale yet known, although our roads are already the best in the world, and we are spending more upon them than any European nation.

At the present time we are making provision for an annual expenditure from the Road Fund of £23 millions as compared with £15 millions in the year in which we took office, while the total expenditure on roads out of rates and taxes amounts to approximately £60 millions a year. The percentages of State contribution to the various classes of roads have been increased, and the problem of rural roads has been met by substantial increases in the grants towards them.

Throughout its tenure of office the policy of the Government has been to encourage and assist highway authorities to pursue a comprehensive and orderly programme of road development, improvement and maintenance.

We intend to pursue this policy, paying special attention to the improvements which will give immediate assistance to our trade and thus bring in a full return for the money expended, rather than to put in hand hasty and ill-considered schemes which could only lead to wasteful and unfruitful expenditure, and could be of no permanent benefit to the unemployed.

Electrical development

If modern industry needs an efficient transportation system, it needs no less a fully adequate supply of electrical power. There has been no more remarkable achievement in recent times than the re-organisation of the generation and transmission of electricity in Great Britain which was effected by the Electricity (Supply) Act. Progress under that Act has been rapid. It was passed at the end of 1926; in March, 1927, the Central Electricity Board was established, and by the coming Autumn detailed schemes will have been prepared covering about 97 per cent. of the population and 98 per cent. of the present sales of current. The placing of contracts in respect of the constructional work on the transmission system has been pressed on, and the total value of orders already placed amounts to £8½ millions, all of which have been placed with British firms. Further substantial orders will be placed during the year and unemployment in the skilled electrical trades is practically non-existent.

Training

While we are thus directing our policy primarily to the permanent restoration of industrial prosperity, on which the solution of the unemployment problem depends, we have also undertaken a wide range of subsidiary measures designed to enable the unemployed, especially in the depressed areas, to find permanent work.

Training Centres have been established which have already enabled thousands of men and women to fit themselves for new employment. The system of juvenile unemployment centres has been greatly developed, and more than 250,000 boys and girls have passed through these centres. As a result of these and other measures, the problem of juvenile unemployment has been largely overcome. There is now little unemployment among boys and girls, except in the depressed mining areas, and, as a result of the arrangements made while we have been in office, practically every boy in these areas can now attend an unemployment centre when he is unemployed, and there be fitted for a carefully chosen job elsewhere.

We shall steadily expand our training system, as need requires, and we shall continue to provide money for public works with due regard to the requirements of industry for which the maintenance of public credit is so necessary.

The past and the future in industry

The policy outlined above has already justified itself. Employment improved under our administration until the Spring of 1926 when, for the first time since the great depression of 1920, the number of unemployed fell below a million. Trade then suffered a severe set-back owing to the General Strike, and the industrial troubles of 1926. In the last two years it has made a remarkable recovery.

In the insured industries, other than the coal mining industry, there are now 800,000 more people employed and 125,000 fewer unemployed than when we assumed office. The coal industry itself is now reviving; many thousands of miners displaced by the re-organisation of the industry have been absorbed into other industries and there are 150,000 fewer miners unemployed than nine months ago.

This recovery has been achieved by the combined efforts of our people assisted by the Government's policy of helping industry to help itself. The establishment of stable conditions has given industry confidence and opportunity.

A new spirit of co-operation is abroad. Fewer days have been lost through trade disputes in 1927 and 1928 than in any year since records were established forty years ago. Negotiations on a friendly basis are proceeding between the partners in industry.

If such co-operation continues with peace at home and abroad, and if full effect is given to the Government's proposals for helping trade, there is every reason to believe that trade and industry will be placed on a sound basis and that men and women will find permanent employment at their proper trades in steadily increasing numbers.

The rights and welfare of the partners in trade and industry

> This peace and revival in industry opens the way to a revision and improvement of the Factory laws.

This is the one pledge we gave at the last Election which we have been unable to fulfil. It was impossible to legislate wisely for industry while still torn by dissensions and harassed by the uncertainties following the troubles of 1926. In our view the time has now arrived for the enactment of a single and clearly drafted statute which shall protect the health, safety and general welfare of the workers without imposing on industry burdens which might retard its recovery.

Factory legislation of this kind will complete the work we have already done to give greater security to the partners in trade and industry. By the legislation we have passed during our term of office we have given both to the business tenant and to shop assistants a measure of security which they have long demanded. By the Trade Disputes Act the Trade Unions were protected against the misuse of the strike weapon for political and revolutionary ends, and the Trade Unionist has been secured against intimidation and coercion in the free exercise of his industrial and political rights. The threat of the Socialist Party to repeal this Act is in itself a ground for asking the support of the workers for the present Government.

Agriculture

Our policy for agriculture has been consistently directed, and will continue to be directed, to the relief of burdens, the finding of markets, the provision of credit facilities, and the development of education and research.

We have crowned the Conservative policy of relieving the essential equipment of agriculture from unfair burdens by the entire remission in England and Wales of local rates on farm land and buildings and in Scotland by an equivalent relief from rates. We have found it possible to advance our programme by bringing this relief into immediate operation. We have thus conferred upon the agricultural industry a benefit of not less than £2½ millions for the year ending October 1, 1929, and nearly £5 millions in a full year. The substantial rebates railway freight charges for certain agricultural traffics which we have also secured by our de-rating scheme, and the special grants made from the Road Fund towards the maintenance and improvement of roads in rural areas, with consequent relief to local rates, are further instances of the same policy of easing the burdens of agriculture.

We have endeavoured to improve the farmer's position by helping him to reform the methods of marketing agricultural produce. We are surveying the whole marketing system of the country. New methods of standardised grading and packing have been introduced and under the Agricultural Produce (Grading and Marking) Act, 1928, agricultural products can now be sold in standard grades under a National Mark. A most successful beginning has been made in the application of the Mark to eggs and certain kinds of fruit and vegetables. Provision has also been made for the marking of imported foodstuffs in suitable cases.

The policy of preference to the home producer has been steadily pressed by the Empire Marketing Board, and is already showing results. In order to give a lead in this matter by direct Government example, we have decided that in future only homefed beef shall be supplied to the Army, Air Force and Navy in Home Ports during the six months October to March, and that during six months after harvest 25 per cent. of the flour used for these services shall be milled from home-grown wheat.

We have initiated a long called-for reform in the finance of British agriculture by the Agricultural Credits Acts under which both long term and short term credits are being provided; considerable advantage is already being taken by the farming community of these provisions.

Large sums have been provided for improving the drainage of agricultural land, and we propose to introduce legislation, based on the Report of the recent Royal Commission, which should give a fresh stimulus to this work.

Recognising that arable farming has been specially affected by the depression in agriculture, we have vigorously supported and developed the infant sugar beet industry, with results which have already exercised a marked influence on the prosperity of agriculture, particularly in the eastern part of England.

We have ensured throughout England and Wales that the minimum and overtime rates of wages of agricultural workers prescribed under the Agricultural Wages Act of 1924 are being paid, and where necessary we have secured the enforcement of the Act through the medium of the Courts.

We have extended the facilities for Small Holdings both for renting and purchase by easy instalments, including a new type of cottage holding, and legislation has also been passed facilitating the provision of allotments. We also propose to afford the public in rural areas improved telephone facilities. The radius from the nearest exchange within which a telephone is provided without extra mileage charge will be extended from 1½ to 2 miles. Call offices will be provided at some 5,000 rural post offices which have at present neither telegraph nor telephone facilities and at more than 1,000 rural railway stations. The electrification of rural areas will be greatly facilitated by the transmission system provided under the Electricity Act.

Taken together these measures constitute a practical policy. They have proved, and will increasingly prove, their value as a contribution to the re-establishment of British agriculture. It is a policy which enables the costs of production to be reduced and the marketing of agricultural produce to be improved.

But such a policy must be assisted by all the resources of modern science and skill. To this end we have greatly extended the provision for agricultural education and research, and have directed the attention of teachers in the elementary and secondary schools to the need for closer co-operation between those schools and the industry of agriculture. The further extension of this work will be one of our main cares.

We are utterly opposed both to nationalisation of the land and to bureaucratic control, the policies of our Socialist and liberal opponents. We do not believe that these expedients can ever overcome the difficulties confronting the agricultural industry, or bring prosperity to those who live by the land.

Fisheries

We recognise the great importance of the fishing industry. We have given and shall continue to give financial assistance towards all forms of research beneficial to the industry, including the search for new fishing grounds and the investigations now being conducted into the preservation of fish, its transport and the use of by-products. A start has been made to develop the fish canning industry.

We are taking steps to help the herring and inshore fishermen by improving harbour facilities, by lightening the burden of existing loans and by the reduction of harbour dues.

Share-fishermen have been included in the National Health Insurance scheme and can now qualify for the Contributory Old Age Pensions.

Social reform

The Conservative Party regards the prosperity of trade and industry, not as an end in itself, but as a means to improve the condition of the people. During our tenure of office we have carried through a great programme of social welfare and have thus prepared the ground for the further programme which we now lay before the country.

Pensions

At the last election a promise was given that a Conservative Government, if returned with an adequate majority, would complete the details of a Contributory Scheme of pensions for widows, orphans and old people at an earlier age, without the irritating enquiries and restrictions that had accompanied the earlier scheme of pensions at 70, and would put this scheme into operation as soon as practicable. That promise was fulfilled in the first nine months of our career and already one and three-quarter million persons have been awarded pensions and allowances under our Act.

Housing and the problem of the slums

We also promised special attention to the vigorous promotion of housing schemes, and the 930,000 houses which have been built during our term of office, providing accommodation for nearly four millions of people, constitute a record in this respect in the history of the world.

Realising that the most pressing need is for houses which can be let at lower rents, we have reduced the subsidy which was keeping up prices, and this measure has been so successful that since it was announced the average cost of a non-parlour house has been reduced by no less than £1. 12 shillings. With this encouragement Local Authorities are now placing fresh contracts, and we shall continue to urge them to build houses for the lower paid workers until the shortage, which for this class still remains acute, is completely overcome. Meanwhile, the success already achieved has made it possible to attack with a new prospect of success the formidable problem of the slums which has hitherto baffled all attempts to find a solution.

Plans for the improvement of the present procedure in slum clearance are far advanced. The present basis of compensation to owners, the unfairness of which has had a delaying effect, will be amended after consultation with the various interests concerned. New powers will be given to local Authorities in England and Wales, enabling them to undertake the re-conditioning of old houses after acquisition and providing for an enlightened system of careful and sympathetic management. Where improvement schemes of this kind are carried out it will be possible so to control the tenancies as to put an end to the exploitation of sub-tenants who occupy furnished or unfurnished rooms and who are often in no position to protect themselves against undue charges. The corresponding problem in Scotland will be dealt with by measures adapted to the special conditions of that country.

Rent restriction acts

The continuance of these Acts in their present form has created hardship for certain owners of small houses. But, whatever modifications may be made to mitigate their difficulties, the protection afforded to tenants by these Acts will not be removed until the shortage of houses has been overcome sufficiently to warrant such a course.

Local government

By the adjustment of financial relations between Local Authorities and the Exchequer an increased national contribution will be directed to the places mostly in need of it. Under the provisions of the scheme the vast majority of ratepayers will gain materially.

Welfare of mothers and children

Under the present administration special attention has been given to mothers and children. The network of ante-natal clinics and infant welfare centres has been greatly extended, and largely owing to these measures infant mortality has been reduced from 75 to 65 per 1,000 of the population. The provisions of the local Government Act may be expected to facilitate further expansion of this service in those places where it is most needed by directing to them an increased proportion of the Exchequer contributions to local expenditure.

We desire, however, that this expansion should be carried beyond the infant welfare centres, whose work is chiefly concerned with children up to one year old. The school medical service is now providing treatment every year for half a million more school children than in 1924, but there is still a gap between the work of this service and that of the infant welfare centres. Existing agencies, such as nursery schools, have done much, and can do more, to solve this problem, but the gap cannot be bridged by these means alone. While encouraging these agencies, therefore, we shall also immediately undertake a comprehensive enquiry into the best methods of providing for the health and welfare of children between one and five years of age.

Another enquiry is already being carried out into the causes of maternal mortality, and it is expected that when completed it will throw fresh light upon this grave and urgent problem. In the meanwhile, the Government have come to the conclusion that the maternity benefit under the National Health Insurance scheme might be more effectively utilised in the preservation of the health and life of mothers, and they purpose to reorganise this provision so as to ensure that proper and adequate midwifery and medical services shall be available to them.

Finally, the national provision for child welfare needs to be completed by measures designed to protect the interests of older children. Several Committees appointed during our term of office have examined this question and have recommended important reforms. One of our first measures in the next Parliament will be a Bill to consolidate and improve the Acts relating to children and young people, and to bring them into conformity with enlightened opinion.

Welfare of the blind

Among the social services which affect only a limited number of the population are the provisions made for the welfare of the Blind. Much has been done to ease the lot of those who are thus afflicted, and many are now enabled by special training to make at least a considerable contribution towards their own support. Pensions are provided at the age of 50 for such as have not sufficient means of their own to be independent, but since at that age it is difficult, if not impossible, for a blind person to take advantage of the training facilities provided, the Government have come to the conclusion that pensions should be made available earlier in life, and if they should be returned to power they will introduce legislation to make the pensionable age 40 instead of 50.

Education

As at the last election, we are issuing a separate statement of our education policy. In that statement we show the progress we have made in carrying out the pledges we gave four years ago, and we renew those pledges. Further, we place before the electors for the first time a complete and balanced scheme of education which has behind it the support both of education reformers and of the trades and industries of the country. This scheme, for which we shall pass the necessary legislation, will offer to all our people the opportunity to pursue a connected course of study from childhood to manhood, and will give to each phase of education – primary, secondary, technical and university – its proper place in one coherent structure. In this task we need the co-operation of all types of school and every kind of educational effort, and we therefore pledge ourselves actively to seek an agreed settlement which will enable provided and non-provided schools to work together for the accomplishment of these reforms upon just terms of partnership. We need, too, the speedy completion of the reconditioning of all defective school premises in the interests of the children who attend them, and we propose to bring forward a special measure for this purpose. We need, finally, the services of a teaching profession enjoying security of remuneration and professional prospects, and we shall endeavour to complete the work in this direction which has already been carried so far during the past four years.

Civil administration

The efficiency of our public administration is an essential factor in our national well-being. The changes that have taken place during recent years and the increase in the numbers of women employed have given rise to many difficult problems affecting the Civil Service. We have decided that the time has come when it should be made the subject of a comprehensive enquiry by a Royal Commission.

Great War pensioners

By the end of this year the country will have spent on Great War Pensions £913 millions, a sum greater in amount than the combined expenditure of France and Germany on the same object.

War pensioners have been relieved by the Government's action from any anxiety that the rates of their pensions might be reduced owing to the fall in the cost of living.

Four hundred thousand officers and men have been given security of pensions for life by the policy of final award which is being, and will be, steadily pursued. Altogether over 800,000 men and women have been made secure in the possession of their war pensions.

Arrangements have been made whereby exceptional cases of all kinds can and do receive pension beyond the seven years' time limit.

The household and the family

Great as are the benefits conferred upon the community by the public social services, the happiness of the individual depends primarily upon the conditions of his home life. During the past four years there has been a substantial improvement in those conditions. Over the working population as a whole wage rates have risen slightly while there has been a marked fall in the cost of living.

The reduction of 6d. in the standard rate of Income Tax, together with the increase in the earned income allowance and in the rates of children's allowances for income tax purposes, has effected a striking diminution in the burden of direct taxation, especially in the case of the family man who is dependent for his livelihood upon his own labours. In the sphere of indirect taxation we have abolished altogether the Tea Duty which has been in existence for over 300 years, and by our rearrangement of the Sugar Duties, we have effected a reduction of 1/4d. a lb. in the price of sugar to the consumer, and this reduction has been doubled in consequence of world market conditions. But these contributions to a reduction in the cost of living are far transcended by the general reduction which has taken place as a result of the Government's policy in returning to the Gold Standard. During our term of office wage rates over the working population as a whole have risen slightly while the cost of living has fallen by 10 per cent. This fall is equivalent to a reduction of £160 millions a year on the household budgets of the insured wage earners of the nation alone, and if it is applied to all wages, salaries, old age pensions and war pensions, the increased purchasing power would be the equivalent of £240 millions a year. It is not surprising that there has been a remarkable growth in the savings and investments of the workers.

This growth in the material prosperity of the home has been accompanied by a series of reforms in our legislation affecting family life. By these reforms, such as the Acts relating to the Adoption of Children, the Guardianship of Infants, Legitimacy and the Age of Marriage, we have sought especially to improve the position of women and children.

Economy

It is the steady improvement in the resources and spending power of the individual home which should form the main object of our national financial policy. Our opponents in all their schemes to gain votes never count the cost in cash or credit. Yet money is the measure of all that can be done. We are told that immense new burdens are to be placed upon the direct taxpayer by the Socialist Party, and formidable drains upon our credit will be made by the Liberals. All this will simply be taken from the common stock, and the saving power and economic energy of the country will be reduced accordingly. We do not think that this is a time for imposing new and heavy taxes and it is certainly most necessary to nourish by every means the financial credit upon which the whole activity of industry and enterprise depends. Instead of placing heavy new burdens upon the taxpayer, the process of strict and steady economies in every branch of the public service must continue to be pursued with the aim of lightening the public burdens and leaving larger sums of money to fructify in the pockets of the people. The large savings which we have made on armaments are already apparent, and it is to be hoped that international agreements and further departmental economies will continue this process in the new Parliament, provided always that national safety is not jeopardised.

Peace abroad

The promotion of peace and disarmament has been the prime object of our foreign policy, and that policy has proved successful over the whole field of foreign affairs. Under the guarantees given by the Treaty of Locarno, security, on which peace depends, has been assured in Europe, and Germany has entered the League of Nations. This security has been extended from Europe to the whole world by the signature of the Kellogg Pact, under which all nations have solemnly undertaken to renounce war as an instrument of policy and so have assumed the obligation to settle international disputes by peaceful means.

The improvement in the international situation wrought by these important treaties leads us to look with confidence for an early advance towards disarmament. We stand for the reduction and not merely the limitation of armaments and in this field we have set a notable example.

Despite the emergence of the Royal Air Force as a third fighting service and the additional defence responsibilities we have assumed for the Mandated Territories, the combined strength of the three Services is to-day substantially lower than the corresponding figure for the Navy and Army before the War.

Along with this reduction in fighting strength, we have progressively reduced the cost of Imperial Defence, despite the considerable programmes of replacement and rearmament in all three Services necessitated by modern conditions. In 1929–30 the total estimated expenditure on Defence Services shows a reduction of approximately £7½ millions as compared with the corresponding cost in 1924–25.

The development of the League of Nations is a cardinal principle of our foreign policy. The importance attached by the present Government to the work of the League is illustrated by the fact that Great Britain has been continuously represented by the Secretary of State for Foreign Affairs on the Council and in the Assembly of the League.

We welcome, as the fruit of this consistent policy, the advance recently made at Geneva towards an international agreement for the reduction of armaments and we greatly hope for a further advance in this direction on the lines of the proposals foreshadowed by the representatives of the United States of America.

As in European and world politics, so also in the special affairs of the Middle and the Far East, we have shown our desire and our ability to settle differences and promote friendly relations. In the case of both Turkey and China, where we were confronted with special difficulties, our policy has fully justified itself; it has re-established old friendships and afforded new opportunities for British export trade.

We shall continue, in every sphere of foreign policy, to act in the closest consultation and co-operation with the Governments of the Dominions. We believe this to be essential if the unity of the Empire and its influence in the councils of the world is to be maintained.

Finally, we stand for the scrupulous execution of all international engagements, in accordance with the traditions of this country.

Conclusion

It is for the electors to judge, in the light of our past record, whether we have not faithfully redeemed the promises which we made four and a half years ago. We have striven consistently to build up industrial prosperity on sound and permanent foundations, and to improve the social conditions of our people. The results can be seen in the steady revival of trade, especially in the great basic industries, and in the reduction in the cost of living. The future destinies of the country rest in the hands of the electorate. I am confident that, with the growth of the new spirit of co-operation in industry, the present trade revival will make steady and even rapid progress, provided that British industry is guaranteed a period of stable government and can thus enjoy that confidence in the future without which trade recovery is impossible. If, as I hope, the Conservative and Unionist Party is returned to power with an independent majority, those conditions can be secured. The alternatives are a Socialist Government with, or without, liberal support, or a state of political chaos and uncertainty through the existence of three parties, none of which has a clear majority over the other two. Either of these contingencies would be disastrous to the welfare of industry and to the welfare of the nation as a whole, and I ask the electorate once again to place their confidence in our Party as the only one which can secure stable conditions and ordered progress along sound and practical lines.

NATIONAL CONSERVATIVE GENERAL ELECTION MANIFESTO 1931

The nation's duty: Mr Stanley Baldwin's general election message

Date of Election	Tuesday 27 October
Party Leader	Stanley Baldwin
Candidates	523
MPs	473
Votes	11,978,745
% of vote	55.2%

It is barely two months since my decision to join the National Government was unanimously endorsed at a meeting of Members of Parliament and Candidates held at the Kingsway Hall in London. At that time we expected that the co-operation then secured would last for only a few weeks, but recent events have rendered it necessary, in my view, that the period of this co-operation should be extended. The Budget has been balanced. Borrowing has been stopped at the cost of sacrifices from every class of the community, sacrifices which are heavy but which, I hope and believe, as the result of a continuance of our policy may be temporary. But we have not yet balanced the Trade Account of the Nation: in other words, we are not yet earning enough to pay for what we have to buy from Overseas. Unless this position can be altered nothing can save us from ultimate bankruptcy.

Our country's safety

We must shrink from no steps to prove the stability of our country and to save our people from the disaster attaching to a currency fluctuating and falling through lack of confidence at home and abroad.

A national mandate

To complete this work it is imperative that the Government should have a national mandate giving it freedom to use whatever means may be found necessary after careful examination to effect the end in view. It is necessary that in place of a small Parliamentary majority we should have a stable Government with a large majority backed by the resolution of a great majority of the electors. The country must show in no uncertain manner that it will have nothing to do with a party whose programme could only convert a situation grave already into one of chaos and catastrophe. Some of the problems that lie before us are wide as the world itself. Some are peculiar to ourselves.

In the international field we have to consider war debts and reparations, disarmament, the unequal distribution of the world supply of gold and the mutual financial dependence of the countries of the world. Those questions may well tax the statesmanship of all nations.

At home the paramount question is that of the adverse Balance of Trade, the redress of which is essential to secure our financial stability. This can be accomplished only by reducing imports., by increasing exports, or by a combination of both.

Tariffs essential

I am prepared to examine any method which can effect what is required. I recognise that the situation is altered by the devaluation of the pound, but in my view the effect of that devaluation can be no valid substitute for a tariff, carefully designed and adjusted to meet the present situation. I shall, therefore, continue to press upon the electors that in my view the tariff is the quickest and most effective weapon not only to reduce excessive imports but to enable us to induce other countries to lower their tariff walls.

The position of Agriculture is one which in my judgement is so desperate as to call for immediate and far-reaching measures of relief. To this end the first step should be assistance to cereal farmers, and we have in no way changed our view that the best form of assistance is by means of a quota and guaranteed price for wheat.

'Farmers must be secured against dumping'

Farmers must be secured against dumping, which has brought so many branches of their industry to ruin. The production of food at home should be increased and the drain of men from the land stopped, and to this end and to make Imperial treaties which may be of enormous value to us as a nation we shall require such a free hand as will allow us to use prohibitions, quotas or duties as may seem most effective in the circumstances.

Empire economic unity

The Problem of the Empire is to secure that economic unity for which we have so long striven. I hope that the reasons which led to a suspension of the Ottawa Conference have been overcome, and that it will be possible for the Canadian Government to renew its invitation. We shall then have a unique opportunity before us in the fact that it will fall to a National Government to accept that invitation.

The ideal of Imperial Economic Unity is widespread to-day, and I am confident that the foundation of such unity will be well and truly laid with such general assent of our people as would have seemed impossible but a few short years ago.

All must help

The National Government has with your help accomplished the first part of its work. We are passing through stern and difficult times; our task will be impossible without the support of the nation.

For that support we appeal with confidence, and in the winning of that support I believe a great part will be played by those I am proud to lead.

NATIONAL CONSERVATIVE GENERAL ELECTION MANIFESTO 1935

A call to the nation: the joint manifesto of the leaders National Government (Stanley Baldwin, J. Ramsay MacDonald and Sir John Simon)

Date of Election	Thursday 14 November
Party Leader	Stanley Baldwin
Candidates	585
MPs	432
Votes	11,810,158
% of vote	53.7%

The decision of the Nation four years ago to put its trust in a National Government formed from various Parties in the State, was a turning point in the history of Britain and has exercised a profound influence upon the course of international events. Under this leadership we have emerged from the depths of depression to a condition of steadily returning prosperity, and the name of Britain stands high in the councils of the world. There now fails upon the people of this country the grave responsibility of exercising a choice which may well prove equally momentous for the future.

The broad issue is whether the stability and confidence which the National Government have built up are to be preserved in a period of special difficulty and anxiety. But we have considered it right, for the information of the Electors, to set forth on behalf of a united Government their general aims and policy on various aspects of home and foreign affairs.

The League of Nations

The League of Nations will remain, as heretofore, the keystone of British foreign policy. The prevention of war and the establishment of settled peace in the world must always be the most vital interest of the British people, and the League is the instrument which has been framed and to which we lock for the attainment of these objects. We shall therefore continue to do all in our power to uphold the Covenant and to maintain and increase the efficiency of the League. In the present unhappy dispute between Italy and Abyssinia there will be no wavering in the policy we have hitherto pursued. We shall take no action in isolation, but we shall be prepared faithfully to take our part in any collective action decided upon by the League and shared in by its Members. We shall endeavour to further any discussions which may offer the hope of a just and fair settlement, provided that it be within the framework of the League and acceptable to the three parties to the dispute –Italy, Abyssinia and the League itself.

Peace and defence

Peace is not only the first interest of the British people; it is the object to which all their hopes and efforts are directed. Our attitude to the League is dictated by the conviction that collective security by collective action can alone save us from a return to the old system which resulted in the Great War. The Covenant itself requires that national armaments should be measured both by the needs of national defence and by the duty of fulfilling international obligations. A Commonwealth which holds the position in the world occupied by the United Kingdom and its partners in the British Empire must always take an influential part in League discussions. But our influence can be fully exerted only if we are recognised to be strong enough to fulfil any obligations which, jointly with others, we may undertake. The fact is that the actual condition of our defence forces is not satisfactory. We have made it clear that we must in the course of the next few years do what is necessary to repair the gaps in our defences, which have accumulated over the past decade, and we shall in due course present to Parliament our proposals, which will include provisions to ensure that the programme, is carried out without either waste or unreasonable profit to contractors.

Limitation of armaments

The defence programme will be strictly confined to what is required to make the country and the Empire safe, and to fulfil our obligations towards the League. All the world knows that Britain will never use her forces for any aggressive purpose. And we shall not for one moment relax our efforts to attain, by international agreement, a general limitation of armaments by every possible means, whether by restriction of numbers or by prohibition of weapons and methods of warfare. Already we have summoned a new Naval Conference to meet in London this year, at which we earnestly hope it may be possible to continue the good work done in this direction at the previous Naval Conferences of Washington and London.

Imperial policy

The Agreements entered into at Ottawa in 1932 marked the beginning of a new epoch in inter-imperial trading relations. The results of those Agreements have increased employment both in the Dominions and in this country, without injuring the rest of the world, and it is our intention further to promote the exchange of goods between ourselves and our partners in the Empire, believing that any increase in their prosperity will always be reflected in an increase in the volume of British trade and employment.

The Colonial Empire also benefited greatly by the arrangements made at Ottawa. The greatest need of the British Colonies to-day is an extension of their markets. Special and sympathetic consideration will be given to the possibilities of providing further facilities to enable them to sell their products to the best advantage in the markets of the world and thereby increase their purchase of British goods.

Overseas trade

While the growing volume of British exports to the Dominions and Colonies has done something to fill the gap left by the shrinkage of international trade since 1929, it still remains true that if our foreign trade could be restored to its former dimensions an immense fillip would be given to employment in this country. It is probable that the reduction of excessive tariffs and the abolition of quotas and of other barriers to international trade will only come about by degrees as general confidence is restored. There are, however, hopeful indications that opinion is moving in the right direction. In the meantime it will be our endeavour to continue the policy of reducing these barriers by means of bilateral commercial treaties, which has already had so beneficial an effect in increasing our exports to the countries with whom we have been able to make trade agreements.

Agriculture

A prosperous countryside is an essential foundation of national well-being. The National Government have from the first recognised that agriculture is not one but many industries, each working under different conditions and requiring different treatment for its improvement. Accordingly, they have had to make use of import duties, levies, or combinations of these devices according to the circumstances of each case. The producers have played their part by organisation and co-operation, and this we have encouraged and helped. So bold a treatment was bound to raise some problems not yet solved, but we can claim that, broadly speaking, our efforts have met with success. The prices received by farmers have recovered by 15 per cent from the low point of two years ago. The agricultural worker in England and Wales has to-day an average wage which is the highest recorded for ten years. At the same time the customer in the shops has been able this year to buy more food for 19s. than could be bought for £1 when the Government took office. Yet it is important for our townspeople to recognise that it is not wise to rely entirely upon foodstuffs brought from overseas. The prudent housewife wants some at least of her supplies from near at hand, where they would be readily available in any circumstances.

It has already been announced that the Government have accepted the principle of unemployment insurance for agricultural workers, and it is our intention, if returned, to introduce legislation to that end.

In all branches of agriculture our policy has been and will remain one of expansion of the home market. As the market expands home production can expand with it, and in this way only can a real opportunity be afforded for new men to make a career on the land.

Fisheries

The Government have recognised the great importance of the fishing industry and have taken vigorous and far-reaching measures to assist the fishermen round our coasts.

Here, again, our policy is to extend the market both at home and abroad. We shall not slacken in our efforts to carry this policy into effect.

Employment

The remarkable fact that more persons are now employed in this country than ever before in its whole history has not sprung from accident or the unfettered operation of natural laws. It has been the result of the deliberate policy of the Government in protecting the home market and in creating a regime of cheap money, which has facilitated enterprise and stimulated industrial expansion. In particular, cheap money, resulting from the increased confidence in Great Britain, has been the most powerful factor in bringing about the phenomenal growth of the building industry, which is the most far-reaching of all home industries in the wide field of employment which it creates. It is probable that the improvement in home trade, which has been so marked a feature of the past four years, has by no means reached its limit. Nevertheless, the Government are constantly working on all kinds of plans by which they may make use of the present favourable circumstances to initiate new enterprises, thereby creating additional employment by use of credit or other resources of the State. The building of the Queen Mary, the subsidy to tramp shipping, the production of oil from coal by the hydrogenation process, and the great scheme of London transport improvements, at a cost of between £30 and £40 millions, are instances in point. Further schemes of a similar character are under consideration, and will, if the National Government are returned to power, be announced from time to time as they mature.

Unemployment assistance

The arrangements under the Unemployment Assistance scheme have received prolonged and anxious consideration by the Government, and, as already stated in Parliament, no alteration will be made in the existing "standstill" arrangements before next spring at the earliest. The Government regard it as important to maintain the existing powers of the Unemployment Assistance Board and the general framework of the Unemployment Assistance Act. They will, however, give effect to any recommendations by the Board for improved arrangements, where these may be shown by experience to be desirable. The "standstill" arrangements are, as they were always intended to be, temporary. They must be replaced by permanent arrangements, which must remedy certain abuses and at the same time avoid hardship to applicants. Any action must be gradual, and must be carried out in full association with local opinion, so as to give effect to reasonable differences in the localities. As regards the Means Test, the Government believe that no responsible person would seriously suggest that Unemployment Assistance, which is not insurance benefit, ought to be paid without regard to the resources properly available to the applicant. The question is not whether there should be a Means Test, but what that test should be. This is a matter which is now under close examination, but in any scheme great importance will be attached to maintaining the unity of family life and, in addition, provision will be made to meet any cases of proved hardship.

Special areas and the coal mining industry

No branch of the Government's activities has been more constantly misrepresented than their work in the Special Areas. From the first they have recognised that in these areas – the unfortunate victims of a contraction in the limited number of great industries on which they were formerly chiefly dependent – the problems of unemployment present features of exceptional difficulty. The removal of these difficulties and the restoration of the areas to their proper position in the normal life of the country must necessarily take time. The Government have shown their determination to grapple with the situation by the appointment of the Special Commissioners, and the granting to them of special powers to facilitate their work. As a commencement, a sum of two million pounds was placed at the Commissioners' disposal, with an intimation that more would be forthcoming as it was required. Already the commitments have considerably exceeded the initial sum, and financial considerations will not be allowed to stand in the way of any practical and reasonable scheme.

It is generally recognised that the depression of the Special Areas has been brought about by the contraction in certain large industries, prominent among which is coal mining. Any improvement in this industry, therefore, while it would affect much larger districts than are comprised in the Special Areas, would bring particular benefits to them. The market for coal has been gradually curtailed by economy in its use, by the growth of competitive fuels and by the introduction of restrictive measures in foreign markets. There are, however, certain directions in which the industry can be made more efficient, and we hope more profitable, for the miner will always rightly command the sympathy of the public in his dangerous calling, and there is no part of the community that would not wish to see employment in the industry improved and the level of wages raised. The Government are convinced that improved selling arrangements, without which there is not the money in the industry to provide a higher rate of wages, should be put into operation and, if given the opportunity, we shall devote our energy to ensuring that measures to attain this object are adopted at an early date. We have further decided to effect the unification of coal-mining royalties, a step which will enable greater progress to be made with the organisation of production and thus improve the efficiency of the industry. Nor shall we neglect the problems of safety in coal mining. A Royal Commission will be set up to examine these subjects afresh, and to consider, not only how the present rules and regulations can best be brought up to date in the light of modern methods, but also how the latest discoveries of scientific research can help to secure the safety of those working in the pits.

The introduction of new industries into the Special Areas is extremely desirable. As a result of the efforts which have already been made by the Special Commissioners, and of other plans which are under consideration, it is hoped to enter upon new industrial developments, including the preparation of a trading estate in which industrialists can find ready-made factories provided with all the necessary services. While every effort will be made to find the maximum amount of employment in the Special Areas, increased attention will be given to the training and transfer of such labour as cannot be provided for locally to other places where greater opportunities will be open to them. It may be observed that the new orders required for defence purposes will undoubtedly bring a considerable volume of work and employment into some parts of the country which hitherto have been most hard hit by the heavy depression, and most backward in feeling the general improvement which has been manifest elsewhere.

Social reform

On the foundations which sound financial policy has laid, new and rapid progress in Social Reform has again become possible. We have already referred to the immense development in housing. In the four years during which the Government have been in office more than 1,000,000 houses have been built. A very considerable proportion are small houses, and a substantial number which are being erected to-day are houses "to let". The Slum Clearance campaign is actively proceeding. Already 420,000 occupiers have been actually rehoused, and transfer to new and well-built homes is now proceeding at the unprecedented rate of over 200,000 persons a year. The first steps have already been taken to deal with the evil of overcrowding in accordance with the provisions of the Acts which have just been placed upon the Statute Book. We shall proceed vigorously with all these efforts.

There are a number of other Social Reforms long delayed by the necessity of first restoring the national finances, which are now ripe for action. The Contributory Pensions scheme has been a boon of inestimable value to large numbers of the people. But it has always been recognised that it was not complete so long as persons with small incomes, but not themselves insurably employed, were unable to share in its benefits. Accordingly the Government will, if returned, supplement the present scheme by arrangements which will permit other men – and women, too – whether working on their own account or not, such as shopkeepers, clerks and other black-coated workers, whose income does not exceed a certain limit, to enjoy the benefits of widows', orphans' and old age contributory pensions on a voluntary basis.

Education must always take a foremost place in social progress, and for some time past the Government have been engaged in drawing up a comprehensive scheme of reform. Full details are being published elsewhere; here it suffices to say that it includes the raising of the school-leaving age to fifteen, with exemptions for those children who can obtain satisfactory employment. Considerable preparations, which include reorganisation of schools as well as the provision of further accommodation, will be necessary before this can be made effective. Financial adjustments will include provisions, by which building grants can be made to non-provided schools towards meeting these obligations, and also increased grants to Local Authorities for school buildings and conveyance of children.

Finally, a great combined effort should now be made to raise still further the general standard of health of the Nation, especially that of the younger generation. It will require a simultaneous attack on many fronts. We must further improve our maternity services and make provision for medical assistance at points where there is a gap in the existing services. We must continue to extend our child welfare services and the provision of Nursery Schools. We must meet the increasing demand, especially from our young people, for further physical exercise and training, both in the schools and after school days are over.

We have prepared plans covering all these aspects of this important subject, and when carried into effect they will go far to ensure that future generations shall have full opportunities for the enjoyment of life that comes from the possession of a healthy mind in a healthy body.

Scotland

Scottish problems will continue to receive sympathetic attention. The programme outlined will be generally applicable to the United Kingdom, but in many spheres separate treatment is necessary to meet the special circumstances of Scotland. In particular, the further improvement of housing in the rural as well as urban areas; the needs of Scottish agriculture; the settling of families, and the finding of work for the unemployed, on the land; the provision of water supply and drainage, especially in the sparsely populated areas; and the further betterment of the fishing industry and of the Highlands and Islands will be the subject of special care and attention.

The choice before the country

The advent to power of the Labour Opposition, pledged to a number of revolutionary measures of which the ultimate results could not be clearly foreseen, would inevitably be followed by a collapse of confidence. The measures we have outlined above can only be carried through if the resources of the country are such as to enable it to support the necessary cost. Those resources must be derived from the income of the country, and that income can only increase if the country can rely on a period in which stability will be assured and confidence remain undisturbed.

The international situation reinforces the same lesson. The influence of Britain among other nations, now so conspicuous, could never be maintained under an Administration drawn from a Party whose leaders of experience in foreign affairs no longer co-operate with it, and which is hopelessly divided on the most important points in foreign policy.

In present circumstances it is more than ever necessary that the British Government should not only be united among themselves, but that they should represent that spirit of national co-operation which will best secure the confidence and respect of the world.

CONSERVATIVE PARTY GENERAL ELECTION MANIFESTO 1945

Date of Election	Thursday 5 July
Party Leader	Winston Churchill
Candidates	624
MPs	213
Votes	9,988,306
% of vote	39.8%

Mr Churchill's declaration of policy to the electors

I had hoped to preserve the Coalition Government, comprising all Parties in the State, until the end of the Japanese war, but owing to the unwillingness of the Socialist and Sinclair Liberal Parties to agree to my proposal, a General Election became inevitable, and I have formed a new National Government, consisting of the best men in all Parties who were willing to serve and some who are members of no Party at all.

It is a strong Government, containing many of those who helped me to carry the burdens of State through the darkest days and on whose counsel and executive ability I have learned to rely.

We seek the good of the whole nation, not that of one section or one faction. We believe in the living unity of the British people, which transcends class or party differences. It was this living unity which enabled us to stand like a rock against Germany when she over-ran Europe. Upon our power to retain unity, the future of this country and of the whole world largely depends.

Britain is still at war, and must not turn aside from the vast further efforts still needed to bring Japan to the same end as Germany. Even when all foreign enemies are utterly defeated, that will not be the end of our task. It will be the beginning of our further opportunity –the opportunity which we snatched out of the jaws of disaster in 1940 – to save the world from tyranny and then to play our part in its wise, helpful guidance.

Having poured out all we have to beat the Germans, holding nothing back, we must now take stock of our resources and plan how the energies of the British people can best be freed for the work that lies ahead.

This is the time for freeing energies, not stifling them. Britain's greatness has been built on character and daring, not on docility to a State machine. At all costs we must preserve that spirit of independence and that 'Right to live by no man's leave underneath the law'.

Britain and the world

The settlement of Europe and the prosecution of the war against Japan depend on decisions of the utmost gravity, which can only be taken by resolute and experienced men. Our alliance with Soviet Russia and our intimate friendship with the USA can be maintained only if we show that our candour is matched by our strength.

We have, during the years of our history, gained the confidence of the smaller nations, because, although our power has been formidable, we have tried to use it with restraint and for high purpose, and have always respected the rights and interests of others. There is no small country which does not welcome our strength. This was plainly shown in the recent events in Greece. The irresponsible attitude towards the interests of the Greek people adopted by many sections of Left Wing opinion is, by its example, a warning not to put the conduct of foreign affairs into untried hands.

The main hope of the world is now founded upon the setting up of a World Organisation strong enough to prevent future wars of aggression whether by the weak or the strong. The United Nations have lately been assembled at San Francisco with the object of devising the necessary machinery. We have taken our full part with other Nations and have acted by natural inclination in full agreement with the United States.

There are still many difficulties to overcome. It would be wrong to pretend that so far full success has been gained. Despair would be a crime. We must persevere by any road that opens towards the uplands on which will certainly be built the calm temples of peace. Our prevailing hope is that the foundations will be laid on the indissoluble agreement of Great Britain, the United States and Soviet Russia.

The British Empire and Commonwealth

We shall base the whole of our international policy on a recognition that in world affairs the Mother Country must act in the closest possible concert with all other parts of the British Commonwealth and Empire. We shall never forget their love and steadfastness when we stood alone against the German Terror. We, too, have done our best for them.

The prowess of the Indian Army must not be overlooked in the framing of plans for granting India a fuller opportunity to achieve Dominion Status We should remember those friends who stood by us in our hour of peril, and should be ever mindful of our obligations towards minorities and the Indian States.

The arrangements made in war for constant mutual consultation with the Dominions and India on all matters of joint interest must be perfected in peace. In particular, the whole subject of Imperial defence must be reviewed in relation to our world responsibilities and to modern weapons. Mutually convenient arrangements must be made to foster Imperial trade.

Movement of men and women within the Empire must be made easier. A two-way traffic should grow. Those who wish to change their homes should be enabled to carry their national insurance rights with them wherever they go. Imperial ties should be knit together by closer personal contact and understanding.

Our record in colonial government is unsurpassed. Our responsibility to the Colonies is to lead them forward to self-governing institutions; to help them to raise their standards of life by agricultural advance, the application of science and the building up of local industries; to improve conditions of labour and of housing, to spread education, to stamp out disease and to sustain health, vigour and happiness. The policy laid down in the Colonial Development and Welfare Acts must be keenly pressed forward. The resources of the Empire need to be developed for the benefit of all its many peoples.

Defence

During a whole year of this great war Britain bore the burden of the struggle alone. She must not lose her position in world affairs now that the war in Europe is won. She cannot afford to break and squander the splendid organisms of defence, Naval, Army and Air, which she has with so much effort brought into existence. Above all the nucleus and special elements of command and research must be kept in the highest position. The three Services must be duly balanced in order to meet all the needs of new weapons and new times. It will not be possible, until a new Parliament has been assembled, to shape in detail the naval, military and air forces under conditions of what we hope will be a lasting peace. There will, first of all, be a prolonged occupation of Germany. We have immediately to relieve many of those who have borne the brunt and long burden of the battle by others who have not, so far, had the honour to go to the front.

I am in agreement with Mr Bevin and other Leaders of the Socialist Party that, until the end of the Japanese War and, I hope, until the World Security Organization has become a reality, all citizens under a democratic government should bear responsibility for defending their Country and its Cause. By a system of national service according to their various aptitudes, our young men must be trained to play their part if danger calls. Only a Britain that is strong and ready to fight in defence of Freedom will count in the high councils of the world and thus safeguard coming generations against the immeasurable horrors of another war.

Four years' plan

More than two years ago I made a broadcast to the nation in which I sketched a four years' plan which would cover five or six large measures of a practical character, which must all have been the subject of prolonged, careful and energetic preparation beforehand, and which fitted together into a general scheme.

This plan has now been shaped, and we present it to the country for their approval. Already a beginning has been made in carrying it out, and the Education Act for which our new Minister of Labour is greatly respected is already the law of the land.

Back from the war

We welcome the opportunity of fulfilling all obligations of Service men and women. The financial engagements, the provision of opportunities for training for careers, and, above all, the plans for treatment and rehabilitation of the disabled will be our duty and our aim.

The broad and properly considered lines of the demobilisation proposals, based on age and length of service, which Mr Bevin has elaborated with much wisdom, will be adhered to, and releases will be made as quickly as the condition of the tormented world permits.

Work

In the White Paper presented to Parliament by the late administration are sound plans for avoiding the disastrous slumps and booms from which we used to suffer, but which all are united in being determined to avoid in the future.

The Government accepts as one of its primary aims and responsibilities the maintenance of a high and stable level of employment.

Unless there is steady and ample work, there will not be the happiness, the confidence, or the material resources in the country on which we can all build together the kind of Britain that we want to see.

To find plenty of work with individual liberty to choose one's job, free enterprise must be given the chance and the encouragement to plan ahead. Confidence in sound government – mutual co-operation between industry and the State, rather than control by the State – a lightening of the burdens of excessive taxation – these are the first essentials.

Homes

In the first years of peace, the provision of homes will be the greatest domestic task. An all-out housing policy will not only make a tremendous contribution to family life, but also to steady employment and to national health. All our energy must be thrown into it. Local authorities and private enterprise must both be given the fullest encouragement to get on with the job.

Prices of materials must be controlled as long as supplies are short. Even so, building costs will be high at first. They must be brought down as rapidly as possible. Subsidies will be necessary for local authorities and for private enterprise alike.

We must add to our building labour force as quickly as we can. The strength of the industry was 1,000,000 men before the war. Now it is down to under 400,000. We have already made our plans to expand it as quickly as possible up to and beyond its pre-war strength.

In blitzed areas the repair of war-damaged houses and the rebuilding of those destroyed will be given high priority. In the first two years, as the labour force grows, we intend to build at least 220,000 permanent new houses and have a further 80,000 under way. We hope to increase this still further, but do not intend to make promises we may not be able to fulfil. As the result of intensive research work that has been carried out by many enterprising firms, a number of new types of factory-made permanent houses and housing equipment is being developed. (The erection of these makes a smaller demand on our scarce building labour than the traditional types.) These will be put into large-scale production with the same energy as was shown in munitions. We must supplement this with at least 150,000 well-equipped temporary houses that can be put up quickly. Our target is 200,000.

So long as there is a serious shortage of houses, rent control must continue on houses controlled at present. The establishment of Tribunals throughout the country to fix fair rents as between landlord and tenant (as recommended by the Ridley Committee) seems to provide the best solution of a long-standing problem.

The rebuilding of badly bombed areas, the general attack on the housing problem and the redistribution of industry demand plans for the use of land which will take into account the needs of each locality and the opportunities offered by national resources. The Government will press forward with the main lines of policy laid down in the Town and Country Planning Acts, including the acquisition of land required in connection with the restoration of blitzed areas on the basis of the 1939 value.

We shall bring forward in the new Parliament proposals for improving the law with regard to compensation and betterment, so as to secure for the future the best use of land in the public interest, including proper reservation of open spaces and the best location of industry and housing.

Food and agriculture

We must produce a great deal more food than we did before the war, because food is scarce in the world to-day, and in any case we shall not be able to buy as much imported food as we did.

A healthy and well-balanced agriculture is an essential element in our national life. British agriculture will be maintained in a condition to enable the efficient producer to obtain a reasonable return on the enterprise and the capital invested, and to enable wages to be paid to the worker sufficient to secure him a proper standard of living.

We must maintain the fertility of the soil; we must be skilful in the use and management of our land for the production of the foodstuffs which it is best fitted to provide, and which are most required to satisfy the nutritional needs of our people.

We need Imperial co-operation, leading to international co-operation, in the orderly production and marketing of food; and within this country we shall have improved systems of marketing of home products and such other arrangements as may be necessary to maintain stability and avoid the evils of recurring scarcity and gluts. For this purpose each product will be treated on its own merits.

Our policy will be one of stable markets and prices. In return for this all occupiers and owners of agricultural land must maintain a reasonable standard of good husbandry and estate management. Within these principles the best results will be obtained by restoring the greatest measure of freedom possible, and allowing full scope for each farmer to make the best use of his land.

The war-time directions and controls will be progressively reduced as our food situation improves and consequently the functions of the County Agricultural Executive Committees will progressively be limited to that of affording leadership, help and advice.

Educational facilities will be developed as fast as the necessary teaching staff and buildings can be made available. The extension of agricultural research will continue. The best scientific advice will be made available to all farmers by the new advisory service.

Provision of smallholdings will be resumed as soon as labour and materials can be spared for men who have gained experience as agricultural workers, and allotments will be encouraged by every reasonable means.

The new Forestry Policy will result in far-reaching and permanent programmes of afforestation. We must take care of our big trees, and make provision for their replacement.

Better housing in country districts is a most urgent need. Large numbers of new cottages in rural areas will be provided, as well as greater facilities for bringing existing cottages and farms up to date. A wide extension of electricity supply, water and sanitation will be undertaken for villages, cottages and farms. No less necessary are better communications, better health services and better social facilities for all who live and work in the countryside. A policy on these lines will secure a prosperous agriculture. That in its turn will bring benefits to town and country alike, and help to provide our people with good food for a steadily improving diet.

Our fishing industry must be restored with intense exertions and at the utmost speed. In war the fishermen have been out after sterner catches, and once again the nation has been well served in danger by their skill and courage. We must rebuild the industry and make it a way of life which will give attractive employment to the fine men it breeds. What we want now is fish, and this must be tackled by every conceivable method.

National Insurance

National well-being is founded on good employment, good housing and good health. But there always remain those personal hazards of fortune, such as illness, accident or loss of a job, or industrial injury, which may leave the individual and his family unexpectedly in distress. In addition, old age, death and child-birth throw heavy burdens upon the family income.

One of our most important tasks will be to pass into law and bring into action as soon as we can a nation-wide and compulsory scheme of National Insurance based on the plan announced by the Government of all Parties in 1944.

In return for a single consolidated contribution there will be new and increased benefits, amongst which is to be an old age or retirement pension of 20/- for single people and 35/- for married couples. Family allowances are one part of the great scheme, and the arrangements made will ensure that men and women serving in the Forces and those disabled will benefit equally with other classes in the community.

The new Ministry of National Insurance has been set up to prepare, administer and control the whole of this great legislation. So massive and complex a task can only be discharged by a large and highly-trained staff, which has to be assembled and accommodated. The specialised experience of the Approved Societies will therefore be drawn upon, and their employees, especially those who have served at the front, must have due consideration.

The scheme will not justify itself to the public unless the service given to them in return for their contributions combines human understanding with efficiency. There must be no queuing up for sickness benefits by those who are entitled to them. The same standard of intimacy in personal relationships must be maintained as formerly.

Health

The health services of the country will be made available to all citizens. Everyone will contribute to the cost, and no one will be denied the attention, the treatment or the appliances he requires because he cannot afford them.

We propose to create a comprehensive health service covering the whole range of medical treatment from the general practitioner to the specialist, and from the hospital to convalescence and rehabilitation; and to introduce legislation for this purpose in the new Parliament.

The success of the service will depend on the skill and initiative of doctors, dentists, nurses and other professional people, and in its designing and operation there will be full scope for all the guidance they can give. Wide play must be given to the preferences and enterprise of individuals. Nothing will be done to destroy the close personal relationship between doctor and patient, nor to restrict the patient's free choice of doctor.

The whole service must be so designed that in each area its growth is helped and guided by the influence of a university. Through such a service the medical and allied professions will be enabled to serve the whole nation more effectively than they have yet been able to do. At the same time Medicine will be left free to develop along its own lines, and to achieve preventive as well as curative triumphs. Liberty is an essential condition of scientific progress. The voluntary hospitals which have led the way in the development of hospital technique will remain free. They will play their part in the new service in friendly partnership with local authority hospitals.

Motherhood must be our special care. There must be a large increase of maternity beds and convalescent homes, and they must be provided in the right places. Mothers must be relieved of onerous duties which at such times so easily cause lasting injury to their health. The National Insurance Scheme will make financial provision for these needs. All proper arrangements, both voluntary and State-aided, must be made for the care of other young children in the family, in order that the energies of the male breadwinner or the kindness of neighbours and relations, which nevertheless must be the mainspring, should not be unduly burdened. Nursery schools and nurseries such as have grown up during the war should be encouraged. On the birth, the proper feeding and the healthy upbringing of a substantially increased number of children, depend the life of Britain and her enduring glory.

Education

The Education Act set forth in the 'Four Years' Plan' has already been piloted through Parliament by Mr Butler. Our task in the coming years will be to remodel our educational system according to the new law, and a vigorous drive will be needed to supply the teachers and the buildings necessary.

Our object is to provide education which will not produce a standardised or utility child, useful only as a cog in a nationalised and bureaucratic machine, but will enable the child to develop his or her responsible place, first in the world of school, and then as a citizen. Many parents will be able to choose the school they like and to play their part with the educational authorities in the physical and spiritual well-being of their children.

Our aim must be to produce the good citizen of tomorrow. Our primary schools call for much encouragement and improvement. Secondary Education for all will have no meaning unless variety, practical training and, above all, quality of standards convince parents that the extra schooling for their children is worth while. Technical education, at all levels, must be greatly extended and improved.

No system of education can be complete unless it heightens what is splendid and glorious in life and art. Art, science and learning are the means by which the life of the whole people can be beautified and enriched.

Overseas trade

Britain relies upon overseas trade for maintaining her people's standard of living. Industry and employment are bound to depend largely on imported raw materials. Even in wartime we have to draw one-third of our food from abroad. Britain's investments overseas and our shipping, which helped to pay for these imports before the war, have been largely sacrificed. In striving for others we have become a debtor nation.

Therefore it is only by greatly increasing our exports and services that we can buy the imports we require, and thus increase the whole vast volume of our internal trade. The exchange of goods and services with Empire countries is our most fertile and natural market.

We must do all we can in various ways to promote international trade, but of course we cannot give up our right to safeguard our balance of payments by whatever means are necessary: in the end the way to sell enough of our exports abroad, both directly and by roundabout trade, is to take full advantage of the great variety of British industry, the inventiveness of British scientists and technicians, the enterprise and experience of British manufacturers and merchants, and the skill of British workpeople and the renowned trustworthiness of their output.

All possible encouragement will be given to the enterprise of individuals and firms to take advantage of export opportunities of all kinds, and nothing must be done to paralyse the spirit of adventure.

Industrial efficiency

The more efficient British industry is and the fuller the use it makes of modern methods and materials, the higher will be the standard of well-being that is possible for our people. We will stimulate scientific research in industry and in the universities, and encourage the scrapping of obsolete plant and methods in every possible way. Taxation must not bear unduly upon new machinery and enterprise.

All that we long to achieve in making good the wartime shortage depends on attaining the highest possible levels of peacetime production as fast as we can. We shall fail in that if the British people, instead of fixing their eyes on production, are led off at this moment into academic and spiteful controversies about Socialism.

We should examine the conditions and the vital needs of every industry on its own merits. We believe in variety, not in standardised and identical structure, still less in bureaucratic torpor. We will not allow drastic changes of ownership to be forced upon industries on no evidence except a political theory, and with no practical regard to the results they may bring. To us the tests will always be – what will conduce most to efficiency, and what will render the greatest service to the community. This is the policy we shall apply, whether it be coal, cotton or the heavy industries.

As against the advocates of State ownership and control, we stand for the fullest opportunity for go and push in all ranks throughout the whole nation. This quality is part of the genius of the British people, who mean to be free to use their own judgment and never intend to be State serfs, nor always to wait for official orders before they can act.

Monopolies

We must guard against abuses to which monopolies may give rise. It is vital that there should be effective protection of the consumers' interests and of the independent business, whether small or large, against any such abuse. Nationalisation involves a State monopoly, with no proper protection for anyone against monopoly power. Neither that nor any other form of unfettered monopoly should be allowed to exist in Britain. The right remedy against harmful restrictive practices is to set up an independent tribunal before which charges of monopoly abuse can be laid. Its work and reports should be public, so that any necessary action in restraint of abuse may be taken by Parliament or otherwise.

Controls

We stand for the removal of controls as quickly as the need for them disappears. Control of labour, of materials and of prices, is necessary in war, when we have to give up much of our freedom in order to make sure that the war machine gets all that it requires. Some of these controls will continue to be needed until normal times return. As long as shortage of food remains, rationing must obviously be accepted: the dangers of inflation also must be guarded against.

As long as any wartime controls have to be retained, they must be made subject to strict Parliamentary scrutiny and sanction. We must watch the interest of the consumer always. Controls, originally imposed on his behalf, tend to bind him down and injure him as soon as circumstances change.

We intend to guard the people of this country against those who, under guise of war necessity, would like to impose upon Britain for their own purposes a permanent system of bureaucratic control, reeking of totalitarianism.

The small man in business

The small man in trade or industry, who adventures all he has in the effort to make a success of the business he undertakes, must be given every chance to make good. His independence of spirit is one of the essential elements that made up the life of a free society. Many thousands of such men have been hit bitterly hard by war. Other men may have jobs to go back to, but the businesses of some of these men are gone, or hanging by a thread.

It will be a definite point in our policy to make certain that the problems of the small man receive special attention. In particular, the returning Service men or women who obtained their livelihood in this way must be given every possible chance to re-establish themselves.

Fuel and power

Coal is owned by the State, and is a wasting asset. The industry, taken by and large, as the Reid Report shows, has fallen behind some of its competitors overseas.

The industrial activities of this country are principally founded on coal. Adequate supplies, as cheap as possible, must be available for our homes, for our factories and for export. We cannot afford to lose a coal export trade. Wartime measures are not suited to peacetime conditions. A new, practical start is needed. The position cannot be remedied by mere change of ownership of the collieries. That offers no solution.

A central authority, appointed by the Minister of Fuel and subject to his general direction, will be set up, to insist that the necessary measures are taken and to provide such help and guidance as is useful. These measures centre upon the proper development and efficient conduct of operations in each coalfield according to the best modern practice. In so far as grouping or amalgamating collieries is necessary for this object, it will be carried through, voluntarily if possible, but otherwise by compulsion.

At the same time in this diversified industry where conditions vary widely, there are often to be found highly efficient undertakings which are sometimes not large: in such cases amalgamation will only be proposed if there are clear advantages to the nation and the industry; we do not propose amalgamation for amalgamation's sake. The making and carrying out of these plans will be undertaken by the industry itself. The duty of the central authority will be to satisfy itself that the scope and effect of the plans conform to national requirements, and it will have powers of enforcement in reserve. This policy will preserve the incentives of free enterprise and safeguard the industry from the dead hand of State ownership or political interference in day-to-day management. It will also provide the necessary sanctions for making sure that the essential improvements recommended in the Reid Report are carried through.

At the same time, increased efficiency must be stimulated in the use and handling of coal and its principal products, electricity and gas. There is room for much greater coordination of the local distribution of these services. Opportunities to increase the nation's resources by harnessing water power also will be scientifically investigated and followed up.

Transport

Transport over land and over sea will have to remain under wartime control for a time. We have still to work out detailed plans to meet the new needs of peace. Road and rail, canals and coast-wise shipping, will be encouraged and helped to bring to a successful conclusion in plans already under discussion for a transport system of the highest efficiency, in which each method would play its appropriate part, with freedom for the public to choose which one to use, and with protection against any risk of monopoly charges.

New proposals for Civil Aviation, based broadly on the White Paper of 1945, will be adopted and speedily brought into operation. This policy will ensure the full development of our Commonwealth and Empire services on the partnership lines already established; there will be co-operation with foreign governments on all overseas services linking our country and theirs; we shall at the same time expand our air services within the United Kingdom, aiming at the most complete network of services in and between England and Wales, Scotland and Northern Ireland.

We shall see to it that air transport undertakings are free to manage the services for which they are responsible and that there shall be ample opportunity for development, and for newcomers to enter the lists in the United Kingdom. It is, of course, our intention that British Air Lines shall use British aircraft and we are satisfied that those aircraft in peace as in war will be second to none.

We must ensure the maintenance of a large, modern and highly efficient Merchant Navy. This country must never forget the debt she owes to her merchant seamen. The men who sailed the convoys to Britain, to Malta, to Russia and all over the world must be sure of steady employment, ships designed to give them good living conditions, good standards of food, and proper provision for their welfare.

There will shortly be a large world surplus of wartime shipping and we shall enter into international consultations for its orderly disposal and for avoiding competitive subsidies after the war.

Money

Our war budget has been rendered possible only by the severest taxation pressing heavily on everybody, by borrowing on a vast scale to meet the passing crisis, by huge Lend-Lease supplies from the United States and by generous gifts from Canada and elsewhere. All this cannot go on.

The State has no resources of its own. It can only spend what it takes from the people in taxes or borrowing. Britain is now a nation of taxpayers. Its record of providing more than half of the national expenditure during the last years of the war from taxation is unsurpassed. The willingness of this generation to bear their fair share of sacrifices must, though we hope for relief, be continued. Our future needs for the war against Japan, for winding up the German war, and the plans for social progress which we are determined to carry out, cause and require a much higher rate of national expenditure than before the war.

This burden must be borne by all citizens as taxpayers. There is no easy way of one section getting great benefits from the State at the expense of another. The nation can have the services it is prepared to pay for. Where all benefit, all will have to contribute. The revenue is not created by waving a magic wand. It is drawn from the fruits of the nation's industry, agriculture and commerce. It is won by work and paid in taxes. The present level of taxation drastically restricts the ability of the ordinary citizen to satisfy his personal desires. It is discouraging to his enterprise and his efforts to better himself by doing the bit extra, for so large a part of anything he gains to be removed by the tax-collector.

It will be our aim and purpose to make an early reduction in taxation in a way that will stimulate energy and permit free individual choice. The Government will re-examine the whole structure of taxation in relation to the level at which expenditure will stand after the war, in order to lighten the burden where it presses most, and simplify the tax system.

We will not permit any monkeying with the people's savings. Our desire is to see property widely spread, and we rejoice that the savings movement, which must go on, has now made almost everyone a property-owner. An object of our financial policy is to keep prices from rising, and make sure that savers do not see the purchasing-power of their savings dwindle.

On a basis of high employment, initiative and hard work on the part of everyone, we can achieve our great Four Years' programme. It is well worth achieving.

Our purpose

Ours is a great nation and never in its history has it stood in higher repute in the world than today. Its greatness rests not on its material wealth, for that has been poured out in full measure, nor upon its armed might, which other nations surpass. It has its roots in the character, the ability, and the independence of our people and the magic of this wonderful island. British virtues have been developed under the free institutions which our fathers and forefathers struggled through the centuries to win and to keep. We of this generation are trustees for posterity, and the duty lies upon us to hand down to our children unimpaired the unique heritage that was bequeathed to us.

This is a country built on family life. War and separation have strengthened, not impaired, the love of home. The children must always come first. The Education Act, school meals, family allowances, all show that Parliament is realising that. Family life is a precious asset to be defended at all costs.

We are dedicated to the purpose of helping to rebuild Britain on the sure foundations on which her greatness rests. In recent generations, enormous material progress has been made. That progress must be extended and accelerated not by subordinating the individual to the authority of the State, but by providing the conditions in which no one shall be precluded by poverty, ignorance, insecurity, or the selfishness of others from making the best of the gifts with which Providence has endowed him.

Our programme is not based upon unproved theories or fine phrases, but upon principles that have been tested anew in the fires of war and not found wanting. We commend it to the country not as offering an easy road to the nation's goal but because, while safeguarding our ancient liberties, it tackles practical problems in a practical way.

THIS IS THE ROAD

The Conservative and Unionist Party's Policy

GENERAL ELECTION
1950

CONSERVATIVE PARTY GENERAL ELECTION MANIFESTO 1950

Date of Election	Thursday 23 February
Party Leader	Winston Churchill
Candidates	620
MPs	298
Votes	12,502,567
% of vote	43.5%

THIS IS THE ROAD

The Conservative and Unionist Party's policy

As Leader of the Conservative and Unionist Party I submit this manifesto of our beliefs and policy to the British electors.

All who cherish the cause of our country at this fateful moment must cast their vote after hard and long thought, and make sure they cast it effectively.

I commend to your attention with confidence this outline of our resolves and desires should we be called upon to assume the responsibilities of Government.
19 January, 1950 Winston S. Churchill

The policy of the Conservative Party, expressed in 'The Right Road for Britain' is to restore to our country her economic independence and to our citizens their full personal freedom and power of initiative. Unless Britain can hold her place in the world, she cannot make her full contribution to the preservation of peace, and peace is our supreme purpose. Britain, wisely led, can bring together the Commonwealth and Empire, Western Europe and the Atlantic Powers into a partnership dedicated to the cause of saving world peace and of preserving democratic freedom and the rule of law.

Present dangers

We can only import the food and raw materials on which we depend by paying for them in goods, services or cash. For the first few years after the war every country wanted all that Britain could make, almost regardless of price. That time is passing. Now Britain can sell abroad only if her goods are high in quality and competitive in price.

Since 1945, Britain has received in gifts and loans from the United States and the nations of the Commonwealth the vast sum of nearly £2,000 millions. But Marshall aid will end by 1952. From that time forth we must pay for all we buy from overseas or suffer the consequences in low standards of living and high unemployment.

The duty of the Government from their first day in office was to husband the national resources, to evoke the greatest efforts from all, to give every chance to enterprise and inventiveness and above all, not needlessly to divide the nation.

The socialist failure

But the Socialists have failed in their duty. National resources have been squandered. Individual effort has been discouraged or suppressed. National unity has been deeply injured. The Government have shrunk from the realities of the situation and have not told the people the truth.

The socialist deception

From the time they acquired power they pretended that their policy was bringing the prosperity they had promised. They tried to make out that before they got a majority the whole history of Great Britain, so long admired and envied throughout the world, was dark and dismal. They spread the tale that social welfare is something to be had from the State free, gratis and for nothing. They have put more money into circulation, but it has bought less and less. The value of every pound earned or saved or paid in pensions or social services has been cut by 3s. 8d. since they took office. It is not a £ but 16/4.

There is no foundation for the Socialist claim to have brought us prosperity and security. Ministers themselves have declared that but for American Aid there would have been two million people unemployed.

During these bleak years Britain has lurched from crisis to crisis and from makeshift to makeshift. Whatever temporary expedients have been used to create a false sense of well being, none has effected a permanent cure. Devaluation is not the last crisis nor have we seen the worst of it yet.

Socialist mismanagement

In 1945, the Socialists promised that their methods of planning and nationalisation would make the people of Britain masters of their economic destiny. Nothing could be more untrue. Every forecast has proved grossly over-optimistic. Every crisis has caught them unawares. The Fuel Crisis cost the country £200 millions and the Convertibility Crisis as much. Ambitious plans have gone awry. Nearly thirty million pounds have already been muddled away on the Groundnuts Scheme. Railway engines were converted to burn oil because coal was scarce and then converted back again because oil was even scarcer. With the same labour force as before the war little more than half as many houses are being built. Despite the promise of the Minister of Health that 'when the next Election occurs there will be no housing problem in Great Britain for the working class', waiting lists for council houses in many districts are longer now than they were five years ago.

Socialism has imposed a crushing burden of taxation amounting to eight shillings of every pound earned in this country. Enterprise and extra effort have been stifled. Success has been penalised. Thrift and savings have been discouraged. A vote for Socialism is a vote to continue the policy which has endangered our economic and present independence both as a nation and as men and women.

The Conservatives and your future

A complete change in the spirit of administration is needed. Only the Conservative Party can make this change. The Socialist Government are temporising with grave economic perils. Britain's difficulties will not be resolved by some trick of organisation, nor will prosperity come as a gift from government. The nation will enjoy in benefit only as much as it is prepared to create by its own effort. With a high spirit, through great endeavours, relying on our native skill, every man and woman must bend their energies to a new wave of national impulse. Only thus can the British people save themselves now and win lasting prosperity for the future. In the last four years the British people have not been shown the way nor given a proper chance to find it. A Conservative Government will guide them along the right road.

THE ECONOMIC CRISIS

Empire Conference

Britain can resolve her economic difficulties not only by reviving her native strength but by fortifying every link with the nations of our Empire and Commonwealth. An Imperial Economic Conference should consider the whole problem of strengthening the resources of the Empire in order to close the dollar gap. This will speed the development of raw materials and foodstuffs. It will promote greater exports of raw materials and manufactured goods to dollar countries. It will seek to encourage the investment of American as well as British capital in the Empire. It will try to reach a permanent settlement of the debts owed by Commonwealth nations to one another, and especially the war-time debts incurred by Britain for defending India and Egypt.

We must rebuild the reserves of the sterling area, of which we are the principal guardians and with our partners enlarge the area of trade over which free exchange prevails.

Enterprise

Britain's own contribution must take the form of larger and more efficient production at lower prices.

Conservatives believe in enterprise. We believe that the quality of daring was never more needed than today. It deserves practical encouragement wherever it is to be found. Only by its exercise can mass unemployment be averted and prosperity attained.

The true value of money must be honestly maintained. The crushing burden of public expenditure must be drastically reduced. Stronger effort, more enterprise and inventiveness, and greater thrift can only be encouraged by lower taxes.

Government expenditure

In order to lower taxes and the high cost of living we must cut down Government spending. We are convinced that substantial savings are necessary and possible. If a tenth or even a twentieth of our enormous national expenditure of three thousand three hundred millions a year were saved, our whole financial position would be relieved, and immediate reductions in taxation could be shared by all. We do not ignore the unpopularity of any kind of saving and the misrepresentation to which it will be subjected, but the task must be faced, and we shall not shirk it.

Cost of defence

An immediate survey of the whole seven hundred and fifty millions of defence expenditure is imperative.

Cost of food

The time has come to restore the business of food purchase to the experienced traders in food and to end direct Government buying. If the experience of other countries is any guide, this change will certainly effect some reduction in the cost of our food. Meanwhile the production of food is rising in many lands, and thus it should be possible to reduce the number of commodities for which rationing remains necessary. Our Conservative policy is clear: to reduce the cost to the taxpayer by the wise buying of food.

The present system of food subsidies is open to the objection that it is indiscriminate in its incidence. Those who need it least get as much as those who need it most. As Mr Eden said in the House of Commons, our principle should be 'that the strong should help the weak and we should not try to aid everybody indiscriminately'.

In any approach to the problem of food subsidies, made necessary by the urgent need to improve the purchasing power of the £, we shall be bound by this pledge. There will be no reduction which might influence the price of food without compensating increases to those most affected. These compensations will take the form, on the one hand, of larger family allowances, pensions and other social benefits, and, on the other, of reductions of taxation, direct and indirect, that will increase incentives among the masses of the people.

Waste and extravagance

Everyone knows that there is enormous waste. There are too many Ministers and Government Departments and there is too much overlapping of functions between them. For example, the work of the Ministry of Civil Aviation should be redistributed between the Transport and other ministries so that a separate Department ceases to exist. The civilian functions of the Ministry of Supply such as state trading in metals, will cease; and others should go to the Board of Trade. The Service Departments should buy their common needs through a joint organisation under the Minister of Defence in order to achieve the most efficient and economical arrangement. Many new Commissions or Committees outside the Ministries must be reviewed to see if they are wanted. There is also plenty of scope for retrenchment – to give only a few examples – in public relations, Information Services, excessive control over local authorities, the county agricultural committees, Government travelling, etc.

In local government we favour more devolution to the boroughs and district councils to avoid the swarms of full-time organisers and supervisors like those who have sprung up in the health services. The cost of hospital administration could be reduced by new methods of financial control including better costing and more publicity for accounts.

Lower taxes

We regard present high taxation as a grave evil. By reductions in expenditure substantial sums will be available for reducing both direct and indirect taxation. As we have already said, our aim and intention is to make sure that extra work, effort and skill on piece-rates and through overtime, instead of being penalised, shall gain their just reward. The restoration of their incentive, not only to the higher ranks of labour, will give a new stimulus to every kind of production and help our export trade. The high taxation of money put to reserve in business hinders many important schemes for improving industrial efficiency. We hope to make sufficient economies to start upon reducing indirect taxation and particularly Purchase Tax on necessities and semi-necessities. Under the present system any reduction of purchase tax entails considerable losses to retailers. This we shall avoid. All reductions in taxation will encourage National Savings.

Unemployment

The Socialists claim that their policy has prevented mass unemployment such as followed the First World War. The conditions often were wholly different. Under the Socialist Government of 1929–1931 unemployment rose violently and reached fearful figures. With all this in our minds our war-time Coalition anxiously probed the future, and all the leading Socialist ministers, including Mr Attlee, Mr Herbert Morrison, Sir Stafford Cripps and Mr Bevin, agreed with their Conservative colleagues that the world demand for goods would, for some years after the fighting stopped, make serious unemployment unlikely. However, we made far-reaching plans, based upon hard experience and new knowledge, to cope with the evil should it come. All this is upon record and was laid before Parliament in 1944. But in addition we have had nearly £2,000 millions given or loaned to us by the United States and Commonwealth countries. Do not forget that Mr Morrison, Mr Bevan and other leading Socialists have declared that without this aid we should have had 1½ to 2 millions unemployed in these last years instead of the present 300,000.

These are strange confessions for public men to make at a time when they are boasting that they have cured unemployment. Stranger still is the charge they make that their Conservative colleagues, with whom they agreed the policy of 1944, actually seek to provoke unemployment in order to get more work out of the wage earners. This is indeed rather shabby. We regard the maintenance of full employment as the first aim of a Conservative Government. How grave will be the consequences of the cessation of American Aid no one can forecast. But if human endeavour can avail we shall succeed.

Post-war credits

We recognise that the repayment of post-war credits is an obligation to be met. Such large sums are, however, outstanding that it will be impossible to repay them all at once without risk of inflation. Meanwhile we shall consider schemes for the repayment of credits to the estates of deceased persons.

Equal pay

We hope that during the life of the next Parliament the country's financial position will improve sufficiently to enable us to proceed at an early date with the application in the Government Service of the principle of equal pay for men and women for services of equal value.

BRITISH INDUSTRY

The Conservative Party will encourage in industry the highest level of efficient production and the most effective partnership between owners, executives and operatives. Today all forms of production and distribution are hampered in a Socialist atmosphere which denies enterprise its reward while making life too easy for the laggards. Monopoly and bureaucracy should give place to competition and enterprise. All enterprises, large and small, should have a fair field.

We shall do everything to help the trade unions to serve the best interests of the nation and their members. The foundation of industrial endeavour must be good human relationships, not impersonal control from aloft and afar. For all those engaged in production we shall provide opportunity, freedom and a fair share of the proceeds, and for the consumer greater variety of choice at prices to suit his pocket.

Power should be more decentralised

On every hand, in local as well as in national affairs, power is being increasingly centred in the Government. The State has obtruded heavily on the individual, his home and his pocket. Almost every incident of daily life is bound by controls which Parliament has had little chance to debate. These controls shelter the sluggish from failure while holding back the adventurous from success. They permit easy profits without insisting on efficiency. They create monopoly and deprive the consumer of the correction of competition.

Britain already knows to her cost that the state monopolies created by nationalisation are rigid, awkward, wasteful and inefficient. Large losses have been made. Monopoly powers are being used to force higher prices on the consumers, who have no effective redress. Responsible initiative is crushed by centralised authority. Frustration and cynicism prevail among the staffs. The power of trade unions to protect their members is being undermined and the freedom of choice of consumer and worker alike is being narrowed. If nationalisation is extended, the creeping paralysis of state monopoly will spread over ever wider sections of industry until the Socialists have carried out their declared aim to nationalise all the means of production, distribution and exchange.

Nationalisation

We shall bring Nationalisation to a full stop here and now. Thereby we shall save all those industries, such as cement, sugar, meat distribution, chemicals, water and insurance which are now under threat by the Socialists.

We shall repeal the Iron and Steel Act before it can come into force. Steel will remain under free enterprise, but its policy on prices and development will be supervised as in recent years by a Board representative of Government, management, labour and consumers.

The nationalisation of omnibuses and tramways will be halted. Wherever possible those already nationalised will be offered to their former owners, whether private or municipal. We shall also be prepared to sell back to free enterprise those sections of the road haulage industry which have been nationalised, and to restore the former system of A and B licences. The limitation of distance on private road hauliers will be progressively eliminated. The present freedom of C licences will remain untouched.

As wide a measure of free enterprise as possible should be restored to Civil Aviation. We shall review the structure and character of the Airways Corporations with that in mind.

We shall drastically reorganise the Coal Industry as a public undertaking by restricting the duties of the National Board and by giving autonomy to the Area Boards. By decentralising the work of the National Board we shall give greater responsibility to the men on the spot and revive local loyalties and enthusiasm. 'British Railways' should be re-organised into a number of regional railway systems each with its own pride of identity and each administered by its own Board of Direction whose members must have varied practical experience of serving public needs. We shall hold ourselves free to decide the future of the Gas and Electricity Boards when we have had more experience of their working.

The consumer must be given greater protection in the industries remaining nationalised. This can be done by a wider use of independent price tribunals, by stricter Parliamentary control of accounts, by finding time for a periodic review of each industry by Parliament and by subjecting them to examination by the Monopolies Commission or some similar body. Ministers' powers to make appointments will be defined and their powers to give directions will be clarified. Every nationalised undertaking will observe the Workers' Charter.

Our special proposals for nationalised undertakings in Scotland are set out later.

Controls

The time has come when controls must be reduced to the minimum necessary as the supply situation improves. Controlled prices should be based on the costs of the more efficient firms and the system of allocating materials put on an up-to-date basis. This will make it easier for new firms to start.

Almost all our neighbours in Europe have ended food, and indeed petrol, rationing. As soon as we have been able to ensure that the prime necessities of life are within the reach of every family and each individual, we shall abolish the existing rationing system.

Monopoly

Through the powers of the Monopoly and Restrictive Practices Act we shall see that the public interest is protected and that prices are not kept up either by inefficiency or by combinations in restraint of trade. We shall bring to the front the question of restrictive labour practices which the National Joint Advisory Committee has had under consideration.

Bulk purchase

It will be our policy to end bulk buying by the State. But we shall honour existing contracts and be prepared, where necessary, to give suitable guarantees for producers in Empire and Commonwealth countries. Wherever conditions permit, we shall reopen the commodity markets which can be a valuable source of foreign currency. The Liverpool Cotton Exchange will be reopened.

Trade unions

We have held the views, from the days of Disraeli, that the Trade Union movement is essential to the proper working of our economy and of our industrial life. Conservatives should not hesitate to join Trade Unions as so many of our Party have already done, and to play their full part in their union affairs. As soon as possible we wish the Trade Unions to regain their function of obtaining for their members a full share of increasing productivity through free collective bargaining. We shall consult with all engaged in industry on how to make more effective the machinery for consultation between industry and the Government.

We shall abolish the direction of labour.

We shall consult with the Unions upon a friendly and final settlement of the questions of contracting out and compulsory unionism, on both of which Conservatives have strong convictions of principle, and on any other matters that the Unions may wish to raise.

Workers' charter

The detailed application of a Workers' Charter designed to give security, incentive and status will be discussed with the Trade Unions and the employers. It is our intention to bring it into effect as early as possible in industry and to extend it to agriculture wherever practicable. Legislation will provide every employee with a legal right to a written contract of service in which, if both parties agree, length of notice may be adjusted to length of service.

The Workers' Charter will lay down the principle that extra effort should always bring extra reward and that promotion shall be by merit. It will encourage schemes of training, both technical and general, for all who may benefit from them. It advocates the widest possible extension, on a voluntary basis, of joint consultation on subjects other than wages and conditions of work, which are already covered by collective bargaining, and will favour schemes of co-partnership and profit-sharing. The main body of the Charter will not be embodied in legislation but will be drawn up as a Code of Conduct and submitted to Parliament for debate and adoption. We shall ensure that this Code is strictly applied in all undertakings under Government control. After due notice has been given, only those employers who observe the Code will obtain public contracts.

Food and agriculture

Home food production must have an assured place in the national economy. We must look to the home farmer and market gardener for a greater quantity and more variety in the nation's food and they will have first place in the home market. We are opposed to the nationalisation of the land and farming by the State.

British agriculture is expected to provide, on a long-term basis, an efficient output at least half as large again as that of pre-war. It should concentrate more than at present on live stock and so help to increase the meat ration.

We shall encourage the fishing industry to set up a White Fish Marketing Board. Renewed efforts will be made to secure an international agreement to stop serious over-fishing.

For farm produce we shall continue the system, which we introduced during the war, of guaranteed prices based upon an annual price review. Wool should be given a guaranteed price and oats the same treatment as other guaranteed products.

Farmers and merchants must be encouraged to work together through Marketing Boards and voluntary associations, while the consumer is protected by the Monopolies Commission and special committees of investigation. Loans to aid in financing new production will be made available through co-operative associations and Marketing Boards. British horticulture must be safeguarded against destructive imports. Small growers in the industry should be encouraged to develop grading and co-operative buying and selling organisations.

We shall vigorously implement the Hill Farming Act and give appropriate incentives to farmers of marginal land.

The duties of the County Committees should be re-examined and their administration and excessive paperwork simplified. Ministers should seek their advice on every problem of production and the use of agricultural land. The Advisory Service must give impartial advice and inspire the trust of farmers. It must be freed from bureaucracy and enabled to attract the best advisers. If necessary, the Universities should be asked to help.

The Ministries of Agriculture and Food must be brought closer together and the present overlapping and conflict eliminated, with a view to their eventual amalgamation. The supply of food from home and overseas supplies must be kept under constant review by a revived Market Supply Committee.

Nationalisation will not reduce the costs of food. Past experience shows that it will increase them. We shall make it our business to see that the housewife gets her food through the cheapest and most efficient channels and that she has first chance of any extra supplies that can be got.

Rural conditions

Houses for the agricultural population must have the necessary priority and subsidies will be given to local authorities and individuals alike. Reconditioning grants will be made available for all rural cottages. As supplies of materials improve, reconditioning will be made compulsory.

Local schemes for water supplies and sewerage should be given the highest priority and administrative delays in the work should be attacked. The countryside deserves its fair share of other modern amenities such as electricity and buses.

Suitable educational facilities will be provided by retaining as many village schools as possible, by teaching rural science in all primary and secondary schools, rural and urban, and by providing adequate facilities for technical education, and grants for village halls. It has always been part of our policy to foster the smallholdings movement. We shall make suitable financial arrangements to encourage small-holders to buy farms.

Land use

Where land is to be chosen for building or for the use of the Fighting Services we shall see that the over-riding test between alternative sites is their capacity for agricultural production.

Forestry

The Minister of Agriculture and the Secretary of State for Scotland should have full responsibility for the Forestry Commission.

Social security

The Social Services were born of Parliaments with Conservative and Liberal majorities. They rest upon the productive effort of British industry and agriculture. The Socialists have by inflation reduced their value and compromised their future. By energetic action they can be saved and their value maintained. Britain can only enjoy the social services for which she is prepared to work.

We are determined to give a solid base of social security below which none shall fall and above which each must be encouraged to rise to the utmost limit of his ability. We shall encourage instead of penalising those who wish to create from their own efforts more security for themselves and their families. We shall foster the ancient virtue of personal thrift.

Property-owning democracy

We intend to help all those who wish to own a house of their own or a small holding. A true property-owning democracy must be based upon the wide distribution of private property, not upon its absorption in the State machine.

Housing

Upon good housing depends the health and happiness of every family. Before the war, under free enterprise with a Conservative government, the nation was getting a thousand new houses every day. The latest Socialist target is five hundred. In fact, the cuts caused by the devaluation of the pound have now reduced the Housing Programme to a figure which will result in 30,000 fewer houses a year than were built in 1931 at the height of the world economic crisis. Moreover, house building is now costing three times as much as it did before the war. We cannot believe that this is the last word in modern planning.

We shall revive the confidence of the Building Industry and greatly widen the scope for the independent builder. The restrictive licensing system as it applies to house building should be removed, but a limit on the size of houses should be kept. Every assistance and encouragement will be given to the Building Societies.

In order to further our aim to help all those who wish to have a house of their own, local authorities will be stimulated to make full use of the Housing and Small Dwellings Acquisition Acts. Only 5 per cent. deposit in cash should be required for the purchase of a house. Certain extra costs like the recently doubled stamp duty should be abolished. Supplies of timber are vital to the whole programme. We intend to abolish the bulk buying of timber.

Houses to rent

Local authorities must continue to play their full part in providing a wide variety of houses and flats for families of every size including smaller dwellings for elderly people. We look to local authorities particularly to be the spearhead of the attack on overcrowding and the slums which we shall resume as soon as possible. Where houses are built with the aid of public funds or public credit, the necessary arrangements will be made to ensure the appropriate standards.

Liberated, and if need be, encouraged private enterprise can be relied upon to meet part of the need for houses to rent if, among future tax reliefs, consideration is given to depreciation allowances for owners of new houses to rent. Modernisation can be encouraged by a more generous system of licensing and by granting tax allowances to cover the cost of conversion.

Rent control must continue until there is no housing shortage at any given level. We shall keep the matter under review.

Town and country planning

We shall drastically change the 1947 Act. It has been shown by experience to have all the defects forecast by Conservatives in debate in Parliament. The present machinery is much too cumbersome, too rigid and too slow. Bad planning and wrong use of land must, of course, be avoided. Bur we must be careful that in seeking to control minor development we do not distract attention from the main structure of the development plans. We shall encourage more elasticity and informal consultation. The high level of the development charge and the uncertainty of its application hamper development. The amount of the charge seems to be often decided by bargaining and not on principle. The incidence of the charge must be reviewed. Any such levy must be fair to all and should be at such a rate that suitable development is not discouraged. We shall also provide an appeal against assessments.

Education

Our main objective will be to bring into operation the reforms set out in our Education Act of 1944. As was originally stated, the whole Act will take a generation to implement. Everything cannot be carried out at once.

Within the existing framework of the Act it will be necessary to discuss with local education authorities and with the Denominations the timetable of the development plans, so that all who take decisions about the future of particular schools may do so with a clear idea as to the date and the circumstances in which their various responsibilities will have to be undertaken. Where necessary we intend to adopt simpler standards for school building. This will help the voluntary schools.

A determined effort must be made to reduce the size of classes particularly in the primary schools. There is grave danger of education losing its meaning if what is happening in some areas is allowed to continue. We must be free to meet this challenge with fresh minds and active policies.

The division of all-age schools into primary and secondary must be pressed forward. We attach special importance to retaining the traditions and, wherever possible, the corporate life of the grammar schools. Every effort should be made to help parents to send their children to schools of their own choice. The status of technical schools and colleges must be enhanced and their numbers increased. We wish to see that the rewards of the teaching profession are such as will continuously attract men and women of high quality.

The Health Service

We pledge ourselves to maintain and improve the Health Service. Every year the Estimates laid before Parliament have been greatly exceeded. Administrative efficiency and economy and correct priorities throughout the whole service must be assured, so that a proper balance is maintained and the hardest needs are met first. In particular the balance of the dental service should be restored so that children and mothers receive attention.

We intend to strengthen the position of the family doctor by restoring his freedom to practise anywhere and by offering a weighted capitation fee to doctors with small lists, especially in rural areas. Appeals against dismissal should be allowed to go to the Courts instead of to the Minister.

The functions and methods of appointment of Boards of management and area hospital boards require a more satisfactory basis. All hospitals within the health scheme should by statute admit the acutely sick, subject to proper safeguards. In capital expenditure priority will be given to the re-opening of beds and improving the conditions of the nursing staff.

Pensions

War pensions

War pensions have been affected by the reduced purchasing power of money. We shall set up a Select Committee to see what improvements should be made, having regard to national resources.

Contributory and non-contributory pensions

There are a number of improvements which ought to be made:

- An increase in the limit of weekly earnings without reduction of pensions from 30s. to 45s. in the case of widows with children and 20s. to 30s. for women pensioners with dependants.
- Assessment of casual earnings of old age pensioners on a monthly instead of a weekly basis.
- Revision of the assumed rates of interest on capital saved by applicants for non-contributory pensions.

Working pensioners

In order to assist those who desire to prolong their working days and thus aid our production effort, a prime aim of our policy will be to provide an optional pension of 10s. a week at the age of 65 for a man and 60 for a woman without a retirement condition and without payment of contributions, other than for industrial injuries if employed, for persons insured for at least five years prior to 5th July, 1948. When they retire, or at the age of 70 for a man and 65 for a woman, they would revert to the normal pension of 26s. a week without any addition for their employment during the previous five years.

Britain and the world

The Socialist Government has failed to make good its claim at the last election that Socialism alone could reach a good understanding with Soviet Russia. 'Left would speak to left,' they said; but in fact today East and West are separated by an Iron Curtain. Socialism abroad has been proved to be the weakest obstacle to Communism and in many countries of Eastern Europe has gone down before it. We are not prepared to regard those ancient states and nations which have already fallen beneath the Soviet yoke as lost for ever.

In China 500 million people have been subjected to Communist dictatorship, and in the new countries of South Eastern Asia free democracy is under heavy Communist pressure.

Too often in the last four years Britain has followed when she should have led. A Conservative Government will go forward resolutely to build, within the framework of the United Nations, a system of freedom based upon the rule of law. For this Britain must continue in ever closer association with Western Europe and the United States. But in the fore-front of British statesmanship stands the vital task of extending the unity, strength and progress of the British Empire and Commonwealth.

The British Empire and Commonwealth

We pledge ourselves to give our active support to all measures to promote the welfare of the British Empire and Commonwealth. We shall do all in our power to develop the new relationships in the Commonwealth with India, Pakistan and Ceylon. The more frequent the meetings between principal ministers from the countries of the Commonwealth the better, and the views of our partners on the desirability of setting up a permanent civil liaison staff will be sought. All Empire and Commonwealth Governments must review the entire field of Imperial defence and discuss together the need for a common advisory Defence Council and a combined staff so as to work together for the standardisation of equipment and methods of training.

We shall welcome and aid the steady flow of United Kingdom citizens to Commonwealth countries provided that it includes a fair cross-section of our population by age and occupation. The greatest possible development of Empire trade is our aim. We offer Empire producers a place in the United Kingdom market second only to the home producer. We claim the right to maintain whatever preferences or other special arrangements may be necessary. We shall be prepared to offer a guaranteed market at a remunerative price for some colonial products, and to concert plans with Commonwealth countries for the long-term expansion of production of food and raw materials. Both British and American investment in the Colonies must be fostered under suitable conditions, in order to develop colonial territories to the advantage of all.

Foreign affairs

We adhere to the ideals set forth in the Charter of the United Nations, and will sustain all agencies designed to promote the social and economic welfare of the peoples of the world.

Hand in hand with France and other friendly powers we shall pursue the aim of closer unity in Europe. The admission of the Government of Western Germany into the Council of Europe will be supported on the understanding that she accepts freely and fully the Western democratic conception of human rights. Among future tasks is the need to make an Austrian Treaty on terms which will safeguard Austrian independence and provide for the withdrawal of Russian forces simultaneously with those of the Western Powers.

Above all we seek to work in fraternal association with the United States to help by all means all countries, in Europe, Asia or elsewhere, to resist the aggression of Communism by open attack or secret penetration.

Defence

Until the challenge to the authority of the United Nations is ended, we affirm the principle of national service. We believe that by wise arrangements its burden may be sensibly reduced without our fighting power being diminished. The reconstitution of the Regular Army will require pay and conditions of service which conform more closely with the standards of civil life. Recruiting for the Auxiliary Forces demands better conditions, accommodation and amenities. We are sure we can get better value for the vast sums of money now being spent.

THE UNITED KINGDOM

Conservatives recognise that both Scotland and Wales have justifiable grievances against the immensely increased control of their affairs from London. Centralised control which ignores national characteristics is an essential part of Socialism. Until the Socialist Government is removed neither Scotland nor Wales will be able to strike away the fetters of centralisation and be free to develop their own way of life.

Scotland

A new Minister of State for Scotland, with Cabinet rank, will act as deputy to the Secretary of State and in order to secure a proper distribution of departmental duties an additional Under-Secretary will be appointed. The whole situation as between Scotland and England in the light of modern developments requires a review by a Royal Commission and this we propose to appoint.

For coal, electricity and railways there should be separate Scottish Boards, which will act in concert with the English Boards but in no way subordinate to them. We also propose a Scottish Gas Commission, responsible to the Secretary of State, to return wherever practicable and desired, the undertakings to local authorities either singly or jointly.

The status of the heads of United Kingdom Departments in Scotland should be enhanced. The powers of local councils must be maintained and strengthened and the supervision of the Secretary of State over them reduced. Wherever Scottish law and Scottish conditions on matters needing legislation differ materially from those in England and Wales, separate Scottish Bills based on conditions in Scotland ought to be promoted.

Wales

A special responsibility for Wales should be assigned to a member of the Cabinet. A strong and diversified industrial structure founded upon mining, iron and steel must form the basis of her future economic security. We must continue to develop a suitable range of light industries. Such local industries as quarrying must be encouraged. Wales will benefit from our policies for hill farming, the more intensive use of marginal land and the other proposals stated in our policy for Wales.

Since the passing of the Welsh Intermediate Act, Welsh education has marched steadily forward giving an example to the whole of the United Kingdom, especially in the secondary sphere. Similar progress is to be observed in facilities for higher technical education in the Principality. We shall make it our special care to foster Welsh culture and the Welsh language.

Northern Ireland

We renew our pledge of faith which all parties have made, to Northern Ireland. We shall not allow her position as an integral part of the United Kingdom and of the Empire to be altered in the slightest degree without the consent of the Northern Ireland Parliament.

THE CONSTITUTION

Conservatives believe in the Constitution as a safeguard of liberty. Socialists believe that it should be used for Party ends. They have brought in measures for changing the constitution of the House of Commons which directly violated the all-Party agreement reached by the Speaker's Conference and were designed to give advantage to their own Party. Without mandate and without good reason they have reduced the powers of the House of Lords and taken the country a long way towards single chamber government. By over-centralisation of power they have gravely weakened our system of democratic local government.

Conservatives are determined to restore our democratic institutions to their former traditions and to their rightful place above party.

House of Lords

It would be our aim to reach a reform and final settlement of the constitution and powers of the House of Lords by means of an all-Party conference called at an appropriate date. It would have before it proposals that:

(a) the present right to attend and vote based solely on heredity should not by itself constitute a qualification for admission to a reformed House;
(b) a reformed House of Lords should have powers appropriate to its constitution, but not exceeding those conferred by the Act of 1911.

House of Commons

The Socialist Party has violated the tradition in that changes in the composition of the House should be made only in accordance with the report of an all-Party conference presided over by the Speaker. To repair this breach of faith, we shall restore, as we have already declared in Parliament, the University constituencies, holding elections immediately after the necessary legislation has been passed.

Local government

It is our aim to restore adequate confidence and responsibility to local government. To that end in consultation with local authorities of all kinds, functions and financial arrangements (including all Government grants) must be reviewed and overhauled. We wish to restore functions to the smaller authorities when reorganised, particularly the personal health services.

Our purpose

In all that we strive to do we shall seek to serve the nation as a whole without fear or favour or subservience to the interests of one class or party.

We intend to free the productive energies of the nation from the trammels of overbearing state control and bureaucratic management. To denationalise wherever practicable, to decentralise as much as possible, to encourage and reward personal responsibility, to give enterprise and adventure their heads: these are the principles on which a Conservative Government will act. Throughout the whole of industry we intend to foster a growing spirit of unity for a common purpose.

National unity

By partisan measures and factious abuse, the nation has been deeply divided in the last five years. A Conservative Government will set itself the task of bringing the people of Britain together once again. We shall act not for a section but for the nation. We shall not be the masters of the people but their servants. The Conservative aim is not enviously to suppress success, but to release energy and enterprise: not maliciously to sow distrust, but to create unity; not to pursue a doctrinaire and ill-considered theory, but to enable the British people to lead their traditional way of life.

Britain of the future

We shall make Britain once again a place in which hard work, thrift, honesty and neighbourliness are honoured and win their true reward in wide freedom underneath the law. Reverence for Christian ethics, self-respect, pride in skill and responsibility, love of home and family, devotion to our country and the British Empire and Commonwealth, are the pillars upon which we base our faith.

The MANIFESTO of the CONSERVATIVE AND UNIONIST PARTY

GENERAL ELECTION
1951

CONSERVATIVE PARTY GENERAL ELECTION MANIFESTO 1951

Date of Election	Thursday 25 October
Party Leader	Winston Churchill
Candidates	617
MPs	321
Votes	13,717,538
% of vote	48.0%

We are confronted with a critical Election which may well be the turning point in the fortunes and even the life of Britain. We cannot go on with this evenly balanced Party strife and hold our own in the world, or even earn our living. The prime need is for a stable government with several years before it, during which time national interests must be faithfully held far above party feuds or tactics. We need a new Government not biased by privilege or interest or cramped by doctrinal prejudices or inflamed by the passions of class warfare. Such a Government only the Conservative and Unionist Party can today provide.

There must be no illusions about our difficulties and dangers. It is better to face them squarely as we did in 1940. The Conservative Party, who since victory have had no responsibility for the events which have led us to where we are now, offers no bribes to the electors. We will do our best to serve them and to make things better all round, but we do not blind ourselves to the difficulties that have to be overcome, or the time that will be required to bring us back to our rightful position in the world, and to revive the vigour of our national life and impulse.

We all seek and pray for peace. A mighty union of nations tread that path together, but we all know that peace can only come through their united strength and faithful brotherhood.

Contrast our position to-day with what it was six years ago. Then all our foes had yielded. We all had a right to believe and hope that the fear of war would not afflict our generation nor our children. We were respected, honoured and admired throughout the world. We were a united people at home, and it was only by being united that we had survived the deadly perils through which we had come and had kept the flag of freedom flying through the fateful year when we were alone. There, at any rate, is a great foundation and inspiration. Everyone knows how the aftermath of war brings extraordinary difficulties. With national unity we could have overcome them. But what has happened since those days?

The attempt to impose a doctrinaire Socialism upon an Island which has grown great and famous by free enterprise has inflicted serious injury upon our strength and prosperity. Nationalisation has proved itself a failure which has resulted in heavy losses to the taxpayer or the consumer, or both. It has not given general satisfaction to the wage-earners in the nationalised industries. It has impaired the relations of the Trade Unions with their members. In more than one nationalised industry the wage-earners are ill-content with the change from the private employers, with whom they could negotiate on equal terms through the Trade Unions, to the all-powerful and remote officials in Whitehall.

Our finances have been brought into grave disorder. No British Government in peace time has ever had the power or spent the money in the vast extent and reckless manner of our present rulers. Apart from the two thousand millions they have borrowed or obtained from the United States and the Dominions, they have spent more than 10 million pounds a day, or 22 thousand millions in their six years. No community living in a world of competing nations can possibly afford such frantic extravagances. Devaluation was the offspring of wild, profuse expenditure, and the evils which we suffer to-day are the inevitable progeny of that wanton way of living.

A Conservative Government will cut out all unnecessary Government expenditure, simplify the administrative machine, and prune waste and extravagance in every department.

The greatest national misfortune which we now endure is the ever falling value of our money, or, to put it in other words, the ever-increasing cost, measured in work and skill, of everything we buy. British taxation is higher than in any country outside the Communist world. It is higher by eight hundred millions a year than it was in the height of the war. We have a population of fifty millions depending on imports of food and raw materials which we have to win by our exertions, ingenuity, and craftsmanship. Since Devaluation it takes nearly twelve hours of work with hands or brains to buy across the dollar exchange what we could have got before for eight hours. We have now to give from one-quarter to one-third more of our life's strength, skill and output of every kind and quality to get the same intake as we did before Devaluation two years ago. We pay more for what we buy from abroad. We get less for what we sell. That is what Socialist Devaluation has meant. This costly expedient has not prevented a new financial crisis.

We are a hard-working people. We are second to none in ability or enterprise so far as we are allowed to use these gifts. We now have the only Socialist Government in the Empire and Commonwealth. Of all the countries in the world Britain is the one least capable of bearing the Socialist system.

The Nation now has the chance of rebuilding its life at home and of strengthening its position abroad. We must free ourselves from our impediments. Of all impediments the class war is the worst. At the time when a growing measure of national unity is more than ever necessary, the Socialist Party hope to gain another lease of power by fomenting class hatred and appealing to moods of greed and envy.

Within the limits of a statement of this kind, it is only possible to deal with some of the main questions now before us. We wish to be judged by deeds and their results and not by words and their applause. We seek to proclaim a theme, rather than write a prospectus. Many years ago I used the phrase, 'Bring the rearguard in.' This meant basic standards of life and labour, the duty of the strong to help the weak, and of the successful to establish tolerable conditions for the less fortunate. That policy is adopted by all Parties to-day. But now we have the new Socialist doctrine. It is no longer, 'Bring the rearguard in,' but 'Keep the vanguard back.' There is no means by which this

Island can support its present population except by allowing its native genius to flourish and fructify. We cannot possibly keep ourselves alive without the individual effort, invention, contrivance, thrift and good housekeeping of our people.

In 1945 I said:

> 'What we desire is freedom; what we need is abundance. Freedom and abundance – these must be our aims. The production of new wealth is far more beneficial than class and Party fights about the liquidation of old wealth. We must try to share blessings and not miseries. The production of new wealth must precede common wealth, otherwise there will only be common poverty.'

It is because these simple truths have been denied and our people duped by idle hopes and false doctrine that the value of our money has fallen so grievously and the confidence of the world in Britain has been impaired. Confidence and currency are interdependent and restoring confidence by sound finance is one of the ways in which the value of our money may be sustained and the rising cost of living checked.

The Conservative aim is to increase our national output. Here is the surest way to keep our people fully employed, to halt the rising cost of living, and to preserve our social services. Hard work, good management, thrift – all must receive their due incentive and reward.

In the wider world outside this Island we put first the safety, progress and cohesion of the British Empire and Commonwealth of Nations. We must all stand together and help each other with all our strength both in Defence and Trade. To foster commerce within the Empire we shall maintain Imperial Preference. In our home market the Empire producer will have a place second only to the home producer. Next, there is the unity of the English-speaking peoples who together number hundreds of millions. They have only to act in harmony to preserve their own freedom and the general peace. On these solid foundations we should all continue to labour for a United Europe, including in the course of time those unhappy countries still behind the Iron Curtain.

These are the three pillars of the United Nations Organisation which, if Soviet Russia becomes the fourth, would open to all the toiling millions of the world an era of moral and material advance undreamed of hitherto among men. There was a time in our hour of victory when this object seemed to be within our reach. Even now, in spite of the clouds and confusion into which we have since fallen, we must not abandon the supreme hope and design.

For all these purposes we support the Rearmament programme on which the Socialist Government have embarked. We believe, however, that far better value could be got for the immense manpower and sums of money which are involved. Special sacrifices are required from us all for the sake of our survival as free democratic communities and the prevention of war.

Our theme is that in normal times there should be the freest competition and that good wages and profits fairly earned under the law are a public gain both to the Nation and to all in industry – management and wage-earner alike. But the vast Rearmament policy of spending five thousand millions in three years on Defence inevitably distorts the ordinary working of supply and demand, therefore justice requires special arrangements for the emergency. We shall set our face against the fortuitous rise in company profits because of the abnormal process of Rearmament.

We shall accordingly impose a form of Excess Profits Tax to operate only during this exceptional period.

At the same time a revision of the existing system of taxation on commercial and industrial profits is required. Relief will be given in cases where profits are ploughed back and used for the renewal of plant and equipment.

We believe in the necessity for reducing to the minimum possible all restrictive practices on both sides of industry, and we shall rely on a greatly strengthened Monopolies Commission to seek, and enable Parliament to correct, any operations in restraint of trade, including of course in the nationalised industries.

I will now mention some other practical steps we shall take.

We shall stop all further nationalisation.

The Iron and Steel Act will be repealed and the Steel industry allowed to resume its achievements of the war and post-war years. To supervise prices and development we shall revive, if necessary with added powers, the former Iron and Steel Board representing the State, the management, labour, and consumers.

Publicly-owned rail and road transport will be reorganised into regional groups of workable size. Private road hauliers will be given the chance to return to business, and private lorries will no longer be crippled by the twenty-five mile limit.

Coal will remain nationalised. There will be more decentralisation and stimulation of local initiative and loyalties, but wage negotiations will remain on a national basis.

All industries remaining nationalised will come within the purview of the Monopolies' Commission and there will also be strict Parliamentary review of their activities.

We seek to create an industrial system that is not only efficient but human. The Conservative Workers' Charter for Industry will be brought into being as early as possible, and extended to agriculture wherever practicable. The scheme will be worked out with trade unions and employers, and then laid before Parliament.

There you have a clear plan of action in this field.

Housing is the first of the social services. It is also one of the keys to increased productivity. Work, family life, health and education are all undermined by overcrowded homes. Therefore a Conservative and Unionist Government will give housing a priority second only to national defence. Our target remains 300,000 houses a year. There should be no reduction in the number of houses and flats built to let but more freedom must be given to the private builder. In a property-owning democracy, the more people who own their homes the better.

In Education and in Health some of the most crying needs are not being met. For the money now being spent we will provide better services and so fulfil the high hopes we all held when we planned the improvements during the war.

The whole system of town planning and development charges needs drastic overhaul.

We shall review the position of pensioners, including war pensioners, and see that the hardest needs are met first. The care and comfort of the elderly is a sacred trust. Some of them prefer to remain at work and there must be encouragement for them to do so.

To obtain more food practical knowledge and business experience must be released to comb the world for greater supplies.

We shall maintain our system of guaranteed agricultural prices and markets and protect British horticulture from foreign dumpers. We have untilled acres and much marginal land. Farmers and merchants should work together to improve distribution in the interests of the public.

Subject to the needs of Rearmament, the utmost will be done to provide better housing, water supplies, and drainage, electricity and transport in rural areas.

The fishing industry will be protected from unrestricted foreign dumping. Every effort will be made by international agreement to prevent over-fishing.

Food subsidies cannot be radically changed in present circumstances, but later we hope to simplify the system and by increases in family allowances, taxation changes and other methods, to ensure that public money is spent on those who need help and not, as at present, upon all classes indiscriminately.

Apart from proposals to help Britain to stand on her own feet by increasing productivity, we must guard the British way of life, hallowed by centuries of tradition. We have fought tyrants at home and abroad to win and preserve the institutions of constitutional Monarchy and Parliamentary government. From Britain across the generations our message has gone forth to all parts of the globe. However well-meaning many of the present Socialist leaders may be, there is no doubt that in its complete development a Socialist State, monopolising production, distribution and exchange, would be fatal to individual freedom. We look on the Government as the servant and not as the masters of the people. Multiplying orders and rules should be reduced, and the whole system kept under more rigorous Parliamentary scrutiny. We shall call an all-Party conference to consider proposals for the reform of the House of Lords.

We shall restore the University constituencies, which have been disfranchised contrary to the agreement reached by all three Parties during the war.

The United Kingdom cannot be kept in a Whitehall straitjacket. The Unionist policy for Scotland, including the practical steps proposed for effective Scottish control of Scottish affairs, will be vigorously pressed forward.

There will be a Cabinet Minister charged with the care of Welsh affairs,

We shall seek to restore to Local Government the confidence and responsibility it has lost under Socialism.

All these and other issues of the day can only be stated briefly in our Party Manifesto. A much fuller account will be given of them in Britain Strong and Free which will be published in a few days.

I close with a simple declaration of our faith. The Conservative and Unionist Party stands not for any section of the people but for all. In this spirit, we will do our utmost to grapple with the increasing difficulties into which our country has been plunged.

Winston Churchill

THE CONSERVATIVE AND UNIONIST PARTY'S POLICY

UNITED FOR PEACE AND PROGRESS

GENERAL ELECTION 1955

PRICE 6d.

CONSERVATIVE PARTY GENERAL ELECTION MANIFESTO 1955

United for peace and progress: the Conservative and Unionist Party's policy

Date of Election	Thursday 26 May
Party Leader	Sir Anthony Eden
Candidates	623
MPs	344
Votes	13,286,569
% of vote	49.7%

A personal statement by the Prime Minister

I took the decision to recommend a dissolution of Parliament and the holding of a General Election after much thought, and for reasons which seem to me of supreme national importance.

One of the greatest figures ever to be Prime Minister of Britain has put aside his burden. I have been called upon to take his place and to lead the Conservative and Unionist Party. It will be my purpose to give effect, in terms of the modern world, to the faith we hold and the principles we defend.

In the year 1955 –in this age of peril and promise –what needs to be done can be carried through only with the trust and goodwill of the people of this country.

This Parliament is already in its fourth year, and it is inevitable that, with a change of Prime Minister, there should be expectation of a General Election. I believe that it is better to face this issue now. Uncertainty at home and abroad as to the political future must be bad for our influence in world affairs and bad for our trade.

Moreover, as is made clear in the pages which follow, we have far-reaching plans for the future of our country. They will take years rather than months to realise, and I need the support of the country to make them possible.

As you know, much of my political life has been concerned with foreign affairs. Twice in a lifetime my generation has seen its world shaken, and almost destroyed, by a world war. Our civilisation could not hope to survive a third. It has been my work to do all I can to prevent such a catastrophe, and this will remain my firm resolve for the whole time I serve you.

But to secure peace we have to do more than just want it or just hope for it. We must be firm and resolute. Weakness can lead only to war or to subjugation without a struggle. Because of this we and our allies have to be militarily strong. We have to accept the burden this entails. However costly, it is a price worth paying to avoid a war.

We must make it certain that any would-be breaker of the peace knows beyond all doubt that aggression will be met, and that at once, by overwhelming retribution. If it is known that we have both the power and the will to deliver such retribution, we can hope that the danger of war will recede and that we can build a lasting peace.

For this reason I have no doubt that we are right to make the hydrogen bomb and it is a source of strength to the country that the Opposition should support us in that step. Mr Attlee, whose Government made the atomic bomb, has agreed that we must possess this newer and still more powerful deterrent. In the face of its destructive power, any group of men would have to be not only bad, but mad, to unleash a war. This fact may be the greatest force for peace.

But our policy needs more than a deterrent. It must have a more positive side. We must seek to remove the distrust which today poisons the atmosphere between East and West.

We have built the unity of the West, and our country has played a leading part in this. We are now ready for wider discussion. We will spare no effort to bring about meetings with the leaders of the Soviet Union and try to agree around the table proposals which will make a fresh advance towards disarmament and security for all peoples. I shall never despair of finding by agreement solutions which will rid the world of fear.

At home we need a new authority if we are to develop the full sweep of our plans, which offer enormous opportunities.

Within the lifetime of the Parliament which is about to be elected the first stage of our programme to produce electricity from nuclear power will be completed. What this means in material progress in Britain, how we plan to effect a steady and accelerating increase in the living standards of every section of our people, is set out in this document. These projects will inevitably take time but they can soon begin to revolutionise our national life.

During the last three and a half years the Conservative Government has achieved many of the aims proclaimed in 1951. We have seen solvency succeed the threat of national bankruptcy. We have seen both employment and earnings reach new high levels. We have seen new houses and new schools and new factories built and building, and soon we shall see new hospitals too. We have seen the social services extended and improved.

Now the time has come for a new effort and fresh advances. To realise them we need a mandate measured not in months but in years. Here are some of the demands we shall have to meet

We must fight with vigour the war on the slums and the war against ill-health and disease. We must equip our rising generation with an education to fit them for the requirements of this new age and to enable them to make the best use of their talents. We must produce more and produce it more efficiently. We must capture new markets overseas. We must save to invest in the future – at home and in the Commonwealth and Empire.

To be successful we need a great national effort in which the fullest use is made of our finest asset – the character of our people. For that character to find its true expression we have to deepen our sense of national unity.

How can this be achieved? One way would be to try to impose it from the top. The Conservative way is to encourage the growth of unity and fellowship in a free and neighbourly society in which the people of every calling work naturally together. I believe that this can be brought about if we develop in this country what I have many times described as a property-owning democracy.

Such ownership can be expressed in the home, in savings or in forms of partnership in industry. It can take many shapes; but the essential theme is clear. We are against increased ownership of power and property by the State. We seek ever wider ownership of power and property by the people. We aim at a community of free men and women working together for the common good.

Anthony Eden

United for peace and progress

Two parties have governed in Great Britain in these post-war years. The effective choice at this Election will lie between these two. Each will present a manifesto of its beliefs and policy. Each will expound its theme at length and at large. But a Party must not only be judged by what it says. It must be judged even more by what it does. Therefore we ask the British people to make this comparison now: Which were better for themselves, for their families and for their country? The years of Socialism or the years of Conservatism that have followed? Let us look at the record.

Socialists had claimed that the political Left would be able to speak to the Soviets in comradeship. This indeed proved an empty boast. They promised that their methods of 'planning' would make us masters of our economic destiny. Yet they allowed one financial crisis after another to rock our land. They pretended that their policy was bringing prosperity. In fact it opened up an endless vista of filling in forms, cutting out coupons, applying for permits, waiting on housing lists and standing in queues.

For six years their meddling and muddling made post-war problems harder and gravely injured our strength. The climax came in 1951, when chronic inflation at home cut more than 2s. off the value of every £ and the worst balance of payments crisis in our history brought the nation to the brink of bankruptcy.

Contrast the position now with what it was in that dark hour. Under Conservative administration we have broken away at long last from the regular cycle of crises. We have proved, by re-establishing confidence in our currency, by maintaining full employment, by restoring housewives choice and by smashing housing records, that Conservative freedom works.

Indeed, we in Britain are producing, building, selling, earning and buying more today than ever before. Personal savings have more than trebled since 1951. Judging by this alone the nation has regained faith in its own future. Abroad, too, we have turned a more hopeful page. Imaginative diplomacy has awakened respect for British leadership, and the new strength and unity of the West should provide the essential basis on which we may seek an understanding with the East.

The successes of Conservatism have now made possible a fine and ambitious target. We believe that the British people have a real chance during the coming twenty-five years to double their standard of living. The future beckons to this generation with a golden finger. Peace can bring abundance for all, if we match the opportunity with the will to prosper.

Conservatives do not pretend that the way ahead is easy. There will be no lack of obstacles and dangers in our path. We shall need every ounce of individual effort and resourcefulness that we can muster. We shall need a spirit of partnership and a firm sense of duty to our country. We shall need a general readiness to save as well as to spend. We shall need a Government that will lead, and not hamper.

Socialists cannot be trusted to provide such a Government. They failed in their six years of office. Their appeal to the Electorate in 1951 was founded, not on constructive policies, but on scares – that we were warmongers, that we would create mass unemployment, that we would slash the social services – which experience has proved were lies. They have spent most of their time in Opposition quarrelling with one another. On vital issues of State policy they cannot speak as a united Party. In so far as they have a programme at all, it consists of a mixture of more and more nationalisation and a return to State restrictions and controls.

We do not question the sincerity of our political opponents. All Parties pray for peace. All Parties desire no less the prosperity and welfare of the people. These ends are not at issue between the Parties. The issue is: Which Party has shown, in practice and in prospect, that it knows and can use the means to secure them? If the lessons of yesterday are remembered, tomorrow can be bright indeed. A vote for Socialism is a vote for the policy which was tried and which failed. To vote Conservative is to invest in success.

In the following pages we outline the constructive proposals of the Conservative and Unionist Party for the next five years, and the main themes of our longer-term policy. Peace and security in the nuclear age; a programme for prosperity; the development of a property-owning democracy, and the strengthening of personal freedom and national unity – these are our principal objectives in conducting the affairs of Government.

Our policy is a policy for Great Britain as a whole. Distinctive needs and aspirations of Scotland and of Wales require special care and they receive separate mention.

Peace and security

Science in our day has unlocked the secret of atomic and nuclear power. The future of our civilisation depends on the use to which mankind puts this knowledge. Never in history have the issues of peace and war been more sharply defined. For the same power that can forge weapons of mass destruction can also confer blessings beyond all our dreams.

Already research, medicine and industry are making great and growing use of atomic material manufactured in Britain. Already our country leads the world in its programme of nuclear power stations for generating electricity. We give our fullest support to President Eisenhower's initiative to develop atoms for peace through an international agency, and will readily contribute from our own resources.

Deterrents and disarmament

Britain, like America and Russia, has also the knowledge and capacity to make nuclear weapons. That we should use this knowledge is not in dispute between the Parties. The Socialist Government made the atomic bomb. The Socialist Opposition has said it shares our view that the possession of the hydrogen bomb is necessary.

Why? Because to have the hydrogen bomb is today the best way of preventing war;

the best and perhaps the only way to convince the Communists that they have nothing to gain, and indeed everything to lose, from aggression, whereas the whole world has everything to gain from peace and general disarmament.

The Conservative Government will continue to strive for world disarmament. To be real, such disarmament must be balanced, all-round and effectively controlled. We cannot agree to one-sided disarmament. The issue is not simply whether to ban the hydrogen bomb. Our disarmament plan makes it plain that this must be done. But banning the bomb alone would make the risks of war not smaller but greater, as long as the Communists retained their superiority in all other arms and in manpower. Therefore we say we must not only abolish nuclear weapons, but also reduce armies and armaments to a point where no one State can threaten the peace. We say too that there must be effective international inspection and safeguards, applying both to nuclear and other weapons. We have made in the United Nations far-reaching and constructive proposals to these ends. Up to now the Communist powers have rejected these proposals. But we do not give up hope; and we shall not give up trying. For general disarmament such as we have described is the only path to lasting peace and safety.

Peace through strength

Meanwhile our interest and duty is to make war less likely by building up, with our allies, the most powerful deterrent to aggression we can achieve. Our defence policy aims to bring each of the Services into line with the strategy of the nuclear age, to arm each with the most modern weapons, to improve conditions of life in the Forces, and to re-shape home defence where the need for civilian services will remain vital.

The Conservative Party does not regard the current two years period of whole time National Service as necessarily having come to stay. Its object is twofold: to ensure that the active forces have enough men to carry out their commitments and to build up trained reserves of skilled men for an emergency. National Service is thus an instrument of our foreign and Imperial policy. But it is not an end in itself. A Conservative Government will continue to suit its application, and the period of service, to the needs of the time.

In our policy of peace through strength we are not alone. With our Commonwealth and Atlantic partners this country serves the common cause of freedom and peace. We and other Commonwealth countries joined with the United Nations in condemning and resisting aggression in Korea. We play a leading part in the Atlantic Alliance, the main shield of peace and the formal expression of Anglo-American solidarity. Britain too by her initiative has helped to create Western European Union, the hub of the alliance between the free peoples of the Continent.

In Western European Union we have undertaken an act of faith without precedent in British history, in that we are pledged to keep our forces on the Continent so long as they are needed by our European allies. This British pledge, following the French rejection of E.D.C, led to the London and Paris Agreements. It has restored the basis of European unity. It has strengthened N.A.T.O by giving America and Canada added confidence in their European partners. It holds out the hope of a new and friendly relationship between France and Germany.

The Soviets began to rearm Eastern Germany seven years ago. In carrying forward the policy set on foot by the Labour Government of bringing the German Federal Republic into the Western defence system, we have erected a barrier to aggression, not to negotiation.

We should be wrong to minimise the fundamental issues of principle that divide us from the Communist world. We cannot ignore the post-war record of Communist subversion and attack, or their world-wide conspiracy to undermine free institutions and to divide and confuse the free peoples. We cannot excuse their denial of the rights of free worship and free expression. Whatever the origins of Communist theory, its practice has led to the extinction of freedom and the enthronement of tyranny wherever it has spread. Only if we are firm in faith and spirit, and united in common purpose with our allies, can we hope to achieve in time something better than a state of cold war.

We are determined to keep our Western Alliance defensive in character, to indulge in no provocation, to take advantage of every chance to settle disputes. In the changed Soviet attitude towards the signature of an Austrian Treaty, which we have repeatedly proposed, we may be seeing a first-fruit of the ratification of the London and Paris Agreements. We hope that this new mood may extend to other outstanding problems. It is still our hope that the Soviet Government can be brought to agree to the unity of Germany on the basis of free elections.

Now ratification is complete and the unity of the West assured, we shall welcome and work for any high-level meeting or conference with the Soviets which seems to be practicable and useful.

Diplomacy and security

It would be a mistake to assume that nothing can be settled unless or until everything is settled. During this period of Conservative Government a fresh spirit of initiative and of refusal to accept stalemate has already been successfully brought to bear on many problems which once seemed insoluble. Not only was Western European Union due to a British initiative, but in the Korean armistice, in the Geneva settlement of the Indo-China war, which could so easily have become a world conflict, and in the ending of the Trieste dispute, our country has played a leading part.

On taking office we faced difficult and dangerous situations in Persia and Egypt. Today there are agreements with both these countries. That with Egypt has enabled us to redeploy our forces. That with Persia has meant that oil is flowing from Abadan once again. Our prestige throughout this area has been restored. Thus we have a better chance to continue helping the countries of the Middle East in their plans both for defence and for economic development, and also to work for a reconciliation between the Arab States and Israel.

In the Formosa Straits we should like to see a guarantee on both sides not to resort to force, and the withdrawal of Chinese Nationalist forces from the coastal islands. This could lead to the reconsideration at an appropriate moment both of Chinese representation in the United Nations and the future status of Formosa.

The South-East Asia Treaty Organisation, guaranteeing the Geneva settlement, is the first step towards collective security in this area. The basic necessity is strength in arms; but social and economic betterment can be a powerful reinforcement in less developed countries which might otherwise be undermined by Communist infiltration.

We shall make a real contribution to the raising of living standards both under the Colombo Plan and through the Agencies of the United Nations.

Commonwealth and colonies

The British Commonwealth and Empire is the greatest force for peace and progress in the world today. It comprises a quarter of the world's population. It contains peoples of every race, of every religion, of every colour, and at every stage of political and economic advance. It represents the most fascinating and successful experiment in government and in international relations ever known.

We are its founder member, and for a large part we are still directly responsible. Other powerful communities have their territories confined within a limited area. The Commonwealth and Empire alone straddles the globe. For us isolationism is impossible.

It is, therefore, of the first importance that machinery for consultation between the self-governing partner members of the Commonwealth, already so close, should be steadily improved and perfected. Five times within less than four years Commonwealth leaders have met together. In their approach to world problems and economic policies an ever closer concord has been established. We are in constant touch on foreign affairs and defence. As opportunity offers, we should like to see Commonwealth Ministers with responsibility for other aspects of public policy, such as the social services, meeting and consulting together. It is the concept of a family council which underlies our relationship and which must and shall endure.

We wish to strengthen the cohesion and influence of the Commonwealth. We uphold the principle of racial partnership, as exemplified in the new Federation of the Rhodesias and Nyasaland so auspiciously launched and increasingly enjoying the confidence of Europeans and Africans. We shall work to raise living standards and to guide Colonial peoples along the road to self-government within the framework of the Commonwealth and Empire. We shall do all we can to insulate these problems from the heat of Party conflict.

Economic development

Commonwealth partnership enabled us to stave off the economic perils that faced the whole Sterling Area at the time the Conservative Government took over. It offers the best hope of prosperity for the future.

Conservative policy will stimulate the flow of private and public capital from London for sound Empire development. Last year alone the Government approved applications for new investment in the Commonwealth to a total of £160 million. In addition there was much private investment in the sterling Commonwealth which did not need Government approval. Great wealth-creating projects are under way in all the Commonwealth countries and in the Colonial territories too.

The peaceful uses of nuclear energy will be of the utmost benefit to Commonwealth and Empire, and we are already helping a number of Commonwealth countries with research and development programmes.

Like all countries of advanced development and democratic tradition, we have responsibilities towards the less fortunate peoples of the world. We have a special responsibility for the welfare and happiness of the seventy millions who live in British Colonies, Protectorates and Trust Territories. We must give them every help in their continuing assault on ignorance, want and disease.

Special arrangements have been made to enable us to help industries in the Colonies by treating them in certain circumstances as though they were industries of the United Kingdom. A powerful contribution to better conditions will continue to be made under the Colonial Development and Welfare Acts which we have recently extended and improved. We shall seek to promote capital investment in the improvement of Colonial communications, the winning of minerals and the modernisation of agriculture, with emphasis on peasant production. Measures to increase food supplies must occupy a high place. Land utilisation and related problems in East Africa have been examined by a Royal Commission whose conclusions will have careful study.

Political progress

From the shores of Africa westwards to the Caribbean and eastwards to the Pacific Islands, the Colonies are thinking of their future. They differ vastly in size, resources and tradition. Each must be helped to solve its own problems. Our administrative and technical officers are doing fine work in fostering political and economic advance. They still have a part to play in the self-governing Colonies, for some of these also need and want their help.

So diverse are the circumstances that it would be unrealistic to lay down a cut and dried time-table for the evolution of political maturity. Our purpose and goodwill in achieving self-government for the Colonies are proclaimed by recent constitutional advances in many parts of the Empire, for example in West Africa. We believe that people in self-governing Colonies will find greater security, prosperity and freedom by remaining part of the Commonwealth. It is well known how easy a prey small, independent countries can be to Communism or adverse economic circumstances. Moreover, it is our responsibility to see that the rights of minorities are fully safeguarded, and self-government can be granted only when we are certain of this. In multi-racial communities we believe that the way to progress must lie through a real racial partnership.

A Conservative Government would work to these ends throughout the Colonies, judging each problem individually and striving to solve it without prejudice. We shall maintain law and order wherever peaceful progress is threatened; doing all in our power to settle rival claims, whether political, religious, or racial, impartially, and with tolerance and humanity.

Programme for prosperity

The economic policy of the Conservative Party is to help create the conditions in which the British people can steadily improve their standard of living. As long as we conduct our affairs wisely and get on with the job of raising the national product year by year, the country can be twice as well off in twenty-five years time as it is now.

So we say: Let us strive to double our standard of living within this period. Let every one have a firmer stake in the fortunes of his country. Let everyone have a fuller chance to earn more and to own more, to get on and to have more enjoyment as well. Given the boon of world peace, all this can be ours, if we will work for it and save for it and so deserve to have it.

How, then, shall we invest in success?

First, we must believe in it. We need throughout the nation an ever-growing sense of partnership and a lively spirit of venture. If we take pride in our work, have confidence in one another, and are ready to give up out-worn attitudes and methods for new, then we are already half-way to success.

Second, we must devote more of our resources to increasing productivity; and this means saving as well as spending. First thought must go to investment in productive forms of capital-factory and farm buildings, plant and machinery, communications and power. This must be matched by far-sighted educational policies to augment our scientific and technical skills.

Third, we must invest in wealth-creating schemes overseas, and especially in the Commonwealth and Colonies. Development of their resources is a practical example of our partnership and will make life better both for them and for us.

Fourth, we must continue to sell more and earn more abroad. Only thus can we pay for the extra raw materials we shall need for rising production, and build up a trading surplus large enough to increase our investment overseas. To expand world trade and our own share in the world's export markets is a foremost task.

Men and women cannot be compelled or commanded or cajoled into greater prosperity. Nor can such prosperity come overnight as a gift of Government. What a Government can do is to encourage people to think and to act in terms of expansion rather than restriction, of freedom rather than control. The Conservative Government alone in post-war Britain has shown its ability and willingness to do that.

Trade not aid

We live by world trade: the more world trade there is, the better we shall live. We share in it, we ship it, we insure it and we help finance it. We have been selling, and we shall have to go on selling, against fierce competition in the markets of the world. The first object of our policy must be to enable British industry to do this in what is likely to remain a buyer's market.

Therefore, we have got rid of a vast range of manufacturing controls and we aim to stay rid of them. British industry must be adaptable, and ready not only to hold old markets but to jump into new ones with new ideas and new products. Freedom from control and a stable home economy are the true foundations of a successful export trade; both would be in peril under Socialism.

For our part, we intend to make our export trade a first charge upon our resources. Without success in this field, neither defensive strength nor social welfare can be achieved, and it is our object to achieve them both.

It is with this in mind that the Conservative Government has taken the lead in organising a move towards a world-wide system of freer trade and freer payments. The two must march together. We must re-establish sterling in a position so strong and respected that it can play its full part as a major international currency.

The solution of the complex problems involved will take time. It requires, in particular, a suitable response from the dollar world, such as the President of the United States has recommended. We in Britain have shown our goodwill and intentions. For example, we have relaxed restrictions on imports from Europe, and re-opened our international commodity markets.

Our aim being to expand trade, we must observe a system of trade rules which makes such an expansion possible. This policy is in harmony with our Commonwealth trade relations, and the Commonwealth countries themselves pursue it. More than half our trade consists of purchases from or sales to the Commonwealth and Empire. We have negotiated special arrangements under the G.A.T.T. in the interests of Colonial industries.

It will be our constant aim to safeguard the special interests of the cotton textile industry in the important interchanges taking place with other Governments particularly concerned.

We have announced our decision that trade relations with Japan should continue to be dealt with by mutually negotiated arrangements, and our desire for a long-term commercial treaty.

We propose to strengthen our defences against unfair trade practices. The Government has taken a leading part in seeking to obtain the elimination or limitation of export subsidies in international trade. Material injury can be caused to domestic industry through the use by other countries of these devices, and we propose to take powers to impose countervailing and anti-dumping duties in such cases and within the terms of our international agreements.

Any country pursuing a policy of economic expansion and full employment faces a constant danger of inflation. The risk is that home demand may take away from the export trade and swell the import bill. Here sound monetary and fiscal policies are powerful weapons. We propose to continue with their flexible use.

An expanding economy

If Britain is to seize the opportunities which our trade policy can open up, economic arrangements at home have got to be as modern and go-ahead as we can possibly make them.

Conservatives neither minimise nor exaggerate the part that Governments can play in bringing these conditions about. It is for the State to give a lead, to provide incentive, support and advice, to protect the public interest and to restrain abuse. But it is certainly no proper function of the State in normal times to go into trade itself, to interfere in the day-to-day running of business, or to tell housewives how to do their shopping. Within broad but well-defined limits of basic public concern, we insist on freedom of action for producers and freedom of choice for consumers.

Full employment

Under Conservative administration a working population of record peace-time size has been kept fully employed, without Socialist controls and without continual inflation. Our record speaks for itself. In the intensely competitive times ahead, continued full employment must mean, not only everyone in a job, but everyone doing their job to the full. Only with a high output–high earnings economy can we maintain and improve our trading position.

The Government has sought, with an encouraging measure of success, to create the right climate of confidence and to foster the idea of a common interest and task. Team-work is an essential driving force of a dynamic economy. There is really only one side in modern industry, and all of us are on it. As Conservatives we have always believed this.

We shall follow up our work for better human relations in industry by discussing with the joint advisory bodies of employers and Trade Unions, and with the British Productivity Council, how best they can increase their status and the scope of their work. We shall encourage such individual employers as are not already doing so, to keep their workpeople regularly and frankly informed of the fortunes and problems of their firm.

We wish to see proper rewards for extra skill, effort and responsibility. Where they are suitable and desired, co-partnership and profit-sharing schemes should be encouraged. They give employees a stake in the prosperity of their firm and so contribute to our concept of a property-owning democracy. We shall continue to assist better training within industry.

We intend to launch a vigorous drive to promote the health, welfare and safety of the working population, with the aid of our new Mines and Quarries Act and of the recently established Industrial Health Advisory Committee. Legislation will be passed to promote a steady improvement of conditions for other workers, including those in transport and in farming, in offices and in shops. We shall also introduce new legislation to safeguard the employment of children.

Equal pay

The Labour Party has been talking about equal pay for as long as anyone can remember; it has taken a Conservative Government to do something about it for its own employees. In fulfilment of our pledge at the last Election, the principle of equal pay for equal work in the public service is now being applied by stages.

Competitive enterprise

We reaffirm our belief in the system of free competitive enterprise. The Conservative Party is strongly opposed to any further measure of nationalisation. We are equally anxious that private enterprise should be free from any reproach of harmful restrictive practices. Many of these practices, on both sides of industry, are relics of the past, quite out of place today.

The Monopolies and Restrictive Practices Commission, first suggested and recently strengthened by the Conservatives, has started on the right path. Its recommendations have been acted upon. The Conservative Government has made a new approach by referring for examination certain practices which cover a wide range of industry. This reference is likely to raise many issues ranging from the existence of private trade courts to the right of proprietors of branded goods to fix a uniform price for their products. These are complex questions. Our policy is to obtain an impartial statement of the facts and their effect on the national interest, and then to take the action appropriate in each case.

Consumer choice

Socialists, the makers of new monopolies, are posing now as the champions of the consumer. Multiply the Ministries and clamp on the controls is what, in effect, they say. But that was precisely their policy after the war. It led, despite heavy food subsidies, paid for out of taxation, to a 40 per cent. rise in the cost of living in six years and to the perpetuation of shortages and queues, ration-books and black markets, snoopers and spivs. All these things will inevitably come back if the Socialists get their way. They seem to think that the British housewife is incapable of deciding for herself; we are sure that it is the customer, and not 'the gentleman in Whitehall', who knows best.

We warned the country at the last Election that it would take time and immense efforts to stabilise the purchasing power of money. We claim to have made progress. The cost of living has risen less in the past three years than in the Socialists' last single year; and, what is more, the standard of living of the great mass of the people has steadily and substantially improved.

Average industrial earnings and social security payments have gone ahead of price rises. Clothes and many household goods are cheaper. We have rejected policies which would deliberately deny to the housewife food in plenty and plenty of choice. But we accept the obligation to continue to work for more stable prices. We are certain that freedom and efficiency are the keys to abundance and to lower cost.

Taxation and investment

Efficiency is powerfully affected by taxation policy. If the toll of taxes is too high, enterprise and thrift are discouraged; and lax Government spending can itself be a root cause of inflation.

In an armed Welfare State the demands on taxable resources cannot be light. This makes it all the more necessary that government, central and local, should be run economically. There are today over 50,000 fewer civil servants and four fewer Ministries than when we took over. Conservatives will persist in the drive for simpler and less expensive administration.

We have already succeeded in making substantial reductions in P.A.Y.E. and the Purchase Tax, and have introduced new allowances to help factory and farm re-equipment. The 1955 budget is one more proof of our determination to reduce where we can the burden of taxation on the individual, on the family and on industry. We hope to make further progress in the years ahead.

We recognise the decline in the standard of living suffered since 1939 by many salaried workers and by many who live on fixed incomes, savings and pensions. They stand to benefit most from the more stable prices and lower taxation which can be expected from a period of sound and steady Government, but which Socialist policies would render impossible. Within the limits set by our economic circumstances, we must seek to bring the structure of the income tax into line with modern conditions, facilitate provision for retirement, and pay regard to cases of hardship among those who have served the State.

The Conservative Party acknowledges the part that budgetary policy can play in stimulating saving and private investment. A striking rise in factory building approvals and in new orders for machine tools has already followed from our system of investment allowances.

We must see to it that manufacturing industry and agriculture are well served. Ample supplies of steel are vital, particularly to our export trade, and the denationalised iron and steel industry, which is breaking production records month by month, has now embarked on a further programme of capital investment and expansion. Up-to-date means of transport and ready sources of power are equally essential. For this purpose, those sections of our economy that remain nationalised must be brought to a higher peak of efficiency. Here again, investment is an important factor.

Transport

We must move our goods swiftly to markets, shops and homes, and to the ports for our overseas trade. In work and at leisure we look to our railways, roads and airways to give us efficient service. It is Conservative policy to see that they do. The spur of competition which we have provided will certainly help. In addition, both railways and roads require vigorous development to make up for the time lost in the years of war and of Socialism.

We shall make it possible for the British Transport Commission to push on with its comprehensive plan of modernisation and re-equipment, so that the railways may earn their own living and a good wage for those who work on them. The public and industry are entitled to a better service.

We have already started on the first big programme of road construction since the war. The first great motorways to be built in this country will help traffic to flow between our cities. But we will not sacrifice safety to speed. Our programme also includes the elimination of hundreds of accident 'black spots'. This will be combined with intensive propaganda, the new highway code and fresh legislation in a drive for greater safety.

Air transport gives us new highways. Experience has shown that a blend of public and private enterprise is best for this service. Close co-operation with shipping can often be of great value. The Airways Corporations will continue to have an important role; we shall ensure that their relationships with independent operators are developed in the interests of traveller, trader and taxpayer.

Fuel and power

Britain built her industrial supremacy on coal. We shall continue to need all the coal we can get. But we must look to new sources of energy as well to meet the demands of an expanding economy.

The peaceful uses of nuclear energy can make an incalculable contribution to the raising of living standards. A new industrial era may indeed be ushered in when the atom has been harnessed to bring everyday heat, light and power to factory, farm and home. Quietly, unobtrusively, our scientists have been working; and the Conservative Government has now become the first in the world to launch a programme of nuclear power stations on a commercial scale. This will be pressed ahead at the utmost speed.

The National Coal Board has now been reorganised. The efficiency of nationalised electricity is also under independent examination.

We intend to increase capital investment in new pits and major reconstruction schemes to four times what it was when we took over in 1951. Greater supplies of good coal would not only be gratifying to the user, including the housewife, but also a substantial help to our balance of payments. We recognise that as far as one can see ahead the demand for coal will outstrip capacity. So we must make coal work harder, and economise in its use, by extending our industrial loan scheme and by other means. We must also supplement our coal with oil, and in particular ensure by progressive conversion of electric power stations that their mounting fuel needs can be met by oil instead of coal.

Science and invention

Our country's prosperity is bound up with her scientific knowledge and the extent to which her industrialists and farmers make use of it. We therefore place a strong emphasis in our educational policy upon the expansion of scientific and technological training. We shall continue to promote and encourage research both in private industry and State establishments.

We regard the widest possible spread of scientific information as a major factor in modern progress. With this in mind we shall take early steps to expand the Patent Office Library into a National Reference Library of Science and Invention, and to develop a National Lending Library of Science and Technology whose facilities will be available to all British firms, large and small.

Agriculture and fisheries

Side by side with the expansion of other productive industries Britain needs a strong and progressive agriculture, and always will do. The Conservative Party gives a pledge to the farming community that so long as we are responsible there will be fair prices for good farming, orderly marketing of the main farm products, and no nationalisation of the land.

By support prices, deficiency payments and other means, we shall uphold the principle of the 1947 Agriculture Act. We have shown, for example with milk, potatoes and eggs, our firm belief in Producer Marketing Boards where these have majority support and safeguard consumers and taxpayers. Marketing arrangements should continue to put a premium on efficiency.

The more efficient our agriculture continues to grow, the better it will be for everyone. The farmer will become more independent. There will be more scope for increased production. The housewife will be better satisfied. And the taxpayer will need to find less in agricultural subsidies, which are now running at the formidable rate of some £250 million a year.

We must, therefore, direct our main effort to the wide range of farm production where the overseas supplier has no natural advantage. We should save unnecessary imports of feeding stuffs by concentrating on grass and ley farming. To encourage good husbandry and to help the small farmer in particular, the wide range of improvement and other production grants must be continued. We shall take care that credit facilities are adequate. There will be further development of the Government's research, education and advisory services. By these and other means we shall provide the knowledge, advice and incentive needed to secure the maximum economic production from our land.

Under Conservative Government country workers are assured of better housing conditions, better schools for their children and more village halls. Three out of every four farms and cottages will be linked to a main electricity supply on the completion of a major five-year programme which we have initiated. We have doubled the amount paid annually in grants for rural water supplies and sewerage; this progress will be kept up, and further funds made available.

We have taken steps within our international agreements which have enabled us to increase the tariffs on a number of horticultural products. With a view to improving the marketing of fruit and vegetables, we shall give close study to the conclusions of the recently established inquiry.

The marketing of home-grown timber is now under review. We wish to see greater use made of the grants available to private woodland owners.

The needs of the fishing industry will have constant attention. Further efforts will be made towards improving international control of over-fishing. Investment in research and the building of new vessels will continue to receive steady Government aid.

The task ahead

This is an age of challenge and opportunity. In the first half of the century we had to sacrifice our wealth and our overseas investments in two world wars: in the struggle for life and freedom we diminished our commercial strength. Now in this second half of the century, more dependent than ever on our foreign trade in an increasingly competitive world, we must venture for livelihood and prosperity. Ours are long-term problems: they cannot be settled and solved automatically by an Act of Parliament, by some trick of organisation, by one short spurt of intense activity. We can never allow a mood of complacency and inertia to settle down upon us.

After these few years of Conservative Government, the economy is in much better shape, and the nation in much better heart. Now we must harness these assets to a new and powerful surge of national effort.

Socialism would merely hinder this task. Instead of thinking how to expand wealth in which all can share, the Socialists continue to 'plan' the equal division of scarcity. Instead of looking forward to the next twenty-five years, they are still parroting the untruths and half-truths of twenty-five years ago. Instead of learning from the many mistakes they made when in office, they are obstinately preparing to repeat them. Their partisan attitudes would create disunity among the people and undermine business confidence. Their policies would involve an increase in Government spending so huge that there could be no saving for purposes of investment. Their immediate contribution to our trading problems would be to nationalise and disrupt some of our most efficient and progressive export industries.

We offer the nation a programme for prosperity; they offer a blue-print for disaster.

Home and family

Britain's greatest asset has always lain in the gifts and character of her people. It must be the purpose of a vigorous and progressive society to enable this asset to be fully and freely developed. Our programme for prosperity can succeed only if the nation is in good heart and good health, well housed and well educated. All must be secure in the possession of a basic standard of life; and all must be free to rise above it as far as their industry and talents may take them.

We denounce the Labour Party's desire to use the social services, which we all helped to create, as an instrument for levelling down. We regard social security, not as a substitute for family thrift, but as a necessary basis or supplement to it. We think of the National Health Service as a means, not of preventing anyone from paying anything for any service, but of ensuring that proper attention and treatment are denied to no-one. We believe that equality of opportunity is to be achieved, not by sending every boy and girl to exactly the same sort of school, but by seeing that every child gets the schooling most suited to his or her aptitudes. We see a sensible housing policy in terms, not of one hopeless Council waiting list, but of adequate and appropriate provision both for letting and for sale.

We wish to develop in our country the idea of a property-owning democracy. That means that people should be owners as well as earners. Our theme is that property, power and responsibility alike must not become absorbed into the State machine, but be widely spread throughout the whole of the community. To this end, we shall encourage home ownership. We shall foster thrift. We shall stimulate a spirit of partnership in industry. We shall maintain the independence of the small trader and landowner and of the professional man. We shall cherish local democracy. We shall strengthen the rights of the individual. The aim and consequence of Conservative policy will be to enable men and women, in all the groups to which they belong, to lead their own lives in their own way within the limits of law and the obligations of good neighbourliness.

Liberty and the law

Justice between citizen and citizen, and justice between citizen and State must be upheld and strengthened.

The Conservative Party regretted that economic difficulties made it necessary for the Socialist Government to defer indefinitely the operation of important parts of the Legal Aid and Advice Act. We are now preparing to extend legal aid to proceedings in the County Courts, and also intend during the life of the next Parliament to introduce the comprehensive scheme for legal advice. We have cut back war-time powers and regulations which trespassed upon British liberties. Seven out of every ten have been eliminated, and we shall take steps to deal with the rest.

We are determined that, in exercising the normal powers of Government in a modern State, a just balance should be struck, and seen to be struck, between the interests of the individual and those of the community. There is no ground for belief that, as a general rule, justice is not substantially done; but we consider that there is room for further improvement in the machinery of tribunals, of public inquiries and of departmental decisions affecting individual interests and property. The public has a right to be assured on these matters. We shall therefore appoint a strong advisory Committee, representative of a wide range of public life and service, to give practical attention to these problems of administrative law and recommend action. We shall ask them to consider as a matter of particular urgency whether changes are needed in the present practice and procedure of compulsory acquisition.

Wherever possible we shall reduce the acreage of land now owned by the State, and shall press ahead with the derequisitioning of Government-held buildings. Local authorities must also restore requisitioned houses and flats to their owners as speedily as possible, without causing hardship to present occupiers.

Houses and amenities

Our aim is to ensure that every family has a decent home to live in. Our Party's pledge to build 300,000 houses a year was derided by our opponents as impossible to fulfil. In fact nearly 350,000 were built last year, and at least as many are likely to be built this year. Already under Conservative Government a million new homes have been provided.

Only under Conservative administration can the nation be sure of a housing policy in line with its needs.

Now that the construction of new homes is going ahead so well, we shall be able to devote a larger part of our resources to the elimination of slums and the modernisation of the older houses. There has been only one full-scale slum clearance drive in British history, and that was when Conservatives were in office in the late thirties. Now, under Conservative Government, there is going to be another. We shall root out the slums at an increasing pace, and aim to rehouse at least 200,000 people a year from them.

People are already benefiting from the repair, improvement and conversion of the older houses in which they live. They should remember that the Labour Party voted in Parliament against the Act which gave recent impetus to this work. The Conservative Government will do all it can to encourage private owners and local authorities to make fuller use of the improvement grants available.

With the abolition of building licences, the competitive efficiency of the private builder can now play its full part in keeping down costs. This will help more people to afford a home of their own. We shall encourage local authorities to adopt schemes which enable the Building Societies to accept a smaller cash deposit. We shall also seek means of including legal costs in the money advanced to house purchasers, and review the rate of the Stamp Duty, particularly on smaller homes.

In this crowded Island we must not build without giving careful thought to where we build. Conservatives will see that good farm land is protected, that big towns are restrained from sprawling haphazardly into the countryside, and that development to relieve over crowded cities takes place where, and only where, there will be work and amenities available for the people who move.

Within the home we wish to see domestic tasks lightened by improved labour-saving and fuel-saving appliances, and the most modern amenities.

More than a thousand new telephones a day are now being installed, and we intend to speed up this record progress.

The new medium of television, which is becoming ever more important in our lives, must not be under monopoly control. Conservatives have ensured that alternative and competing television programmes will soon be available. Measures to improve reception of sound broadcasts where necessary must also go forward.

Education

The most urgent problem in education since the war has been to provide for the huge rise in the school roll. Under Conservative Government a record number of new schools has been completed and a record number of teachers recruited. We have kept pace with the growth in the school population. Now we can draw ahead, bring down the size of classes, improve existing buildings and equipment, and extend facilities for scientific and technical training.

In the next five years we shall provide at least another million new school places, mostly in secondary schools. In this period we intend to complete the reorganisation of all-age classes in the rural areas and make good progress with reorganisation in the towns. We shall also tackle the problem of the slum schools.

Local authorities have been given greater freedom to improve existing schools. More generous assistance is now available to voluntary schools, whose religious teaching is of the utmost importance. Grants will continue to be given for playing fields, community centres and youth clubs. In all this expansion we shall see that no money is wasted.

Under the Conservatives the number of teachers has increased by 6,000 a year. In the next five years we aim at least to maintain this rate and so secure the reduction in the size of classes. We are anxious that the status and rewards of the teaching profession should continue to attract men and women of high attainment and character. We are working out with the teachers' representatives and local authorities an up-to-date pensions scheme.

What matters in education is the development of the child's talents and personality, not the forwarding of a political theory. To prepare for the increasing opportunities of the modern world we need all three kinds of secondary school, grammar, modern and technical, and we must see that each provides a full and distinctive education. We shall not permit the grammar schools to be swallowed up in comprehensive schools. It is vital to build up secondary modern schools, and to develop in them special vocational courses, so that they and the technical schools offer a choice of education that matches the demands of our expanding economy. Parents should have the chance before the eleven-plus examination to discuss with teachers and the local education authority which school is likely to suit their child best. There must be proper provision for the later transfer of children from one type of school to another.

We accept the case that family allowances should be paid as long as a child is at school. A system of increased maintenance allowances will be introduced for senior pupils who might otherwise leave school before finishing an advanced course.

We shall build more technical colleges and seek the co-operation of industry in making their day courses a success. Further funds will be made available for major or specialised developments in higher technological education.

Conservatives will continue to guarantee the present freedom of the Universities from Government interference. We favour greater uniformity in the scales of County awards to University students.

Good health

New hospital building was completely neglected by the Socialist Government. A start is now being made. Plans have been announced and will be carried out over the next few years for the building of new hospitals, both general and mental, and for the extension and modernisation of many existing hospitals. We are making special arrangements to replace worn out and obsolete hospital plant and equipment. We shall seek to open new beds where they are most needed, to recruit extra staff and to provide better facilities. We desire to see steady progress in all forms of preventive work. These are our priorities: we rank them higher than free wigs or free aspirins.

We believe that private practice and contributory schemes have a part to play with the National Health Service and we shall therefore maintain the system of hospital amenity and hospital pay beds. We have cut away restrictions on voluntary effort in the hospital service. We shall continue to give every encouragement to voluntary work.

We welcome the increase in the provision of dental treatment, especially for mothers, children and young people, and we wish in co-operation with the profession to push forward with preventive measures.

The problems of the elderly must concern us all. In particular we shall encourage local health authorities to build up their home help services and to provide half-way houses for the old.

We shall introduce legislation to give effective status to those, known as medical auxiliaries, who assist doctors in investigation and treatment.

We are anxious to provide the best National Health Service the country can afford.

We set up the Guillebaud Committee to study the problems involved and await its recommendations.

The steady fall in infant and maternal mortality rates is a wonderful measure of the nation's better health. Quarter by quarter the records are being broken. We are winning the fight against tuberculosis. Still a great challenge remains for all concerned with the prevention and cure of disease. We shall make sure that adequate funds are available for medical research, and in particular that hopeful lines of inquiry into cancer and polio are urgently pursued.

Air pollution is an enemy to good health, and can cause death. We wholeheartedly accept the need for a national 'clean air' policy. The use of smokeless fuels must be encouraged wherever they can readily be made available, and comprehensive legislation on smoke abatement will be introduced.

Pensions and benefits

The nation has assumed very large obligations towards the pensioners of tomorrow; and tomorrow there will be very many more pensioners. For every 10 people of working age there are now 2 of pensionable age; but within a quarter of a century there will be 3. If during this period Britain can increase her national wealth and resources, by the policy of investment and enterprise which we advocate, these obligations can be met. But if wealth is dissipated, enterprise hampered and severe inflation brought about again by Socialist short-sightedness, the whole of our National Insurance scheme would be undermined and ultimately destroyed.

In its first year of office the Conservative Government increased virtually all social service payments. This year it has again raised pensions and benefits, and fully restored the purchasing power that Parliament intended they should have when the main rates were fixed after the war. Insurance pensioners, war pensioners and public service pensioners can be sure that a Conservative Government will continue to give the most constant attention to their interests and needs.

It is our wish to avoid any change in the present minimum pension ages. But these ages do not necessarily represent the limit of working life. With the aid of its National Advisory Committee the Government will continue to encourage the employment, without regard to age, of all who can give effective service and wish to do so.

Local government

The social policy we have outlined will make heavy demands on the energies and capacity of local authorities up and down the country. They must be strong and well-equipped if they are to carry out these responsibilities effectively.

The problems of local government finance will receive our urgent attention. They must be considered afresh in the light of present-day conditions. When the effects of the new valuations can be fully measured, we shall review the proportion of the rate burden falling upon the different groups of those who occupy property and we shall consider whether any changes are needed to remove injustice. We shall examine possible ways of supplementing the rate, including the revision of Government grants. A fundamental and continuing duty will rest upon every local Council to run their services economically and to see that ratepayers and taxpayers get full value for money.

After first seeking to establish the widest measure of common ground between local authorities of all kinds, the Conservative Government in the coming Parliament will introduce effective machinery for adapting local government to modern needs. In so doing we shall give full weight to valuable local traditions.

The proper allocation of functions must be considered at the same time. As Conservatives we believe that, consistent with efficiency and economy, local government should be as local as possible. So long as we are in office, there is no danger from proposals to strip local government of further powers. On the contrary, we shall seek to secure a wider range of interesting and constructive work for the smaller authorities. Only in this way can we continue to attract to local government the ablest men and women, and ensure that services closely touching the daily lives of everyone are not subjected to impersonal control from aloft and afar.

Scottish affairs

It is our general theme that within the Union the responsibility for managing Scottish affairs shall be in the hands of Scotsmen.

We have ensured that a senior member of the Government shall be constantly in Scotland, and have already transferred from Whitehall to Scotland a variety of additional responsibilities. Next year, in accordance with the recommendation of the Royal Commission on Scottish Affairs, the Secretary of State will take over the care of Scottish roads and bridges. Where further measures of this kind are shown to be in the best interests of Scotland, we shall not hesitate to adopt them.

Industry and employment

Each year since the Unionists took office, the number of people at work in Scotland has grown and now stands at a record level. As part of our policy for maintaining full employment, we aim to attract the widest variety of new industrial enterprise to the areas where it is most needed. We shall review the facilities now available for the building of small and medium-sized factories. We shall see that Scotland continues to receive her fair share of defence and other contracts.

Scottish needs will be fully assessed in framing our new programmes of road construction and railway modernisation. Approval has been given to the building of the Whiteinch–Linthouse Tunnel under the Clyde, and we have announced that a start will be made within the next four years on the construction of a Forth Road Bridge or Tube.

Countryside and Highlands

Within the framework of our agricultural policy, the special requirements of farming on Scottish hill and marginal land will receive particular attention. The measure we have passed to assist the reconditioning of farm workers' houses must continue to be used with vigour. Still faster progress must be made in bringing water supplies to the rural areas, and the funds available for this purpose will be increased.

We are certain that the Crofting Counties can make a growing contribution to the national wealth. Every practicable step will be taken to improve the prosperity and welfare of the Highlands. We are giving particular attention to the special importance of road works.

We shall maintain, and where necessary extend, measures to modernise and increase the efficiency of the Scottish fishing fleets.

Building and rebuilding

Never before in Scottish history has the rate of house-building been so high as in these years of Unionist Government. We fully recognise the compelling seriousness of Scotland's housing problem. We are determined to root out the slums, redevelop the overcrowded and decayed areas in our towns and cities, and rehouse the people in modern homes. We intend to ensure that this redevelopment will provide balanced communities with all the necessities for a full life. This policy, together with house-building throughout Scotland, will receive impetus from a reform of the Scottish rating system.

We propose to expand the hospital building programme and in particular to provide more accommodation for the old, the chronic sick, the mentally ill and those with tuberculosis.

We also propose to speed up the school building programme. We shall aim at the establishment of local technical colleges in Scotland, and make increased provision for developments in higher technological education in our great cities. Thus we shall train our youth of today to meet the challenge of tomorrow, and enable Scotland to maintain a proper place in the forefront of twentieth-century progress.

Welsh affairs

The appointment of a Minister for Welsh Affairs in the Conservative Government has ensured that Welsh interests and problems are represented at the highest level with a force and directness which previous methods of co-ordination had been unable to achieve. At the same time, a steady policy of administrative devolution has been followed. This policy should go on and, if possible, go further.

The Council for Wales and Monmouthshire is engaged in a detailed examination of the arrangements for conducting Government business in Wales, and we shall consider, in the light of the Council's advice, such further changes as it may be practicable and advantageous to make in the present system.

Education

We are sympathetic to all measures designed to preserve Welsh culture and educational tradition. We shall continue to give strong encouragement and support to the teaching of the Welsh language and to the use of Welsh as a medium of instruction in schools.

Employment and development

Unemployment under the Conservative Government has touched the lowest levels ever recorded in Wales in time of peace. We recognise the need for imaginative and tireless attention to the stubborn problems that remain. We shall do everything in our power to improve the competitive position of the Development Area and the South Wales ports, and to attract suitable industry to North-West Wales.

The Conservative Party is determined to promote a more stable economy and fuller development of resources in rural Wales. A thorough investigation of agricultural problems and land use is now in progress and action will be guided by the recommendations which emerge.

We shall press forward with the building and reconditioning of houses and the extension of sewerage, water supplies and electricity. Where the improvement of now unadopted roads in livestock rearing areas would materially assist farm economy, new grants will be made available for the purpose.

We wish to increase the extent and the pace of afforestation in Wales. This can provide employment for the younger generation, not only in forestry itself, but in the many dependent industries that will grow up around the forests. Co-operation between farmers, private woodland owners and the Forestry Commission can make this policy a success.

Constitutional questions

The Constitution of the United Kingdom is the essential safeguard of our democratic government and way of life. We intend that it should retain its rightful place above Party politics.

Northern Ireland

We renew the pledge of faith to Northern Ireland. We shall not allow her position as an integral part of the United Kingdom and of the Empire to be altered in the slightest degree without the consent of the Northern Ireland Parliament.

House of Lords

It has long been the Conservative wish to reach a settlement regarding the reform of the House of Lords, so that it may continue to play its proper role as a Second Chamber under the Constitution. The Labour Party's refusal to take part in the conversations we have proposed on this subject must not be assumed to have postponed reform indefinitely. We shall continue to seek the co-operation of others in reaching a solution. We believe that any changes made now should be concerned solely with the composition of the House.

House of Commons

It will also be our aim to achieve all-Party agreement to amend the rules governing the redistribution of Parliamentary constituencies. We hold the opinion that a longer interval between general reviews would be more appropriate, and that mathematical equality between electorates ought not to be an over-riding consideration.

The nation's choice

We confidently commend to the judgement of the Electorate the policy and principles we have outlined in these pages.

It is our profound belief that the British nation has a high destiny and a glorious future before it. In stemming the tide of Communism, promoting the concord of nations and finding the way to peace, Britain has a central and crucial part to play. A great mission and adventure await us in the Empire and Commonwealth where rich resources can bring prosperity and plenty to all our peoples and to all our friends. At home, the high standards of life we now enjoy may be doubled within a generation, by enterprising work, by far-sighted investment – and by wise leadership.

Who can believe that the Socialists today, out-moded in thought and divided in counsel, are fitted to give such leadership? They still cling to the broken reed of nationalisation; we work for a property-owning democracy. They rely on officialdom; we rely on enterprise. Their policy is to multiply restraints; our policy is to multiply opportunities. Themselves divided, they would divide the nation. We Conservatives place our political faith in the unity of our country, in the neighbourliness of its spirit, in the vigour of its character, and in the liberties of its subjects.

PRICE: ONE PENNY

THE MANIFESTO OF THE CONSERVATIVE & UNIONIST PARTY

The next five years

AS LEADER OF THE CONSERVATIVE AND UNIONIST PARTY I submit this Manifesto to the judgment of my fellow countrymen and women.

This constructive programme—indeed its very title—will show you that we do not intend to rest in the next five years upon the achievements of the past. We must both defend and develop the great gains that we have made. Our policy can be simply stated: PROSPERITY AND PEACE.

I do not remember any period in my lifetime when the economy has been so sound and the prosperity of our people at home so widely spread; but we must also do what we can to extend a generous helping hand to the Commonwealth family and others overseas.

As for peace, it is of course the supreme purpose of all policy. I have lived through two wars and all my efforts are directed to prevent a third. Events of the last few months give me hope that we may be moving into a more constructive period. Vital international negotiations lie ahead and I ask you to continue to entrust them to a Conservative Government.

Harold Macmillan

The Conservative Record

Eight years ago was a turning point in British history. The Labour Government had failed in grappling with the problems of the post-war world. Under Conservative leadership this country set out upon a new path. It is leading to prosperity and opportunity for all.

The British economy is sounder today than at any time since the first world war. Sterling has been re-established as a strong and respected currency. Under Conservative government we have earned abroad £1,600 million more than we have spent. Our exports have reached the highest peak ever. Overseas, mostly in the Commonwealth, we are investing nearly double what we could manage eight years ago. Capital investment at home, to build for the future, is over half as large again. To match this, and make it possible, people are saving more than ever before.

The paraphernalia of controls have been swept away. The call-up is being abolished. We have cut taxes in seven Budgets, whilst continuing to develop the social services. We have provided over two million new homes and almost two million new school places, a better health service and a modern pensions plan. We have now stabilised the cost of living while maintaining full employment. We have shown that Conservative freedom works. Life *is* better with the Conservatives.

In the international field, thanks to the initiative of the Conservative Government, the diplomatic deadlock between East and West has now been broken. The Prime Minister's visit to Russia in February began a sequence of events which has led to the present easing of tension. The proposed exchange of visits between President Eisenhower and Mr Khrushchev is the most recent proof of this. It is our determination to see that this process continues and to make a success of the important negotiations which we trust will follow.

The main issues at this election are therefore simple: (1) Do you want to go ahead on the lines which have brought prosperity at home? (2) Do you want your present leaders to represent you abroad?

Sharing Prosperity

Conservative policy is to double the British standard of living in this generation and ensure that all sections of society share in the expansion of wealth.

While we have been in charge of the nation's affairs, many more of the good things of life have been enjoyed by families large and small, and so long as we remain in charge they will be able to fulfil many more of their hopes and ambitions. But this is not enough. Conservatism is more than successful administration. It is a way of life. It stands for integrity as well as for efficiency, for moral values as well as for material advancement, for service and not merely self-seeking. We believe that, in this spirit and as a contribution to world peace, we British must make a big and sustained effort to help others, particularly within the Commonwealth, climb nearer to our own high level of prosperity.

By raising living standards and by social reform we are succeeding in creating One Nation at home. We must now carry this policy into the wider world where the gap between the industrialised and the under-developed nations is still so great. This can be done by individual service, by increased trade and by investment, public and private.

Under Conservatism annual investment overseas has been more than one per cent of the national income. We want to do better than this, but to do better requires more than a warm heart; we must earn a bigger surplus on our trade overseas.

So at the very forefront of our programme for the next five years we

CONSERVATIVE PARTY GENERAL ELECTION MANIFESTO 1959

The next five years

Date of Election	Thursday 8 October
Party Leader	Harold Macmillan
Candidates	625
MPs	365
Votes	13,749,830
% of vote	49.4%

Foreword

As Leader of the Conservative and Unionist Party I submit this Manifesto to the judgement of my fellow countrymen and women.

This constructive programme –indeed its very title –will show you that we do not intend to rest in the next five years upon the achievements of the past. We must both defend and develop the great gains that we have made. Our policy can be simply stated: Prosperity and Peace.

I do not remember any period in my lifetime when the economy has been so sound and the prosperity of our people at home so widely spread; but we must also do what we can to extend a generous helping hand to the Commonwealth family and others overseas.

As for peace, it is of course the supreme purpose of all policy. I have lived through two wars and all my efforts are directed to prevent a third. Events of the last few months give me hope that we may be moving into a more constructive period. Vital international negotiations lie ahead and I ask you to continue to entrust them to a Conservative Government

Harold Macmillan

The Conservative record

Eight years ago was a turning point in British history. The Labour Government had failed in grappling with the problems of the post-war world. Under Conservative leadership this country set out upon a new path. It is leading to prosperity and opportunity for all.

The British economy is sounder today than at any time since the First World War. Sterling has been re-established as a strong and respected currency. Under Conservative government we have earned abroad £1,600 million more than we have spent. Our exports have reached the highest peak ever. Overseas, mostly in the Commonwealth, we are investing nearly double what we could manage eight years ago. Capital investment at home, to build for the future, is over half as large again. To match this, and make it possible, people are saving more than ever before.

The paraphernalia of controls have been swept away. The call-up is being abolished. We have cut taxes in seven Budgets, whilst continuing to develop the social services. We have provided over two million new homes and almost two million new school places, a better health service and a modern pensions plan. We have now stabilised the cost of living while maintaining full employment. We have shown that Conservative freedom works. Life is better with the Conservatives.

In the international field, thanks to the initiative of the Conservative Government, the diplomatic deadlock between East and West has now been broken. The Prime Minister's visit to Russia in February began a sequence of events which has led to the present easing of tension. The proposed exchange of visits between President Eisenhower and Mr Khrushchev is the most recent proof of this. It is our determination to see that this process continues and to make a success of the important negotiations which we trust will follow.

The main issues at this election are therefore simple:

1 Do you want to go ahead on the lines which have brought prosperity at home?
2 Do you want your present leaders to represent you abroad?

Sharing prosperity

Conservative policy is to double the British standard of living in this generation and ensure that all sections of society share in the expansion of wealth.

While we have been in charge of the nation's affairs, many more of the good things of life have been enjoyed by families large and small, and so long as we remain in charge they will be able to fulfil many more of their hopes and ambitions. But this is not enough. Conservatism is more than successful administration. It is a way of life. It stands for integrity as well as for efficiency, for moral values as well as for material advancement, for service and not merely self-seeking. We believe that in this spirit and as a contribution to world peace, we British must make a big and sustained effort to help others, particularly within the Commonwealth, climb nearer to our own high level of prosperity.

By raising living standards and by social reform we are succeeding in creating One Nation at home. We must now carry this policy into the wider world where the gap between the industrialised and the underdeveloped nations is still so great. This can be done by individual service, by increased trade and by investment, public and private.

Under Conservatism annual investment overseas has been more than one per cent of the national income. We want to do better than this, but to do better requires 'more than a warm heart'; we must earn a bigger surplus on our trade overseas.

So at the very forefront of our programme for the next five years we place these three essential conditions of success – a strong pound, expanding trade and national unity.

The pound

Sterling is the currency in which nearly half the world's trade is done. Our paramount aim will be to maintain international confidence in it as a sound and stable medium of exchange.

We shall use flexible monetary and other measures to achieve the right balance in the home economy, to keep the cost of living as steady as possible in the interests of the housewife, and to ensure that our goods and services are available at prices the world will pay.

Trade opportunities

We shall concentrate on the further promotion of the export trade.

Half our trade is with the Commonwealth, and the new Commonwealth Economic Consultative Council will provide further opportunities for expansion. We shall continue to take steps to increase the flow of trade with America in which for the first time in a century our exports have exceeded our imports. We are about to join an economic association of Seven European countries; our aim remains an industrial free market embracing all Western Europe. The recent trade agreement we made with Soviet Russia is already leading to more orders for British machinery and other goods.

Unity

Prosperity depends on the combined efforts of the nation as a whole. None of us can afford outmoded approaches to the problems of today, and we intend to invite the representatives of employers and trades unions to consider afresh with us the human and industrial problems that the next five years will bring.

Employment and economic change

So long as Conservative policies of sound currency and expanding trade are continued, and unity at home maintained, full employment is safe. But patches of local unemployment can be created by swift changes in markets, methods and machines. Our policy is to welcome technical progress, which can lead to dramatic increases in prosperity and leisure, but at the same time to deal with the problems it brings.

Our first major Bill in the next Parliament will be one to remodel and strengthen our powers for coping with local unemployment. This will be done in three ways – by ensuring that we can act anywhere in Britain where high local unemployment shows up; by adding to the places where we can now offer help, those where there is a clear and imminent threat of unemployment; and by offering capital grants to encourage the building of new factories where they are most needed, as an addition to subsidising the rent of Government-built factories. This policy will also feature the clearing of sites to make a district attractive to new industry.

These measures will be of particular help to Scotland and Wales. We shall continue to help the Government of Northern Ireland to deal with the special problem there.

Many individual industries have to adjust themselves to new conditions. The Government will play its part in assisting the aircraft industry to increase its sales, and will help in fostering research and development. Shipping and shipbuilding depend on expanding world trade which our policies are directed to encourage. We shall do all we can to assist them in their problems, and also intend to support the replacement of the Queen liners.

Reorganisation and re-equipment of the Lancashire cotton industry have got away to a good start. With the help of the Act we have passed, it can have a prosperous future. It is a condition of grants under this Act that compensation is paid to displaced operatives.

As part of our policy of easing general mobility of labour, measures will be taken to encourage re-training. Part of the capacity of the Government Training Centres will be used to make a direct contribution towards the provision of adequate opportunities for apprenticeship. We shall also continue our support of the Industrial Training Council which we took the initiative in setting up.

Many educational, industrial and official bodies have made provision since the war for management courses. We should welcome the creation of an Advanced Business School at one of the universities.

Policy for progress

We are determined to keep Britain a great and go-ahead country, leading the world in important branches of technology, and translating its technological advance into productive capacity with a high and rising rate of investment.

This is how we shall set about this task in the next five years.

Technical advance

One Cabinet Minister will be given the task of promoting scientific and technological development. Whilst it would be wrong to concentrate all Government scientific work into a single Ministry, this Minister for Science will have responsibility for the Department of Scientific and Industrial Research, the Medical and Agricultural Research Councils and the Nature Conservancy, the atomic energy programme, and the United Kingdom contribution to space research.

The development of nuclear energy for peaceful purposes will be pressed ahead. A conference will be called of those concerned in industry and education to forward the spread and understanding of automation. We shall encourage new inventions and the development of new techniques.

Under the railway programme over 3,000 new diesels will be delivered into service by 1965, 8,000 miles of track re-laid, and electric traction increased by 60 per cent. We shall go ahead with a 'round-the-world' telephone cable in co-operation with the Commonwealth, and maintain our lead in telecommunications by building a new large cable-laying ship.

Modern roads

The rising volume of traffic, a yardstick of rising prosperity, must be matched by an intensive drive to build better and safer roads. Our road programme is already the biggest we have ever had in this country. Over the next five years it will be twice as big as over the last five years.

Our first priority in England and Wales will be to complete the five major schemes and motorways, which with their urban links and through routes will provide the framework of a new road system. In Scotland we mean to complete the Forth Road Bridge, the two Clyde Tunnels and the reconstruction of the Carlisle–Glasgow–Stirling trunk road, and to speed up the programme of Highland road development.

At the same time there will be a country-wide drive to improve the existing road network and new schemes to relieve congestion in the towns. Severn and Tay Bridges will both be started.

The land

Farming in Britain today is efficient and prosperous. Great progress has been made possible by our system of long-term price guarantees and the payment of grants for modern buildings, equipment and techniques. This policy will be developed so as to ensure stability to farmer and farm worker.

We give a pledge that the long-term assurances to agriculture contained in our 1957 Act will continue for the life-time of the next Parliament. In the light of experience, we shall consider, in close consultation with the leaders of the industry, any improvements and developments in agricultural policy including the small farmers scheme. We shall continue to promote the well-being of the British fishing industry.

We confirm that horticulture must have support comparable with that given to agriculture generally. We shall continue to use the tariff as the main instrument of protection. Legislation will be passed to provide improvement grants of £7½ million and to help reform horticultural marketing, including a streamlining of the operation of the central London markets.

In the next five years, 300,000 acres will be planted by the Forestry Commission. Encouragement will continue to be given to private woodland owners. We attach importance to the prosperity of this industry, which would be further assured by the establishment of an effective marketing organisation.

There will be continued improvement in amenities for families who live on the land – a further extension of water, sewerage and electricity supplies, and better housing and schools. We have set up a Committee to help us solve the problem of public transport in the countryside.

Nationalised industries

We are utterly opposed to any extension of nationalisation, by whatever means. We shall do everything possible to ensure improved commercial standards of operation and less centralisation in those industries already nationalised. In addition, we shall review the situation in civil aviation, and set up a new licensing authority to bring a greater measure of freedom to nationally and privately owned airlines.

To further the development of the Post Office as a modern business, we propose to separate its current finances from the Exchequer. Direct Ministerial responsibility to Parliament and the status of Post Office employees as Civil Servants will be retained.

Public administration

In addition to our proposals regarding the Minister for Science, we shall from time to time make such changes in the functions of Ministers as are necessary to suit modern needs.

We shall maintain our policy of giving special regard to the distinctive rights and problems of Scotland and Wales. Transfer of administrative work from London will be carried further as opportunity allows.

We look forward to reforming and strengthening the structure of local democracy, in the light of reports from the Local Government Commissions for England and Wales.

The whole administrative system of town and country planning will be reviewed afresh with the aim of simplifying procedure, achieving improvements and reducing delays.

Opportunity and security

Conservatives want everybody to have a fuller opportunity to earn more and to own more – and to create a better life for themselves and their children.

We shall proceed in the next Parliament with our policy of reducing whenever possible the burden of taxation.

We shall encourage facilities for the small investor to have a stake in British industry.

Education

During the next five years we shall concentrate on producing a massive enlargement of educational opportunity at every level. The necessary work is already in hand. Four programmes, each the biggest of its kind ever undertaken in Britain, are gathering momentum.

Training colleges for teachers, which will now provide a three-year course, are being expanded by nearly two-thirds so as to get rid of over-large classes; the number of students at universities is to be further increased by at least one-third; new technical college buildings are opening at the rate of one a week; and we shall spend some £400 million by 1965 to improve the quality of our school buildings.

We shall defend the grammar schools against doctrinaire Socialist attack, and see that they are further developed. We shall bring the modern schools up to the same high standard. Then the choice of schooling for children can be more flexible and less worrying for parents. This is the right way to deal with the problem of the 'eleven-plus'. Already, up and down the country, hundreds of new modern schools are showing the shape of things to come. Our programme will open up the opportunities that they provide for further education and better careers to every boy and girl; and by 1965 we expect that at least 40 per cent will be staying on after fifteen.

We have appointed a Committee to review the system of awards to students from public funds, including the present 'means test', and improvements will be made when it has reported.

Good housing

Our housing policy, so successful in the past, will be pressed ahead with vigour in the future so as to deal with up-to-date priorities These are the clearance of the slums, the relief of overcrowding, and the needs of the old. By 1965 we intend to re-house at least another million people from the slums.

The local authorities will continue to play a big part along with private enterprise in meeting housing needs; but we reject as costly and bureaucratic nonsense the Socialist plan to take into council ownership millions of privately rented houses.

In the next Parliament we shall take no further action to decontrol rents. More houses must be built and recent rent legislation given time to have its full beneficial effect in increasing house-room.

In the last eight years, 750,000 families have bought their own new homes, and we want to see the process go on. Also, up to £100 million will be advanced by the Government to building societies for loans on older houses – and we shall consider increasing this figure if need be.

Good health

As part of a major policy to promote good health, we shall not only clear the slums, but also wage war on smog by effective use of the Clean Air Act, and tackle the pollution of rivers and estuaries. We shall offer vaccination against polio to everyone up to the age of forty and to all specially vulnerable groups. Prevention of accidents on roads and in the home will be subjects of sustained campaigns.

On the curative side there will be a big programme of hospital building. We already have sixteen new general or mental hospitals and some fifty major extension schemes under way; over the next five years our target is to double the present capital programme.

The level of doctors' and dentists' pay in the health services will be considered as soon as the Royal Commission has reported. We shall also be ready to consider with representatives of the professions their status in the health services.

Local authorities will be encouraged to develop their health and welfare services. We shall set up a National Council for Social Work Training to help recruit and train the extra social workers who will be needed.

Security and retirement

The rates of retirement pensions, which we have increased three times, have now a real buying power over ten shillings higher than in 1951. We pledge ourselves to ensure that pensioners continue to share in the good things which a steadily expanding economy will bring.

Our new pensions scheme will put national insurance on a sound financial footing, concentrate Exchequer help on those with the lowest earnings, and enable men and women with higher earnings to make increased provision for old age. At the same time, we are encouraging the growth of sound occupational pension schemes.

The weekly amount that can be earned without deduction of pension, by those who have retired or by widowed mothers, will be further increased. We shall continue the preferential treatment which our recent legislation has provided for widows and their children. Those disabled in the service of their country will remain the subject of our special care. Particular attention will be given to providing more suitable vehicles for the badly disabled. We shall continue to ensure that those dependent on national assistance have a share in the country's increasing prosperity.

Not only will our housing programme cater more and more for the needs of the old, but we shall also try to make it easier for them to go on living at home. For example, better provision will be made for a 'meals on wheels' service for the old and infirm. The extension of the home help service and the provision of holiday rest homes will be encouraged.

The use of leisure

Two out of three families in the country now own TV, one in three has a car or motor-cycle, twice as many are taking holidays away from home – these are welcome signs of the increasing enjoyment of leisure. They are the fruits of our policies.

But at the same time all this represents a challenge to make the growth of leisure more purposeful and creative, especially for young people.

Our policy of opportunity will therefore be extended. In particular, we propose to reorganise and expand the Youth Service. Measures will be taken to encourage Youth Leadership and the provision of attractive youth clubs, more playing fields and better facilities for sport. We shall do more to support the arts including the living theatre. Improvements will be made in museums and galleries and in the public library service. Particular attention will be given to the needs of provincial centres.

Liberty under the law

We believe that it is by emphasis on the home, enlargement of educational opportunity, development of services for youth and a spread of the responsibilities of property that national character can be strengthened and moral standards upheld. In addition, we shall revise some of our social laws, for example those relating to betting and gaming and to clubs and licensing, which are at present full of anomalies and lead to abuse and even corruption.

It will continue to be our policy to protect the citizens, irrespective of creed or colour, against lawlessness.

We intend to review the system of criminal justice and to undertake penal reforms which will lead offenders to abandon a life of crime. A scheme for compensating the victims of violent crime for personal injuries will be considered.

The Legal Aid and Advice Acts will be extended to remaining courts and to certain tribunals, and the present income and capital limits will be reviewed to ensure that help is not denied to anyone who needs it.

We shall appoint a Committee to review the working of the Companies Act in the light of present conditions. Action will be taken to protect the public against the sale of sub-standard goods and to amend the law on weights and measures.

We mean to make quite sure that the Press have proper facilities for reporting the proceedings of local authorities.

In all these matters we shall act to strengthen Britain's traditional way of life, centred upon the dignity and liberty of the individual.

Our duty overseas

Whilst one hundred million people in Europe alone have, since the war, been forcibly absorbed into the Communist bloc and system, six times that number have been helped to nationhood within the British Commonwealth. It is our duty to ourselves and to the cause of freedom everywhere to see that the facts are known, and that misrepresentation about British 'colonialism' does not go unchallenged. Progressive expansion of overseas information services will remain our policy.

The Conservative Government will continue to work out in the Commonwealth the pattern of a community of free and sovereign nations. Next year Nigeria, and before long the West Indies, will acquire independence.

We shall discuss with our partners in the Commonwealth plans to deal with the status of members too small to be fully self-supporting and self-governing.

An advisory Commission, under Lord Monckton's chairmanship, is being set up in preparation for the review of the Constitution of the Federation of Rhodesia and Nyasaland which is to take place in 1960. Our central aim in multi-racial countries is to build communities which protect minority rights and are free of all discrimination on grounds of race or colour. If democracy is to be secured, education must underpin the franchise; and the rapid expansion of education is the Commonwealth's most pressing need. We therefore undertake to increase training facilities for teachers and to make more English books available; and we will play a leading part in financing the new Commonwealth scheme of exchange scholarships and fellowships.

We emphasise the part that individual service can play. The need for teachers, doctors and technicians of every kind is almost unlimited, and an appeal to the adventurous spirit of youth must be made. We shall encourage the professions and industry to help those willing to do so to serve for a few years in the overseas Commonwealth without prejudice to their careers at home.

Further British capital will be made available through loans and grants for sound Commonwealth development. The Colombo Plan and other schemes of technical cooperation will be assisted to the full. We shall back the proposal for a new International Development Association. The Conservative Government will continue to support the United Nations' agencies in relieving poverty and combating disease, and will substantially increase the British contribution to the United Nations' Special Fund for economic development.

Policy for peace

The next few years and even months will be critical and perhaps decisive. As a result of our policies the great powers of the world have closer contacts both personal and official than for a long time. Provided we use flexibility of method without abandoning firmness of principle, a great opportunity lies before us. Peace with justice is our aim.

United Nations

Peace cannot finally be secure until there is a world instrument with the power and the will to deal with aggression and ensure that international agreements are carried out. In view of the deep divisions between East and West, this is necessarily a long-term aim. We shall continue trying to build up the United Nations' strength and influence, but recognise that progress in improving East–West relations is an essential preliminary. Meanwhile, we shall give all our support to the work of conciliation and mediation which the United Nations' machinery is well fitted to carry out.

Relations with Russia

We are opposed to the Communist system as being wholly contrary to the basic principles of our freedom and religious faith. We believe that if peace can be preserved these principles will not only survive in our own part of the world but spread. Owing to the destructiveness of modern warfare, both sides have in common a greater interest in peace than ever before. If humanity is to survive both must therefore learn to live together. With this aim we have worked for a steady improvement in our relations with the Soviet Union. The steps we have taken to expand trade, promote personal contacts and discussions and improve means of communication will be pursued.

Our alliances

Meanwhile it remains vitally important to maintain our defensive alliances throughout the world. In Europe while we will work for the inspection and reduction of armaments in areas to be agreed, we are opposed to plans which would alter the military balance and so weaken NATO.

We have sought to keep the alliance united on matters of principle and flexible in its diplomacy. For example, over Berlin we are resolved that the two and a quarter million West Berliners shall preserve their freedom to choose their way of life. Subject to that, we are ready to work out new arrangements to improve the existing situation.

The armed forces

Our armed forces are being reorganised on a voluntary basis and extensively re-equipped to suit them to the needs of the present day. The pay and living conditions of the Services have been vastly improved and we intend to keep them in line with standards in civilian life.

Disarmament

The power of modern weapons is appalling; but the fact that a nuclear war would mean mutual destruction is the most powerful deterrent against war. It is, however, war itself, not a particular weapon, which is the true enemy. Our aim, therefore, is to move forward by balanced stages towards the abolition of all nuclear weapons and the reduction of the other weapons and armed forces to a level which will rule out the possibility of an aggressive war. In doing this we must stick to the principle that disarmament can be effective only if it is subject to a proper system of international inspection and control. To. this end, we have just reached agreement with the Soviet Union on a new body to consider disarmament and report to the United Nations. We shall place before it our comprehensive proposals.

Nuclear tests

On British initiative the Conference of experts met last year and reached agreement on some aspects of controlling the suspension of nuclear tests. This was followed by the present Geneva Conference and no nuclear weapon tests have taken place since the Russian tests in November 1958. At the Conference, effective systems have been worked out for supervising a ban on nuclear tests in the air and under water, though more work is still to be done on supervising a ban on tests underground.

We have three objectives, achievement of each of which would be a great prize:

1 The end of atmospheric tests and all that that implies. Since agreement in principle has been reached about the feasibility of controlling a ban on atmospheric tests, we see no reason why any such tests need ever be undertaken again by the nuclear powers. It was in this hope that we suspended our tests.
2 The establishment of the first experiment in a system of international control, which may lead to effective measures of disarmament, both nuclear and conventional.
3 The abolition under effective control of tests of all kinds.

This is a realistic and constructive approach. It maintains British influence in world affairs unimpaired and paves the way for wider agreements in the future.

The alternative

Vital issues of defence and foreign policy divide the Socialists in Opposition and would continue to divide them if returned to power. Remember their record at home! What have they to offer today that was not tried and found wanting when they last held office?

The country is disillusioned with nationalisation; but a Labour Government would extend it. People are glad to be free of controls; but a Labour Government would clamp them on again. Everyone welcomes stable prices and lower taxes; but a return to Socialism is bound to mean a return to inflation and higher taxes. Britain lives by her trade; but Socialism would disrupt business at home and undermine confidence abroad.

The Socialists have learnt nothing in their period of Opposition save new ways to gloss over their true intentions. Their policies are old-fashioned and have no relevance to the problems of the modern world. Our policies look to the future and offer the best hope of prosperity and peace with justice.

manifesto
manifesto
manifesto

CONSERVATIVE PARTY GENERAL ELECTION MANIFESTO 1964

Prosperity with a purpose

Date of Election	Thursday 15 October
Party Leader	Sir Alec Douglas Home
Candidates	630
MPs	304
Votes	12,000,396
% of vote	43.4%

Foreword by Sir Alec Douglas Home

As Leader of the Conservative and Unionist Party, I submit this Manifesto to my fellow countrymen and women.

Its object is to declare the principles for which Conservatives stand and to show how we propose to translate them into action. Part of it is a record of achievement, and that is deliberate. For work well done carries conviction that our policies for the future will succeed. Our philosophy is to use what is good from the past to create a future which is better.

But these pages are not an introduction to an easy, sheltered life. No country has an inherited right to wealth or influence. Prosperity has to be worked for. The future will be assured only if our people recognise the simple economic rules which must be kept by a country dependent on earning its living in a competitive world. This manifesto points the way.

Throughout, you will find a constant theme. It is the creation of a social and economic climate in which men and women can develop their personalities and talents to their country's benefit as well as their own. Conservatives believe that a centralised system of direction cramps the style of the British people. Only by trusting the individual with freedom and responsibility shall we gain the vitality to keep our country great.

Such greatness is not measured in terms of prosperity alone. What counts is the purpose to which we put prosperity. The Conservative purpose is clear from our record and from our programme. It is to raise the quality of our society and its influence for good in the world. We are using the growth of wealth to expand opportunities for the young, to provide more generously for the old and the sick and the handicapped, to aid developing countries still battling against widespread poverty, and to maintain the strength on which national security and our work for peace depend.

In a world as dangerous as that in which we live it can make no sense whatever for Britain unilaterally to discard her strength. We therefore reject the idea of giving up our nuclear arm. We adopt instead a balanced policy of strength and conciliation: strength to be used to stop wars before they start; conciliation to reach areas of agreement with the Soviet Union and the Communist world which will replace tension and potential conflict. The Nuclear Test Ban Treaty was one such achievement. We mean to work for more until the danger of war is eliminated. The way will be rough but we will persevere. I ask you to conclude that we should retain British power and influence so that they may be used for such high purpose.

In short, I trust that the values for which Conservatives stand and the policies which we intend to follow commend themselves to the imagination and the common sense of the British people.

Working for peace

Our policy of peace through strength has brought Britain safely through years of tension and danger. It contributes to the security of the free world. It provides the realistic basis for better relations between East and West. It keeps this country in her rightful place at the centre of international affairs.

The Socialists, by contrast, would relegate Britain to the sidelines. They are as always deeply divided on international and defence issues – so divided that they dared not even discuss them at their last party conference lest an open quarrel should break out. Nuclear abdication is the only policy on which they can unite.

Diplomacy and disarmament

The Nuclear Test Ban Treaty of 1963 has been welcomed throughout the world. Both the United States and the Soviet Union have acknowledged how much it owed to the Conservative Government's initiative and perseverance. But if Labour Party policy had been carried out, and our country had no longer been a nuclear power, there would have been no British role to play. We should have been without influence and without voice. The Conservative Party will not cast away by unilateral action this vital contribution to Britain's diplomacy and defence.

We are ready and anxious not only to stop all tests but to discard further armaments – if other nations agree to do the same and give convincing proof that they are doing so step by step with us. That is what we are trying to achieve in the general disarmament negotiations. That is what we pledge ourselves to work for.

Following upon the test ban treaty, the Russians, Americans and ourselves have this year agreed to limit production of fissile materials for military purposes. In accord with our allies, we shall seek other areas of agreement with the Soviet Union – for example, on non-dissemination of nuclear weapons and observation posts against surprise attack. It would be wrong to raise false hopes, for the Russians are stubborn negotiators and these are difficult matters. But we are determined to maintain the momentum of constructive discussion which has already done much to bring nearer an end to the cold war.

Defence and deterrence

A Conservative Government will firmly uphold Britain's world-wide interests and obligations. In recent months we have been called upon to defend Malaysia and South Arabia and to render assistance in East Africa and Cyprus. These crises have demonstrated the effectiveness of our defence organisation and the skill and spirit of our fighting Services. We shall continue to ensure that they are equipped to respond swiftly and successfully to challenge.

Over 90 per cent of our defence effort is devoted to conventional arms. But in the nuclear age no money spent on increasing the size or improving the conventional equipment of our forces could by itself secure the defence of these islands. The only effective defence is the certainty in the mind of any enemy that there is no prize he could ever win by our defeat which could compensate him for the destruction he would suffer in the process. Conservatives do not accept the view that we could never be threatened on our own, or that an enemy will always assume we shall have allies rushing to our side.

Britain must in the ultimate resort have independently controlled nuclear power to deter an aggressor. We possess this power today. Only under a Conservative Government will we possess it in the future.

We have put into practice the concept of interdependence within the Atlantic alliance by assigning our V-bombers to Nato but subject to our right to deploy them at discretion if supreme national interests are at stake. The Polaris submarines when operational will be assigned in the same way and subject to the same reservation.

Western unity and the UN

We remain convinced that the political and economic problems of the West can best be solved by an Atlantic partnership between America and a united Europe. Only in this way can Europe develop the wealth and power, and play the part in aiding others, to which her resources and history point the way.

Entry into the European Economic Community is not open to us in existing circumstances, and no question of fresh negotiations can arise at present. We shall work, with our EFTA partners, through the Council of Europe, and through Western European Union, for the closest possible relations with the Six consistent with our Commonwealth ties.

The principles laid down in the Charter of the United Nations are as valid today as when we signed it. We shall use our influence to see that these principles are implemented. Our contribution to the UN's economic and social agencies and to its work of conciliation and peace-making is second only to that of the United States. We shall work for the establishment of its present peace-keeping machinery on a more permanent basis.

The role of the Commonwealth

The Prime Ministers' Conference this summer reflected the vigour and increased the strength of the modern Commonwealth. In a few weeks' time it will comprise 20 nations, 13 of whom will have achieved their independence since the Conservatives took office.

This historic evolution is now reaching its final stages. Of our remaining dependencies many are well on the road to sovereignty. A number have multi-racial populations presenting special problems. Others are too small to bear the burdens of separate statehood. In each case we shall work for a fair and practical solution which will protect the interests of the peoples concerned.

The organisation of government in this country and the machinery of Commonwealth co-operation will be brought into line with new conditions. We propose next year to merge the Colonial Office with the Commonwealth Relations Office, and it and the Foreign Office will be staffed from a single Diplomatic Service. We shall give full support to the Commonwealth Secretariat whose establishment was agreed at the Prime Ministers' Conference. We also intend to set up a Commonwealth Foundation to develop contacts between professional bodies in the Commonwealth, and will give increased assistance to the Commonwealth Parliamentary Association.

Trade and aid

Today the Commonwealth faces two world challenges. One is political: the opportunity to show by example that peoples of different races can work together in amity and confidence. The other is economic: the need to build up in developing territories more prosperous and hopeful conditions. We shall succeed in the political task only if we also succeed in the economic. For it is the gap in living standards between the industrialised and the developing that gives racial conflict its cutting edge.

The prime need of developing countries is for trading opportunities, and here Britain leads the world. No country is so liberal in providing them with access to her markets. At the United Nations trade and development conference this year we played a crucial role in securing the adoption of recommendations to help them expand, export and earn. Our consistent aim is wider world trade and an improved world monetary system to sustain it.

Under the Conservatives since 1951, £1,400m. has been provided in Government aid, preponderantly to the Commonwealth. Last year it reached the record level of £175m., more than double what it was six years earlier. Private investment has been providing substantial amounts. As the British economy expands, so the level of aid will progressively rise. We shall also support voluntary endeavour, of which the Freedom from Hunger Campaign has been a splendid example.

Technical co-operation

But aid is more than money. Just as vital is the sharing of knowledge and experience. We have multiplied our technical assistance more than sixfold in six years. We set up the new Department of Technical Co-operation in 1961 to give impetus to this work.

More than 50,000 students from developing countries were in full-time courses in Britain last year, while some 19,000 British men and women were serving in the developing countries under our Government's auspices. An important feature has been the growing opportunity for young people to find scope for their energy and idealism in voluntary overseas service. Through the initiative of voluntary organisations, and with increasing Government support, the numbers are rising fast.

At the 1964 Commonwealth Education Conference we offered a big increase in capital assistance for high education in the Commonwealth during the coming five years. We shall also vigorously pursue our proposals for a Commonwealth medical conference, and for increasing Commonwealth co-operation in development projects and in the training of administrators.

In these ways we shall seek both to help the developing countries and to strengthen Commonwealth links.

Growth without inflation

In 13 years of Conservative government the living standards of the British people have improved more than in the whole of the previous half-century.

The working population is up by two million and over 98 per cent are in jobs. Rising incomes and lower taxes have made possible a spectacular increase in spending on the essentials, the comforts and what were once regarded as the luxuries of life. At the same time personal savings have grown from £100m. in 1951 to nearly £2,000m. last year – providing funds for the modernisation of Britain, security for the individual, and substance to the Conservative concept of a property-owning democracy.

We do not claim that these benefits are the gift of the Government. What we do claim is that the Government has created conditions in which individuals by enterprise and thrift have gained these benefits for themselves and the country. These are the conditions we shall maintain.

An expanding economy

We shall give first priority to our policy for economic growth, so that Britain's national wealth can expand by a steady 4 per cent per year. We recognise that this involves a high level of imports, and we are prepared to draw on our reserves whilst our exports, both visible and invisible, achieve a balance with them. By new arrangements with the International Monetary Fund, the European banks and the United States, we have strengthened the defences of sterling against speculative attack which could put a brake on progress. But the long-term problem of the balance of payments can only be solved by bringing our trading economy to the highest pitch of competitiveness and modern efficiency.

Exports and prices

We have improved the services provided for export firms, given them the fullest credit insurance facilities in the world, and established the National Export Council to aid their efforts. But basically our capacity to sell abroad depends on competitive prices.

No country has succeeded in keeping post-war prices completely steady, but Britain in recent years has done far better than most. Our aim is an economy in which earnings rise in step with productivity and do not outpace it. An effective and fair incomes policy is crucial to the achievement of sustained growth without inflation. We shall take a further initiative to secure wider acceptance and effective implementation of such a policy. In addition, a downward pressure on prices will be increasingly exerted by Conservative measures to stimulate industrial competition.

NEDC and planning

We have set up the National Economic Development Council, bringing together Government, management and unions in a co-operative venture to improve our economic performance. This has been followed by the establishment of Economic Development Committees for a number of individual industries.

NEDC gives reality to the democratic concept of planning by partnership. In contemporary politics the argument is not for or against planning. All human activity involves planning. The question is: how is the planning to be done? By consent or by compulsion?

The Labour Party's policy of extended State ownership and centralised control would be economically disastrous and incompatible with the opportunities and responsibilities of a free society. Conservatives believe that a democratic country as mature as ours must be self-disciplined and not State-controlled, law-abiding without being regulation-ridden, co-operative but not coerced.

Modernisation and competition

Record progress is being made in modernising industry. Today capital investment in new factories, construction, plant and equipment is twice as high as when the Socialists left office. Our financial incentives for this purpose are now the best in the world, and we shall see that tax policies continue to stimulate industrial innovation.

Science and industry

Britain's total spending on civil scientific research and development has more than trebled since the mid-1950s. In this effort Government and industry have shared.

We shall further improve the organisation for promoting civil science by setting up new research councils. An industrial research and development authority will be formed to undertake basic and applied work of importance to industry.

Economic efficiency and increasing leisure have always depended on supplementing human with mechanical effort, and increasingly mechanisation must extend to the control systems which link and co-ordinate the machines. It is an important feature of our policy to encourage the wider spread of automated equipment. The National Research Development Corporation, with extended powers and finance, will be helped to sponsor the application of such new techniques in industry.

Whilst recognising the Government's obligation to assist in these ways, we are convinced that the rapidly changing world of industrial technology is the last place for Socialism. It calls for a flexibility, and a response to new ideas and requirements, which a system of free competitive enterprise is best suited to provide. The Conservative Party is utterly opposed to any extension of nationalisation, whether outright or piecemeal. We propose to complete the denationalisation of steel. Industries in public ownership will continue to be developed as modern businesses.

Competition and the consumer

In private industry and trade we intend to stimulate the forces of competition which make for efficiency and bring down prices. Abolition of resale price maintenance, save in cases where it can be shown to serve the public interest, will have this effect on retail trade. In the next Parliament our first major Bill will be one to strengthen the Monopolies Commission, speed up its work, and enlarge the Government's powers to implement its recommendations. It will enable us to deal with any merger or takeover bid likely to lead to harmful monopoly conditions.

We shall reform the Companies Act, so as to take account of modern developments and give added protection to investors.

Competition and free choice are the customers' most effective safeguards. We welcome the many signs of growing consumer awareness and influence, and have established and will finance the Consumer Council as a spokesman for these interests. We shall follow up our reform of hire purchase and weights and measures by improving merchandise marks legislation, and by strengthening the Sale of Goods Act so as to secure greater protection for shoppers in such matters as warranties and guarantees.

The restrictions on shop hours, which are particularly inconvenient for the growing number of women at work, are being reviewed. Our aim is to achieve greater flexibility in the present arrangements, while maintaining necessary safeguards for shop-workers.

Full employment

We believe that a growing and competitive economy must redeploy its resources to meet or anticipate changes in markets, methods and machines. But the interests of those who work in industry must be fully safeguarded in the process. Otherwise responses to change could act as a brake on modernisation and rising standards.

Redundancy and retraining

The Government is helping industry to plan its manpower requirements ahead so that unnecessary redundancies are avoided. Our new Contracts of Employment Act gives employees for the first time statutory rights to a minimum period of notice. We attach great importance to the wider extension of arrangements whereby redundant workers are compensated by their employers through severance payments.

In the next Parliament we shall reform the unemployment benefit under the national insurance scheme. Men and women with earnings above a minimum level will be able to receive for some months a graduated supplement to their flat-rate benefit. Their total benefit will thus be more closely related to their normal standard of living, and those unable to find a new job right away will be protected against a sharp fall in income. Some workers who fall ill may suffer comparable financial hardship, and a similar change will be made in sickness benefit. Our detailed scheme will be put forward when we have completed our discussions with representatives of the interests concerned.

We are at present carrying through in Government training centres a doubling of the facilities for retraining men and women in new skills. In addition, the industrial training boards which are being set up under our new legislation will stimulate industries particularly those that are expanding to provide greatly improved systems of apprenticeship, training and retraining.

Regional development

Our programme of regional development will expand employment prospects, make the maximum use of national resources and spread prosperity more evenly throughout the United Kingdom. In this way, the potentialities of each region can be developed to the utmost and at the same time its characteristics retained.

This programme combines the provision of better communications, up-to-date social services and improved amenities with generous inducements to build new factories, install modern equipment and provide fresh jobs where they are most required. Its object is to make each region a more efficient place to work in and a more attractive place to live in. Our studies for this purpose now cover Wales, Scotland and most of England.

In central Scotland and north-east England we are already carrying out programmes without precedent in conception and scale. Their impact is evident in the renewed activity and growing buoyancy of these areas which are looking, not towards the problems of the past, but to the technological developments of the future. Thus the places which pioneered the first industrial revolution will become full partners in the second.

In south-east England our programme will ensure proper development to meet the needs of the natural growth of population. New cities and towns and urban expansions will be built to provide work and homes away from the capital. Consultations are now being held about the location and size of these developments, which will be carried out without prejudicing growth elsewhere. We are determined to check the drift to the south and to achieve a sound balance over the whole country.

A Conservative Government will continue to control immigration from overseas according to the numbers which our crowded country and its industrial regions can absorb. We shall ensure that the working of the Commonwealth Immigrants Act, which we passed in 1962 against bitter Labour Party opposition, is fair and effective.

Industrial relations

All these measures to protect and expand employment should help reduce industrial disputes. They also highlight the lack of justification in present conditions for many restrictive practices of labour.

The trade unions have a vital responsibility to diminish such handicaps to Britain's competitive strength. We shall continue to seek their co-operation in matters of common interest and to work in partnership with them through NEDC.

Recent decisions in the courts have thrown into prominence aspects of the law affecting trade unions and employers' associations. The law has not been reviewed since the beginning of the century, and it will be the subject of an early inquiry.

Britain on the move

We shall press ahead with improving and reshaping the transport system to fit the needs of a modern Britain.

The first essential is to make the best possible provision for the increase in private motoring which prosperity brings. Since the 1959 election we have carried out a 600m. programme of new road building. During the next five years £1–50m will be devoted to this purpose.

On our present plans the first thousand miles of Britain's motorway system will be completed in 1973. In addition we shall improve hundreds of miles of trunk roads. A modern system of road signs will be installed, and we shall concentrate on measures to increase safety.

We are putting particular emphasis on reducing traffic congestion in towns. In the longer term, we shall apply the principles of the Buchanan Report to comprehensive campaigns of town replanning. As an immediate step, expenditure on urban roads will be trebled. In London big improvements in traffic flow have resulted from overall management by the Traffic Management Unit: we shall arrange with the other major conurbations for the same methods to be applied by them.

Public transport

We shall complete the Victoria Underground line, and will encourage the development and use of new techniques for public transport in the towns. In six rural areas pilot schemes are being started to provide better bus services in some cases with financial support from the Government and county councils. By mid-1965 we hope to extend such schemes to other parts of the countryside.

Under the Beeching Plan we are producing an economic railway system able to attract suitable traffic off the roads by its own efficiency. A faster and more reliable rail service is increasingly being provided on the busy main lines for passengers and freight, and millions of pounds have already been knocked off the railway losses. We shall not consent to the closure of any service where this will damage economic development or cause undue hardship. Alternative bus services, with facilities for luggage, will be provided where necessary.

Sea and air

Britain's ports are now entering a new era when great development schemes will be carried through to the benefit of our trade. We have supported our shipowners against foreign interference and passed the Shipping Contracts Act which will protect British interests. We affirm our faith in the future of the shipbuilding industry whose current prospects have been much improved by our credits scheme.

We intend to press ahead with negotiations for the Channel Tunnel so that an early start can be made.

In developing efficient air communications we believe that a combination of public and private enterprise is best. We shall encourage the growth of a network of internal air services and airports to meet local needs.

Progress on the land

On our farms productivity has been rising by 5 per cent a year. Output is approaching twice what it was before the war. Modernisation is proceeding apace under the Farm Improvement Scheme and the Small Farmers Scheme.

British agriculture is efficient and competitive, and makes an indispensable contribution to our economic and social strength.

Agriculture and horticulture

The Conservative Government has evolved a system of support which has provided a sound basis for this progress. It is being adapted now to changed world conditions. Agreements have been reached with our overseas suppliers to regulate imports of cereals and bacon, and we shall continue to work for a stable market for meat. These policies are in line with our desire to conclude world-wide agreements for key commodities. Together with the improvement we shall bring about in marketing arrangements for home products, they will assure British farmers of a fair share of a growing market.

In developing our policies we shall continue to uphold the principles of the 1947 and 1957 Agriculture Acts. With imports regulated and home production more effectively related to market needs through standard quantity systems, greater weight can be given to farmers' returns at future price reviews. The long-term assurances under our 1957 Act will continue throughout the life of the next Parliament.

Our new deal for horticulture will strengthen the industry's ability to compete. We offer substantial aid to growers to adopt the most up-to-date production and marketing methods. Horticultural markets in major cities will be rebuilt, and the sites better related to modern traffic conditions. This will help to get the produce to housewives quicker, fresher and cheaper.

Forestry and fisheries

The Forestry Commission will carry through a long-term programme of planting. especially in areas where expansion can bring social and employment benefits. We will continue our help to private woodland owners. We have extended British fishery limits in accordance with the recently negotiated convention, and will further promote the technical progress and prosperity of the fishing industry. Powers of river authorities to ensure proper conservation of fisheries will be extended. With the aid of river authorities and the new Water Resources Board we shall develop a national policy of water conservation, so ensuring adequate supplies to meet increasing demand.

Ways and means

The programme we propose for the next five years is an ambitious one; but we know it can be achieved, for it is based on 13 years of solid progress. It embraces rising investment in the modernisation of Britain, on the lines we have described, and rising expenditure on the social services.

The money must be found from two sources: the savings of the nation and the contributions of taxpayer and ratepayer. We have never disguised that the cost will be heavy. No programme worthy of this country can be cheap. But it must be kept within bounds, and related to the growth of the national income. Our proposals are based on our target of a 4 per cent annual growth rate, and on maintaining a high level of savings.

One thing is quite certain. The Labour Party's promises would cost many hundreds of millions more than our programme. At the same time their policies would discourage enterprise and savings. The result could only be renewed inflation and rapidly rising taxes.

Incentives to save

To secure a still higher volume of savings, a Conservative Government will introduce new incentives. In particular we aim to devise a contractual savings scheme, giving attractive benefits to those who undertake to save regularly over a period of years. We shall also encourage the successful efforts which are being made to widen the field of share ownership.

Taxpayer and ratepayer

We shall continue to reform the tax system, both on companies and on individuals, to make it less complicated and fairer in its incidence.

Local authority services are expanding in response to public need and demand, but in some instances and areas the cost is outpacing the capacity of householders to pay. We recognise that a reform of the rates is required. The precise scale and methods will be determined as soon as our full inquiries, now in progress, are complete. These inquiries which could not have been undertaken effectively until revaluation had been carried through, cover the whole rating system, potential sources of local authority finance, the impact of rates now, and the current Exchequer grants.

In the light of these studies we shall ensure that the cost of local government, and particularly of education, is fairly apportioned between ratepayers and taxpayers, as well as making changes in the system of grants. In carrying out these and any other necessary reforms, we shall bear specially in mind those householders living on small fixed incomes.

Opportunity for youth

Education is the most rapidly developing feature of our social outlay. Its share of the expanded national wealth has risen since 1951 from 3 per cent to 5 per cent, and will go on rising. This reflects our view of education as at once a right of the child, a need of society, and a condition of economic efficiency. It also matches a tremendous upsurge in educational ambition and attainment.

Educational expansion

Our aim is to see that suitable education or training is available to every boy and girl up to at least 18. These are the steps we shall take:

1 The minimum school-leaving age will be raised to 16 for all who enter secondary school after the summer of 1967. This, which we looked forward to in the 1944 Education Act, is not to be just 'another year at school'. The whole school course will be refashioned to give a wider and deeper education.

2 More and more who have the ability to benefit will stay on to 17 and 18 and go forward to higher education. This will be made possible by our plans for the universities, colleges of advanced technology, higher technical institutions and teacher training colleges. There will be places for 100,000 extra students by 1968, and for a steadily growing number after that.

3 For those leaving school to start work at once, we shall further develop the Youth Employment Service and encourage the appointment by schools of careers advisers of high calibre, as well as improving industrial apprenticeship and training. Steps will be taken to increase the number of industrial workers under 18 who are released during the day to attend technical and other courses. We shall continue our great expansion of technical colleges.

Buildings and teachers

The building of new schools and the modernising of existing ones will be pressed ahead. The rising school population will put heavy pressure on our resources, but we are determined to devote a share of each year's programme to improving conditions in the older primary schools.

The training colleges will be producing by 1970 three times as many new teachers as in 1958, and the larger numbers going on to higher education will mean more teachers later on. We shall sustain our successful campaign for the return of qualified married women to teaching. Improved machinery will be established for the negotiation of teachers' salaries.

Research and organisation

We shall continue to encourage educational research and provide extra funds for this purpose.

Of the many different forms of secondary school organisation which now exist, none has established itself as exclusively right. The Socialist plan to impose the comprehensive principle, regardless of the wishes of parents, teachers and authorities, is therefore foolishly doctrinaire. Their leader may protest that grammar schools will be abolished 'over his dead body', but abolition would be the inevitable and disastrous consequence of the policy to which they are committed. Conservative policy, by contrast, is to encourage provision, in good schools of every description, of opportunities for all children to go forward to the limit of their capacity.

The Youth Service

Beyond the gates of school, college and factory, young people need ample facilities for social activity and outlets for adventure and service. As we promised in 1959, the Youth Service has been rejuvenated through the building of new clubs and the training of capable leaders. We shall press forward with this work, encourage more courses of the 'Outward Bound' type, and foster schemes whereby young people can assist the elderly.

Re-shaping social security

Under Conservatism the value of social security benefits has outpaced both prices and average earnings; under Socialism they were eaten away by inflation. We pledge ourselves to ensure that those receiving such benefits continue to share in the higher standards produced by an expanding economy.

Help will be concentrated first and foremost on those whose needs are greatest. Special insurance provision has already been directed to widows with children. When next we make a general increase in benefits, we shall give preferential treatment to the older pensioners.

Priorities and improvements

Those who work after retirement age, and widows at work, have benefited from a steady relaxation of the earnings rule. In the next Parliament we shall again progressively raise the amounts they can earn without deduction of pension.

Our graduated pension scheme, started in 1961, embodied the principle that retirement pensions should be more closely related to individual earnings. As we have explained, we are now proposing to extend this principle to benefits for the early months of unemployment and sickness, and we shall give similar help to widows during the early months of widowhood.

General review

All these proposals will make important improvements in the existing social security system. This system was framed 20 years ago, and in the light of pre-war experience. Since then there have been dramatic changes in economic conditions and social needs. We therefore propose to institute a full review of social security arrangements, so that their subsequent development may be suited to modern circumstances.

The review will not be confined to the national insurance scheme, but will include industrial injuries insurance, the varying provisions for widows, and the method of supplementing benefits.

Pension rights

In organising social security the State ought not to stifle personal and family responsibility or the growth of sound occupational schemes. Socialist plans would do precisely that. We Conservatives welcome the valuable additional security which occupational schemes provide, and will help to preserve such pension rights for people changing jobs.

We shall continue to make special provision for war widows and those disabled in the service of their country. The level of pensions for retired members of the armed forces and other Government servants will be adjusted as necessary. In the next Pensions Increase Act we shall reduce the age at which such pension increases are payable from 60 to 55.

The housing programme

One family in every four is living in a new home built under the Conservatives. More than half of the million houses classified as unfit when our slum clearance drive began have been replaced. One third of the 2,500,000 older houses capable of improvement have been given a new lease of life with the aid of Government grant.

This is a vast achievement; but there is much more to do. We are again speeding up progress on every front. Here are the main points of our programme:

1. *Expansion in house-building*
   Since 1951 homes have been built at an average rate of 300,000 a year. We shall build about 370,000 this year. Next year we shall reach our new target of 400,000. This will be sustained, and will enable us to overtake remaining shortages, while keeping pace with the needs of a more prosperous, younger-marrying, longer-living and fast-increasing population.

2. *Slum clearance and urban renewal*
   In the towns and cities where most remaining slums are concentrated, clearance rates are being doubled. We aim to clear by 1973 virtually all the known slums. As each authority completes this task, we shall go on to redevelop out-dated residential areas.

3. *Modernising older houses*
   Already 130,000 sound older houses are being modernised each year. The 1964 Housing Act provides for systematic improvement in older areas, with powers of compulsion where landlords are not persuaded to co-operate by the better grant arrangements. In this way we shall step up modernisation to 200,000 a year.

4. *Increasing home ownership*
   Owner-occupation has spread to 44 per cent of families. Conservatives will encourage its continued increase. Land registration leads to reduction of legal fees involved in house purchase: we shall hasten this process, aiming to complete it first in built-up areas and then for the whole country.

5. *Co-ownership and cost renting*
   Co-ownership schemes provide most of the advantages of owner-occupation for a much smaller deposit and lower out-goings. We have set up a Housing Corporation which will release £300m. to housing societies, building for co-ownership and for renting without subsidy and without profit.

6. *Local authority housing*
   We intend to revise the system of housing subsidies. Provided authorities charge proper rents, with rebates for those who cannot afford them, they will be able to plan ahead confidently and maintain necessary programmes especially for slum clearance, relief of overcrowding new and expanded towns, and the needs of the elderly – without burdening the rates.

7. *Improved building methods*
   Our long-term plans give the construction industries confidence to expand and modernise. Through the voluntary consortia of local authorities and our National Building Agency they are enabled to introduce up-to-date methods and tech-

niques which save site labour and increase productivity. We shall reform the laws governing building standards and safeguard the quality of houses for owner-occupation.

8 *Supply of land*
Our regional studies, showing land needs for twenty years ahead, will enable planning authorities to release ample land in the right places and without damage to the green belts. This substantial increase in the supply of land will do more to stabilise land prices than anything else.

Where major developments are in prospect – such as the many new towns and town expansions which are being started or proposed – land will be acquired well in advance and made available to private and public enterprise as necessary.

The Finance Act 1962 brought short-term land transactions within the sphere of ordinary taxation. In considering any further measure to tax land transactions, the test must be that it should not adversely affect the price or the supply of land.

We reject the Labour Party's 'Land Commission' as an unworkable and bureaucratic device, which would dry up the voluntary supply of land and slow down all our housing and building programmes.

9 *Rent control*
In the next Parliament we shall take no further steps to remove rent control. Additional safeguards for tenants will be provided if shown to be necessary by the inquiry into rented housing in London.

A healthy nation

The past thirteen years have seen improvements in the nation's health greater than in any comparable period. These advances we owe to medical science and the skill of the healing professions. They could only have been achieved against a background of rising living standards and continuously expanding health services such as Conservative Government is providing.

Hospital and health plans

The Conservative Hospital Plan will ensure that every man, woman and child in the country has access to the best treatment. We aim to build or rebuild some 300 hospitals of which over 80 are already in progress, and carry through 400 major schemes of improvement. Priority will be given to additional maternity beds, so that every mother who needs to will be able to have her baby in hospital. There will be no question of closing any existing hospital unless or until there is satisfactory alternative provision.

Those not needing hospital care will be properly looked after by community services. Local authorities are expanding these under our health and welfare plan. Support for old people living at home will come from increasing numbers of health visitors, home nurses, home helps and social workers. For those who can no longer manage on their own, there will be modern, specially designed accommodation. Provision for the physically and mentally handicapped is being brought up to date and will be greatly increased. New maternity and child welfare clinics are being built throughout the country.

In these plans for the nation's health, the scope for voluntary service will be emphasised, and we shall concentrate on the human approach which can make all the difference when a person is sick, handicapped or lonely.

Cure and prevention

A working party is now considering how best we can help the crucial work of the family doctor. Terms and conditions of service, methods of payment, the number of patients on doctors' lists, and their access to hospitals and other facilities will be reviewed, so as to raise still further the standards of good doctoring. We shall improve and bring up to date the law controlling the safety and quality of drugs. We shall also continue our campaigns against the enemies of good health, by eliminating slum environments, reducing air pollution, and cleaning the rivers and beaches.

The quality of life

There is an enormous growth in the variety and richness of leisure-time activity. Appreciation of the arts, hobbies and handicrafts of every kind, physical sports, home and foreign travel – these and other pursuits are increasing year by year. They are a cheerful measure of rising prosperity. For the 'affluence' at which Socialists sneer is enabling people, not only to satisfy material wants, but to develop their interests and their feel for the quality of life.

The Arts

The Government has trebled since 1951 the amount of money provided for the arts. Recently we have helped to bring the National Theatre into being, multiplied several times over the grants to museums and galleries for purchasing works of art, and done much to preserve and open to the public old and lovely houses. We shall continue to expand this support and to increase the resources of the Arts Council. We shall also seek to promote higher standards of architecture and civic planning, and commission works by contemporary artists for public buildings.

Broadcasting and television

Broadcasting in Britain has always been regarded as a medium for providing information, education and entertainment. For all these elements to find effective expression, viewers and listeners must be given the widest possible choice of programmes. This is why we introduced ITV, authorised BBC 2, and have licensed experiments in Pay-as-you-view television by wire.

We wish to extend the range of choice still further. That will be our object when considering proposals for the fourth television channel and for the establishment of a system of local sound radio.

Sport

Capital outlay for sport and physical recreation has increased fourfold in four years. But there remains a need in and around the towns and cities for many more sports grounds, playing fields, running tracks, swimming baths and gymnasia. Local authorities have been advised on how to combine with their neighbours for the larger projects, and a substantial programme will be authorised.

Countryside Commission

In the countryside we must satisfy the need for recreational facilities without harm to rural and farming interests.

We propose to set up a countryside commission with sufficient resources to secure the positive care of countryside and coast, including the national parks. It will be charged with promoting the systematic clearance in these localities of derelict land and other eyesores. Whilst strictly safeguarding secluded areas, the commission will advise planning authorities on the designation of recreation areas where boating, climbing, gliding and similar activities will be welcome.

Freedom and order

The consistent aim of Conservative policy is to uphold the British way of life, centred upon the dignity and liberty of the individual.

To this end we swept away Socialist restrictions and restored freedom of enterprise and choice. We safeguarded individual rights at tribunals and inquiries along the lines suggested by the Franks Report. We have made reforms in the composition of the House of Lords, the procedure of the House of Commons, and the structure of local government. We have taken measures to protect the public against lawlessness and introduced compensation for the victims of violent crime. We intend to continue this work of modernising our institutions and strengthening the rule of law.

Modernising institutions

We shall propose to the newly elected House of Commons the immediate establishment of a select committee to consider further reforms in parliamentary procedure. It will be asked as matters of priority to review the methods for scrutinising public expenditure and to consider ways of speeding up the passage of many technical and relatively uncontroversial law reform Bills which we intend to bring forward. It will also have the opportunity to consider whether adequate means are available to Members of Parliament to secure the redress of genuine complaints of maladministration.

A Conservative Government will call an all-party conference presided over by the Speaker to review electoral law. Among the changes it should consider is an extension of postal voting, since two-thirds of the nation now take holidays away from home.

In completing the reorganisation of local government, we shall aim to produce a system giving full scope to local knowledge, and capable of discharging within our regional plans the increasing responsibilities inseparable from rising population, living standards and car ownership.

We have appointed a committee to advise us on the best methods to stimulate and finance social studies both basic and applied, and we shall take action as soon as it reports.

Upholding law

We shall continue to build up the strength of the police forces, and see that they are equipped with every modern scientific aid. A royal commission has been set up to report on sentencing policies and the most effective methods for the treatment of offenders. We have asked it to give urgent priority to the growing problem of crime among the young. Meanwhile, we have increased the penalties for malicious damage and the compensation to those who suffer from this form of hooliganism.

The system of after-care will be developed on comprehensive lines, to save offenders from returning to crime.

Much juvenile delinquency originates in broken or unhappy homes. We shall continue to support the work of marriage guidance. Local authorities will be encouraged, in co-operation with voluntary bodies, to develop their services of child care for young people deprived of normal home life and affection.

We shall extend legal aid to all care and protection cases in juvenile courts and, as resources permit, to tribunal cases beginning with the Lands Tribunal.

The United Kingdom

We are issuing, simultaneously with this manifesto, special statements recording our achievements and plans in Scotland and in Wales. These demonstrate our regard for the distinctive rights and problems of each nation. They also show how our programmes are designed to secure the even spread of prosperity throughout Great Britain.

A Conservative and Unionist Government will continue to support the Government of Northern Ireland in developing and diversifying the economy, and so providing new employment. It is a cardinal principle of our policy that Northern Ireland's partnership with Great Britain in the United Kingdom shall remain unchanged so long as that is the wish of the Parliament at Stormont.

The nation's choice

We have now shown the extent to which, by building upon past progress, fresh advances can be made with a Conservative Government in the next five years. But we warn the nation that both the gains of the past and the hopes of the future would be imperilled by Socialism. On examination, what the Labour Parry have to offer is not a 'New Britain', but a camouflaged return to the dreary doctrines which had already proved a failure when they were last dismissed from office. What we are offering is an extension of that prosperity – prosperity with a purpose – which our policies have been proved to achieve.

ACTION not words
THE NEW CONSERVATIVE PROGRAMME

CONSERVATIVE PARTY GENERAL ELECTION MANIFESTO 1966

Action not words: the new Conservative programme

Date of Election	Thursday 31 March
Party Leader	Edward Heath
Candidates	629
MPs	253
Votes	11,418,433
% of vote	41.9%

Foreword

I present to the people of Britain a manifesto which is also a blueprint. It is a blueprint not for a year but for a full Parliament I am determined to promise nothing that we cannot achieve. I know that we shall inherit from the Labour Government a weak economic position, and I intend to give first priority to the management of our economy, to the strengthening of Britain's competitive position in world markets and to the repayment of the heavy burden of debt which they have incurred.

Equally I am determined to break away from the growing constraint of Socialism and the dreariness which stems from it: from the pattern of inflation and stagnant production which has been created.

I want to see our social services recognise the overriding claims of those in most need. I want to see choice become once more part of the pattern of life of the individual. I want to see our country with confidence in itself and in the future taking its place in the European Economic Community.

These are the things we must achieve. This manifesto points the way. I ask now for your confidence so that we can put it into effect I call not for words –but for action.

Edward Heath

Our new Conservative programme

This is what we are going to do:

- Get the economy straight, check rising prices, and restore expansion.
- Reform the trade unions.
- Remodel the Welfare State.

- Get the nation properly housed.
- Restore respect for Britain and lead her into Europe.

The Labour record

In October 1964 the Labour Government came to power promising action. Since then we have had many more promises. And many words. But the one thing we have not had is action. For eighteen months we have been waiting while the Labour leaders talk. But their words have had little relation to the facts.

The Labour Government has had its opportunity and it has failed. It's easy enough to say 'Let's be fair to Labour. Give them another chance.' But it would be taking an immense chance with everybody's future to do so. We cannot afford to sit and wait for the other failures and blunders that will be coming our way if Labour is left in charge.

Just look at their record. The Labour leaders have failed to tackle the fundamental economic and social problems at home. Abroad Britain's reputation has declined under their clumsy and uncertain touch. In the High Street prices are rising. Up go rates and taxes, down go standards of service on the buses and trains and in other public industries. The road programme is held up. The universities and technical colleges have had to cut back their expansion plans. The housing target has been missed. Mortgage rates are higher than ever. Complicated tax penalties are sapping individual enterprise. Production in industry is stagnating.

It is a depressing catalogue. It is hard to see how any one of us, whatever our job or whatever our attitude to politics, can be satisfied with the situation into which we have now drifted. Nor can anyone be content to let this sort of thing go on. This is not the kind of Britain we want.

All those who really believe in this country must know in their hearts that we can do far, far better, given energy and imagination. And not only for ourselves, but for our families, our communities and for the millions overseas who rely on a strong and free Britain.

The Conservative way ahead

The alternative to Labour drift is less talk and gimmickry, and more positive action. The alternative is a government team which means what it says and knows what it intends to do: a government that doesn't run away; an honest government.

Our first aim is this: to run this country's affairs efficiently and realistically so that we achieve steadier prices in the shops, high wages and a really decent standard of social security.

With sensible and determined action and our new Conservative policies we can reach these goals. But we have to be quite clear what this means. It means that we must give every man and woman a chance to play a decisive and worthwhile part in restoring Britain's health and strength and confidence. It means that our best brains must be encouraged and rewarded so that they can get on and succeed. It means that there must be a war on inefficiency and waste in the public industries – as well as in Whitehall and in the town hall. It means that pride, self-confidence and efficiency must replace the suspicion and the 'who cares?' attitude which weaken industry and hold us all back.

Now to get to these goals here are the action programmes which we will be starting on as soon as we form a government.

- First, the next Conservative Government will not hesitate to take all the measures necessary to deal with the immediate economic situation. Our new economic programme will make a prices and incomes policy really effective.
- Second, we will use tax incentives to encourage individual men and women to earn and save more for themselves and their families.
- Third, our new policies for competition will inject fresh vitality into British industry, keeping prices down and quality up, and giving the housewife the service she deserves.
- Fourth, we will be launching new industrial policies, involving major reforms of both management and unions. At last the barriers in the way of higher productivity and higher earnings will be brought down.
- Fifth, we will be making big changes in the organisation of our government and public services.
- Sixth, we will start new programmes for speeding up the spread of prosperity to the English regions, Scotland, Wales and Northern Ireland.
- Seventh, the strategy of the new Conservative Government will be to throw everything this country has in skill, resources and brainpower behind the things at which Britain is best. We intend to see British quality again become the pace-setter in world markets and British services again become the envy of the world. And we intend to bring in the men who can do the job.

We intend to reform both British management and British trade unions.

Everyone is fed up with pointless strikes and outdated management. We reject the argument that there is a clash between the interests of management and workpeople. Higher wages, good profits and competitive products are in the interests of both. Efficient production and stable prices are what the customer wants.

Here are the action programmes we shall be introducing to bring this about.

- First, we will be transforming industrial relations by introducing a new Act covering the trade unions and employers' associations.
- Second, we will be turning the heat on restrictive practices by both management and labour so that men and women can do a decent job unhampered by the fears and restrictions which belong to another age.
- Third, we want to see better job prospects with greater security of incomes and pensions in the new high-wage low-cost economy.

We intend to revitalise our Welfare State so that those most in need get the most help and so that our money is used sensibly and fairly. We will be working to a fresh pattern of social priorities to meet new needs and help build our community on more responsible lines.

We want to see more generous help for those who have special needs not yet met by the Welfare State. We want to see family life strengthened by our Conservative social policies. We intend that there should be full equality of opportunity but not that we should all be equally held back to the pace of the slowest. Our policies are designed to bring higher quality and wider choice into our lives. We reject the kind of outdated thinking which leads to cuts in university and college expansion in order to provide free drugs for all.

Here are the action programmes which make up the new Conservative social policy and which will fulfil our aims.

- First, an entirely new social security strategy designed to concentrate better care and the biggest benefits on those most in need.
- Second, wider ownership – not only of houses but of pension rights and other forms of capital as well.
- Third, full educational opportunity, putting the needs of the individual child before Party doctrine. The first thing is to get more colleges and schools built, particularly primary schools, and more teachers trained.
- Fourth, an all-out attack on the rising wave of crime which today besmirches our society.
- Fifth, fair treatment for immigrants combined with stricter control of entry.
- Sixth, more regional administration with strong and modernised local government.
- Seventh, better conditions for the car driver, the commuter and the travelling public generally.
- Finally, a countryside preserved where it is beautiful and transformed where it is ugly and derelict.

We intend to see that this entire nation is decently housed. Our aim is more choice in housing. We are determined to see house prices in reach of those eager to buy homes of their own. We are determined to see that the needs of people for rented accommodation are more effectively met.

Here are the action programmes we intend to launch.

- First we will raise the housing target to an annual rate of 500,000 homes by the end of 1968. We reached our target before, and we will hit it again. We will make use of every new method that works to get the houses up and keep the prices down. And there will be major reforms in planning procedure to increase the supply of land for building.
- Second, we will encourage more people to buy their own homes – by aid with deposits or help with interest payments or by assisting with the purchase of older houses.
- Third, the next Conservative Government will speed up council house building for slum areas. And we will insist on sensible local authority rent policies.

We are determined to give Britain a respected place in the world again and lead her into the European Community. Britain must be part of a wider grouping if she is to exert her full influence in the world. British industry must have far bigger markets if it is to develop on the scale required in so many cases by modern technology. This can best be achieved by Britain becoming a member of an enlarged European Economic Community to which she herself has so much to contribute.

A strong Britain can provide a powerful trading partner, and a growing source of skill, knowledge and capital, for the other members of the Commonwealth. This way also lies the best chance of Britain helping the developing countries. That is why we shall seize the first favourable opportunity of becoming a member of the Community.

These are our aims. The detailed proposals which follow show how we will achieve them. Together they form a powerful new strategy-based on sound Conservative principles – to replace words with action, and promises with achievements.

Blueprint for a parliament to ensure prosperity with steadier prices . . .

- Get taxes down again so as to encourage hard work and enterprise.
- Encourage wider ownership. Drastically revise Labour's ill-prepared tax changes which penalise saving and go-ahead companies.
- Get better management by improving management education at all levels.
- Reform company law – doing the whole job instead of Labour's inadequate proposals.
- Mount a new attack on restrictive business practices which hurt the public interest. Close the legal loop-holes Labour have left open.
- Speed up and give more punch to the Monopolies Commission. And cut tariffs wherever it can be shown that competition from abroad is needed to deal with monopolies.
- Set up a Small Business Development Bureau to help small firms start and grow.
- Step up opportunities to train and retrain for better, more highly paid jobs. Build up the Youth Employment Service into a Careers Advisory Service for adults as well as young people.
- Help the housewife with new legislation on misleading 'guarantees' and more vigorous use of safety standards for food and household goods.
- Abolish the out-dated restrictions on the hours during which shops can open on week days.
- Start a new drive to put the customer first in the nationalised industries and to increase efficiency in these and other public services.
- Stimulate the new technological industries at which Britain excels. Provide the aerospace industry with a stable long-term programme based on European co-operation.
- Stop the war in Whitehall between rival economic Ministers with conflicting policies. Put one man in charge with one firm policy which hangs together.
- Start a war on waste in Government. Establish a Cost Effectiveness Department to introduce new management techniques into all Government Departments. Use sophisticated computer techniques to study the feasibility of Government projects.
- Make greater use of the knowledge available in the universities and industry in the formation of Government policy. In particular, enlist scientists, the universities and industrial consultants to help us prevent waste of taxpayers' money.

To improve industrial relations . . .

- Pass a new Industrial Relations Act and establish a new Code of Good Industrial Relations Practice.
- Ensure that agreements between unions and employers are kept by making them legally enforceable.
- Establish a Registrar of trade unions and employers' associations. See that their rules are fair and meet the interests of the public.

- Set up a new Industrial Court to deal with industrial disputes and claims for damages against unjust dismissal.
- Introduce measures to deal with restrictive labour practices.
- Repeal the Trade Disputes Act 1965 so as to help prevent intimidation.

To provide better transport . . .

- Speed up the building of motorways with the aid of increased productivity in the road building industry.
- Resume the task of increasing railway efficiency and of reducing the railway deficit.
- Give independent airlines new opportunities to develop inter-city services.
- Improve the traffic flow of big cities and the efficiency of public transport by traffic management and by building off-street parking.
- Get on with the modernisation of our ports. End the casual employment system. Reduce the number of different employers. Improve working relations – for example, see that better welfare facilities are provided.

To help agriculture . . .

- Give Britain's farmers scope to supply a bigger share of the home market for food.
- Move over gradually from Exchequer deficiency payments to a system of import control.
- Maintain the support given by the Agriculture Acts throughout the transition stage, and ensure continued support in any legislation required to implement our new proposals.
- Keep production grants and special help (e.g. small farms, farm improvements and hill farms).
- Modernise the main horticultural markets, give continued support to co-operation and encourage better marketing techniques.

To get into Europe . . .

- Work energetically for entry into the European Common Market at the first favourable opportunity.
- Prepare for entry by relating the development of our own policies to those of the Common Market, wherever appropriate.
- Encourage co-operation with other European countries in joint projects which need not await our membership of the Common Market: particularly where large-scale scientific and technological resources are called for.

To provide most care for those in need . . .

- See that everyone has a good pension with their job, on top of the State basic pension.
- Ensure that everyone can either transfer or preserve their pension when they change jobs.
- Give more generous help to children in families where the income is below

minimum need, to the very old, to the chronic sick, to the severely disabled and to others most in need.

- Improve rehabilitation and retraining for the disabled.
- Help people who have put by some savings, by raising the amount which can be disregarded before a supplementary pension is granted.
- Continue to ease the earnings rule.
- Provide a pension for those too old to be covered by National Insurance.
- Combine the Ministry of Health, the Ministry of Pensions and National Insurance and the National Assistance Board into a single Department with local officers who would have a positive duty to seek out those needing help whether in cash or in care. The new Department would have a research organisation to pin-point changing needs.
- Establish inspectors of welfare to improve co-ordination between local authority, hospital and voluntary services.
- Encourage voluntary service.
- End the present rigid age barrier of 50 which prevents some widows who have been out of employment for many years from getting any pension at all.
- Give special help to areas where there is the most need – for example, bad housing and oversized school classes.
- Restore – subject to wide exemptions (such as the elderly, chronic sick, disabled, expectant and nursing mothers) – prescription charges. Use the savings for higher social priorities including the hospital and medical service.
- Improve the health service by giving family doctors closer contact with hospitals and with local health and welfare services. Improve conditions for doctors.
- Review all public service and Armed Forces pensions every two years to ensure that they maintain their purchasing power. Reduce to 55 the age at which increased pensions become payable. Bring the pensions of those who retired before 1956 up to the same level as if they had retired then with appropriate increases since. Give special treatment to war pensioners and their widows.

To provide better education . . .

- Get more teachers especially for the primary schools by expanding the Colleges of Education, enabling part-time teachers to qualify for pension, and giving more encouragement to married women who want to return to teaching.
- See that more teaching aids are made available.
- Give back to local authorities the freedom to make small improvements, for example, an extra classroom or better sanitation.
- Encourage local education authorities to provide as full a range of courses as possible in all their secondary schools.
- Judge proposals for reorganisation on their educational merits. Strongly oppose hasty and makeshift plans, especially in the big cities, for turning good grammar and secondary modern schools into comprehensive schools.
- Give improvements to primary school accommodation priority over projects for building new comprehensive schools where adequate secondary accommodation already exists.
- Give parents as much choice as possible by having diversity in the pattern of

education. Give independent schools of high standing the opportunity to become direct grant schools, thus narrowing the gap between State schools and fee paying schools.

- Establish an Educational Television Centre to encourage the best use of television – broadcast and closed circuit – in schools, colleges and universities.
- Restore the university and further education buildings programmes cut by the Labour Government.

To house the nation . . .

- Speed up house building. Reach our target of a rate of 500,000 new homes a year by the end of 1968. Use modern building methods and speed up planning procedures.
- Help home buyers by these three methods, as appropriate:
  - Helping with their deposits.
  - Enabling people below the standard rate of tax who are buying their home to deduct from the interest payments on their mortgages an amount similar to the tax relief obtained by those who pay tax. People eligible for the present tax allowance will have the option of continuing it.
  - Introducing again the scheme for Exchequer help for the buying of older houses through the Building Societies.
- Give home buyers a guarantee of good workmanship.
- Accelerate housing for the elderly.
- See that council house subsidies are concentrated on those who really need them.
- Increase council house building for slum clearance.
- Expand the work of Housing Associations, so as to provide more good homes, at reasonable prices.
- Introduce depreciation allowances to help provide more homes to rent.
- Maintain rent control where there is a shortage of houses.
- Legislate to allow ground leaseholders to buy or rent their houses on fair terms except where the property is to be redeveloped.
- Take £100 million off the rates – equivalent to one-tenth of the rate bill.

To beat the crime wave . . .

- Place responsibility for law and order and for the war against crime on the Home Secretary and the Secretary of State for Scotland.
- Set up a central staff within the Home Office responsible for police strategy, intelligence and equipment.
- Accelerate the amalgamation of local police forces and establish a clear chain of command. Within a national force of this kind, local loyalties can and will be preserved.
- Ensure that the police have the organisation, manpower and equipment to do the job.
- Make offenders pay restitution for the injuries and damage they have done. Replace many short-term sentences by substantial fines.

- Preserve the Juvenile Courts and expand the methods available for dealing with the problems of young people.
- Train those in prison to become useful members of the community.

To deal with the problem of immigration . . .

- Ensure that all immigrants living in Britain are treated in all respects as equal citizens and without discrimination.
- Introduce a conditional entry system which will control the initial time during which a new immigrant may stay, until permission is granted either permanently or for a further limited period.
- Strengthen the arrangements for health checks for immigrants.
- Require all immigrants to register the names of any dependants who might at any time wish to join them, so that their numbers will be known. In the case of new immigrants the number of dependants will be an important factor in deciding whether entry will be permitted.
- Help immigrants already here to rejoin their families in their countries of origin, or to return with their families to these countries, if they so wish.
- Combine stricter control of entry with special help where necessary to those areas where immigrants are concentrated.

To build a better country and widen opportunities for recreation . . .

- Plan the coast and countryside in such a way as to increase their natural beauty, increase the holiday attractions of Britain, and encourage provision for the growing numbers who leave the towns to sail, ski, climb, picnic or go caravaning.
- Create a new Coast and Countryside Commission with the powers to get on with the job, using the resources of both public authorities and private enterprise.
- Open more inland water for recreation, provide more access for visitors to the National Forests, and secure a national network of camping and caravan sites.
- Encourage the development of regional recreation areas, largely financed by private investment, on the model of the Lea Valley Scheme.
- End the existing confusion and duplication of effort between at least five Ministries in Whitehall, by setting up within the Ministry of Housing and Local Government a Recreation Department.
- Provide more choice and competition in broadcasting.
- Encourage the arts, particularly in the provinces. Promote high standards of architecture and civic planning.

To deal with the special problems of each area . . .

- Develop fully the resources of each region and maintain its character in consultation with local organisations. Accelerate action on regional studies.
- Develop the growth zone idea which Labour has abandoned. Strengthen the public services in these areas by greater investment in communications, homes, schools and hospitals. Provide financial inducements for new industry.

- Improve amenities: provide powers to clear away the industrial dereliction of yesterday.

To bring new prosperity to Scotland . . .

- Expand Government Training Centres and technical education programmes in order to provide the new skills which our new industries need.
- Make a greater allocation of funds for education in the Highlands, the Borders and other country areas.
- Concentrate development in those areas where it is most needed and will do the most good.
- Restore the cuts which the Labour Government has made in Scottish road-building and pursue policies which will stop transport costs rising so fast.
- Encourage competition on Scottish air routes and ensure that the Highlands have services timed to suit the people who live and work there.
- Make a top priority the clearance of the remaining slums in Glasgow, Edinburgh, Dundee and other cities by every type of building – private building, council building and housing associations.
- Introduce sensible rent schemes for local authority housing.
- Make the best use of our land resources outside the central belt by supporting the hill farmers, encouraging the expansion of forestry and planning special tourist areas.
- Make the Scottish Tourist Board a more professional body and use it to stimulate the growth of the industry.
- Modernise local government and its finance.

To bring new prosperity to Wales . . .

- Tackle the problem of depopulation in mid-Wales by constructing first class road communications from Shrewsbury to Cardigan Bay, by attracting new industries, and by revitalising existing towns and developing mid-Wales as an area of high amenity and a tourist attraction.
- Develop the coastal road in North Wales from Queensferry to Caernarvon.
- Encourage new industrial development in North and South Wales and the development of the South Wales ports under a group system.
- Give special attention to the needs of the hill farming community.
- Maintain a Secretary for Wales in the Cabinet.
- Overhaul the structure and organisation of Local Government in Wales.
- Legislate to allow ground leaseholders to buy or rent their houses on fair terms except where the property is to be redeveloped.
- Expand higher education in Wales and grant independent status to each university college. The university college of Cardiff, the Welsh college of Advanced Technology and the National School of Medicine will form the Civic University of Cardiff.
- Encourage and foster the culture and arts which are the characteristic of the Welsh people.

To bring new prosperity to Northern Ireland . . .

- Co-operate with the Northern Ireland Government in:
  - Seeing that Northern Ireland, as an integral part of the UK, shares fully in the economic growth of the rest of the country; in particular, that the counties west of the Bann share in growing prosperity.
  - Improving basic services, such as the new road programmes now being planned.
  - Offering inducements to new industry to raise employment.
  - Promoting the interests of Ulster farmers, bearing particularly in mind the size of holdings and their distance from the rest of the British market.

To strengthen the Commonwealth . . .

- Break the deadlock in Rhodesia by initiating talks with Mr Smith and his colleagues for the purpose of obtaining a constitutional settlement, without any prior conditions on either side.
- Strengthen and expand existing Commonwealth links by making full use of the Commonwealth Foundation, by encouraging the professional, legal, medical and educational Commonwealth Conferences and by acting on their recommendations where appropriate.
- Encourage voluntary service overseas.
- Help Commonwealth development by technical and other assistance, by joint or bi-lateral projects and by ensuring that all aid given is used to its maximum effect.
- Work for the expansion of world and Commonwealth trade through the UN Trade and Development Board and the Kennedy Round tariff negotiations.

To help preserve world peace . . .

- Make our contribution to NATO. Fulfil our treaty obligations in the Middle and Far East.
- Maintain a combination of nuclear and conventional arms related to our financial resources to enable us to defend ourselves and to honour these commitments. In particular, go on with the building of the new aircraft carrier.
- Maintain properly equipped Regular forces together with reserve forces – including the Territorial Army – suitable reorganised for their supporting roles.
- Seek, with our allies, every means and opportunity of bringing an end to hostilities in the Far East, thus reducing the pressure on our resources in that area.
- Seek to make the United Nations a more effective instrument for keeping peace.
- Renew Conservative support for the admission of Communist China to the United Nations.
- Give a new impetus to disarmament by pressing for an extension of the Nuclear Test Ban Treaty to underground tests and an agreement to prevent the spread of nuclear weapons.

A Better Tomorrow

The Conservative programme for the next 5 years

CONSERVATIVE PARTY GENERAL ELECTION MANIFESTO 1970

A better tomorrow

Date of Election	Thursday 18 June
Party Leader	Edward Heath
Candidates	628
MPs	330
Votes	13,145,123
% of vote	46.4%

Foreword

This Manifesto sets out the policies of the Conservative Party for a better Britain. It provides a programme for a Parliament. How fast we can go will depend on how difficult a situation we find when we take office.

But good government is not just a matter of the right policies. It also depends on the way the government is run. This is something which I have thought about deeply. Indeed, it has been one of my main interests since I entered the House of Commons in 1950.

During the last six years we have suffered not only from bad policies, but from a cheap and trivial style of government. Decisions have been dictated simply by the desire to catch tomorrow's headlines. The short-term gain has counted for everything; the long-term objective has gone out of the window. Every device has been used to gain immediate publicity, and government by gimmick has become the order of the day. Decisions lightly entered into have been as lightly abandoned.

It is not surprising that under this system several senior Labour Ministers have at different times left the Government in disgust at the way it is run. It is not surprising that whenever I have travelled abroad in recent years friends of Britain have told me of their sadness at the way in which our reputation has shrunk. It is not surprising that young people in this country looking at politics for the first time should be suspicious and cynical.

I am determined therefore that a Conservative Government shall introduce a new style of government: that we shall re-establish our sound and honest British traditions in this field.

I want to see a fresh approach to the taking of decisions. The Government should seek the best advice and listen carefully to it. It should not rush into decisions, it should use up-to-date techniques for assessing the situation, it should be deliberate and thorough. And in coming to its decisions it must always recognise that its responsibility is to the people, and all the people, of this country.

What is more, its decision should be aimed at the long term. The easy answer and the quick trick may pay immediate dividends in terms of publicity, but in the end it is the national interest which suffers. We have seen that too often in the recent past

Finally, once a decision is made, once a policy is established, the Prime Minister and his colleagues should have the courage to stick to it. Nothing has done Britain more harm in the world than the endless backing and filling which we have seen in recent years. Whether it be our defence commitments, or our financial policies, or the reform of industrial relations, the story has been the same. At the first sign of difficulty the Labour Government has sounded the retreat, covering its withdrawal with a smokescreen of unlikely excuses. But courage and intellectual honesty are essential qualities in politics, and in the interest of our country it is high time that we saw them again.

So it will not be enough for a Conservative Government to make a fresh start with new policies. We must create a new way of running our national affairs. This means sweeping away the trivialities and the gimmicks which now dominate the political scene. It means dealing honestly and openly with the House of Commons, with the press and with the public.

The decisions which a Government has to take affect the livelihood and perhaps the lives of millions of our fellow citizens. No-one has any business to take part in public life unless he is prepared to take such decisions with the seriousness which they deserve.

This is my strongest personal conviction, and I shall not be content until it is the guiding principle of the government of this country.

Edward Heath

A better tomorrow

This election is about Britain's tomorrow. The choice of a Government for the next five years will go far to determine the future of our country right through the seventies and beyond.

The failures of today

The nation now knows what five years of Labour rule can mean. Hundreds of thousands of extra families suffering the hardship and insecurity of unemployment. Increasing problems of poverty and homelessness. Pensioners helpless as they watch the extra shillings eaten up by the fastest price rise for twenty years. Housewives struggling to make ends meet. £3,000 million a year of extra taxation equivalent to £3.10. 0d a week for every family. A devalued £. A new load of foreign debt, some of it stretching ahead into the twenty-first century.

Britain has paid many times over in lost opportunity for the benefit of any improvement on our overseas trade account. The nation has lost £12,000 million in potential wealth as the result of Labour's failure to maintain expansion. That's about £750 for every family in the country.

Our economy has expanded more slowly than that of any other comparable country in the world. Almost everywhere in Western Europe and North America the standard of living grows faster than in Britain. International experts are predicting that if these trends are allowed to continue Britain will soon be the poorest major country in the

West. As a nation, we have been starved of achievement. We have become conditioned to failure.

To pay our way, normal in Conservative years, now seems like a miracle. High unemployment is no longer the exception but the rule. We have become resigned to the value of the £ in our pockets or purses falling by at least a shilling a year. For a year to pass without a crisis has become cause for congratulation.

Yet before these locust years of Labour, we had the Conservative years of rising prosperity. Years when Britain's industry expanded faster. When the standard of living grew three times as fast. When prices rose more slowly. When unemployment was low. When tax rates were cut time after time. When pensions rose twice as fast as prices. When the social services at home advanced more rapidly, and Britain played a proper part in helping poorer countries overseas.

Conservatives are proud of yesterday's achievements. Angered by today's failures. Determined that tomorrow shall be better again.

We remember 1966, when the strengthening balance of payments which was Labour's true inheritance was smothered by the disastrous irresponsibility of a Party whose one concern was electoral success. Before the election, surplus and smiles. Afterwards, savage tax increases, the wage freeze, and a headlong plunge into deficit, devaluation and debt. It need not and must not be allowed to happen again.

Labour has nothing to offer

Labour's policies for the future are their policies of the past. Nothing to curb the rise in prices. Nothing to cut the human waste of unemployment. Nothing to see that extra social help goes where the need is greatest.

More taxes. More blanket subsidies. More state ownership. More civil servants. More government interference.

No new encouragement to earn and save. No new incentive to invest and expand. No new policy to bring about better relations in industry. No new deal for our farmers.

Just the mixture as before.

They have little to boast of in their record. Even less to put forward for the future. So they talk, instead, of their ideals.

But just what are those ideals?

What ideal is it that leads a government to policies that double the rate of unemployment?

What ideal is it that makes it impossible for so many young couples to afford a home of their own, sets out to prevent people buying the council house they live in, and brings about the biggest drop in house-building in a quarter of a century?

What ideal is it that makes the poor get poorer, and three times votes down pensions for the over-eighties?

What ideal is it that breaks our country's word abroad, weakens our defences, leaves our friends in the lurch, and cuts down our overseas aid?

What ideal is it that has to be propped up by rigging electoral boundaries?

What ideal is it that leaves a litter of broken promises wherever it goes?

Labour must answer for itself. But whatever its ideals may be, they have nothing in common with the values which Conservatives proclaim.

The Conservative way

We want to build a better Britain. A Britain we can all be proud of. A Britain in which future generations will be happy to live. A Britain which other nations will admire.

We want a country which makes the fullest use of all its human and material resources to build a new prosperity. A country which uses that prosperity wisely and well, helping the elderly and those in need, providing new educational opportunity for our children, investing for the future as well as giving us a fuller life today. A country confident in itself, playing a full part in the world's affairs, accepting and meeting its responsibilities to others.

We want a society in which material advance goes hand in hand with the deeper values which go to make up the quality of life. A society which cares for its cities, towns and villages, its rivers, its coast, its countryside.

We want people to achieve the security and independence of personal ownership, greater freedom of opportunity, greater freedom of choice, greater freedom from government regulation and interference. A responsible democracy based on honest government and respect for the law.

Despite all the failures and frustrations of recent years, Britain is still the best country in the world in which to live. But at best we have been marking time, at worst slipping back. It could and should be so much better.

Programme for a Parliament

In this Manifesto we present our policies to end the retreat and begin instead a new advance. Our policies are not, like Labour's, a collection of short-lived devices. They make up a strategy for the next five years – a programme for a Parliament. Nor are they a set of promises made only to be broken. The last Conservative Government kept all its promises. So will the next.

We start with the economy because this remains the key. The true problem in social policy is not that we spend too much but that with Labour stagnation we can afford too little. Britain now faces the worst inflation for twenty years. This is mainly the result of tax increases and devaluation. In implementing all our policies, the need to curb inflation will come first. For only then can our broader strategy succeed.

Our theme is to replace Labour's restrictions with Conservative incentive. We utterly reject the philosophy of compulsory wage control. We want instead to get production up and encourage everyone to give of their best.

- We want an economy based on more jobs, higher wages that are well-earned, and lower costs.
- We will reduce and reform taxation, giving first priority to reducing income tax so that people will keep a fairer reward for their work.

- We will create the basis for these reductions by giving new incentive to saving and by cutting out unnecessary state spending.
- We will strengthen responsible trade unions and good management by establishing fair, up-to-date rules for industrial relations.
- We will greatly increase opportunities for men and women to train for new and better jobs.
- We will stop further nationalisation, and create a climate for free enterprise to expand.
- We will introduce effective regional development policies to bring prosperity to every part of our country.
- We will give agriculture a real opportunity to increase production.

These are policies to enable people and government to work together to create new national wealth. Only on the secure basis of this foundation can we help everyone to build a better tomorrow for themselves and their families.

Our education policy will give greater priority to the primary schools, where an inadequate start can so easily destroy the chance that every child must have to develop its talents to the full.

We will reverse the decline in building, make home ownership easier again, and concentrate Government subsidies where they are most needed.

We will give priority to those most in need – the over-80s without pensions, the elderly, the disabled, the chronic sick, the children in families below the poverty line.

Our policies will reduce the causes of racial tension, and we will ensure that there will be no further large-scale permanent immigration.

We will protect Britain's interests overseas, and play our part in promoting peace and progress in the world.

These policies will strengthen Britain so that we can negotiate with the European Community confident in the knowledge that we can stand on our own if the price is too high.

A new opportunity

The aim of these policies is to create the new opportunity for a better tomorrow.

- A better tomorrow with living standards rising again at a reasonable rate so that every family can enjoy a fuller life.
- A better tomorrow for all: for the families that are homeless today, for the unemployed; for the children still in poverty, and for the old and the lonely.
- A better tomorrow with greater freedom: freedom to earn and to save, freedom from government interference, freedom of choice, freedom from fear of crime and violence.
- A better tomorrow in a better Britain: with the beauty of our countryside preserved and improved, with our towns and cities made more pleasant to live in.
- A better tomorrow with a deeper appreciation of the quality and goodness of life.

Our nation has so much to be proud of and so much to offer. All we need now is a new opportunity that will allow the people of Britain to create for themselves a better tomorrow.

Our programme

These are our plans for making tomorrow better than today.

Lower taxes

We will reduce taxation. We will simplify the tax system. We will concentrate on making progressive and substantial reductions in income tax and surtax. These reductions will be possible because we will cut out unnecessary Government spending and because we will encourage savings. And as our national income rises we will get a larger revenue with lower tax rates.

We will abolish the Selective Employment Tax, as part of a wider reform of indirect taxation possibly involving the replacement of purchase tax by a value-added tax.

The value-added tax, already widely adopted in Western Europe and Scandinavia, is in effect a general sales tax, operated in a way which allows for desirable exemptions – for example, exports. It could help to make our system of taxes on spending more broadly based, less discriminatory, and fairer in its impact on different types of industry and service. It would not apply to food, except for those few items already subject to purchase tax. It would not apply to normal farming activities, nor to very small businesses; and special arrangements would be made for housing. No Opposition could commit itself finally in advance of an election to a major new tax of this kind which would need detailed consultation with the civil service.

Labour's betterment levy has increased bureaucracy and put up the price of land and houses. We will do away with it and collect any tax due on a sale of land through the capital gains tax, with exemption for owner-occupiers.

We will end the tax nonsense which makes some married couples pay more tax on their joint earnings than they would if they were not married. We will repeal the Labour changes which have imposed new penalties on children's income and disallowed the interest on many loans as a deduction from income for tax purposes.

We will encourage the flow of private funds to charities including voluntary social service, sport and the arts.

Labour has put tax rates up by over £3,000 million. We are determined to reverse this process. High taxation discourages effort and saving, deadens the spirit of enterprise and causes many of our best brains to leave the country.

In the thirteen years of Conservative prosperity we cut tax rates by £2,000 million – as well as doubling expenditure on the social services. We have done it before: we can do it again.

More savings

When savings go up, taxes can come down. If savings had increased as fast during the last six years under Labour as they did in the previous six years with the Conservatives, taxation could now be £2,000 million lower – the equivalent of the whole of the selective employment tax and more than two shillings off income tax.

We will encourage all forms of saving, and saving at every level of earnings. Every family should be able to accumulate savings to give security and independence, to provide for their old age and their children's future.

Our tax policies will stimulate savings. We will introduce a more imaginative contractual savings scheme designed particularly to attract new savings. Our plans for more home ownership and an extension of private and occupational pension schemes must mean higher personal savings. We have already done much and will do more to develop a 'property-owning democracy': now we must also progress towards the capital-owning democracy of the future, for individuals and families who save and accumulate wealth serve the nation as truly as they serve themselves.

Controlling government spending

Under Labour, there has been too much government interference in the day-to-day workings of industry and local government. There has been too much government: there will be less.

We will reduce the number of Ministers. We will reduce the number of civil servants: under Labour their numbers have grown by over 60,000. The Land Commission will be abolished. The functions and responsibilities of all departments and government agencies will be systematically rationalised. There will be cost-reduction plans for every single Ministry in Whitehall, and the widespread application throughout government of the most modern management, budgeting and cost-effectiveness techniques. Some present government activities could be better organised using competent managers recruited from industry and commerce. Plans to achieve this new style of government are well advanced. It will be more efficient and less costly.

Detailed policies set out in this document will also lead to reductions in the weight of government spending.

Steadier prices

The cost of living has rocketed during the last six years. Prices are now rising more than twice as fast as they did during the Conservative years. And prices have been zooming upwards at the very same time as the Government have been taking an ever-increasing slice of people's earnings in taxation. Soaring prices and increasing taxes are an evil and disastrous combination. Inflation is not only damaging to the economy; it is a major cause of social injustice, always hitting hardest at the weakest and poorest members of the community. The main causes of rising prices are Labour's damaging policies of high taxation and devaluation. Labour's compulsory wage control was a failure and we will not repeat it.

The Labour Government's own figures show that, last year, taxation and price increases more than cancelled any increase in incomes. So wages started chasing prices up in a desperate and understandable attempt to improve living standards.

Other countries achieve a low-cost high-wage economy. So can we. Our policies of strengthening competition will help to keep down prices in the shops. Our policies for cutting taxes, for better industrial relations, for greater retraining, for improved efficiency in Government and industry – all these will help to stimulate output. This faster growth will mean that we can combine higher wages with steadier prices to bring a real increase in living standards.

Under the last Conservative Government, wages rose twice as fast as prices, living standards rose three times as fast as they have under Labour, and Britain achieved one of the best records in Europe for steady prices.

The Labour Government's policies have unleashed forces which no Government could hope to reverse overnight. The first essential is for the new Government to give a new lead. We will subject all proposed price rises in the public sector to the most searching scrutiny. If they are not justified, they will not be allowed. In implementing our policies, we will give overriding priority to bringing the present inflation under control.

Fair deal at work

There were more strikes in 1969 than ever before in our history. Already in the first three months of 1970 there were 1,134 strikes compared with 718 in the same period last year, when the Labour Government said the position was so serious that legislation was essential in the national interest. This rapid and serious deterioration directly stems from Labour's failure to carry through its own policy for the reform of industrial relations.

We will introduce a comprehensive Industrial Relations Bill in the first Session of the new Parliament. It will provide a proper framework of law within which improved relationships between management, men and unions can develop. We welcome the TUC's willingness to take action through its own machinery against those who disrupt industrial peace by unconstitutional or unofficial action. Yet it is no substitute for the new set of fair and reasonable rules we will introduce.

We aim to strengthen the unions and their official leadership by providing some deterrent against irresponsible action by unofficial minorities. We seek to create conditions in which strikes become the means of last resort, not of first resort, as they now so often are.

Our new Act will establish clear rights and obligations for unions and employers. It will lay down what is lawful and what isn't lawful in the conduct of industrial disputes. It will also introduce new safeguards for the individual – the right of appeal against unjust dismissal by an employer or unjust action by a union.

The framework of law we will establish will provide for agreements to be binding on both unions and employers. A new Registrar of Trades Unions and Employers' Associations will ensure that their rules are fair, just, democratic, and not in conflict with the public interest. In the case of a dispute which would seriously endanger the national interest, our Act will provide for the holding of a secret ballot and for a 'cooling-off period' of not less than sixty days.

Associated with our new Act will be a Code of Practice laying down guidelines for good collective agreements and standards for good management and trade union practices in the individual company.

Training for better jobs

We want to help people seeking new and better jobs. This involves provision for redundancy, opportunities for retraining, the maintenance of living standards during retraining, and assistance – particularly with housing – for those who have to move. Existing arrangements are inadequate: they will be improved. We will stimulate a massive retraining programme for men and women in industry. We will closely examine the work of the Industrial Training Boards and the operation of the levy/grant system, so as to root out unnecessary bureaucracy and ensure the full support of industry and the closest co-operation with further and higher education.

We will also encourage wider and better provision for management training. Modern industry imposes new and heavy burdens on all levels of management. Good management is essential not only for efficiency and the proper use of capital resources, but also for the creation of good industrial relations.

Industrial progress

Competitive free enterprise ensures choice for the consumer. Profitable free enterprise provides the resources for both capital investment and higher wages. We will pursue a vigorous competition policy. We will check any abuse of dominant market power or monopoly, strengthening and reforming the machinery which exists.

We reject the detailed intervention of Socialism which usurps the functions of management and seeks to dictate prices and earnings in industry. We much prefer a system of general pressures, creating an economic climate which favours, and rewards, enterprise and efficiency. Our aim is to identify and remove obstacles that prevent effective competition and restrict initiative.

We will sharpen the disclosure requirements in the accounts of public companies subject to an exemption procedure and reduce them for most private companies, and will institute an inquiry into other aspects of company law. As prosperity increases we will progressively reduce restrictions on overseas investment.

Small businesses have had a raw deal from Labour. They have had to suffer higher and more complicated taxes, and waste more time filling up forms. Our policies for reducing taxation and reducing government interference in industry will reduce the heavy burdens on the small firm. We will decide the best method of providing advice and encouragement for small businesses in the light of the Bolton Report.

We are totally opposed to further nationalisation of British industry. We will repeal the so-called Industrial Expansion Act which gives the Government power to use taxpayers' money to buy its way into private industry. Specific projects approved by Parliament will continue to be given Government support. We will drastically modify the Industrial Reorganisation Corporation Act.

The quality and cost of transport services affect the fares and prices everyone pays. We will continue an expanding road programme, improving in particular roads in Scotland, Wales, the South West, and the development areas. 85 per cent of the freight throughout the country is carried by road. Cheap and efficient service must be combined with high standards of public safety. We will repeal the Labour Government's law which would prevent lorries driving more than 100 miles without a specially obtained licence.

We will progressively reduce the involvement of the State in the nationalised industries, for example in the steel industry, so as to improve their competitiveness. An increasing use of private capital will help to reduce the burden on the taxpayer, get better investment decisions, and ensure more effective use of total resources.

The railways have a vital part to play in the modernisation of the transport system. They need to provide new passenger facilities, interchanges with the car and bus, and freight depots outside the urban areas. Shipping lines, hotels, parking facilities, catering services, vacant land, can all be developed more effectively in partnership with private enterprise. This will give better service to the public.

We will prevent the waste of £76 million on the nationalisation of the ports. We will end the uncertainty hanging over both large and small ports by giving them the freedom to build, in competition with each other but co-ordinated through a strong central authority.

The bureaucratic burden imposed upon industry by government departments, agencies and boards has steadily increased in recent years. We will see that it is reduced.

We will encourage investment through tax allowances or reductions rather than by means of grant – with differential arrangements in favour of the development areas. And the more flexible system of grants under the Local Employment Acts will be retained as an important part of our regional policy. These changes will be subject to transitional arrangements and will not in any way be retrospective. Special assistance for particular industries like shipping will be continued.

Prosperity for all areas

We regard an effective regional development policy as a vital element in our economic and social strategy; economically, because both prosperous and less prosperous areas are affected by the present regional imbalance and waste of resources it involves; socially, because we are not prepared to tolerate the human waste and suffering that accompany persistent unemployment, dereliction and decline.

We will stimulate long-term growth by increasing the basic economic attraction of the areas concerned. This is a markedly different approach from that followed by Labour, who have five separate and often unco-ordinated government departments spending very large sums of money with little regard to the practical effect. Despite the Government's lavish spending of the taxpayer's money during the last six years, in Scotland, Wales, and most regions of England there are hundreds of thousands fewer jobs. Since 1966, the country has experienced the longest period of high unemployment since the 1930s.

We will link expenditure more closely to the creation of new jobs, especially in industries with growth potential, and to improvements in the economic facilities of the development areas. We will maintain regional assistance to each development area. We will initiate a thorough-going study of development area policy as was recommended by the Hunt Committee. We will phase out the Regional Employment Premium, taking proper account of existing obligations and commitments. We will maintain financial incentives for investment in the development areas, making greater use of the powers given by the Local Employments Acts, and these powers will also be used where appropriate in the intermediate areas. We will give fairer treatment to the service industries and to commerce. We will give special attention to the needs of the development areas in our plans for a massive increase in retraining facilities.

Some resources could with advantage be switched from the present general subsidies towards the better training schemes and the infra-structure needed to make both development and intermediate areas more attractive to live in – and to invest in. More skilled workers, good housing, better schools, and first-class communications provide a surer long-term answer to the problems of regional development than indiscriminate financial hand-outs.

We will continue to provide financial assistance to the Northern Ireland Government so that all parts of Northern Ireland may enjoy the full benefits of United Kingdom prosperity.

Food and farming

Farmers are frustrated and disgruntled. Labour has failed to allow British agriculture to expand and prosper. We will provide new opportunities for the farming community to increase production, improve their incomes, and make a further massive contribution through import-saving to the balance of payments.

We will retain the Annual Price Review system, the production grant system, and the marketing boards, but will introduce levies on imports in order to enable us to eliminate the need for deficiency payments in their present form. These levies, variable at very short notice, will deal effectively and immediately with dumping from overseas and will thus do away with the old cumbersome and slow procedures. The changeover will be spread over at least three years. The present support system will be maintained in full throughout this transitional period, although its cost will decline. Thereafter it will continue in the form of a 'fall-back' guarantee. Before the new system is introduced, there will be full discussions with our international suppliers and with the farmers' unions.

This fundamental change will provide much-needed scope for agricultural expansion. The resultant small increase in food prices will amount to just over a penny in the £ per year on the cost of living for three years – a small increase in comparison with the five shillings in the £ rise of the last six years. The Exchequer will benefit by some £250 million, which can be used for tax reductions and for selective improvements in social security payments.

We will free from rates all buildings which a farmer uses for producing food from his land.

We will continue to encourage the development of British horticulture through the Horticultural Improvement Scheme. We will also maintain, and where appropriate expand, statutory provision through the Central Council for Agricultural and Horticultural Co-operation, to encourage better and more uniform marketing of horticultural produce.

A thriving and expanding forestry industry can reduce dependence upon costly imported timber and can, particularly in Scotland, make good use of difficult land and provide a comparatively high level of employment.

We will promote the prosperity of the fishing industry, and will ensure that the home fishing industry is enabled to compete effectively in British markets without unfair competition from dumped imports.

Homes for all

New drive and impetus is urgently needed to reverse the biggest decline in the housing programme for a quarter of a century. Labour has failed to honour its pledge to build 500,000 houses a year by 1970. It is scandalous that this year, as last year, fewer houses will be completed than in 1964 when Labour took over. And far fewer are under construction. One million people to whom Labour promised a new home by 1970 are still waiting.

Our vigorous new housing drive for the 1970s will have three main objectives:

- To house the homeless, to concentrate on slum clearance and to provide better housing for those many families living without modern amenities.
- To bring about a great increase in home ownership so that the majority of our nation fulfil their wish to live in a home of their own.
- To see that the tenant, whether of a private property or of a council house, receives a fair deal.

Under the present subsidy system, too little help goes to the homeless and the badly housed; too little help also goes to provide housing for the elderly and the disabled. We will re-negotiate the housing subsidy system so that the full weight of Government assistance goes behind tackling the worst areas of our housing problems.

The problem of the homeless is concealed by unrealistic official statistics. We will lay down a more sensible definition, and then make sure that families without a home or living in intolerable conditions receive priority. We seek a big increase in the programme of modernisation of our older houses, in co-operation with movements such as Shelter. We will, in consultation with the voluntary housing movement, give a new momentum to housing associations, co-ownership and cost-rent groups. This movement, if encouraged and assisted in its organisation and financing, can do much to cope with and to care for the problems of the elderly and the homeless.

Too often those confronted with housing problems have nowhere to turn for advice. Housing advisory centres will be set up in co-operation with voluntary housing organisations and the local authorities. People will then have an easy means of discovering how they can apply for a council house or an improvement grant, how they can obtain a mortgage, how the 'fair rent' system works, or where to contact a housing association or a cost-rent society.

The number of new houses built for owner-occupation has declined month by month. The increase in the cost of new houses and the highest mortgage interest rates in our history have prevented thousands of young people from becoming owners of their own homes. Labour promised cheaper houses and lower mortgage interest rates. But today the mortgage repayments on the average-priced new house are £3 per week more than when Labour came to power.

Our policies to abolish the Selective Employment Tax and to abolish the Land Commission, and to get more land released for building, will help to keep down house prices. We will make both the 100 per cent mortgage scheme and the mortgage option scheme more flexible. The improvements we will make to the Save As You Earn scheme will encourage a larger flow of funds into building societies.

We will encourage local authorities to sell council houses to those of their tenants who wish to buy them. Thus many council house tenants of today will become the owners of their own homes tomorrow. As a result, more money will be immediately available for the local authorities to provide housing for the aged, for the disabled, and for those on the housing lists.

Our policies for encouraging home ownership will also mean that more council house tenants can move into homes of their own, thus releasing their council houses for those in need. The present system of government council house subsidies is wasteful and inefficient; all too often those receiving subsidies are better off than those who pay for them through rates and taxes. We will change the system so that subsidies are used for adequate rent rebates for those tenants who cannot afford to pay fair rents, and also for slum clearance and other essential programmes.

We will maintain the security of tenure provisions of the 1965 Housing Act, and the fair rent system. We will continue the process – started under Labour's Housing Act of 1969 – of their gradual extension to the remaining controlled tenancies.

We will review and improve the machinery of compensation to see that it is fair and just to those whose property is compulsorily purchased or adversely affected or blighted by road and redevelopment schemes.

Social service advance

The fundamental problem of all Britain's social services – education, health, provision for the old and those in need – is the shortage of resources.

Of course money isn't everything. Much will always depend on the devoted work and care of teachers, doctors, nurses, welfare workers of all kinds, both professional and voluntary. But too often today their most dedicated efforts are frustrated and undermined by inadequate facilities and never-ending worry about finance.

With Labour's economic stagnation it is little wonder that in many cases these problems are getting steadily worse. The slow-down in economic growth which Labour Government has brought has already cost our country some £12,000 million in lost production. Even one-tenth of the revenue lost by the Government as a result of this stagnation would have paid for 100 hospitals and 1,000 schools.

In our last five years of Government, spending on the social services increased at a much faster rate in real terms than in the five years of Labour Government. Taking account of rising prices, Selective Employment Tax, the family allowance clawback, and the increased cost of unemployment benefit, our spending increased 36 per cent compared with only 25 per cent under Labour.

Our aim is to develop and improve Britain's social services to the full: here too, tomorrow must be better than today.

Immediately we can help by establishing more sensible priorities. But the only true solution is to increase what we can afford. The theme and purpose of our policies for the economy are to enable government and people to work together to create new national wealth. Only then will there be a firm foundation for new social advance.

Better education

In education above all the problem of resources is crucial. The number of children in the schools is rising. More and more are qualifying to go on to colleges, polytechnics and universities. That they should be able to develop their abilities to the full is not only right in itself but a vital national investment in the future.

Within the education budget itself, we shall shift the emphasis in favour of primary schools – the foundation on which all later education and training is built. We also recognise the need for expansion of nursery education. This is especially important in areas of social handicap, such as the poorer parts of our large cities, where it is so vital to give children a better start.

In secondary education, a number of different patterns have developed over the years, including many types of comprehensive school. We will maintain the existing rights of local education authorities to decide what is best for their area.

They will take into account the general acceptance that in most cases the age of eleven is too early to make final decisions which might affect a child's whole future. Many of the most imaginative new schemes abolishing the eleven-plus have been introduced by Conservative councils.

Local councils must ensure that the education they provide is the best for the children, taking into account the suitability of the buildings, the supply of staff, the travelling distances involved, the advice of teachers, and the wishes of parents and local electors. And they must be certain that they provide properly for the late developer. And they will naturally be slow to make irrevocable changes to any good school unless they are sure that the alternative is better.

We believe that the proper role of the central government is to satisfy itself that every local education authority provides education which will enable a child's talents and abilities to be developed to the full, at whatever age these may appear. All children must have the opportunity of getting to 'O' level and beyond if they are capable of doing so. We therefore believe that Labour's attempt to insist on compulsory reorganisation on rigid lines is contrary to local democracy and contrary to the best interests of the children.

We will raise the school leaving age to sixteen as planned. Opportunities should be given to some children, under the authority of their head teacher, to take advantage in their final year of the facilities available in colleges of further education.

We will encourage the direct grant schools. Many of these schools have an excellent record and provide opportunities which may not otherwise be available for children of academic ability, regardless of their parents' income.

Parents must have the freedom to send their children to independent schools if they wish.

The demand for higher and further education in universities, polytechnics and other colleges will increase during the 1970s. We will expand the number of places available.

Concern about teacher training is widespread. We will institute an inquiry into teacher training, as the Plowden Committee recommended. We wish the teaching profession to have a career structure which will attract recruits of high quality into the profession, and retain them.

Care for those in need

Between 1951 and 1964, Conservative Governments increased pensions five times, and the real value of the basic State pension rose by 50 per cent. We will review retirement pensions every two years to ensure that they at least maintain their purchasing power and that pensioners' living standards are properly protected.

The next Conservative Government will take urgent action to give some pension as of right to the over-eighties who now get no retirement pension at all. We will improve the benefits payable to those who are seriously ill or disabled, and introduce a constant attendance allowance for the most seriously disabled. We will improve the present situation where a woman who is just over fifty when she is widowed gets a pension but a widow just under fifty gets nothing.

We will continue to ease the earnings rule for retirement pensions and we will also increase the additions to the pension which can be earned by postponing retirement beyond the minimum age.

We believe that everyone should have the opportunity of earning a pension related to their earnings. But, in contrast to the Labour Party, our view is that, for the great majority of people, this can and should be achieved through the expansion and improvement of occupational schemes. And we will ensure that everyone can take their pension rights with them when they change their job.

There are some people who may not be covered by an occupational scheme, and for them there will be a reserve earnings-related State scheme over and above the basic flat-rate scheme. But this is intended as a reserve scheme, and all approved occupational schemes will be enabled to contract out of it completely under simple conditions.

Labour's complicated pension scheme would be unfair to existing pensioners and would harm the pension prospects of the twelve-and-a-half million members of occupational schemes. It would severely damage the growth of savings and mean ever-increasing taxation.

Our proposals will be fair to those who are now old, and also fair to those now working. Under Labour's scheme their pension prospects would depend upon the willingness of future generations to pay an ever-increasing pensions bill through mounting taxation. Under our proposal, a growing part of the future cost of pensions will be met through genuine savings.

Retirement pensions, sickness, unemployment, widowhood and industrial injuries benefits will continue to be paid as of right, and without means tests, in return for National Insurance contributions. These contributions will be graduated according to earnings, and the present flat-rate contributions – which have become a heavy burden on the lower paid during recent years – will be abolished.

We will lower the age at which public service and armed forces pension increases become payable to fifty-five, and the pensions of those who retired before 1956 will be brought up to the same level as if they had retired then with appropriate increases since. The purchasing power of public service pensions will also be protected by a two-yearly review. Special treatment will be given to war pensioners and their widows.

We will take firm action to deal with abuse of the social security system. We will tighten up the administration so as to prevent the whole system being brought into disrepute by the shirkers and the scroungers.

We will tackle the problem of family poverty and ensure that adequate family allowances go to those families that need them. A scheme based upon negative income tax would allow benefits to be related to family need; other families would benefit by reduced taxation. The Government has exaggerated the administrative problems involved, and we will make a real effort to find a practical solution. If this can be done, it will increase incentive for those at work, and bring much-needed help to children living in poverty. We welcome the recently announced improved rates of supplementary benefit.

More emphasis is required on the provision of care for the elderly, the chronic sick and handicapped people, and particularly on the expansion of those services which provide help in the home. We welcomed the Seebohm Report's recommendations on local authority social services and supported the legislation which followed. We will, in consultation with the local authorities, improve local social services so that help is more readily available to those in need.

We recognise the important contribution to social welfare that volunteers and voluntary organisations are already making, and we believe there is scope for considerable expansion and development. We are convinced that many of the social problems that now scar society can only be solved through a genuine partnership of effort between statutory and voluntary organisations – between the professional and the volunteer.

We will give active support, both financially and legislatively, so that new opportunities may be created in co-operation with the local authorities for all those – and in particular the young people and the retired people – who want to do voluntary social work.

As a result of the slow rate of economic growth under Labour, the resources going into the Health Service are inadequate. There are too many outdated hospitals, too many old people not getting the care they need in their own homes, too many mentally ill people either in overcrowded hospital wards or getting insufficient care through local community services. And too many of those working in the health service lack a decent career structure.

We will improve the administration of the health service so that its three main branches – hospitals, general practitioners, and local health services – are better co-ordinated. This will mean better value for money and better care for the patient. We will also improve the ways of dealing with suggestions and complaints from both patients and staff.

In forward planning for health, we will put more emphasis on community services. This will enable more people to be looked after at home where they are happier, rather than in hospitals and residential institutions. We will increase the number of health centres and encourage more group practice to improve the working conditions for doctors.

Labour see 'danger' in the growth of private provision in health and welfare. We believe it right and proper that people should be free to provide for themselves and their families if they wish.

Race relations and immigration

Good race relations are of immense importance. We are determined that all citizens shall continue to be treated as equal before the law, and without discrimination. Our policies for education, health and housing will help to reduce the causes of racial tension. The sooner prosperity returns, the sooner additional resources will be available to tackle the problems of poverty, decay and squalor in our towns and cities. Local authority services are under great strain in many of the towns and cities where large numbers of immigrants have settled. We believe that additional funds should be made available to these local authorities in order that they can deal with these problems effectively without placing heavy burdens on their ratepayers.

We will establish a new single system of control over all immigration from overseas. The Home Secretary of the day will have complete control, subject to the machinery for appeal, over the entry of individuals into Britain. We believe it right to allow an existing Commonwealth immigrant who is already here to bring his wife and young children to join him in this country. But for the future, work permits will not carry the right of permanent settlement for the holder or his dependants. Such permits as are issued will be limited to a specific job in a specific area for a fixed period, normally twelve months. There will of course be no restrictions on travel.

These policies mean that future immigration will be allowed only in strictly defined special cases. There will be no further large-scale permanent immigration.

We will give assistance to Commonwealth immigrants who wish to return to their countries of origin, but we will not tolerate any attempt to harass or compel them to go against their will.

Government and the citizen

The Government in Whitehall is overloaded, and as a result people in the regions grow increasingly impatient about the decisions being made in London which they know could be better made locally. Under our new style of government, we will devolve government power so that more decisions are made locally.

Scotland, with its distinct identity, traditions and legal system, is particularly conscious of these problems.

The Report of the Committee set up under Sir Alec Douglas-Home offers a new chance for the Scottish people to have a greater say in their own affairs. Its contents, including the proposal for a Scottish Convention sitting in Edinburgh, will form a basis for the proposals we will place before Parliament, taking account of the impending re-organisation of local government.

We are publishing separate manifestos for Scotland and Wales.

We reaffirm that no change will be made in the constitutional status of Northern Ireland without the free consent of the Parliament of Northern Ireland.

We support the Northern Ireland Government in its programme of legislative and executive action to ensure equal opportunity for all citizens in that part of the United Kingdom. We will provide the military and other aid necessary to support the Royal Ulster Constabulary in keeping the peace and ensuring freedom under the law; with the Ulster Defence Regiment as a strong and efficient reserve force capable of playing a significant role in maintaining peace and security.

The independence of local authorities has been seriously eroded by Labour Ministers. On many issues, particularly in education and housing, they have deliberately overridden the views of elected councillors. We think it wrong that the balance of power between central and local government should have been distorted, and we will redress the balance and increase the independence of local authorities.

We are convinced of the need for reform of the present structure of local government. Unfortunately, the Terms of Reference given to the Redcliffe-Maud and Wheatley Royal Commissions which examined this problem in England and in Scotland respectively were restricted. As a result, the crucial questions of devolution of power from the central government and of local government finance were not adequately dealt with in their Reports. We believe that these matters must be considered and that those concerned in local government must be fully consulted before final decisions are made.

We will bring forward a sensible measure of local government reform which will involve a genuine devolution of power from the central government and will provide for the existence of a two-tier structure. There will be full consultation about the pattern of boundaries and the effect of changes upon existing resources of local government

We will ensure that the legitimate interests of existing local government staff are fully safeguarded in any changes made in the structure of local government. Similarly, reductions in the number of civil servants can be achieved by restricting recruitment and allowing the normal processes of retirement and resignation to reduce numbers. Adequate financial compensation will be paid to any civil servant or local government officer made redundant, and the career prospects of those who are transferred will be safeguarded.

Traditionally, changes in Parliamentary constituency boundaries are made on the recommendation of the impartial Boundaries Commission. The Labour Government has broken this tradition in order to gain an unfair advantage at this election. We will return to the previous honest and fair system.

Freedom under the law

Protection of the individual citizen is a prime duty of government. Urgent action is needed to check the serious rise in crime and violence. The Labour Government cannot entirely shrug off responsibility for the present situation since they restricted police recruitment at a critical time.

The best deterrent to crime is the likelihood of being caught. We will strengthen the police force. We will restore the prison building programme, taking special care to provide secure detention for the most dangerous criminals.

In some respects the law needs modernising and clarifying, and needs to be made less slow and cumbersome, particularly for dealing with offences – forcible entry, obstruction and violent offences concerned with public order – peculiar to the age of demonstration and disruption. A Conservative Government will do this.

We will also change the law so that the demonstrator who uses violence, or the criminal who causes personal injury or damages property, will be obliged to compensate his victim in addition to fines or other punishments imposed by the Courts.

A tolerant and civilised society must continue to permit its citizens to assemble, march and demonstrate in support of the ideals and principles they believe in. Our purpose is to protect the citizen against disruption of lawful activities and, to that end, we will immediately institute an inquiry into the law affecting trespass. Such a reform of the law would in no way inhibit the peaceful use of the right to demonstrate or strike.

We will eliminate unnecessary secrecy concerning the workings of the Government, and we will review the operation of the Official Secrets Act so that government is more open and more accountable to the public.

The functions and powers of government have expanded so much in recent years that the traditional safeguards for the citizen no longer suffice. Although we will reduce government activity and interference, a better system of control and examination of decisions by civil servants, public bodies and local authorities which affect individual citizens is also needed. Parliament during recent years has often passed government legislation which has infringed individual rights and given wide discretionary powers to Ministers and their civil servants. We will closely examine ways of safeguarding more effectively and equitably the rights and freedom of the individual citizen.

A Conservative Government introduced equal pay for women in the teaching profession, in local government, and in the non-industrial Civil Service in the 1950s. We have supported and sought to improve the equal pay legislation.

But this alone does not ensure genuine equality of opportunity. Many barriers still exist which prevent women from participating to the full in the entire life of the country. Women are treated by the law, in some respects, as having inferior rights to men, we will amend the law to remove this discrimination.

We will clear away the remaining anomalies in family law and make fairer provision for women in the event of separation or bereavement. We will help deserted wives by improving the enforcement of maintenance orders.

A better environment

Economic growth and technological innovation are the principal means of achieving a continuing improvement in our standard of living. But the effects of technological change can sometimes lead to a deterioration in the natural environment and in the quality of life. The public are rightly concerned about these dangers.

We will improve the machinery of government for dealing with these problems. We will review existing legislation to ensure proper and sensible control in the future. The damage of the past must be repaired. The worst scars are in and around our industrial cities and towns. We will ensure that the natural beauty of our British countryside and seashore is conserved and wildlife is allowed to flourish.

We intend to launch a major campaign in which government, local authorities and voluntary organisations will combine to produce a healthier, pleasanter Britain. We will vigorously pursue international agreements for the safeguarding and improvement of the environment. We will set clearly defined aims and target-dates for the achievement of cleaner air and rivers, and for the clearance of derelict land.

The arts, broadcasting and sport

We will continue to give full financial support and encouragement to the Arts. The Arts Council will be strengthened so that it can take a more active role in stimulating regional co-operation and in establishing effective regional arts associations. Local authorities will be encouraged to play a larger role in patronage of the Arts. We recognise the vital importance of private patronage. We will devote special attention to those areas of artistic life such as museums and music colleges which face particularly acute problems.

We believe that people are as entitled to an alternative radio service as to an alternative television service. We will permit local private enterprise radio under the general supervision of an independent broadcasting authority. Local institutions, particularly local newspapers, will have the opportunity of a stake in local radio, which we want to see closely associated with the local community.

We will ensure that the British Broadcasting Corporation continues to make its effective and essential public service contribution in both television and sound broadcasting. Equally, we will ensure that the independent television companies are not prevented from providing a responsible service by too high a government levy on their income.

The Sports Council is fulfilling an important function in carrying out research and advising the Government on capital investment in recreation by local authorities, and on grant-aid to voluntary organisations. We will make the Sports Council an independent body, and make it responsible for the grant-aiding functions at present exercised by the Government.

A stronger Britain in the world

If we can negotiate the right terms, we believe that it would be in the long-term interest of the British people for Britain to join the European Economic Community, and that it would make a major contribution to both the prosperity and the security of our country. The opportunities are immense. Economic growth and a higher standard of living would result from having a larger market.

But we must also recognise the obstacles. There would be short-term disadvantages in Britain going into the European Economic Community which must be weighed against the long-term benefits. Obviously there is a price we would not be prepared to pay. Only when we negotiate will it be possible to determine whether the balance is a fair one, and in the interests of Britain.

Our sole commitment is to negotiate; no more, no less. As the negotiations proceed we will report regularly through Parliament to the country.

A Conservative Government would not be prepared to recommend to Parliament, nor would Members of Parliament approve, a settlement which was unequal or unfair. In making this judgement, Ministers and Members will listen to the views of their constituents and have in mind, as is natural and legitimate, primarily the effect of entry upon the standard of living of the individual citizens whom they represent.

We will stand by our alliances and strengthen our defences. We will continue to make our contribution to the forces of NATO and will seek to revitalise this organisation which is basic to the defence of Britain.

In the past, British forces in the Gulf, and in Singapore and Malaysia, have helped to ensure stability beneficial to the countries concerned and without which Britain's valuable interests would not have flourished. By unilaterally deciding to withdraw our forces from these areas by the end of 1971, the Labour Government have broken their promises to the Governments and peoples of these areas, and are exposing these British interests and the future of Britain's friends to unacceptable risk.

We have proposed a five-power defence force to help maintain peace and stability in South-East Asia. We will discuss this with our allies and Commonwealth friends – Australia, New Zealand, Malaysia and Singapore. Similar talks will be held with leaders in the Gulf.

We are satisfied that all these peacetime defence needs can be fulfilled by our Regular forces without the need for conscription. We deplore the destruction of the Territorial Army, and will provide adequate volunteer reserve forces for the defence and security of these islands.

We believe that Britain must in the last resort retain independent control of its nuclear weapons to deter an aggressor; as at present, those assigned to NATO can be withdrawn if supreme national interests are at stake.

We will foster the development of official and unofficial links within the Commonwealth, believing that this unique organisation can be a force for peace and understanding. We believe that the independence of each of its members must be respected, and that their internal affairs and individual responsibilities are matters for their individual decision alone, and that jointly they should only consider those matters freely agreed upon as being of common interest.

We will give the United Nations full, constructive but not uncritical support. We will seek to build on its successes and to remedy its shortcomings. We intend to go on working for sound schemes of disarmament and arms control.

Labour has failed to solve the Rhodesian problem, to the detriment of all concerned. We will make a further effort to find a sensible and just solution in accordance with the five principles which we have consistently maintained.

Britain must play a proper part in dealing with world poverty. We will ensure that Britain helps the developing countries:

- by working for the expansion of international trade;
- by encouraging private investment overseas;
- by providing capital aid and technical assistance to supplement their own efforts.

We have accepted the UNCTAD target for aid to developing countries, and will increase the British programme as national prosperity returns. We will re-examine the objectives and performance of the programme so that the maximum mutual advantage is gained.

The choice

The choice before the electors today is not just between policies and programmes. It is about the way of life our country shall follow in the next five years, and far beyond that.

In purely practical terms, it is a choice between another five years of the kind of incompetent, doctrinaire Government we have had for nearly six years and a new and better style of Government.

Faced with any problem, the instinctive Socialist reaction is to control, to restrict, and to tax. We aim to reduce the burden of taxation, and to extend individual choice, freedom and responsibility.

Socialists believe in the extension of the power of the State: government today is trying to do too much, managing too much, bringing too much to the centre for decision. We plan to clear away from Whitehall a great load of tasks which has accumulated under Socialism; to hand back responsibilities wherever we can to the individual, to the family, to private initiative, to the local authority, to the people.

It is also a choice between a Government which by its conduct has done much to discredit the value of the politician's word, and an alternative Government which is determined to restore honesty and integrity to political life.

Under a Conservative Government, the gap between the politician's promise and government performance will be closed, so that people and government can be brought together again in one nation united in a common purpose – a better tomorrow.

Firm Action for a Fair Britain

The Conservative Manifesto

1974

CONSERVATIVE PARTY GENERAL ELECTION MANIFESTO: FEBRUARY 1974

Firm action for a fair Britain

Date of Election	Thursday 28 February
Party Leader	Edward Heath
Candidates	623
MPs	297
Votes	11,868,906
% of vote	37.9%

Today we face great dangers both from within our own country and from outside. The problems are formidable, but there is no reason why they should overwhelm us.

The assets of the British people are great. Not simply our technical skills and our natural resources, but also, more important than these, the strength and stability of our institutions and the determination of our people in moments of crisis to ensure that good sense and moderation prevail. If we are to make the best use of those assets it is essential that the affairs of this country are in the hands of a strong government, able to take firm measures in defence of the national interest. This means a Conservative Government with a renewed mandate from the people and with a full five years in which to guide the nation safely through the difficult period that lies ahead. That is why we need a General Election now. Once the General Election is behind us then we must put aside our differences and join in a common determination to establish and maintain a secure, civilised fair society.

The danger from outside

The world has changed dramatically since we last sought the support of the electorate. In the last two years there has been a dramatic rise in the world price of almost all the essential raw materials and foods which we have to import from overseas. Many of these prices have doubled in the past year alone, making it impossible to stem the rise in the cost of living. Now on top of these increases comes the huge increase in oil prices, which in turn will affect the cost of almost everything that we produce or buy in this country.

Fortunately, as far as energy is concerned, Britain will in the long run be able to cope better than most. We have plentiful supplies of coal and natural gas. We are well advanced in the development of nuclear power. Above all, within five years from now we should be able to satisfy the greater part of our needs with our own oil from the seas around our shores, provided we make the determined effort that will be necessary.

But let no one suppose that as a nation we can deal with the immediate problem without hardship and sacrifice. It will impose a greatly increased burden on our balance of payments, and for the time being will make us poorer as a nation than we would otherwise have been. What we must continue to ensure is that any sacrifices are shared equitably and that hardship does not fall on those least able to bear it. If the situation requires further action – whether it be in the field of public expenditure or of tax or monetary policies – we shall not hesitate to take it. But the basis of our firm action will be fairness.

The danger from within

Events from overseas have held us back. They will not destroy us. What could destroy, not just our present standard of living but all our hopes for the future, would be inflation we brought upon ourselves. Despite the unprecedented sharp rise in world prices, price increases in the shops have, as a result of our counter-inflation policies, been much less than would otherwise have been the case. We have also made sure that those worst hit by rising prices, in particular pensioners, are better protected than they have ever been before. But we have also had to deal with the inflation which comes as a result of excessive wage increases here at home. For more than two years we tried strenuously to deal with this problem by voluntary means. In particular we asked trade unions and employers to join us in working out a voluntary scheme to prevent one group of workers using its industrial strength to steal a march over those working in other industries. Then other groups are inevitably provoked into leapfrogging. And so it goes on, with the old, the weak and those who do not or will not strike, suffering more at each turn of the inflationary screw.

In the end, after all our talks, although we agreed on objectives, the trade unions could not agree with us on a voluntary means of achieving them, and we had to ask Parliament for statutory powers over pay and prices to hold the line against inflation.

Stages 1 and 2 of that policy, which are now completed, proved more successful than our critics thought possible. The rise in prices due to internal causes was sharply reduced – to a greater extent, indeed, than in most other countries.

Now, in Stage 3 nearly six million workers have concluded wage agreements within the approved limits. The special position of the mineworkers has been recognised by an offer, within Stage 3, of a size which few other groups of workers can hope to achieve.

It is a tragedy that the miners' leaders should have turned down this offer. The action taken by the National Union of Mineworkers has already caused great damage and threatens even greater damage for the future. It must be the aim of any responsible Government to reach a settlement of this dispute at the earliest possible moment. The choice before the Government, and now the choice before the country, is clear. On the one hand it would be possible to accept the NUM's terms for a settlement. The country must realise what the consequences of this would be. It would mean accepting the abuse of industrial power to gain a privileged position.

It would undermine the position of moderate trade union leaders.

It would make it certain that similar strikes occurred at frequent intervals in the future.

It would destroy our chances of containing inflation.

The alternative is to reach a settlement with the NUM on terms which safeguard the nation's interests as well as the miners. The basis of that settlement must be fairness.

The terms must be fair to the miners, but they must also be fair to the nearly six million workers who have now accepted settlements within the limits of our counter-inflation policy and the many others who are prepared to do so.

They must be fair to the even greater number of people who have no union to stand up for them and who rely on the elected government to look after their interests.

A Conservative Government with a new mandate and five years of certain authority ahead of it would be in a good position to reach such a settlement.

The present offer by the National Coal Board remains on the table. It can be accepted at any time.

We have accepted the principles of the Pay Board's report on relative rates of pay between one group of workers and another. We have already set up machinery for the examination of major claims about relative pay levels, based on the Pay Board.

As its first task, this new machinery will conduct a full examination of the miners' case within this framework. It will take due account of the relative claims of other groups, many of whom – such as nurses and teachers – gave evidence during the preparation of the Relativities Report. Moreover, we are prepared to undertake that whatever recommendation the new body makes on the miners' case can be backdated to the first of March.

It will be completely free to take evidence from any quarter and to decide upon its recommendations. So it will be impartial and it will be thorough. And it will be fair, not only to the miners, but to everyone else.

But whatever settlement is reached, the fact must be faced that, for a time, our nation's resources will be stretched to the limit, and those most in need of protection against inflation must have first claim on them.

This Conservative Government has already moved from a two-yearly to an annual review of pensions and all other benefits. We will now move to a six monthly up-rating of pensions and other long-term benefits. This will have to be paid for by the community as a whole, out of higher contributions which must be shared fairly amongst all the people.

A fair and orderly policy for pay and prices, for pensions and benefits meets the economic needs of the country. But at the same time, it must be matched by a fair and orderly way of dealing with our industrial relations.

The foundations for better relations in industry were laid in the Industrial Relations Act. We have never pretended that it would be easy to implement. But other industrial countries have found that good industrial relations require a proper framework of law and we are sure that Britain is no exception. We shall therefore maintain the essential structure of the Industrial Relations Act, but we shall amend it in the light of experience, and after consultation with both sides of industry, in order

- to meet any valid criticisms;
- to make conciliation a pre-condition of court action;
- and to provide more effective control for the majority of union members by ensuring that they have the opportunity to elect the governing bodies and national leaders of their unions by a postal ballot.

We shall also seek to improve industrial relations by bringing in new legislation, following discussions with both sides of industry, designed to make large and medium-sized firms introduce a wider measure of employee-participation.

The best way of curbing the majority of extremists in the trade unions is for the moderate majority of union members to stand up and be counted. But the fact remains that a small number of militant extremists can so manipulate and abuse the monopoly power of their unions as to cause incalculable damage to the country and to the fabric of our society itself. Moreover, it is manifestly unfair that those who do not go on strike are, in effect, obliged to subsidise those who do. It is no part of our policy to see the wives and children of men on strike suffering. But it is only right that the unions themselves, and not the taxpayer, should accept their primary responsibility for the welfare of the families of men who choose to go on strike; and, after discussions with trade unions and employers. we will amend the social security system accordingly.

The General Election that is now upon us is a chance for the British people to show the world that at a time of crisis the overwhelming majority of us are determined not to tear ourselves apart, but to close ranks. It is a chance, in other words, to demonstrate that we believe in ourselves as a nation.

This is our aim:

- a Britain united in moderation, not divided by extremism; a society in which there is change without revolution;
- a Government that is strong in order to protect the weak;
- a people who enjoy freedom with responsibility;
- a morality of fairness without regimentation;
- a nation with faith in itself, and a people with self-respect.

We are a great nation, with a long and eventful history behind us. We have survived grave perils in the past, and we can do so again now. But to do so, two things are needed, as they have always been: a united people, prepared to put aside our differences to fight the common threat; and a strong Government, able to do whatever is necessary to carry out the people's will.

In the pages that follow we set out our record over the four years since we were voted into office, our proposals for the future, and the nature of the choice now facing the nation.

Although we have not been able to do as much as we would have liked, and the problems which face us are immense, the record of the progress we have made so far, despite all the difficulties, both national and international, that have beset us, is important in two ways.

First, looking back, it provides a fair basis for a comparison with the record of our predecessors. Second, looking ahead, the achievements of the past four years provide the solid foundation for our further progress once the present difficulties are overcome.

Until the present crisis hit the country, the living standards of the British people, since we took office in 1970, had been rising more than twice as fast as they did during the period of the former Labour administration. One of the cruellest consequences of inflation is the unfair way in which it hits some groups in the community far harder than others. But despite the hardship caused by rising prices, for the great majority of the people of this country, the pronounced rise in living standards was a reality; and with the expansion of the nation's economy came a welcome restoration of Britain's strength in the world.

This prosperity has now, for the time being, been blighted by the effects of the three-day week, forced upon us by the need to ration electricity so as to prevent our power stations from running out of coal altogether as a consequence of the industrial action taken by the National Union of Mineworkers.

And even when the need for the three-day week is over, we must still, for some time to come, and in common with many other countries, expect a pause in the rise in our living standards; since, for the time being, all the extra national wealth created will be needed to pay for the higher cost of essential imports, notably oil, and will not, therefore, be available for increased prosperity at home.

This obviously has particular implications for those of our programmes and objectives which necessarily involve substantial Government expenditure, where everything is dependent on the economic resources available. Here the crisis makes it more essential than ever to avoid easy but irresponsible promises beyond what the country can at present afford. We have, therefore, undertaken a full and realistic review of all our policies in the light of the changed conditions faced by the Western world as a whole. As a result, in framing our specific proposals, we have concentrated on indicating what our priorities in the next Parliament will be; on outlining, in each field, those programmes that will be given first claim in present economic circumstances.

But while this means that the next year or two will inevitably be arduous and difficult, further ahead, provided we work together as one nation and stand firm against inflation, we can look forward to an economy more soundly based than we have known since the war, thanks to the increasing availability of North Sea oil. In addition to going a long way towards solving the energy crisis, this promises radically to transform our balance of payment position.

Meanwhile, during the difficult period that lies ahead, we shall continue to take special care to protect the pensioners, the lower paid, and those in need.

It may be that we are able to do more than is promised in this manifesto. That will depend, in part, on world economic forces beyond our control; but, more than anything else, it will depend on our ability to work together as one nation and on the extent of our success in winning the vitally important battle against inflation. Meanwhile, at this critical time in our nation's affairs, we believe it to be right to err on the side of caution; to promise too little rather than too much.

Beyond this, however, there is something that no crisis can change or slow down. That is our vision of the Britain in which we believe, the ideal which will inform all that we do.

A Britain united in moderation, not divided by extremism. A society in which there is change without revolution. A Government that is strong in order to protect the weak. A people who enjoy freedom with responsibility. A morality of fairness without regimentation. A nation with faith in itself, and a people with self-respect.

Holding the line against inflation

Our consistent aim since taking office has been, and remains, to safeguard and enhance the well-being of the British people.

Throughout that period, and never more so than today, the gravest threat to our national well-being has been the menace of unrestrained inflation. This was a legacy we inherited from our predecessors. In our 1970 Election Manifesto, we pledged that 'we will give overriding priority to bringing the present inflation under control', but warned that 'the Labour Government's policies have unleashed forces which no Government could hope to reverse overnight'.

We reduced Labour's rates of indirect taxation, which bore directly on prices. We made unprecedented efforts to obtain the co-operation of trade unions and employers in formulating an effective voluntary pay and prices policy. When agreement on this proved impossible, we sought and obtained the consent of Parliament to control pay, prices and profits by law.

But our warning that the battle against inflation would not be quickly or easily won has proved even truer than we feared at the time. For on top of all the problems we inherited, we have had to absorb an unprecedented rise in the world prices of almost all the essential foods and raw materials that we are obliged to import from overseas. It is this, and not membership of the Common Market, which has led to the substantial rise in the price of food in the shops.

When we took office nearly four years ago, prices were not merely rising alarmingly: the rate of increase was steadily accelerating. As a result of our policies so far, we have been able to reduce the rise in prices due to internal causes and, therefore, within our own control as a nation.

But the rate at which prices are rising is still dangerously high, and on top of everything else we now have to absorb a four-fold increase in the price of oil. This makes it all the more vital that we hold the line against inflation caused by excessive wage settlements at home.

We shall, therefore, press ahead with the pay and prices policy, if necessary stiffening it in the light of the developing economic situation.

We shall ensure that the Price Commission has the powers it needs to protect the consumer from unnecessary price rises, and we will examine further means of controlling the rise in prices of key items of food in the household budget.

We shall renew our offer to the TUC and CBI to join us in working out an effective voluntary pay and prices policy, ultimately to replace the existing statutory policy, in the management and evolution of which both sides of industry would jointly participate.

Meanwhile, however, it is manifestly unfair that those who do not go on strike are, in effect, obliged to subsidise those who do. It is no part of our policy to see the wives and children of men on strike suffering. But it is only right that the unions themselves, and not the taxpayer, should accept their primary responsibility for the welfare of the families of men who choose to go on strike; and after discussions with trade unions and employers, we will amend the social security system accordingly.

Beating the energy crisis

Well before the current oil crisis emerged in the aftermath of the Arab–Israeli War of October 1973, we were developing, as a matter of urgency, a new and comprehensive energy policy.

Our objective was, first, to reduce our hitherto growing dependence on imported oil and, second, among home-produced sources of fuel and power, to plan for the proper balance between coal, North Sea oil, natural gas and nuclear power.

To this end we had already:

(a) Passed the Coal Industry Act, to provide massive funds for the industry's modernisation and substantial extra money for miners' pensions and other benefits; thus, for the first time in twenty years, providing the coal mining industry and those who work in it with a secure future;
(b) Accelerated the exploitation of the vast proven oil reserves in the British sector of the North Sea and set up the Scottish Petroleum Office under a Scottish Minister to co-ordinate all on-shore developments;
(c) Initiated negotiations to purchase the entire natural gas output of the Frigg field in the Norwegian sector of the North Sea;
(d) Merged Britain's nuclear power station capacity into a single new company, the National Nuclear Corporation, and agreed with the NNC and the Central Electricity Generating Board to build a new generation of atomic power stations.

In the light of the post-October 1973 energy crisis, and in particular the rocketing price of imported oil, still further steps were needed. Accordingly, we set up a Department of Energy under a Secretary of State, whose long-term goal is to achieve national self-sufficiency in energy.

The first oil from the British sector of the North Sea is due to be landed this year and by 1980 the North Sea should be supplying the greater part of our national needs. In full co-operation with private enterprise, we will press ahead with the extraction and landing of North Sea oil, and prospecting for Celtic Sea oil, as fast as is technically and humanly possible. Labour's irrelevant and disastrous proposal to nationalise our offshore oil would needlessly deprive Britain of an invaluable source of capital, skills and experience, and would cause confusion and delay when the nation can least afford it.

Britain has pioneered nuclear power technology. Already we generate a higher proportion of our electricity in nuclear stations than any other European country, and we shall shortly be announcing the details of our new nuclear power station programme.

We are working out with the National Coal Board an expanded investment programme for coal. We shall press ahead with the rapid development of the newly discovered coalfield in Selby, Yorkshire – the largest and richest unworked seam in Europe.

The new Department of Energy is urgently examining every possibility for increasing our own national energy resources – including the use of methane gas, solar power and tidal power. However successful we are in developing the main sources of energy, the greater the range of available sources and the less vulnerable we shall be.

The new Department is also working out the details of a major energy conservation programme, and will announce steps to ensure the maximum efficiency in the use of expensive fuel. We will give a strong lead on improving standards of building design so as to make the best use of fuel. We will encourage higher insulation standards in homes, offices and factories.

As a result of the measures already taken and those now proposed, we shall be better placed in terms of energy supplies than most other nations. However, while we should thus enjoy secure supplies of the fuels the nation needs, we cannot escape from the higher cost of those fuels. The days of cheap energy are gone for good.

Taken as a whole, our measures throughout the field of energy will set a secure pattern for the future. But the nation's position must also be safeguarded in the short term. We have already concluded an important agreement with Iran to procure a substantial quantity of oil in exchange for British exports.

We shall continue to work both within the framework of the European Economic Community and in the wider context of consumer/producer collaboration to ensure an adequate flow of oil from the major producing countries, so long as our dependence on overseas sources of supply remains.

Industry, agriculture, and the regions

In present circumstances, energy policy must necessarily take pride of place in the Government's programme to provide the essential long-term framework for soundly based industrial and agricultural expansion. But other aspects, to which we have rightly given priority in the past, will not be forgotten or neglected.

During the past four years we have introduced a wide range of new measures to bring new life to some of the older and decaying industrial regions of Britain, both for the benefit of the people of those regions and of the economic health of the nation as a whole.

Through the Industry Act, through free depreciation, and in other ways, we have provided more effective financial incentives for industrial expansion in these areas than they have ever previously enjoyed; and we have set up the Industrial Development Executive to ensure that these incentives give the greatest value for money.

We have greatly increased the programmes for improving housing and the social services in these regions, and for clearing away the scars of dereliction; and we have given them special priority in the provision of industrial training. We have also greatly improved their transport links.

An important source of new help for the regions over the years ahead should derive from our membership of the European Community. We attach importance to a substantial fund devoted to Community Regional Development, and a decision is to be taken early this year.

For the nation as a whole, we have introduced the Training Opportunities Scheme, to meet the needs of an economy in which rapid technological change and new patterns of demand shut down old jobs and open up new ones. We have nearly trebled the numbers being trained and retrained under Government auspices in Government Training Centres. Our Employment and Training Act has provided industry with help in increasing its own training, related to actual labour needs, through the newly established Manpower Services Commission.

We shall continue to expand the Training Opportunities Scheme, and continue to modernise the employment services. We have announced new legislation to bring up to date the law dealing with the health and safety of people at work. We have announced a massive ten-year expansion and modernisation programme for the steel industry.

After nearly four years of Conservative Government the British aircraft industry has the biggest order book in this century. In technology, in research and in production we have established skills and abilities which provide us with immense opportunities within Europe and throughout the world to see that this industry plays an important role in the future commercial success of Britain.

We are the first Government to have given special attention to small firms, appointing a Minister with special responsibility for them. We have implemented the majority of the Bolton Report recommendations, especially in the field of taxation. We do not believe that, in business, bigger is necessarily better.

Agriculture

We reaffirm our traditional Conservative support for British agriculture, which over the past four years, has enjoyed a marked resurgence of confidence.

The past year has seen some sections of our agriculture doing well, while others, such as the dairy industry, have been affected by the sharp rise in the price of feeding-stuffs. The particular problem of milk producers is being dealt with in the Price Review to be announced very shortly.

The long-term prospects for the expansion of British agriculture have never been better. Membership of the European Economic Community, for the great majority of British farmers, is, and will continue to be, of enormous benefit, ensuring an enlarged market for farm produce, increased returns to efficient farmers and better protection from market fluctuations. Our current balance of payments problems make a healthy home agriculture more important than ever. Considerable opportunities for expansion exist, and our policies will continue to recognise this.

Industrial relations

But the Achilles heel of the British economy has long been, and continues to be, industrial relations. It is largely because of this that our economic progress since the war has consistently lagged behind that of most other industrial nations – and will continue to do so in the future, with grave consequences, unless a major improvement in industrial relations can be secured. It is in large part because of this that we find ourselves in the present crisis, the gravest since the war.

By setting the pound free in the present unsettled situation, we have liberated the economy and the nation from the restrictions of being pegged to an unrealistic exchange rate. By drastically cutting taxation, we have liberated the economy and the nation from the stultifying imposts of Socialism.

But we have not yet been able to liberate the economy and the nation from the disruption, the inflation, and the inefficiency caused by bad industrial relations.

The need for action on this front was recognised by our predecessors, who first set up a Royal Commission to inquire into the subject and then prepared a major Bill to reform trade union law – only to withdraw it in an abject and humiliating surrender to trade union pressure. This disastrous incident has played a large part in creating the present situation.

In accordance both with our pre-election pledges and with the clear will of the majority of the British people, one of our first steps on taking office was to act where Labour had capitulated.

The Industrial Relations Act represents the first thorough-going reform of trade union law in modern times. Its purpose is to provide for an up-to-date and realistic legal framework for industrial relations, to strengthen responsible trade union leadership, to guarantee fundamental trade union rights, to provide remedies hitherto unavailable for the peaceful solution of disputes about negotiating rights, and to safeguard the individual from the abuse of power, whether by management or unions. Although it is a matter for national regret that its usefulness has been limited by the refusal, so far, of most trade unions to co-operate in its working, it is nevertheless already having some significant effects. More than 15,000 people have made use of remedies it provides to protect individual rights and the National Industrial Relations Court – although supposed to be banned by the unions – has dealt with almost 1,000 cases.

Other industrial countries have found that good industrial relations require a proper framework of law and we are sure that Britain is no exception.

We shall therefore maintain the essential structure of the Industrial Relations Act, but we shall amend it in the light of experience, and after consultation with both sides of industry, in order (a) to meet any valid criticisms; (b) to make conciliation a precondition of court action; and (c) to provide more effective control for the majority of union members by ensuring that they have the opportunity to elect the governing bodies and national leaders of their unions by a postal ballot.

We shall also seek to improve industrial relations by bringing in new legislation, following discussions with both sides of industry, designed to make large and medium-sized firms introduce a wider measure of employee-participation. We have set up a steering group drawn from the Government, the CBI and the TUC to study methods to improve job satisfaction.

Taxation

In our 1970 Election Manifesto we promised both to reduce and reform taxation. Both these pledges have been carried out to the letter.

Whereas our predecessors, during their term of office, increased tax rates by £3,000 million a year, we have cut tax rates by an even greater amount.

Food has been relieved of tax altogether. The biggest cuts in income tax have been made by increases in the personal allowances, which give the largest relief, proportionately, to the less well-off taxpayer. Many people with small incomes have been relieved of income tax altogether. We have also reduced the rate of tax on the first slice of income from savings, which has helped those – usually elderly – living on small fixed incomes, who have been particularly hard hit by rising prices.

In the field of tax reform, we have unified income tax and surtax in a single graduated system of personal tax, in a form that can be simply understood. We have reformed company taxation, so as to end Labour's discrimination against the ordinary shareholder. And we have replaced both Purchase Tax and SET by a 10 per cent Value

Added Tax – the lowest standard VAT rate in Europe. No new tax is ever popular, and VAT is no exception. But it is fairer and less onerous than the taxes it replaced.

Our record on tax reduction and tax reform speaks for itself. Obviously in the present grave situation it would be irresponsible to make any commitments about tax rates. But what we can promise is that the burden of taxation on everyone in Britain will be far less than it would be under Labour, which is committed to a hugely expensive programme of state take-over, a massive expansion of public expenditure far beyond what the nation can afford, and to a belief in high taxation as an end in itself.

We shall continue our programme of tax reform with the Tax Credit Scheme. We will introduce legislation in the next Parliament in order to implement the scheme as soon as the economic situation allows.

The separation between the systems of taxation and social security has proved, in recent years, an increasingly difficult obstacle to the creation of a fair society. In particular, it has made it difficult to give sufficient help to those who, while not in acute poverty, are nonetheless struggling and hard pressed.

The Tax Credit Scheme will bring the two systems – of taxation and social security – together in a single coherent scheme, which will greatly alleviate this problem and bring immediate help to those now affected by it.

The introduction of the scheme will further simplify and modernise our tax system, and bring substantial savings in the cost of administration. For social security, it will represent the most important advance since the implementation of the Beveridge Report more than a generation ago.

The first step would be to pay tax credits for children, including the first child, for whom mothers at present receive no family allowance at all. These child credits, which will be paid to the mother, will be worth more than the existing income tax child allowances and family allowances which they will replace. Mothers will get cash each week through the Post Office, in exactly the same way as they cash the existing, but less valuable, family allowances.

When fully implemented the tax credit scheme:

- will provide a positive social benefit in cash to millions of hard-pressed families with low incomes, especially where there are children;
- will give credits as a right – automatically and without a means-test;
- will relieve hundreds of thousands of pensioners from the need to claim supplementary benefit and give a significant increase in income to another 3 or 4 million pensioners.

Helping the pensioner

In the four years since we took office, we have:

(a) Increased pensions every year. Labour only increased pensions every other year.
(b) Paid, in each of the last two years, a Christmas bonus as well. Labour never did.
(c) Seen to it that, each year, the increase in the pension was greater than the increase in the cost of living; so that each time there has been a real increase in pensioners' living standards. During the last five years of Labour, the real purchasing power of the pension actually fell.

(d) Paid a pension to those over-80s to whom Labour denied one altogether.

In addition, we have raised the amount that pensioners may earn without having their pension reduced. We have improved the allowance which helps many of those on supplementary pensions with the cost of heating their homes.

We have lowered the age at which increases in public service and armed forces pensions become payable, and we have further improved the position of war pensioners and their widows. Public service pensions, armed forces pensions and supplementary pensions are all now reviewed every single year, together with the main National Insurance benefits.

We have undertaken to give compensation to those public service pensioners who have been adversely affected by the provisions of the statutory pay and prices policy, and to allow similar steps to be taken by private occupational schemes.

We are acutely conscious of the hardship suffered by many pensioners as a result of inflation. That is why, for pensioners in particular, the most important section of our programme for the next Parliament is our pledge to hold the line against inflation. Nevertheless, so far as the actual pension is concerned, we shall continue in the next Parliament the progress we have made so far. We shall continue to give the pensioner first priority in the entire field of social service expenditure.

We have already moved from a two-yearly to an annual review of pensions and all other benefits. We will now move to a six monthly up-rating of pensions and other long-term benefits. We shall, of course, continue to ensure that pensions are increased by at least as much as the cost of living.

We shall continue to relax the earnings rule during the next Parliament. Our ultimate objective is to abolish it altogether.

What we shall not do is compete with the Labour Party in an auction of promises which we do not believe can be kept. We are confident that a dispassionate comparison of our record with that of our predecessors speaks for itself.

Finally, in addition to doing our best to fulfil the community's responsibility to those already retired or approaching retirement, we shall press ahead with our new pensions scheme, which will, in the long term, completely transform the financial prospects of those no longer at work. From next year, everyone in employment will be building up the right to a second pension, related to their earnings, on top of the basic State pension. For most people this will be provided through schemes run by the companies where they work; but there will be a reserve State scheme for those who cannot otherwise be properly covered.

The scheme for a second pension will include proper protection of pension rights on change of job, better provision for widows, and some safeguard against rising prices. It will ensure that, for future generations of the retired, there will no longer be such a big drop in income which is so often the biggest single problem for those ceasing to work today.

This new scheme will greatly improve the pension prospects for women in employment, for many of them will be able to earn a second pension for the first time and many, too, will get a second widow's pension also for the first time. Married women in employment will retain their right not to pay the full contribution to the basic State scheme.

Meeting special need

A consistent feature of our social security policy since we first took office has been the bringing of new help to particular groups in society, hitherto insufficiently recognised by Governments, who have need of special help, whether in cash or in care.

Thus we have:

(a) Introduced, for the first time, a range of additional 'invalidity' benefits for wage-earners who cannot work because of long-term illness or incapacity;
(b) Introduced, for the first time, special tax-free attendance allowances for seriously disabled people who need a great deal of care and attention;
(c) Introduced, for the first time, a Family Income Supplement for low wage earning families with children;
(d) Introduced, for the first time, a widow's pension for women, without young children, who were widowed between the ages of 40 and 50.

We are, however, conscious of how very much remains to be done in meeting cases of special need, particularly so far as the disabled are concerned. We shall be carrying out by this autumn our statutory duty to report to Parliament on our proposals for improving the cash provision for the disabled, including the possibility of a disablement income.

We recognise the serious problem of acute family deprivation which exists in certain parts of the country – the inner city areas, some of our older industrial areas and, indeed, some of the new housing estates where there live families rehoused from the central parts of the cities. These areas often contain many of the various forms of deprivation – bad housing, the most out-dated school buildings, the oldest hospitals, lack of community facilities and a bad environment generally – coupled with an inability to cope amongst the families concerned, sometimes, but not always, caused by poverty.

We shall therefore start a new drive to bring more resources into these areas, both to improve living conditions and the environment generally, and to provide a wide range of advice and help to the families concerned. We will concentrate this help on the worst areas; and give more opportunity for local people to play a part in the affairs of their community.

In these and other deprived inner city areas we shall place special emphasis on housing needs and the setting up of comprehensive advice centres, in partnership with the significant contribution already being made by independent voluntary agencies.

In London, these problems are becoming intensified by a shortage of men and women to operate most public services and to teach in the schools. We have therefore referred the whole question of the London Allowance payable to teachers and other public servants to the Pay Board, and will act on the Board's report as soon as we receive it.

We shall provide family planning within the National Health Service. We shall continue to improve the services for the old, the disabled, the mentally ill and the mentally handicapped at home, in the community and in hospital. We shall publish a White Paper on services for the mentally ill. We have increased greatly the numbers of home helps, district nurses and health visitors. We shall improve the services for children and legislate on adoption. We have set in hand help for the deaf and the arthritic and rheumatic. We shall act as necessary on the Finer Report on one-parent families when it is received.

We have much expanded the National Health Service. We have reformed its administration to improve services to the patient. We shall implement the principal recommendations of the Briggs Report on nursing, while preserving the identity of the health visitor. We will take any steps considered necessary to improve hospital complaint procedures in the light of the Davies Report.

Our hospital, health centre and social service building programmes are all much larger in real terms than those of our Labour predecessors. We plan to supplement the District General Hospital network by a network of community hospitals, basing them where practicable on some of the existing smaller local hospitals. We aim to continue reducing the waiting time for non-urgent surgery.

We reject Labour's proposal to abolish private practice and private provision in association with the National Health Service. This is unacceptable in principle and in practice would only reduce the skills available to patients as a whole.

Throughout the entire field of meeting special need, we are particularly conscious of the valuable work done by voluntary organisations, and we shall continue to help them without compromising their independence. To this end, we will review the legal framework within which charities operate.

Housing

The high level of interest rates in an inflationary world has inevitably put difficulties in the way of the expansion of home ownership to which we remain firmly committed. Nonetheless, since 1970, about a million families have become home-owners for the first time, bringing the total to more than half the families in Britain.

Over the first three full years since we took office, we have provided two million new or improved homes. This is 500,000 more than Labour provided in the previous three years, for which they were responsible.

The number of new home-owners would have been still larger had certain Councils not opposed the sale of Council houses to those Council tenants who were willing and able to buy them with the help offered by the Government.

Subject to a right of appeal by the local authority to the Secretary of State on clearly specified grounds, we shall ensure that, in future, established Council tenants are able, as of right, to buy on reasonable terms the house or flat in which they live.

- We have made an agreement with the building societies which will ensure in the long term greater stability in the flow of funds for house purchase, and the building societies have agreed to introduce as soon as possible a scheme to enable first-time purchasers to pay less in the early years of their mortgage. We shall also seek other new ways to help young married couples to become home-owners earlier, including new ways of channelling the funds of leading financial institutions into the finance of house purchase.
- We will provide new powers and more funds for the Housing Corporation and the voluntary housing movement. This will provide dwellings for both letting and

co-ownership, and include new arrangements for people with special housing problems.

- We shall provide more houses for renting in areas of housing need.
- We will ensure that both the local authorities and nationalised industries release housing land for mixed schemes of public and private development.
- We will continue with our slum clearance programme designed to clear the slums by 1982.
- We will continue our programme to improve older houses and will give extra incentives for the selective improvement of areas of bad housing stress. Legislation will be carried through to give greater emphasis to the housing needs of inner urban areas.
- We will strengthen action to cope with homelessness in areas of special need by co-operation with the local authorities in the efficient use of existing permanent and temporary accommodation and the provision of specially designed hostels.
- We intend to pay particular attention to the housing needs of the elderly and the disabled who often need sheltered housing.

Our Housing Finance Act has, for the first time, brought fairness between one tenant and another by concentrating help with the rent on those areas and those families who most need it. Today, by law, and for the first time, every family in a rented home – whether council or private, unfurnished or furnished – can get such help if they need it.

This help has to be paid for. This has meant rent increases for the better off tenants who had hitherto often been enjoying bigger subsidies than many poorer families. But with nearly two million tenants already receiving rent rebates or allowances, a large number of families are now paying less rent than before the Act was passed.

At present, owner-occupiers with more rooms than they need are deterred from letting, unfurnished, any part of their houses. We will consider whether to remedy this by restoring to them the ability to regain possession. This would help provide more accommodation for renting.

- We will keep security of tenure for all those who already have it.
- We have announced the severest financial penalties ever on property profiteering, with special reference to empty office buildings.

Gains by individuals from the development value of property will now be subject to income tax, up to the top rate of 75 per cent, in place of the former flat rate of 30 per cent. As before, this will not apply to the principal home of an owner-occupier. Development gains by companies will be taxed as income at the full 40 per cent Corporation Tax rate, instead of 30 per cent. For the first time unrealised gains from property will be taxed by treating the first letting as a disposal for tax purposes.

We are also committed to taking new powers to deal with empty office premises. These will enable the Minister to take possession of, and manage, premises that have been unoccupied for more than two years. In addition, local authorities will be empowered to levy rates on unoccupied buildings at up to 100 per cent, and at a higher rate than this for certain empty commercial premises.

We wholly reject Labour's policy of preventing any further extension of freehold home-ownership by the nationalisation of every acre of land for new building.

Improving the environment

Right at the start of the last Parliament we set up, for the first time, a Department of the Environment, which remains the only such ministry in the world with so wide a range of powers and resources. As a result, we are now acknowledged world leaders in environmental action in caring for towns, cities, villages, rivers and the countryside.

Conservative policy is to protect our environment where it is good, and to improve it where it is not good enough. We have already done much to achieve this. The Green Belt has been greatly extended. More than 100 new country parks have been opened since 1970. 'Operation Eyesore' has improved the local environment in thousands of towns and villages. Millions more trees have been planted. For every acre of derelict land cleared each year under Labour, we have cleared over three. We have set up a Nature Conservancy Council.

Clean air policy was at a standstill when Labour left office; we have more than doubled the number of Smoke Control Orders, bringing clean air and more sunlight to millions more people, especially in the North. Labour neglected the rivers – we have been improving their condition at an average rate of nearly three miles a week.

To reduce, still further, pollution of all kinds, we shall carry forward our legislation to cut down noise and establish quiet zones in urban areas; to accelerate the cleaning up of our rivers and estuaries; to curb fumes and smoke from vehicles; and to deal more efficiently with waste, especially toxic waste. We shall encourage the recycling of waste so as to conserve scarce resources and reduce imports.

- We shall further extend and protect the Green Belt.
- We shall strengthen the legislation necessary to protect and extend conservation areas, protect historic buildings and their gardens, control demolition, and preserve more carefully trees and archeological sites.
- To supplement conservation areas in the towns and cities, we shall empower local authorities to designate environmental and amenity areas in all parts of the country.
- We shall continue our drive to bring derelict land back into beneficial use. We shall further strengthen the Countryside Commission.

Transport

Continued growth of traffic has brought with it problems as well as advantages; and has in particular made necessary an increasing reliance on public transport. We have recently announced a massive five-year programme for the railways to provide a modern network with a secure future and the opportunity to regain freight traffic from the roads.

- We shall modify the bus licensing system so as to give greater freedom for new forms of local transport in country areas, while safeguarding existing services.
- We are already working to establish a system of lorry routes to keep heavy vehicles

out of towns and villages and away from narrow country lanes where they have no business to be. With this as our priority, we shall complete the major road network as soon as the economic situation allows.

- We have given the new county authorities powers to enable them to fix their own transport strategies and priorities.
- We will continue to take all possible steps to diminish noise and other nuisances caused by new roads and the traffic which uses them.

Better education

Conservatives have accorded high priority in the national budget to the needs of education. Above all we are concerned to provide not merely more education but better education. Better education is not only a matter of resources. It is a matter of standards and of attitudes.

We have advanced in every sector of education but have attached special importance to primary schools, believing that it is the early years that so often determine a child's future progress. In the next Parliament we shall continue to give priority to the early years of education.

We shall gradually extend free nursery schooling throughout the country so that within ten years it should be available for all three- and four-year-old children whose parents wish them to have it. We shall encourage pre-school playgroups; their emphasis on involving the parent is particularly valuable.

Our second priority will continue to be special schools for the handicapped. We have substantially increased the building programme for new schools. Work will soon begin on the enquiry into special education which was announced at the end of 1973.

In secondary education we shall continue to judge local education authorities' proposals for changing the character of schools on their merits, paying special regard to the wishes of parents and the retention of parental choice. We believe it to be educationally unwise to impose a universal system of comprehensive education on the entire country. Local education authorities should allow genuine scope for parental choice, and we shall continue to use our powers to give as much choice as possible.

- We will defend the fundamental right of parents to spend their money on their children's education should they wish to do so.
- We shall continue to support the direct grant schools. They have helped to provide increased opportunities for able children irrespective of their parents' means.
- We shall maintain the right of parents to choose denominational education for their children if they so wish.

The expansion of further and higher education will be less rapid than planned because of the reduced demand for places and the prevailing economic circumstances, but numbers will continue to increase. The review of students' grants is proceeding and we shall continue to improve the parental income scale so that parents on a given income will pay less towards the grant.

As soon as economic circumstances permit, we will improve the opportunities for adult education in the light of the Russell Report.

We believe that the aims of the Youth Service should be more clearly defined. We shall, therefore, be discussing its future development with the local authorities and voluntary bodies who mostly provide this service, and aim to ensure that decisions about the future of the Service take fully into account the views of the young people themselves. Given the right impetus, the Youth Service can do a great deal to widen the scope for young people to play a full and constructive part in local affairs and activities wherever they live and work.

Because of our concern over reading standards in schools we have set up an enquiry under Sir Alan Bullock to report on all aspects of the teaching of English, including the written and spoken word. The conclusions are expected later in the year. A research study on mathematical standards is also in hand.

We share the public concern about indiscipline and truancy. Investigations are being conducted into these problems, and we shall examine their findings as a matter of urgency.

Higher standards of education can only be achieved through more and better trained teachers. There are now some 60,000 more teachers in the schools than there were three years ago; we are carrying out the objectives of the James Report, which was itself set up as a result of a promise in our last manifesto.

We wish to move the debate away from the kind of school which children attend and concentrate on the kind of education they receive.

The arts, broadcasting and recreation

We shall continue to give the fullest support and encouragement to the arts, on which we are already spending £50 million a year, more in fact than any previous government. At a time when economic stringency is necessarily limiting our material objectives it is more important than ever to improve the quality of life.

The arts must be centred on the nation not on the capital. Generous grants have gone to the regions in the past. Major arts centres will be established in Cardiff and Edinburgh.

In accordance with the pledge in our 1970 election manifesto, we are introducing a network of independent local radio stations, under the general supervision of the Independent Broadcasting Authority, with local newspaper participation. Four of these stations are already in operation. We will bring forward proposals for the allocation of a fourth TV channel when economic circumstances permit.

We shall give further impetus to the Sports Council, whose powers and funds we have already greatly expanded. Professional football clubs as well as amateur sports organisations will be encouraged to join with local authorities and voluntary bodies in the redevelopment of town centre grounds for multi-purpose recreational needs.

Protecting the rights of the individual

The rights of the individual citizen need to be protected both against the power of the State and against other large and powerful bodies – whether commercial undertakings, trade unions, or any other centre of power. We have recognised this need in our measures so far, and will continue to do so in the next Parliament.

We have acted decisively to protect the individual consumer. We have passed the Fair Trading Act to increase the powers of the new Monopolies and Mergers Commission and set up a Director-General of Fair Trading, under the Act, to deal with unfair trading practices of all kinds. We have legislated to impose stricter standards on insurance companies. We have, for the first time, appointed a Cabinet Minister for Consumer Affairs, and have introduced new legislation to prevent the consumer from having his legal rights undermined by the small print of so-called 'guarantees'. We have also legislated against the abuse known as pyramid selling. We have made it easier for consumers to get cheap and speedy settlement of small claims in the County Courts.

In the next Parliament, we shall continue to act in defence of the consumer over a broad front. We will act to improve the effectiveness of the nationalised industry consumer councils, to prevent confusion over metrication by insisting on specific unit pricing of goods in the shops, and in a wide range of other fields. In particular, we shall bring forward the Consumer Credit Bill, which will require hire purchase agreements to show the true rate of interest, prevent the unsolicited mailing of credit cards, and, in general, comprehensively reform the law on consumer credit.

We shall carry through our proposals for new legislation to reform company law by requiring of companies a much fuller disclosure of information to the individual – whether shareholder, employee or a member of the general public. By this measure, we will make British free enterprise the most open in the world. We will have created a system of free enterprise more socially responsible to the public, and with the power of the consumer greatly enhanced.

- We have appointed a Health Service Commissioner or 'ombudsman' to investigate individual complaints about the National Health Service. We will be introducing a similar system for complaints against local authorities.
- Citizens' rights in Britain are far more extensive than most citizens' awareness of those rights. This is particularly serious in the deprived central areas of many of our large cities. In these and other 'stress' areas we shall set up comprehensive advice centres, readily accessible to those who need help.
- We have substantially improved the arrangements for consulting the public in advance of major planning decisions, such as large redevelopment schemes and the route to be followed by road schemes.
- We have greatly extended the scope of compensation payable to those whose property is adversely affected by developments such as road schemes. We have provided for special extra compensation payments where a home-owner or a tenant loses his home as a result of development.
- We shall also reform the licensing laws in the light both of the Erroll Report and of public reaction to it.
- We have legislated to remove discrimination against women over a wide range of the law.
- We have introduced equal rights of guardianship for women.
- We have taken special steps to ensure that movement towards equal pay for women is not held back by the provisions of our counter-inflation policy.
- We have improved the enforcement of maintenance payments to divorced or deserted wives.
- We will introduce major new legislation to end discrimination against women at work, and to set up an Equal Opportunities Commission to investigate other aspects of discrimination against women, and to recommend further action.

- We have taken steps to bring about more effective co-ordination of the work of local authority social workers, doctors, teachers and all relevant professional staff in detecting and preventing the ill-treatment of small children. We will urgently study the report of the Committee of Enquiry into the death of Maria Colwell, to see what further measures may be needed.
- We shall strengthen existing safeguards in relation to the adoption of children, following broadly the recommendations of the Houghton Report.
- We shall introduce a reform of the abortion law, in the light of the forthcoming Lane Committee Report.
- We will also, where necessary, act to ease restraints on publication under the present laws of contempt of court and defamation where these restraints do not infringe the rights of the individual. We will bring forward proposals to preserve the privacy of the citizen against unauthorised or unjustifiable intrusion, in the light of the Younger Report.

Other achievements and proposals concerned with the rights of the individual citizen appear elsewhere in this manifesto. Indeed the preservation and enhancement of individual freedom within a framework of responsibility are an underlying theme of all Conservative policy.

It is expressed in our determination to keep taxation as low as possible, so as to give the individual wage-earner greater freedom to spend or save what he earns as he thinks fit; in our Industrial Relations Act that gives new rights to individual trade unionists; in our proposals for giving employees a right of participation in the firms for which they work; in the importance we attach to parental choice in education; and in a housing policy that emphasises the freedom and independence that comes from home-ownership.

Local government

- We have carried through the most important reforms of local government this century. We will continue those reforms by the appointment of local ombudsmen.
- We will review the electoral provisions for London boroughs in the context of the arrangements for the rest of the country.
- We favour a frank disclosure of local government finances to the people; for example, the publication by each local authority of a Balance Sheet, a Budget Statement, and annual spending programmes. Local government services have continued to expand during our term of office, but we have increased central Government's help to the ratepayers to meet the costs of that expansion. We have substantially increased rate relief to the householder. Three million ratepayers will benefit from the more generous rate rebate scheme we have introduced.
- We will, if necessary, change the law and practice relating to the conduct of members and officers in local government wherever the possibility arises of a conflict between their official positions and their private interests.
- We will strengthen and improve the regional offices of Government. Local authorities and the regional economic planning councils will be encouraged to work more closely together so that the views and needs of the regions can more effectively influence national decisions.

- We are studying the Report of the Kilbrandon Commission.
- We are publishing separate manifestos for Scotland and Wales.

Law and order

Protection of the law-abiding citizen is a prime duty of the State. We have given higher priority to the support of law and order and the reduction of crime than any Government for many years. The overall volume of crime in the country has been dropping for the first time for nearly 20 years, and although within this total, crimes of violence are still rising alarmingly there are some encouraging signs even in this field – for example, the marked drop in 1973 in the number of robberies and muggings.

- We have increased and strengthened the police force. In real terms we are spending today over 15 per cent more on the police than in 1970. For the first time we have over 100,000 men and women in the Police Forces of England and Wales and they are backed up by an extra 7,000 civilians.
- We have reviewed the powers available to the Courts. We have increased the maximum penalties for offences involving the use of firearms and for crimes of vandalism. We have widened and strengthened the powers of the Courts to order convicted criminals to compensate their victims. We have provided new non-custodial forms of punishment whereby offenders can be required to do useful work for the community.
- We have substantially increased the size of the Probation Service and will continue to do so.

In the next Parliament we shall continue to give the highest priority to policies aimed at reducing crime and supporting freedom under the law. The further strengthening of the police will be of particular importance.

- We shall maintain the impetus of our measures of law reform. We shall review the law against violent crime in the light of the Criminal Law Revision Committee's forthcoming report on offences against the person. We will further improve the legal aid and advisory services.
- We will place the Criminal Injuries Compensation Scheme, first introduced by a Conservative Government, on a permanent statutory basis.
- We shall provide for the introduction of an independent element in the procedure for complaints against the police.
- The growing display of indecent material in public places gives offence to many people. Accordingly, we shall bring forward our Bill to prohibit this, and to tighten up the law against sending through the post unsolicited matter of an indecent nature.
- We shall reform and liberalize the Official Secrets Acts, while retaining those provisions essential for the protection of national security.

Having reviewed the law on picketing, we have come to the conclusion that the present law as recently clarified by the Courts is adequate both to protect the right of genuinely peaceful picketing and to penalise abuse. But we believe that the lawful limits to peaceful picketing need to be more clearly and widely known. We shall therefore publish a document setting out the law on this subject in the belief that this will be an assistance both to the observance and enforcement of the law.

We deplore the encouragement to politically-motivated law-breaking given by the Labour Party's pledge to remove, retrospectively, the penalties incurred by Clay Cross councillors for serious breaches of the Housing Finance Act. A Conservative Government will continue to uphold the rule of law.

As a people, we live in the freest democracy in the world, with a tradition of individual liberty within the law and of peaceful change. If that tradition is to be maintained, as we are determined that it shall be, it must not be abused. In particular, we reaffirm our conviction that a criminal act does not cease to be criminal by virtue of being committed ostensibly for political ends.

Immigration and race relations

By passing the 1971 Immigration Act, against the combined opposition of the Labour and Liberal Parties, we have provided the country with the necessary means for preventing any further large-scale permanent immigration and also with important new powers for preventing illegal immigration. The Act became fully operative in January 1973 and its effects in reinforcing all the other administrative action we have taken are already becoming evident. Thus the number of new immigrants admitted in 1973 was the lowest since control was first introduced by the previous Conservative Government more than a decade ago.

We intend that this decline shall continue. At the same time within this declining figure we are honouring our obligations to the categories of people in the Commonwealth for whom we have special responsibilities – namely the close dependent relatives of immigrants settled here lawfully before the new Act came into force and those people who, because of our imperial past, possess citizenship of this country and no other.

We have also set in hand a review of British nationality law, and dependent on its outcome, new legislation to replace present British Nationality Acts may be one of the measures required in the life of the next Parliament.

When we came to power in 1970, there were about 1.5 million coloured people lawfully and permanently settled in this country. The great majority are here to stay. Their children are being born and brought up here and Britain is the only country they know as their own. The harmony of our society in the future depends to an important extent on the white majority and the coloured minority living and working together on equal terms and with equal opportunities. We shall therefore pursue positive policies to promote good race relations.

The first need for this purpose was to reassure everyone that new immigration was being brought down to a small and inescapable minimum. But beyond that we shall take further action to improve conditions in the stress areas in the centres of many of our industrial towns and cities where immigrant communities frequently concentrate and where the local inhabitants have long had to endure poor housing and a deprived environment.

Working for peace in Northern Ireland

For the best part of five years now, our British soldiers have carried out their duties superbly. Despite every kind of difficulty and provocation, they have succeeded, with exemplary restraint, in restoring and maintaining a substantial measure of law and order, in crushing the terrorist IRA leadership in Northern Ireland, and in creating the conditions that have made a political solution possible. No other army in the world could have achieved what they have done: no praise is too high for them.

In March 1972 conditions in Northern Ireland had reached the point where we were obliged temporarily to suspend the Province's Parliament and institute a period of direct rule from Westminster, appointing a Secretary of State for Northern Ireland. After almost two years of unceasing effort, the extremists were isolated and a reconciliation was brought about between the responsible political leaders of the Protestant and Catholic communities in the Province.

This eventually resulted in a successful agreement at the tripartite meeting at Sunningdale in December 1973.

In spite of the violence in Northern Ireland, industry there has shown a remarkable resilience. In 1973 unemployment dropped substantially, the number of industrial disputes was the lowest for a decade, and the rate of growth of industrial production was the highest in the United Kingdom. These achievements were made possible by a massive programme of Government aid and by the united determination of workers and management in the Province.

On January 1, 1974 the new Northern Ireland Executive took office. It is still a tender plant. But the fact remains that those who used to be political opponents are today working together on the new Executive in Northern Ireland to bring a better life to their strife-torn Province.

This has been possible, above all, as a result of firm but fair Government action which has succeeded, against all the odds, in mobilising the silent majority of moderate opinion in Northern Ireland to assert itself against extremists of all kinds.

In the next Parliament we shall continue, in the same spirit, to build on the progress we have already achieved.

Britain, Europe and the world

The prime objective of our foreign policy is to preserve peace and maintain the security and prosperity of the British nation. In order to achieve this we need friends and allies. In the last 4 years, sometimes in very difficult circumstances, Britain has made or consolidated friendships in the Far East, China, the Indian Sub-Continent, Africa and the American Continent. Progress has lately been made in re-establishing a proper relationship with the Soviet Union. A successful Commonwealth Conference has recently been held in Ottawa.

Above all, by successfully negotiating British membership of the European Community, we achieved a major national objective which had eluded successive British Governments of both Parties for more than a decade.

We have now been a member of the Community for a little over a year. While it is therefore far too soon to attempt a complete assessment of the implications for Britain of this historic step forward, it is already clear that we are better able to secure our national interests both economic and political within the Community than would have been possible had we remained outside. Firms throughout the country have felt the benefit of British membership for their export trade.

Every aspect of world affairs underlines the need for a Europe which is united and can carry the maximum weight in the councils of the world. Whatever our internal differences, we must increasingly learn to speak strongly with one voice which can be heard among the greatest powers, and which can play its part in evolving mutually beneficial policies towards the rest of the world, including the developing countries. This is what membership of the Community is about. It means increasing economic strength for each member and above all the certainty that there will be partnership instead of rivalry and no more wars having their origin in Western Europe.

Meanwhile, by its very nature, the Community continues to develop and evolve. In particular, just as Britain has to adapt to the Community, so the Community has to adapt to Britain.

Since becoming a member, we have been a full and effective participant in the making of Community decisions. We have made it clear that we are not satisfied with every aspect of Community arrangements, and have sought – and will continue to seek – changes where these are desirable.

A Conservative Government will urge on our Community partners the need to extend the scope of Community action into industrial policy, technological collaboration and social and environmental questions. This is necessary if the full benefits of the larger market are to be reaped, and if we are to realise the full potential of the Community as an instrument for improving the life of the people.

We have already been instrumental in securing a decision in principle to set up a European Regional Development Fund, a considerable proportion of which will be devoted to helping the less prosperous regions of Britain. We have been pressing hard within the Community for a sizeable fund, and a decision is to be taken early this year.

The Community's Common Agricultural Policy provides British agriculture with very real opportunities for expansion. But in a number of ways the Common Agricultural Policy is now manifestly in need of reform; and we shall continue to work so that the necessary changes can be made.

The Conservative delegation to the European Assembly has already made a telling impact. We shall continue to work for ways in which the Community's institutions can be improved in order to make them more responsive to public opinion and to reinforce democratic control. Meanwhile, we will ensure that Parliament at Westminster can play a full and effective part in the consideration of Community proposals in their formative stage.

Renegotiation of the Community in the sense of reforming its practice and redefining Britain's place in it, is a continuous process, which can only be conducted from within, and in which we are already playing a full part. Renegotiation in the sense of British withdrawal, which is what a section of the Labour Party seeks, would be a disaster for which future generations would never forgive us.

Community membership has been of major importance for our foreign and defence policy as a whole, providing us with a new dimension and a new voice in world affairs. We reaffirm our full support for the Atlantic Alliance within which we shall continue to seek still closer European co-operation in defence and procurement.

The problems presented to Europe and all the developed and developing countries by the increased price of oil need to be tackled both in Europe and through wider international consultation. A new understanding must be sought between consumers and producers in which plans for industrial development and investment to mutual advantage would play an important part.

We shall continue to play our full part in the United Nations. We shall continue to maintain close relations with our fellow-members of the Commonwealth, based on a common heritage and mutual independence. We shall seek to play our part in helping economic development in the poorer parts of the world. It is essential for Britain as a trading nation that the momentum of development in the Third World should not slacken.

We remain committed to try to reach a settlement in Rhodesia in accordance with the five principles. We trust that, meanwhile, Europeans and Africans in Rhodesia will make rapid progress towards agreement on constitutional changes which would enable independence to be granted by the British Parliament and sanctions to be lifted.

We shall seek to help the cause of peace in the Middle East. We reaffirm our belief that the integrity of the State of Israel must be maintained, and at the same time we will continue to give our support for withdrawal from occupied territories, in accordance with the relevant resolutions of the United Nations.

We will continue to play a full part in the negotiations over Mutual and Balanced Force Reductions and in the Conference on Security and Co-operation in Europe where we will insist on some movement in the field of an increased flow of information and ideas and people between East and West. While progress towards détente must be our purpose we note with concern the continuing expansion of all branches of the Soviet armed forces – especially its rocket forces and its navies on the high seas. We therefore need to maintain the NATO alliance and ensure that it is sufficiently strong to deter any breach of the peace.

We shall maintain the effectiveness of the British nuclear deterrent. We shall continue to ensure that the morale and effectiveness of our armed forces are maintained at the highest possible level. This is vital if we are to retain our security, which is essential to all our aspirations.

The alternative – and the choice

We have set out in this manifesto our proposals both for dealing with the grave crisis now facing the nation and for building, once the crisis is overcome, on the solid progress made before it broke. We believe that these proposals – firm but fair, based on realism and moderation – are what the British people desire and the situation demands. They are also utterly different from those of the Labour Party.

The Labour Party today faces the nation committed to a left-wing programme more dangerous and more extreme than ever before in its history. This commitment to extremism is no accident. In part, it has occurred as a reaction against the manifest failure of its policies of gimmickry and so-called pragmatism when it was last in office. But, even more, it has occurred because the moderates within Labour's ranks have lost control, and the real power in the Labour Party has been taken over, for the first time ever, by its extreme Left wing. And this in turn has been made possible by the dominance of a small group of power-hungry trade union leaders, whose creature the Labour Party has now become.

The Labour Party today is committed to massive increases in taxation for all – rich and poor alike – not simply as a means to an end, but as an end in itself. It is pledged to increase income tax, not just for the 'rich', but for millions of ordinary wage and salary earners. It has threatened to increase VAT on a wide range of household goods and services, which would bring particular hardship to those less well off. It has promised to levy heavier taxes on the self-employed.

Labour's policy for industry is one of massive nationalisation on an unprecedented scale. In addition to taking over a number of named industries, Labour is pledged to nationalise key firms in other industries and threatens to take over any profitable firm throughout manufacturing industry. In what would remain of private industry, it is explicitly committed to taking power to issue arbitrary State 'directives' to any company and, if it sees fit, to put in a Government 'trustee' to run the firm. It has also talked glibly of nationalising banks, building societies and insurance companies – which would mean taking over the savings of the people.

Labour is committed to an irresponsible programme of public expenditure, costing on its own admission some £6,000 million a year, over and above the huge cost of its nationalisation plans. This was far in excess of what the national economy could afford even before the present crisis. In education, it seeks doctrinaire uniformity throughout the State system, and would abolish the independent schools. It is similarly committed to abolishing freedom of choice in medical care. It is committed to preventing any further extension of freehold home ownership, by taking over all the land on which future homes can be built. It is also committed to indemnifying, at the taxpayers' and ratepayers' expense, those law-breakers of whom it politically approves. Never before in its history has the Labour Party shown such open contempt for the rule of law.

The total effect of Labour's present policies would be to wreck the economy, undermine the free society, and accelerate the present inflation beyond the point of no return. It has no effective policy whatever for dealing with the crucial problem of wage inflation. It is committed to abandoning the legally-backed pay and prices policy; but all it has to put in its place are the outdated and divisive nostrums of class warfare.

It is not surprising that the moderates in Labour's ranks, who formerly held the balance of power in their bitterly divided Party, opposed each and every one of these extremist policies. But on each and every occasion, the moderates were defeated by the now ascendant Left wing, and these policies became firm official commitments. However slick the public relations smokescreen, this is the reality of declared Labour Party policy – and they mean what they said.

In short, the return of a Labour Government at the present time would be nothing short of a major national disaster. The choice before the nation today, as never before, is a clear choice between moderation and extremism. We therefore appeal, at this critical time in our country's affairs, for the support of the great moderate majority of the British people, men and women of all Parties and no Party, who reject extremism in any shape or form. For extremism divides, while moderation unites; and it is only on the basis of national unity that the present crisis can be overcome and a better Britain built.

PUTTING BRITAIN FIRST

A national policy from the Conservatives

CONSERVATIVE PARTY GENERAL ELECTION MANIFESTO OCTOBER 1974

Putting Britain first

Date of Election	Thursday 10 October
Party Leader	Edward Heath
Candidates	623
MPs	277
Votes	10,464,817
% of vote	35.8%

A national policy

The dangers now facing Britain are greater than any we have seen since the last war. These dangers are both economic and political.

Over recent months prices have been rising at an annual rate of over 20 per cent, and on present policies they will rise as much next year. This means that in two years the pound will be worth only 55p. Unemployment is rising rapidly, and the deficit in our balance of payments this year will be £4,000 million. By the end of the 1970s, on present forecasts, we are likely to owe £15,000 million for oil alone.

At the same time the rule of law is threatened, and there are conflicts within the nation. If we do not solve our economic problems, our political difficulties will be made worse. And if we do not tackle our political problems, our economic problems will be insoluble. Our main aim therefore is to safeguard the existence of our free society.

For inflation at its present pace threatens not only the standard of living of everybody in the country, but also the survival of our free and democratic institutions. No major democracy has ever survived such a catastrophic rise in the cost of living. We cannot be sure that we would be the exception.

In any case inflation and rising prices tear society apart. They destroy the confidence of people in one another and the future; they distort the existing relationships within our country; they poison the social environment; they wipe out people's savings; they imperil our economic system; they lead in the end to high unemployment and to widespread, if not national, bankruptcy; and they bring particular hardship and misery to the most vulnerable people in the land.

And that is not all. Another consequence of inflation is that financial manipulations often provide much greater scope for gain than solid hard work. This in itself breeds disillusionment and frustration. Lack of confidence in the currency leads to lessening respect for the law: hence sectional groups are starting to take the law into their own hands and to pursue their ends with a ruthless disregard for the interests of others.

Finally, inflation weakens international confidence in sterling and intensifies the balance of payments crisis. In a few years time North Sea oil should give us an advantage over many of our competitors. But if we rely too much on borrowing from abroad to finance our payments deficit, our gains from North Sea oil will be mortgaged for many years ahead, and our hopes for prosperity based upon that oil will be dashed.

Inflation is therefore a moral and political evil as well as a social and economic evil. Everything else is secondary to the battle against inflation and to helping those who have been wounded in it.

There is no quick or simple way of defeating inflation. We do not claim to have any easy solution. Indeed, no government can beat inflation by itself.

The only way the battle can be won is by the Government and the people of this country uniting on a national policy. In the interest of national unity we will not reintroduce the Industrial Relations Act. Equally, no government should pursue a policy of wholesale nationalisation for party ends nor seek to further the interests of only a section or a class of the population. And certainly our economic condition is far too grave for our country to be subjected to a divisive and dogmatic attack upon the private enterprise sector of our economy.

Inflation has dogged Britain since the war because as a country we have too often paid ourselves more than we earn. Lately this chronic inflation has been made acute by the explosion in the world price of food and raw materials.

We need to bring back confidence in our currency; we need to stop paying ourselves more than we produce; and we need to produce more than we have produced in the past. To restore confidence in our currency we propose a comprehensive price stabilisation programme. This will use every tolerable means available to fight inflation. We will rigorously control public spending and the money supply and there must be restraint in prices and incomes.

Because of the economic crisis there is no room for any early improvement in living standards. But our aim is to protect people's real income as far as it is possible to do so – by increasing pensions and other long-term benefits every six months, by developing new forms of savings protected against inflation, and by pay arrangements which take account of rises in the cost of living.

This is a far better way of protecting the interests of people at work than the excessive increases in some wage settlements over the last few months. These merely feed inflation and lead eventually to heavy unemployment. We believe that our attempt to protect the real value of wages, combined with the responsible self-interest of trade unions, should make a voluntary policy on pay and prices effective. But no government could honestly say that it will never be necessary to use the law in the national interest to support an effective policy for fighting inflation. In the absence of a viable prices and incomes policy any government would have to take harsher financial and economic measures than would otherwise be needed.

Restraint and restriction are only palliatives. The best way of solving Britain's economic problems is by increasing our productivity and expanding British agriculture. It is only by producing more wealth that we can significantly help those who need help: the poor, the sick and the old. There is enormous scope for improving productivity, and our taxation and industrial policies will be directed towards this objective.

Yet only part of our troubles are economic, and inflation is not the only threat to our free way of life. Modern industrial society is fragile. It is vulnerable to the terrorist and the anarchist. But at present an even greater danger is the short-sighted selfishness of some powerful groups. The great technological advances of this century have closely integrated our economy and the whole organisation of national life. This integration has brought immense material advantages, but by laying society open to disruption it has brought weakness as well. The whole is at the mercy of a part to an extent unimagined even a few years ago. Nevertheless no part of the nation can exist by itself. Disruption may bring temporary advantage to a few, but all are hurt in the end. The nation is diminished and impoverished by it.

Trade unions are an important estate of the realm. We shall co-operate closely with them, and we hope that our proposals for industrial partnership will lead to close and effective co-operation both with employees and management. But we shall not be dominated by the trade unions. They are not the government of the country.

We believe that the survival of a mixed economy is vital to national prosperity. If all economic power were in the hands of politicians and civil servants, if all economic and industrial decisions were taken in Whitehall, Britain would become a dictatorship. An all-powerful government is the end of freedom.

A mixed economy ensures the diffusion of power. That is the only way we can prevent the abuse of power. Hence, the destruction of the mixed economy would entail the destruction of our democratic liberties, and the end of our parliamentary democracy.

Obviously the struggle against inflation and the gravity of Britain's economic predicament prevent us from doing immediately all the things we should like to do. Like everyone else, governments must practise restraint.

In the present economic emergency it would be irresponsible for any government to pretend that there can be general increases in public spending in real terms. This means having to postpone many of the things we would like to do straightaway. Only as we overcome our economic difficulties will it be possible to carry through the proposals in the second part of this Manifesto which involve expenditure. These proposals therefore are all subject to this important qualification.

But we will act now in three areas which have been particularly hard hit by inflation and which in one way or another affect the basic livelihood of every family in the country – pensions, housing and food production. Our plans for these, which are set out later, will cost money; and in order to prevent inflationary consequences, it may be necessary to make cuts in public spending or increases in taxation. But as Britain's economic position improves, our general objective will be to reduce the burden of taxation.

Our policies will lead to a united nation. We shall uphold the law and the authority of Parliament. It is in Parliament, not in the streets, that national policies must be worked out and disputes resolved.

Our nation still possesses great moral reserves. Our patriotism, our knowledge that what unites us is far more significant than what divides us, our pride in our way of life and in our institutions, our sense of history, our idealism, our wish to make our country better and to improve the lot of our fellow citizens – all these feelings and beliefs remain strong in Britain. But they can only be properly summoned to the service of our nation by a government that commands the confidence of the country because it puts the country first.

The Conservative Party, free from dogma and free from dependence upon any single interest, is broadly based throughout the nation. It is our objective to win a clear majority in the House of Commons in this election. But we will use that majority above all to unite the nation. We will not govern in a narrow partisan spirit. After the election we will consult and confer with the leaders of other parties and with the leaders of the great interests in the nation, in order to secure for the government's policies the consent and support of all men and women of good will. We will invite people from outside the ranks of our party to join with us in overcoming Britain's difficulties. The nation's crisis should transcend party differences.

In any event, as a national Party we will pursue a national policy in the interests of the nation as a whole. We will lead a national effort. In normal times the party struggle is the safeguard of freedom. But the times are far from normal. In a crisis like this, it is the national interest which must prevail. We will ensure that it does. For all the people.

The challenge

We believe that, working together as a nation, we can solve our problems. It will not be easy. It will demand restraint and sacrifice. It will mean postponing some of our plans and recognising that we shall only be able to do all the things we want if our economic and industrial policies succeed. That should not prevent us planning for the future; and in this second part of the manifesto we set out some of our longer-term and more ambitious aims in addition to our immediate proposals for tackling the crisis.

Paying for our programme

If we are going to make further advances in both individual prosperity and social provision, then we need first to set our economic house in order. But there are some things – housing, pensions and food production – which we believe have to be done now. In order to pay for these extra commitments immediately we may have either to make public spending cuts elsewhere or to raise taxes to meet the cost. But our general objective for taxes is simple: we aim to lower them. We are happy for this promise to be matched against our record. Nevertheless, we give warning that in the present economic climate it might prove necessary to raise some taxes in order to pay for immediate objectives.

Politics is about people

Our plans are firmly rooted in our belief that government and politics are about people. As Conservatives, we have always acted on the principle that government has a clear responsibility to help and protect those who cannot look after themselves. At the same time, we believe that the strength and value of any society lie in individual freedom, effort and achievement. These complementary themes are more relevant than ever today.

People feel increasingly frustrated and even oppressed by the impact on their lives of remote bureaucracy, and of events which seem to be entirely beyond their control or that of our democratic institutions. What is more, there is a serious political challenge from the Left to that fine balance between economic freedom and social provision which has made this country such a civilised place to live in: the balance between giving everyone the chance to achieve and excel and looking after those who cannot look after themselves.

We do not believe that the great majority of people want revolutionary change in society, or for that matter that the future happiness of our society depends on completely altering it. There is no majority for a massive extension of nationalisation. There is no majority for the continued harrying of private enterprise. There is no majority for penalising those who save, own property or make profits. People are not clamouring for Whitehall to seize even greater control over their lives. They want more choice and diversity, not less.

People want to be helped to achieve, not encouraged to envy. They want a decent home – and most of them want to own it themselves. They want security for their families. They want to be fairly rewarded for hard and responsible and useful work. They want to be protected from the ravages of inflation. They want decent schools for their children and a say in how they are taught. They want to be able to retire in comfort, free from financial worries. They want to live in a society where excellence and compassion go hand in hand, and where the rules and the laws are made and upheld by the free Parliament of a free people. The achievement of such a society will be the aim of the next Conservative government.

PEOPLE AND PRICES

The first priority

The first priority for any government must be to defend the value of the currency and to bring inflation down from the present ruinous rates. This cannot be done overnight; it cannot be done by using only one weapon; and it cannot be done without united effort. If it is not done, the effects on every family will be calamitous.

Controlling public spending

We will bring in a comprehensive price stabilisation programme which will use every tolerable means available to fight inflation. There must be restraint in prices and incomes and we will rigorously control public spending and the money supply, which is a vital, though not the only, part of our counter-inflation armoury. We will look hard at local government expenditure which has rocketed in the last few years.

The Price Commission

We will continue the work of the Price Commission, which we set up, but we will review the Price Code to make it more flexible, to stimulate investment and to help provide jobs. In a time of roaring inflation, price controls are necessary. But if they are too rigid, the money needed by companies to stimulate investment and to help provide jobs dries up. More efficient industrial effort is to the long-term advantage of the consumer. We will also encourage competition between companies and will build on the reforms introduced by our Fair Trading Act.

Incomes

Every reasonable person knows that if we pay ourselves higher wages than we can afford, sooner or later we shall have to pay higher bills than we can afford. There is the very real danger of a worsening wages explosion this autumn and winter at precisely the time when world prices are starting to ease. At the moment when we might stand a chance of getting on top of inflation, it would be madness to give another twist to the inflationary spiral. We must therefore as a matter of urgency, work out with the trade unions and the employers a fair and effective policy for prices and incomes. We believe that the great majority of the trade union movement will be prepared to work with the democratically elected government of the country for the public good. If after all our efforts we fail to get a comprehensive voluntary policy, we shall need to support the voluntary restraint that is achieved with the back-up of the law. It would be irresponsible and dishonest totally to rule this out, but the various methods no less than the principle would need to be widely discussed. In the absence of an effective prices and incomes policy any Government would have to take harsher financial and economic measures than would otherwise be necessary.

A better industrial forum

To build a more responsible partnership between government, the unions and the employers, we must strengthen the existing National Economic Development Council as a better industrial forum. One of its main tasks will be to discuss how much of the nation's resources are available for pay, for investment, for exports and for public spending.

Fairer rewards for hard work and responsibility

We would also try to reach an agreement on a new, fair and sensible system for adjusting the relative rates of pay between different groups without adding to inflation. There is a widespread acceptance that those who do particularly demanding work should enjoy an improvement in their relative pay. Yet without some national, independent body on pay relativities, this kind of improvement will prove difficult if not impossible.

Income protection

For our price stabilisation programme to succeed, it must enjoy the consent of the British people. This means offering them some assurance of income protection so that, as far as possible, incomes keep pace with the cost of living to help safeguard real living standards. Our programme involves:

- Moving from an annual to a six-monthly increase in retirement pensions, public service pensions and other long-term benefits.
- Seeking new forms of saving schemes for the small saver protected as far as possible against inflation. We will extend the principle of special indexed and inflation-proofed savings.

- Pay arrangements for wage and salary earners to take account of increases in the cost of living.

This is the only fair and honest approach at a time when there is no immediate prospect of an increase in living standards. It protects the interests of pensioners, trade unionists and employees. We have considered taking our income proposals much further and introducing full-scale indexation, which has a growing number of advocates. We do not believe that this would be the best way of protecting people from inflation if all it did was to help us to live with inflation rather than cutting back the rate of inflation itself. Nevertheless, while we are tackling the crisis it is right to take some practical steps to help protect living standards and savings, and this we propose to do.

Food prices

Food prices make up a large part of every family's budget, and we know that the rise in the cost of food over the last few years largely caused by events outside the control of this country or outside the Common Market has hit many people hard. The present Government's answer has been essentially political and cosmetic. Their food subsidies have proved wasteful. Only £1 out of every £4 has gone to those in real need and the subsidies are being paid for by taxes on a whole range of goods and services which figure in the budget of every ordinary family. It would have been better to help the less well-off families direct. With the urgent need to stabilise prices we accept that it will be necessary to retain these subsidies for the time being.

More home-grown food

In the longer term, if we want more stable food prices in the shops and a healthier balance of payments the answer must be a considerable expansion of British agriculture. Given the right lead and help from government, our farmers and farmworkers are capable of making an even greater contribution to our economy than ever before. In today's unpredictable world, it is vital that they should. What British agriculture needs above all is reassurance and confidence about the future.

After 1970, British agriculture enjoyed a remarkable resurgence of confidence. The result was a healthy increase in the supply of home-grown food for the consumer. But in recent months the industry has suffered severely as a result of the uncertainty over Europe caused by the present Government and their failure to take action to deal with the grain crisis and inflation.

Our farmers must be given the necessary confidence as rapidly as possible to expand their industry once again. To do this, a Conservative government will undertake an immediate review of agriculture, both nationally and on a Community basis, followed by a cash injection as in 1970. We shall have thorough consultations with the industry over the serious problems caused by the rise in feedingstuff costs, and restore a guarantee for beef producers. We will work out with the industry a more efficient system of marketing. We will continue to press for improvements in the European Common Agricultural Policy and work to safeguard the interests of horticulturalists and other specialist producers. We shall remove the immensely damaging threat of Labour's wealth tax proposals to the family farm. Our aim is to ensure that at a time of uncertainty over world food supplies, the British housewife can enjoy the benefits of more home-grown food that those who work on the land are certainly capable of producing.

The Restrictive Trade Practices legislation has led to some unexpected difficulties for agricultural cooperatives. We shall introduce amendments to ensure that such organisations are able to carry out the sensible purposes for which they exist.

The fishing industry

It is also in the national interest, and in the interest of every housewife, to safeguard our fishing industry. The overriding need here is to conserve stocks. We support the move towards internationally agreed limits of 200 miles. In order to protect our waters and our fishing industry from over-fishing by foreign boats, we made special arrangements to protect the interests of inshore fishermen during our negotiations for entry into the European Community. When these arrangements come up for review in 1982, we will make sure that the special interests of the inshore industry continue to be protected.

PEOPLE AND INDUSTRY

Encouraging efficient production

The most positive element in our price stabilisation programme will be measures to encourage efficient production. There are no short cuts to building a new prosperity. There is no alternative to improved efficiency, higher productivity and increased production. No government, whatever its colour, can simply switch on economic growth by itself. It depends on the hard work, skills and enterprise of the British people.

Our taxation and industrial policies will therefore be designed to encourage firms to invest more money in new plant and machinery in our factories. It is here that we have fallen behind other industrial countries. In the last few months, investment and industrial confidence have received a terrible and deliberate battering. Taxation has clawed back much of the cash which industry needs. Threats of nationalisation have destroyed confidence. It is time to call a halt to these immensely damaging policies. Above all, we must recognise that in a mixed economy like ours, economic success depends very largely on private enterprise. One of the most valuable things we could do for industry would be to assure it that for several years ahead, there would be no threat of new nationalisation or more state direction.

We will introduce a major reform of company law as proposed during the period of our last administration.

Help for the regions

We want a partnership with industry based on trust, not a relationship of hostility and compulsion. One important ingredient of that partnership must be continuity of policy; when policies are endlessly chopped and changed, investment plans are damaged. That is why, for example, we intend to continue the regional policies which we pursued in office. In less than two years these provided or safeguarded over 50,000 jobs in schemes which received selective assistance under our Industry Act. We will seek to rebuild confidence in the regions, offering to industry continuity of assistance in order to achieve a real break-through in solving long-term problems. The now threatened rise in unemployment will be especially heavy if we do not succeed in restraining inflationary wage demands. This makes sensible policies for helping the regions more vital than ever.

Small businesses

We want also to help the small, often family-owned businesses which form the backbone of British enterprise. They employ a third of workers in the private sector and are immensely important to the economic life of Britain and to future industrial growth. The last Conservative government recognised their importance by appointing, for the first time, a Minister with specific responsibility for small businesses and by implementing many of the recommendations of the Bolton Committee on Small Businesses. In the recent Parliament, the Conservative Opposition won improved tax relief for small businesses which the Labour government opposed. A new Conservative government will keep under review the profit levels under which small firms are entitled to relief on corporation tax.

The impact of wealth and gifts taxes

Small businesses often face the problem of long-term finance. We will therefore set up an enquiry, to report within twelve months, into the availability and adequacy of long-term finance for small firms. Small businesses are also vulnerable to capital taxation and estate duty. The present government's proposed wealth tax and gifts tax could lead to the break-up of many small firms and a loss of jobs for those employed in them. In our overall reform of capital taxation, we will seek to find ways of shielding small businesses from taxes that might otherwise cripple them, destroy jobs and harm the economy.

Too many small businesses are being squeezed out of city centres in redevelopments. To help prevent this, we will ask all planning authorities to take into account the social contribution of small shopkeepers and other small concerns when considering city-centre redevelopments.

Inflation accounting

There are other areas where we would seek early co-operation with industry. Inflation at the present rate has a seriously distorting effect on company profitability, given the methods of accounting generally employed in Britain today. As a result, companies are finding themselves paying taxes on profits which are to a considerable extent paper profits and do not reflect real values. This is damaging to the economy since it means a further drain on funds for investment. The last Conservative government set up the Sandilands Committee to report and make recommendations on methods of inflation-accounting. We hope that this Committee will be able to produce its Report very soon and we will encourage it to do so. As soon as it reports, we will enter into immediate discussions with industry and the accounting profession on a changeover to methods of accounting which more accurately reflect company profitability.

Incentives for greater productivity

We also want to consider with industry ways of improving productivity. There is enormous scope in Britain for doing this, and the impact on our national prosperity and on that of every family would be considerable. We shall therefore examine straightaway the possibility of introducing in this country the sort of national scheme which operates in France for giving a fair share of the increased profits made by individual firms to those whose efforts produce improved performance and to those who make their contribution by investing their savings in new factories and new machinery.

Self-sufficiency in energy

The energy industries are specially vital to our economic performance, as events over the last year have shown. The days of cheap and abundant energy have gone for good. But Britain is more fortunate than most other industrial countries in having substantial natural reserves of coal, oil and gas. There are two clear lessons to be learned from last year's energy crisis: first, the urgent need to make Britain as self-sufficient in energy as possible; secondly, to make sure that Britain is able to depend on a variety of different sources of energy.

Coal

We support the general strategy for coal agreed during 1974 with the industry. Our aim will be to make the industry viable so that it can provide an assured and prosperous future for all those who work in it. An important element will be the establishment of a productivity scheme.

North Sea oil

In exploiting the oil reserves around the United Kingdom, there are three essential requirements. First, the British people must retain control of, and enjoy, the maximum benefits from our off-shore oil. The answer is not to spend £2,000 million or more of the taxpayers' money in nationalising 51 per cent of the industry. Nationalisation is inefficient, hugely expensive and totally unnecessary. The desired results can be achieved just as effectively, and far more cheaply, through taxation and regulation. Taxation will provide Britain with revenue from the oil. A Conservative government will, therefore, block the existing corporation tax loopholes and introduce a new additional tax on North Sea oil profits. At the same time, our proposed new regulations will give the government all the control that it needs. We will establish an Oil Conservation Authority to act as a watchdog. Its job will be to regulate exploration for oil, investment, production and sales in accordance with general policy directives laid down by the Government.

Scotland and North Sea oil

Secondly, the Scottish people must enjoy more of the financial benefits from oil, and they must be given a far greater say over its operation in Scotland. We will, therefore, establish a Scottish Development Fund. This will provide immediate cash help to solve the problems created by oil development, but beyond that it will lay the foundation for Scotland's long-term economic prosperity. We will move the Oil Production Division of the Department of Energy to Scotland and encourage the oil industry to locate their UK production headquarters in Scotland.

No delay

Thirdly, we must produce enough oil to meet Britain's needs by 1980. This means allowing the oil industry to press ahead with the minimum of hindrance, with the development of our oil resources. Already, the threat of nationalisation is causing considerable delay in the development of North Sea oilfields.

Nuclear power

We will carry through the recently announced pilot programme of nuclear power stations based on the British designed 'heavy water' system. We believe that a larger nuclear programme must be initiated at an early date. In all nuclear matters, safety and reliability must be our paramount considerations.

Energy saving

Events over the last year have highlighted the need for energy conservation. There is a lot that government can do to help and give a lead, for example by encouraging adequate home insulation and by giving the necessary support for research and development. But big savings of energy, which will help the nation's balance of payments and everyone's pocket, can only be made if the whole country makes some contribution. People often ask – 'What can we do to help beat the crisis?' One really useful thing that many of us could do is to cut down voluntarily on the amount of energy that we use, particularly oil. We will start urgent talks with every interest – local authorities, industry, voluntary agencies, consumer groups and so on – with this objective.

PEOPLE AT WORK

Partnership in industry

We want to promote partnership between government and industry, and partnership between those who work together in industry. It is on this that our chances of overcoming the country's economic difficulties and laying the foundations of a new prosperity for everyone will depend.

The law and industrial relations

Governments of both parties have tried to establish a new legal framework within which industrial relations could develop. As we have said elsewhere, we still believe that our own legislation was soundly based and unfairly attacked, but in view of the hostility which it aroused we will not reintroduce it. We accept the Trade Union and Labour Relations Act, introduced by the present government and sensibly amended by Parliament, as the basis for the law on trade union organisation and as the legal framework for collective bargaining. We hope that our decision will help create a better climate for industrial partnership.

Employee participation

To strengthen this partnership, we will lay a formal duty on all large and medium-sized firms to consult employee representatives on a wide range of subjects. This is necessary not only for economic reasons but also because a better understanding is important in its own right. We want to leave the precise methods and procedures as flexible as possible, but we have it in mind that the subjects covered should range from disciplinary and dismissal procedures and redundancy arrangements to consultations about methods of working, and profit-sharing and share-ownership schemes. These proposals should lay the foundation for future developments in employee participation at every level of the enterprise, but it is much too soon to be dogmatic about the exact form of participation in management.

Much can be learned about the right to consultation at work from the success achieved by certain companies. The government in particular will need to set a clear example with its own employees and the nationalised industries will be expected to play their part.

Other rights at work

We will protect and extend other rights of workers, after consultations with both sides of industry. Our objectives are:

- to give employees the right to hold union meetings on the premises of their employer;
- to give union members the opportunity to elect the leaders of their union by a postal ballot, with adequate help from the government to cover the expense;
- to seek effective ways of providing government assistance for the training of shop stewards and union officers;
- to seek ways of regulating the conduct of picketing based on the strict arrangements adopted by the National Union of Mineworkers in February 1974.

Redundancy payments

We also believe that the time is now overdue for a review of the system of payments for redundancy and the arrangements for redundancy in general. We must take account of developments in Europe, and consider relating payments to need, linking arrangements for redundancy with arrangements for industrial retraining, and improving the arrangements for collective redundancy.

Strikes and the taxpayer

We believe it is right that the unions themselves should accept a significant share of the responsibility for the welfare of the families of men who go on strike, and that the whole burden should not fall on the taxpayer. Equally, it is right that the families of strikers should not suffer unnecessary hardship. We will discuss with trade unions and employers how best to meet these two aims.

Job satisfaction

Much of the friction in our industrial relations is a symptom of the frustration and boredom found in many jobs in modern industry. The scope for improving job satisfaction is considerable. The primary responsibility must rest with management. A Conservative government will accordingly bring together government, management and the trade unions, to promote research into ways of improving and extending job satisfaction and to give advice. This will benefit individual workers, industrial relations in general and the community at large by improving the tone and atmosphere of our industrial civilisation.

PEOPLE AND TAXES

A responsible approach to taxation

We believe as Conservatives that people should keep as much of what they earn as is consistent with the responsibility of government to provide adequate services for the whole community. This is the most practical way to reward and therefore encourage effort, and it provides the best guarantee of individual choice and freedom. In present circumstances it would be irresponsible to promise large reductions in tax rates; and as we said earlier, if we cannot find the money to pay for additional programmes through cutting spending on other things it may be necessary to increase some taxes in the short term. But, as circumstances allow, we shall reduce the burden of tax on individuals and industry alike, as we have done in the past.

Above all, the tax system must be fair, and be seen to be fair. The last Conservative government went a long way towards making it fairer. Higher personal allowances gave proportionately more help to the less well-off taxpayers. The unified system of income tax brought relief to retired people living on small investment incomes.

Our proposals for helping older people and low income groups through personal allowances and the tax credit scheme respectively will be found later in this Manifesto.

Taxation on capital

We shall also seek to bring greater fairness into the whole system of taxation on capital. We do not oppose this in principle – for example, we already have in this country death duties and capital gains tax. What we do oppose are ill-considered and damaging additional burdens piled on top of existing penal and comprehensive taxes. Britain already has higher taxes on both capital and income than other countries – with a top rate for income tax of 98 per cent. Tax on tax on tax: this is a prescription, not for a fairer society, but for a poorer and more bitter one. It is wrong to reform capital taxation in a piecemeal way without full consideration of the effects. We will examine the whole system of taxation on capital with the aim of making the system more fair, less a matter in its application of chance or skill in avoidance, and less damaging to the thrift, saving and investment on which our future depends.

The last Conservative government raised the starting point for estate duty so that property passing from husband to wife (or vice versa) is exempt up to £30,000. An important part of our reform of capital taxation will be to extend this limit so that no estate duty is payable until the death of the surviving husband or wife. At present, relations sharing the family home may be forced to sell it in order to meet estate duties on the death of parents, brothers or sisters. We shall extend the relief at present enjoyed by widows or widowers to safeguard the matrimonial home to cover close relatives living in the same house.

PEOPLE AND RATES

People pay tax not only to national government but to local government as well in the form of rates. Local authority expenditure has been growing faster than the economy as a whole. Although on average 60 per cent of this expenditure is met by grant from the taxpayer, the burden on the domestic ratepayer has risen sharply. The rating system itself has come under increasing criticism because it does not reflect people's ability to pay.

Further heavy increases in rates are forecast. In these circumstances Conservatives will take the following steps.

Transferring expenditure

First, we shall transfer to central government in the medium term, the cost of teachers' salaries up to a specified number of teachers for each local education authority. Expenditure on police and the fire services will qualify for increased grants from the Exchequer. We shall see that this saving is passed on to the ratepayer.

Fairer taxes

Secondly, within the normal lifetime of a Parliament we shall abolish the domestic rating system and replace it by taxes more broadly based and related to people's ability to pay. Local authorities must continue to have some independent source of finance.

PEOPLE AND THEIR HOMES

Tackling the nation's housing needs is second only to the fight against inflation on our agenda.

Two main objectives

We have two main objectives. First, we want to see that enough homes are provided for the families that need them. This means, among other things, trying to ensure a steady flow of funds for the construction industry and concentrating help where it is really needed – for example, in the inner city areas where our proposal for establishing Social Priority Areas (set out in more detail later) will greatly help.

Secondly, 51 per cent of houses are at present owner-occupied. There are many families who would like to own their home but for one reason or another cannot do so. It is our purpose to extend the opportunities for home ownership to as many of them as possible. The Conservative ideal is a property-owning democracy.

Mortgage rates

The first part of our programme for doing this is to reduce the interest rate charged by building societies to home buyers to 9½ per cent and ensure that it does not rise above that figure. At the moment, societies have to offer those who are saving money with them the going interest rate for their investment. Without government action, any rise in this rate is passed on virtually automatically to the home buyer. But by varying the rate of tax payable by the building societies (known as the composite rate) when interest rates in general rise, the Government can enable the societies to attract sufficient funds without passing on the full increase in the rate to the purchaser. This step will help all home buyers – both new buyers and those existing buyers who have to struggle to find the extra money each month for the increased mortgage repayments for which they were unprepared.

A number of questions have been raised about the liquidity and reserve ratios of building societies, the legal restrictions on them, and the possibility of widening their powers so that they can operate more flexibly. In order to settle these matters, we shall set up a one year enquiry to sit full-time and to make recommendations to the government on the future role and structure of the societies.

Help with the deposit

Our second proposal is to give first-time purchasers of private houses and flats special help in paying the deposit. We will start a Home Savings Grant Scheme in which people who save regularly with building societies under schemes approved by the government will receive a grant proportionate to their savings. The Government will contribute £1 for every £2 saved up to a given ceiling.

This scheme would take at least two years to mature in order to give builders sufficient time to increase the supply of homes for sale. Without this, the extra grant would raise prices since more money would be chasing the same number of homes.

Several kinds of low start mortgages are already available. We shall encourage a greater variety of house purchase schemes to fit different circumstances.

Sale of council houses and flats

Our third proposal for extending home ownership is to give a new deal to every council tenant who has been in his home for three years or more. These tenants will have the right to purchase their homes at a price one-third below market value. The community will no longer tolerate the attitude of councils which, for narrow partisan reasons, stand in the way of their tenants becoming homeowners. We will therefore place a duty on every council to sell homes on these terms – giving their tenants what amounts to a 100 per cent mortgage with no deposit. It is of course only right that a tenant who buys his home should surrender the appropriate portion of any capital gain if he re-sells it within five years.

Voluntary housing movement

We shall support the voluntary housing movement and the Housing Corporation, both of which have benefited from new measures originally introduced in our Housing and Planning Bill. Housing Associations will continue to provide dwellings to rent as an alternative to local authorities.

Rents

We will continue the freeze on rents until the end of the year. When we have examined the reports of the Rent Scrutiny Boards, we will consider how increases can gradually be implemented in the light of our policies for fighting inflation. Families in need, whether in furnished or unfurnished accommodation, will continue to receive help with their rent as provided for the first time by law under the Conservative Housing Finance Act.

Modernising older houses

A policy of maintaining and modernising older houses is often preferable to demolition and rebuilding. The original scheme for home improvement was subject to certain abuses but these have now been removed. In all, our improvement programme resulted in 1 million homes receiving grants under the last Conservative government. We will continue this programme since it is exceptionally important to keep our older houses in good condition and to keep established communities together.

PEOPLE IN RETIREMENT

Inflation hits the old and the retired especially hard and in our tax and social service policies we must do all we can to protect them. And in a compassionate society they, like people in need, have the right to look forward to a better standard of living.

Six-monthly reviews

We will act first to protect the value of the pension. With prices rising as fast as they are, annual reviews are too infrequent. A Conservative government will therefore increase retirement pensions (as well as other long-term benefits) and public service pensions every six months. We will make sure that the burden of paying for improved pensions is fairly shared. The self-employed in particular should not have to face the huge increases in contributions proposed by the present government. Our development of inflation-proofed savings schemes will help those who want to add to their retirement pension by putting money aside during their working lives.

Second pension scheme

The pension prospects of millions of people in employment have been damaged by the present government's decision to abandon the Conservative Second Pension Scheme. Under the Conservative scheme, which was all set to come into operation, twelve million people would have started building up a second pension from April 1975. The present government has put a stop to this. The next Conservative government will reactivate the Second Pension Scheme to start as soon as possible, and at the latest by April 1976. With this as a foundation, we shall introduce further improvements, in particular to make still better second pension provision for women. We will make sure that married women in employment retain their right not to pay the full contribution to the State basic scheme.

Higher personal allowances for older people

We recognise the special needs of older people, often trapped by rising expenses that they cannot escape, and without the opportunity to increase their incomes as younger people can. Therefore, when we can afford to do so, we shall introduce higher personal tax allowances for people over 65. This will give a real rise in after-tax income to many older taxpayers who at present pay tax at a penal rate of 55 per cent immediately their income becomes subject to tax.

Abolition of the earnings rule

We believe that the earnings rule is socially harmful as well as widely resented. It discourages able men and women, merely because of their age, from making a contribution to society which would help both them and the rest of us. We have relaxed the earnings rule in the past and we will relax it further. We will abolish it as soon as resources allow.

PEOPLE IN NEED

Priorities and inflation

The record of the last Conservative government in giving new help to people in special need was by any reckoning remarkably successful. But rising standards only highlight the inadequacies that still persist. And inflation makes them worse. To tackle all these will cost money – and, as we have said throughout, cash and resources will be severely limited over the next few years. This underlines the need, greater now than ever, for establishing a clear set of priorities.

Our first priority in the social services, as we have made clear, is to look after the pensioners and other families dependent on long-term social security benefits by reviewing these benefits every six months. This is the best way of protecting them against rising prices, and it must be our first task.

The tax credit scheme

The speed at which we can carry out our other main social policies will depend largely on the economic situation and the resources that become available. But the centre-piece of our social programme will be the Tax-Credit scheme – the most advanced anti-poverty programme set in hand by any western country. This scheme will provide cash help, related to family circumstances, automatically and without special means test. It will be of special help to pensioners and to hard-pressed families with low incomes, especially where there are children. Our intention is to ensure that ultimately no family in the land need remain in poverty. Tragically the present government have set their face against this scheme. We will establish the framework for tax credits as soon as we can and bring the scheme into effect in stages, as economic circumstances permit.

Child credits

As a first step towards establishing the tax credit scheme, we will introduce a system of child credits when economic circumstances allow. These will be available for all children, including the first child. Child credits will take the place of the family allowances and tax allowances. The whole of the new child credits will be payable to mothers in cash in exactly the same way as existing family allowances, the only difference being that they will be worth more.

Single-parent families

Single-parent families face many financial and social problems, to which the Finer Report has recently drawn attention. We are studying the Report very carefully and will take action in the light of its recommendations.

Chronically sick and disabled people

One of the particular achievements of the last Conservative government was to introduce new benefits for chronically ill and severely disabled people. We shall continue this work. As resources become available, we shall establish as of right, a new benefit – modest to begin with, but a start – for those disabled people who have never been able to undertake regular work and for married women so disabled that they cannot look after their homes and families. We shall also improve the vehicle service for disabled people in the light of the Sharp Report: the minimum aim must be to see that all those who now qualify for 'three wheelers' will be able to exchange them for cars if they wish to do so.

Earnings rule

We will relax the earnings rule in relation to supplementary benefit so as to enable widows to make a real contribution to the living standards of their families, and we will see that the earnings of children at school are entirely disregarded.

The National Health Service

The National Health Service now faces acute difficulties, which are made all the worse by the impact of inflation. In present economic circumstances, it will not be easy even to maintain existing standards. That is why it is so wrong to reject any acceptable method of channelling additional resources into Britain's health services. The present government's commitment to scrap all Health Service charges at a cost of £100 million is bound to make the problems of the National Health Service worse. For the same reason we reject the present government's plans for abolishing private practice in association with the National Health Service. This is unacceptable in principle; it would also reduce the skills available to patients generally and would cost nearly £30 million a year. We shall safeguard the right of people to make provision for their own health and that of their families. What is now needed in the National Health Service is a period of comparative stability, founded upon the reorganisation that we carried through, which must now be allowed to settle down.

On pay there is considerable criticism of the working of the Whitley Council system in determining salaries and conditions of service in the National Health Service. We will therefore set up an independent inquiry to make urgent recommendations for the improvement of the system. A Conservative government will back-date to last May the recommendations of the Halsbury Committee on the pay of nurses and related medical professions. But the problems on pay that have arisen in the National Health Service only underline the need for a policy to help workers throughout the public sector to be paid comparable rates of pay to those earned by workers in the private sector. This may mean channelling more money into wages and salaries, at the expense of buildings, if we are to avoid a total collapse of the National Health Service. In this way, for instance, we could implement the principal recommendations of the Briggs Report on nursing, while preserving the identity of the health visitor.

Special needs

There are additional areas requiring special help when the country can afford it. A Conservative government will give priority to services for old people, disabled people, mentally ill people, and mentally handicapped people, at home, in the community and in the hospital. We will build on the record of the last Conservative Government in providing improved services for deaf people, and continue to improve the rehabilitation services. We will take what action may be necessary, in the light of the Report on the death of Maria Colwell, to detect and prevent the ill-treatment of small children. We will improve the law relating to adoption following broadly the recommendations of the Houghton Report.

Voluntary social service

In implementing our policy of identifying and meeting special need, we will continue to respect and help the voluntary organisations in their invaluable work. To this end, we will review the legal framework within which charities operate, a review that is long overdue. We will also develop the special unit that we set up when we were in government to help encourage voluntary service throughout the community.

WOMEN – AT HOME AND AT WORK

Child credits for mothers

Among those worst hit by the ravages of inflation are mothers, whose house-keeping money often fails to keep pace with the higher prices in the shops. Housewives will therefore stand to gain most from the success of our price stabilisation programme. In addition, as we have already said, we plan as part of our tax credit scheme to introduce new child credits for all children, including the first. These will be worth more than the existing family allowances and will be payable to mothers in cash at the Post Office.

Women at work

The last Conservative government took steps to ensure the effective implementation of Equal Pay for women at work by the end of 1975.

We stand by the principle of equal pay for women.

Women in retirement

Women have had a rough deal over pensions from the present government, which has abandoned the last Conservative government's Second Pension Scheme. One of the purposes of this scheme was to improve greatly the pension prospects for women in employment – enabling many of them to earn a second pension for the first time and to get a second widow's pension, also for the first time. A Conservative government will reintroduce the scheme. We will also maintain the right of women not to pay the full contribution to the basic State scheme, and retired women who want to do part-time jobs will of course greatly benefit from our eventual abolition of the earnings rule.

Widows

In relation to supplementary benefit, we also intend, as we have said, to relax the earnings rule so as to enable widows to make a real contribution to the living standards of their families. Widows, as well as separated and deserted wives, with children to bring up, will benefit from the action we take in the light of the Finer Report.

The right of a woman to be treated equally

The last Conservative government made considerable progress in strengthening women's rights. In pensions, social benefits, taxation, maintenance payments and guardianship of children, we introduced a succession of new rights for women. We also announced our intention to set up an Equal Opportunities Commission, the biggest single step towards a society of real equality for men and women taken by any government since women won the vote. Only the timing of the election prevented its implementation. We remain committed to setting up an Equal Opportunities Commission with powers to enquire into areas of discrimination and to report to the Government on the need for future action.

CHILDREN, PARENTS AND SCHOOLS

The quality of education

Many parents are deeply worried about the quality of the education which their children receive – in particular about standards of learning, conduct and discipline. These problems have accumulated over the years in an atmosphere over-charged with politics. Too often, the debate over education has centred on the kind of school rather than on the quality of the education provided; and too few parents have been allowed any real say over their children's education.

Children's needs must come first

The Conservative approach towards education is clear and distinct. Our overriding concern is with the educational needs of the children. Our first objective will therefore be to preserve good schools of whatever kind. We are in no way against comprehensive schools: what we oppose is the ruthless imposition of these schools, regardless of local needs and in defiance of parents' wishes. Typical of this approach is Labour's circular, which hits the building programmes of local authorities which have not gone comprehensive. The next Conservative government will withdraw this. We will expect local authorities to make their schemes of reorganisation sufficiently flexible to include grammar and direct grant schools of proven worth. This will help to meet the needs of bright and able children, especially those from disadvantaged areas. We will scrutinise zoning arrangements to ensure that they do not restrict or eliminate choice.

The eleven-plus examination is arbitrary. But selection where necessary must be flexible so as to allow the transfer of children from one school to another at a variety of ages.

Raising standards

We must take speedy action to raise standards of teaching and education. This will involve a considerable strengthening of the system of schools inspection. More inspectors will need to be recruited. National standards of reading, writing and arithmetic will be set. And the training period for teachers should give more attention to teaching the three basic skills and how to maintain discipline.

Comprehensive schools

Comprehensive schools have been a continuing source of controversy. This controversy should be settled by a fair and dispassionate examination of their performance, their size and their structure. A Conservative government will set up such an enquiry, as a matter of urgency, to report speedily.

Direct grant schools

The direct grant schools are particularly valuable. They combine high academic standards with a wide social mix. The present government is currently examining ways of destroying these schools. A Conservative government will instead strengthen them by re-opening the direct grant list, by considering the introduction of a complete system of assisted places so that every parent pays only according to his or her means, and – when economic circumstances allow us to do so – by raising the capitation grants to take account of increased costs.

The school-leaving age

Since the raising of the school-leaving age, the problems of truancy and indiscipline have become more acute. We remain committed to the principle of education up to sixteen, but believe that it should be applied more flexibly. One possibility, which we will want to examine closely, is to allow children of fifteen the opportunity of taking up an apprenticeship or training as a first step towards taking a job.

A charter of parents' rights

An important part of the distinct Conservative policy on education is to recognise parental rights. A say in how their children are to be brought up is an essential ingredient in the parental role. We will therefore introduce additional rights for parents. First, by amending the 1944 Education Act, we will impose clear obligations on the State and local authorities to take account of the wishes of parents. Second, we will consider establishing a local appeal system for parents dissatisfied with the allotment of schools. Third, parents will be given the right to be represented on school boards – by requiring a substantial proportion of the school governors and managers to be drawn from, and elected by, the parents of children currently at school. Fourth, we will place an obligation on all head teachers to form a parent-teachers association to assist and support teachers. Fifth, we will encourage schools to publish prospectuses about their record, existing character, specialities and objectives.

Teachers

Better standards in schools will mean raising the status of the teaching profession. We will consider sympathetically the recommendations of Lord Houghton's Committee on Teachers' Salaries. As steps towards raising the professional status of teachers, we will encourage the movement to an all graduate profession, the implementation of the recommendations of the James Report on In-service Training and the establishment of a professional council for teachers to regulate their own affairs. We will also stimulate local authorities to provide houses for teachers where this is necessary.

Tasks for the future

For the moment, we cannot afford as a country to do all the things we want for children and young people – in their schools, colleges and universities. But when we have got on top of our present economic difficulties we will complete the work we have started for the younger children – replacing and modernising old primary schools (especially in the rundown areas of our towns and cities), developing further the pre-school facilities for children, and helping handicapped children. We will also want to ease the financial problems faced by our universities and see that teachers in polytechnics, with the same qualifications as those at universities, receive the same salaries. In addition our aim will be to finance the polytechnics and colleges of education in a similar way to the universities.

YOUNG PEOPLE

Young people want many of the same things as their parents – a decent home to start married life in, the opportunity to earn a rising standard of living, a fair reward for what they do, a decent environment, the chance to go as far as their abilities will take them. But the problems that are special to young people are not being adequately dealt with by central and local government.

The need for co-ordination

We therefore think that it is time to establish a special unit to co-ordinate the actions of government departments as they affect the needs and aspirations of young people.

Youth and Community Bill

We will re-introduce the Youth and Community Bill, which, among other things, provides local reviews of existing arrangements in the field of housing, employment, leisure and advice services as they relate to young people.

Housing

We will give special help to first-time house buyers as we have said in more detail earlier. We should also recognise that young people working in our cities are more mobile and have a special housing need which has been aggravated by the actions of the present government in introducing the Rent Act. We will encourage the voluntary housing movement to provide accommodation in inner city areas which will meet their needs. We will also encourage the growth of hostel accommodation and student co-operative dwellings. Local authorities should consider the needs of young people in planning their housing provision.

Employment

The youth employment service has over the years provided invaluable help to thousands of school leavers. But too many young people still receive inadequate guidance in choosing their first job and insufficient help with the difficult move from school to work. We will accordingly undertake a review of the youth employment service in order to strengthen it and make it even more responsive to the needs of young people. We will also examine ways of improving the co-ordination of vocational guidance services in general, including the Manpower Services Commission, the adult occupational guidance unit, and the careers service profession. We want to see more young people in their last year at school given the opportunity to try out prospective jobs with the help and participation of local industries. For those in need of special help and support we will expand the Community Industries Scheme.

Community service

Most young people wish to have a greater say in the decisions affecting their lives, and many also wish to give service to the community. It is important to see that they are given opportunities to serve on bodies which influence daily life, particularly where the Government itself makes the appointments.

The young in urban communities are subject to special stresses. Those with immigrant parents may have additional problems because of the cultural differences between their family life and the society they live in. We will use the urban aid and community development programmes to support cooperative schemes, involving local authorities, voluntary agencies and the communities themselves.

Students

When we review student grants, we will reduce the amount that parents have to contribute and we will end the discrimination against married women students. It is unfair that, while some students can get a grant as of right from a local authority, other students only get a grant if the local authority chooses to give one. As soon as economic circumstances allow, we will review the present arrangements with the aim of ending these unfairnesses in the provision of grants. We will encourage the formation of student housing associations.

PEOPLE AND THEIR ENVIRONMENT

For some unfortunate people environment means the slum they live in or the slag heap which looms at the bottom of their garden. For others it means stricter controls over pollution or conserving the world's finite resources; clearing more derelict land or encouraging family planning; giving more people the chance to go to concerts and galleries or raising the quality of broadcasting. The term covers a whole complex of questions which in one way or another affect the quality of our lives. Our approach to these problems as Conservatives is based on our belief that many things should be conserved, and on our belief in the dignity of the individual. We do not accept that, by becoming more prosperous, we will destroy the quality of our environment. We believe, to the contrary, that properly controlled and directed growth can and will improve the environment, not least of those who at present have too low a standard of living to enjoy many of the good things of life.

Building on our record

In 1970 we set up the first Department of the Environment in the world and became world leaders in a policy to protect the environment when it was good and to improve it when it had been spoilt or polluted. We will build on our record by:

- leading a determined, properly co-ordinated effort on a national scale to make far greater progress in the recycling of waste products;
- carrying through the drive to clear derelict land;
- pressing on with measures to prevent pollution of all kinds, and improving the methods for monitoring potentially dangerous matter;
- seeking methods of avoiding waste and unnecessary consumption of fuels and energy, for example, by helping to raise the standards of house insulation.

Family planning

The last Conservative government appointed the Population Panel and for the first time provided a complete family planning service within the National Health Service. We believe that it is the responsibility of government to provide such a service and to tell people the facts about our population. But we must leave it to every family to decide what use to make of the family planning service.

Transport

We want to preserve a proper balance between the interests of road and rail transport and between those of the private motorists and public transport. We will re-introduce our plans to modify the bus licensing system so as to give greater freedom for new forms of local transport in country areas. We will also extend the establishment of a system of lorry routes to keep heavy vehicles out of towns and villages and away from narrow country lanes. We will naturally continue to take all possible steps to diminish noise and other nuisances caused by new roads and the traffic which uses them, and also to improve road safety wherever possible.

Towns and cities

There are still parts of Britain, especially the inner city areas, which suffer acute squalor and deprivation – poor housing, dilapidated schools, substandard social and welfare services and a general lack of amenities. It is not surprising that these conditions have led to an increase in juvenile crime and vandalism.

What is needed is a major concentration of help in these areas, brought together in an effectively co-ordinated programme. We will first ask local authorities, in consultation with voluntary organisations, to propose Social Priority Areas. Our aim will then be to bring about a major transformation in these areas, by improving housing conditions, replacing or improving out-dated schools and building up the local social services and amenities. We will give more opportunity for local people to play a greater part in the affairs of their community. In particular we will make sure that more tenants are involved in running their council estates.

Advice centres

People are frequently unaware of their rights as citizens. They often find themselves being passed from one office to another receiving only discouragement. To help meet this problem we will set up advice centres, in partnership with the independent voluntary agencies which are already making a useful contribution.

Better race relations

In many urban areas, in particular, social harmony depends on the white and the coloured communities living and working together on equal terms and with equal opportunities. A Conservative government will pursue positive policies to promote good race relations. This means, among other things, seeking remedies for the problems faced by coloured people, especially adolescents, in employment and in education (for example, in the teaching of the English language). The Government must take the lead and set an example, but local authorities, employers, trade unionists and voluntary organisations have an important part to play.

Strict immigration control

Better community relations, however, depend also on reassuring people that immigration is being kept down to the minimum. In the interests of good race relations, and for the benefit of immigrants already in Britain, as well as for the wider community, a Conservative government will follow a policy of strictly limited immigration. Abuse of immigration control is unfair, particularly to immigrants who have arrived lawfully. While honouring commitments already made, we will discuss with the representatives of the immigrant communities steps to be taken against abuse. In all our policies our aim will be to keep in the closest touch with the immigrant communities.

Nationality law

We shall carry forward the review of British nationality law. Dependent on its outcome, new legislation may be required in the life of the next Parliament.

The arts, sport and broadcasting

At a time when economic conditions necessarily impose limits on public spending, we will nevertheless continue to give as much help as we can to the arts, to sport and to broadcasting, and we will be particularly keen to encourage local effort and involvement. As we have promised before, we will introduce legislation to establish a Public Lending Right for authors.

PEOPLE IN SCOTLAND AND WALES

A recurring theme in our programme is the need to recognise that people want more freedom and more control over their own lives. This is what has shaped our policies for Scotland and Wales.

In Scotland we will:

- set up a Scottish Assembly;
- give the Secretary of State for Scotland, acting with the Scottish Assembly, the power to decide how to spend Scotland's share of the UK budget;
- establish a Scottish Development Fund, as stated earlier, to provide substantial help with both the new problems created by oil, and with Scotland's old deprived areas;
- transfer the Oil Division of the Department of Energy to Scotland.

In Wales, we will:

- increase the powers and the functions of the Secretary of State for Wales and ensure that Wales' share of the UK budget is spent in accordance with decisions taken in Wales and the Welsh Office;
- establish a new Select Committee of Welsh MPs entitled to meet in Cardiff as well as at Westminster;
- strengthen the functions of the Welsh Council and reconstitute its membership so that the majority will be elected from the new County and District Councils.

In Scotland and Wales we are publishing separate manifestos, setting out these plans and others in more detail.

PEOPLE IN NORTHERN IRELAND

Our troops are still heavily engaged in Northern Ireland. They have carried out their difficult and dangerous task with superb courage, discipline, and skill. No other body of men in the world could have done so well. But the more police duties can be carried out by the police, the more we can reduce the strain on the Army, and the more soldiers we can withdraw from Ulster.

Yet it would be fatal to withdraw the Army before its work is done. And while our troops are risking their lives, they must have the support of the necessary emergency powers.

We recognise that Ulster is at present under-represented at Westminster, but obviously any change in that representation must await an agreement on the future devolution of government in Northern Ireland.

The next Conservative government, like the last, will work for peace and consent in Northern Ireland. There can be no military solution without a political solution that is fair to both the majority and the minority communities. Equally there can be no political solution unless terrorism is curbed and the law is respected and upheld by all. There must be partnership between the communities. We will seek the closest co-operation with the Republic, but Ulster is, of course, part of the United Kingdom.

PEOPLE AND THE LAW

The law under attack

Through the centuries, the law in Britain has acted as the defence of the small man against the great, of the weak against the strong. If we cannot depend on the protection of the law, enacted by the free Parliament of a free people and enforced impartially between one man and another, then our security and our freedoms alike are without foundation. In a world of growing turbulence, individuals more than ever need the law's protection against the might of the powerful and irresponsible. But recently the law has been under attack, and those attacks have all too often been condoned and even endorsed by members and supporters of the present Government. Respect for the law cannot be selective. At a time when there are too many people prepared to take the law into their own hands, a Conservative government, backed by public opinion, will uphold the rule of law. Without law, there can be no freedom.

Strengthening the police

We will need to take vigorous action to deal with the lawlessness and the growth of terrorism which confront us in the 1970s. The new Conservative government will strengthen the police force, our principal defenders against internal attack. We will improve the career prospects throughout the whole police service, to provide greater incentives for policemen to remain in the force until retirement. We will launch a new recruitment drive to increase the numbers of Special Constables who can play an invaluable role in supporting the regular police. We support the introduction of an independent element into the procedure for investigating complaints against the police.

Young offenders

A strengthened police force will be in the forefront of the continuing battle against crime. But additional measures are needed to tackle the growth in crime committed by young persons, especially in our towns and cities. The Children and Young Persons Act of 1969 is now in need of review and amendment. The courts must be enabled to deal more effectively with persistent juvenile offenders – for example, football hooligans – and the range of available institutions must be improved. We need more community homes providing both secure accommodation and an environment for encouraging young offenders to become useful members of the community. All these steps will help to prevent today's young apprentices in crime from becoming tomorrow's professional criminals.

Crime prevention at the roots

A Conservative government will review fines, taking account of the change in the value of money and of trends in sentencing. We will pursue the policy we started of dealing with offenders in the community when it is both possible and sensible to do so. Our programme for channelling additional help and resources into the deprived areas of our cities and towns will also, by creating a better environment, play a valuable part in combating crime at the roots. We will further strengthen and expand the probation service.

Processions and demonstrations

We will review the Public Order Act 1936 to ensure that it is adequate for the control of processions and demonstrations.

Protecting people from indecent display

The growing display of indecent material in public places gives offence to many people. Accordingly, we will reintroduce our Bill to prohibit this and to tighten up the law against sending through the post unsolicited matter of an indecent nature.

Redress against officialdom

In the complex and powerful modern State, control of administrative decisions that can adversely affect the individual has become increasingly important. There have been some valuable recent developments in Britain such as the spread of the Ombudsman system. But we believe our legal structure still needs further reform in order to strengthen its power to defend the citizen aggrieved by the State. We will pursue reform of administrative law in the light of our experience of the extended Ombudsman system and of the forthcoming proposals of the Law Commission.

Law reform

The framework of freedom and civilised life is the law. All our daily activities are dependent on it. We propose to give a high priority to keeping the law clear and up to date. Law reform may seem a dull subject but it does affect the rights of all of us. Here are some examples of needed reforms.

Needed reforms

Our extradition laws, based on a century-old statute, are cumbersome, out of date, and in some conditions unworkable. We also need to reform the licensing laws taking into account public reactions to the Erroll Report. The law on compensation for personal injury needs attention and is at the moment being studied by a Royal Commission. The law affecting 'squatters' has been shown to be inadequate. Finally the drafting of our laws frequently lacks clarity, and this means that they are inaccessible and are difficult to interpret. We propose to secure greater simplicity and clarity in statute law in the light of the forthcoming report of the Renton Committee on the Preparation of Legislation.

Improving justice

When in office we substantially improved the machinery of justice. We will continue to do so and will review the machinery and jurisdiction of Magistrates' Courts in the light of the forthcoming James Report. When the economic situation permits, we favour the phased extension of Legal Aid to proceedings before Tribunals on certain defined principles.

Privacy and official secrets

When in office we implemented some of the Younger Report's recommendations on privacy (for example, on the secrecy of people's credit ratings) and were working on further aspects of it. We were also working on the security implications of the Franks Report. When returned to office, we will take up the unfinished work and present the country with further firm proposals.

Speaker's conference on electoral reform

In a democracy, it is essential that Parliament and our parliamentary institutions should enjoy the confidence of the people. That is why, for example, we have brought forward plans for giving people in Scotland and Wales a greater say in running their own affairs.

But confidence in Parliament has been strained by two developments. First, there have been the attempts by industrial monopolies and others to do as they want, regardless of the democratically expressed will of the people, and of the actions of a democratically elected government. Second, there have been those who have questioned whether our electoral system ensures that Parliament and the legislation it passes reflect the wishes of the people. We will propose the establishment of a Speaker's

Conference to examine our electoral system and to make recommendations. In addition to considering our present voting system and alternatives, we would like the Speaker's Conference to examine the question of representation in the European Parliament, which many people think should be decided by direct election.

THE BRITISH PEOPLE AND THE WORLD

Defending Britain

We live in dangerous times. As much as in the past Britain must be able to defend herself and her way of life. To us, aggressive war may be unthinkable. To some other countries, it is an acceptable way of gaining their ends. Now we face the ever increasing danger of both national and international terrorism. In these circumstances the national interest demands the maintenance of adequate defence forces. Moreover, we must take all necessary steps to protect our energy supplies in the North Sea.

The NATO Alliance

Throughout the last few years the Soviet armed forces in the West have continued to grow and there has been a vast expansion of the Russian navy. Unquestionably the NATO alliance, which has provided peace in Europe for 25 years, remains crucial to our security, and so the Conservative Party believes that Britain should continue to play a leading role within the alliance. We shall see that Britain's nuclear deterrent remains effective.

Efficiency and morale

The efficiency and high morale of the armed forces, which have been so outstandingly demonstrated in Northern Ireland, are of paramount importance. We must improve conditions of service for those who make the defence of this country their career. We will take action to tackle the difficulties which have arisen in the provision of housing for servicemen at the completion of their regular service. We will maintain the efficiency and improve the equipment of the Reserve Forces which play a vital role in the preservation of Britain's security.

Britain and the world

Conservative foreign policy has always had two main objectives: first, to maintain the security of Britain and the protection of British interests; and, secondly, playing our full part in the Commonwealth, to gain as many friends and allies in the international community as possible. Such a policy contributes to stability throughout the world. It also creates the necessary conditions for the expansion of our trade.

Conservative achievements in foreign policy

The last Conservative government helped to strengthen NATO, but we also promoted the process of détente. We played a leading part in the Conference of Security and Co-operation in Europe. We opened Ministerial talks with the People's Republic of China. We greatly improved our relations with the countries of the Middle East and the Persian Gulf.

The Common Market

But by far the most historic achievement of the last Conservative government was to bring about British entry into the European Community. Membership of the EEC brings us great economic advantages, but the European Community is not a matter of accountancy. There are two basic ideas behind the formation of the Common Market; first, that having nearly destroyed themselves by two great European civil wars, the European nations should make a similar war impossible in future; and, secondly, that only through unity could the Western European nations recover control over their destiny – a control which they had lost after two wars, the division of Europe and the rise of the United States and the Soviet Union.

All recent governments of this country have concluded that membership of the community is essential for British interests. These decisions were not lightly taken. They were preceded by prolonged study of the facts. The terms secured by the last Conservative government were supported by those members of the previous Labour government most qualified to judge them. The country's long-term interests should not now be sacrificed to short-term party interests.

The dangers of withdrawal

An overwhelming majority of British exporters and businessmen favour our membership of the Common Market. The Community provides an enormous home market for our industries and membership of the biggest trading bloc in the world. Just as we need military allies, so we need political and economic allies. British withdrawal would mean the abandonment of export opportunities, the decline of industrial development in this country and the loss of jobs. Withdrawal would give us less power and influence in the world not more. Withdrawal would confront us with the choice of almost total dependence on others or retreat into weak isolation. We reject such a bleak and impotent future for Britain.

Negotiation

Within the Community, there is a continuous process of negotiation in order to take account of the interests of Britain and to deal with the problems of the community as a whole. This process will go on: it ensures that no member state carries an unfair burden. We will present the results of negotiation to Parliament at every stage in accordance with Britain's constitutional practice.

Conservatives have been playing their full part in the European Parliament to protect British interests, improve Community policy and make Europe more democratic.

A central part of future Conservative policy will be to work realistically for closer European unity in all the areas of Community policy which can be of benefit to Britain. In this way we can make our contribution to a peaceful, prosperous and democratic Europe.

Europe gives us the opportunity to reverse our political and economic decline. It may be our last.

The
Conservative
manifesto
1979

CONSERVATIVE PARTY GENERAL ELECTION MANIFESTO 1979

Date of Election	Thursday 3 May
Party Leader	Margaret Thatcher
Candidates	622
MPs	339
Votes	13,697,690
% of vote	43.9%

Foreword

For me, the heart of politics is not political theory, it is people and how they want to live their lives. No one who has lived in this country during the last five years can fail to be aware of how the balance of our society has been increasingly tilted in favour of the State at the expense of individual freedom. This election may be the last chance we have to reverse that process, to restore the balance of power in favour of the people. It is therefore the most crucial election since the war. Together with the threat to freedom there has been a feeling of helplessness, that we are a once great nation that has somehow fallen behind and that it is too late now to turn things round. I don't accept that. I believe we not only can, we must. This manifesto points the way. It contains no magic formula or lavish promises. It is not a recipe for an easy or a perfect life. But it sets out a broad framework for the recovery of our country, based not on dogma, but on reason, on common sense, above all on the liberty of the people under the law. The things we have in common as a nation far outnumber those that set us apart.

It is in that spirit that I commend to you this manifesto.

Margaret Thatcher

OUR FIVE TASKS

This election is about the future of Britain – a great country which seems to have lost its way. It is a country rich in natural resources, in coal, oil, gas and fertile farmlands. It is rich, too, in human resources, with professional and managerial skills of the highest calibre, with great industries and firms whose workers can be the equal of any in the world We are the inheritors of a long tradition of parliamentary democracy and the rule of law.

Yet today, this country is faced with its most serious problems since the Second World War. What has happened to our country, to the values we used to share, to the success and prosperity we once took for granted?

During the industrial strife of last winter, confidence, self-respect, common sense, and even our sense of common humanity were shaken. At times this society seemed on the brink of disintegration.

Some of the reasons for our difficulties today are complex and go back many years. Others are more simple and more recent. We do not lay all the blame on the Labour Party: but Labour have been in power for most of the last fifteen years and cannot escape the major responsibility.

They have made things worse in three ways. First, by practising the politics of envy and by actively discouraging the creation of wealth, they have set one group against another in an often bitter struggle to gain a larger share of a weak economy. Second, by enlarging the role of the State and diminishing the role of the individual, they have crippled the enterprise and effort on which a prosperous country with improving social services depends. Third, by heaping privilege without responsibility on the trade unions, Labour have given a minority of extremists the power to abuse individual liberties and to thwart Britain's chances of success. One result is that the trade union movement, which sprang from a deep and genuine fellow-feeling for the brotherhood of man, is today more distrusted and feared than ever before.

It is not just that Labour have governed Britain badly. They have reached a dead-end. The very nature of their Party now prevents them from governing successfully in a free society and mixed economy. Divided against themselves; devoid of any policies except those which have led to and would worsen our present troubles; bound inescapably by ties of history, political dogma and financial dependence to a single powerful interest group, Labour have demonstrated yet again that they cannot speak and dare not act for the nation as a whole.

Our country's relative decline is not inevitable. We in the Conservative Party think we can reverse it, not because we think we have all the answers but because we think we have the one answer that matters most. We want to work with the grain of human nature, helping people to help themselves – and others. This is the way to restore that self-reliance and self-confidence which are the basis of personal responsibility and national success.

Attempting to do too much, politicians have failed to do those things which should be done. This has damaged the country and the authority of government. We must concentrate on what should be the priorities for any government. They are set out in this manifesto.

Those who look in these pages for lavish promises or detailed commitments on every subject will look in vain. We may be able to do more in the next five years than we indicate here. We believe we can. But the Conservative government's first job will be to rebuild our economy and reunite a divided and disillusioned people.

Our five tasks are:

1 To restore the health of our economic and social life, by controlling inflation and striking a fair balance between the rights and duties of the trade union movement.
2 To restore incentives so that hard work pays, success is rewarded and genuine new jobs are created in an expanding economy.
3 To uphold Parliament and the rule of law.
4 To support family life, by helping people to become home-owners, raising the standards of their children's education, and concentrating welfare services on the effective support of the old, the sick, the disabled and those who are in real need.

5 To strengthen Britain's defences and work with our allies to protect our interests in an increasingly threatening world.

This is the strategy of the next Conservative government.

RESTORING THE BALANCE

Sound money and a fair balance between the rights and obligations of unions, management and the community in which they work are essential to economic recovery. They should provide the stable conditions in which pay bargaining can take place as responsibly in Britain as it does in other countries.

The control of inflation

Under Labour prices have risen faster than at any peacetime period in the three centuries in which records have been kept, and inflation is now accelerating again. The pound today is worth less than half its 1974 value. On present form it would be halved in value yet again within eight years. Inflation on this scale has come near to destroying our political and social stability.

To master inflation, proper monetary discipline is essential, with publicly stated targets for the rate of growth of the money supply. At the same time, a gradual reduction in the size of the Government's borrowing requirement is also vital. This Government's price controls have done nothing to prevent inflation, as is proved by the doubling of prices since they came to power. All the controls have achieved is a loss of jobs and a reduction in consumer choice.

The State takes too much of the nation's income; its share must be steadily reduced. When it spends and borrows too much, taxes, interest rates, prices and unemployment rise so that in the long run there is less wealth with which to improve our standard of living and our social services.

Better value for money

Any future government which sets out honestly to reduce inflation and taxation will have to make substantial economies, and there should be no doubt about our intention to do so. We do not pretend that every saving can be made without change or complaint; but if the Government does not economise, the sacrifices required of ordinary people will be all the greater.

Important savings can be made in several ways. We will scrap expensive Socialist programmes, such as the nationalisation of building land. We shall reduce government intervention in industry and particularly that of the National Enterprise Board, whose borrowing powers are planned to reach £4.5 billion. We shall ensure that selective assistance to industry is not wasted, as it was in the case of Labour's assistance to certain oil platform yards, on which over £20 million of public money was spent but no orders received.

The reduction of waste, bureaucracy and over-government will also yield substantial savings. For example, we shall look for economies in the cost (about £1.2 billion) of running our tax and social security systems. By comparison with private industry, local direct labour schemes waste an estimated £400 million a year. Other examples of waste abound, such as the plan to spend £50 million to build another town hall in Southwark.

Trade union reform

Free trade unions can only flourish in a free society. A strong and responsible trade union movement could play a big part in our economic recovery. We cannot go on, year after year, tearing ourselves apart in increasingly bitter and calamitous industrial disputes. In bringing about economic recovery, we should all be on the same side. Government and public, management and unions, employers and employees, all have a common interest in raising productivity and profits, thus increasing investment and employment, and improving real living standards for everyone in a high-productivity, high-wage, low-tax economy. Yet at the moment we have the reverse – an economy in which the Government has to hold wages down to try to make us competitive with other countries where higher real wages are paid for by higher output.

The crippling industrial disruption which hit Britain last winter had several causes: years with no growth in production; rigid pay control; high marginal rates of taxation; and the extension of trade union power and privileges. Between 1974 and 1976, Labour enacted a 'militants' charter' of trade union legislation. It tilted the balance of power in bargaining throughout industry away from responsible management and towards unions, and sometimes towards unofficial groups of workers acting in defiance of their official union leadership.

We propose three changes which must be made at once. Although the Government refused our offer of support to carry them through the House of Commons last January, our proposals command general assent inside and outside the trade union movement.

Picketing

Workers involved in a dispute have a right to try peacefully to persuade others to support them by picketing, but we believe that right should be limited to those in dispute picketing at their own place of work. In the last few years some of the picketing we have witnessed has gone much too far. Violence, intimidation and obstruction cannot be tolerated. We shall ensure that the protection of the law is available to those not concerned in the dispute but who at present can suffer severely from secondary action (picketing, blacking and blockading). This means an immediate review of the existing law on immunities in the light of recent decisions, followed by such amendment as may be appropriate of the 1976 legislation in this field. We shall also make any further changes that are necessary so that a citizen's right to work and go about his or her lawful business free from intimidation or obstruction is guaranteed.

The closed shop

Labour's strengthening of the closed shop has made picketing a more objectionable weapon. In some disputes, pickets have threatened other workers with the withdrawal of their union cards if they refuse to co-operate. No union card can mean no job. So the law must be changed. People arbitrarily excluded or expelled from any union must be given the right of appeal to a court of law. Existing employees and those with personal conviction must be adequately protected, and if they lose their jobs as a result of a closed shop they must be entitled to ample compensation.

In addition, all agreements for a closed shop must be drawn up in line with the best practice followed at present and only if an overwhelming majority of the workers involved vote for it by secret ballot. We shall therefore propose a statutory code under Section 6 of the 1975 Employment Protection Act. We will not permit a closed shop in the non-industrial civil service and will resist further moves towards it in the newspaper industry. We are also committed to an enquiry into the activities of the SLADE union, which have done so much to bring trade unionism into disrepute.

Wider participation

Too often trade unions are dominated by a handful of extremists who do not reflect the common-sense views of most union members.

Wider use of secret ballots for decision-making throughout the trade union movement should be given every encouragement. We will therefore provide public funds for postal ballots for union elections and other important issues. Every trade unionist should be free to record his decisions as every voter has done for a hundred years in parliamentary elections, without others watching and taking note.

We welcome closer involvement of workers, whether trade unionists or not, in the decisions that affect them at their place of work. It would be wrong to impose by law a system of participation in every company. It would be equally wrong to use the pretext of encouraging genuine worker involvement in order simply to increase union power or facilitate union control of pension funds.

Too many strikes

Further changes may be needed to encourage people to behave responsibly and keep the bargains they make at work. Many deficiencies of British industrial relations are without foreign parallel. Strikes are too often a weapon of first rather than last resort. One cause is the financial treatment of strikers and their families. In reviewing the position, therefore, we shall ensure that unions bear their fair share of the cost of supporting those of their members who are on strike.

Labour claim that industrial relations in Britain cannot be improved by changing the law. We disagree. If the law can be used to confer privileges, it can and should also be used to establish obligations. We cannot allow a repetition of the behaviour that we saw outside too many of our factories and hospitals last winter.

Responsible pay bargaining

Labour's approach to industrial relations and their disastrous economic policies have made realistic and responsible pay bargaining almost impossible. After encouraging the 'social contract' chaos of 1974–5, they tried to impose responsibility by the prolonged and rigid control of incomes. This policy collapsed last winter as we warned that it would. The Labour government then came full circle with the announcement of yet another 'social contract' with the unions. For five years now, the road to ruin has been paved with such exchanges of promises between the Labour government and the unions.

To restore responsible pay bargaining, we must all start by recognising that Britain is a low-paid country because we have steadily become less efficient, less productive, less reliable and less competitive. Under this Government, we have more than doubled our pay but actually produced less in manufacturing industry. It will do yet further harm to go on printing money to pay ourselves more without first earning more. That would lead to even higher prices, fewer jobs and falling living standards.

The return to responsibility will not be easy. It requires that people keep more of what they earn; that effort and skill earn larger rewards; and that the State leaves more resources for industry. There should also be more open and informed discussion of the Government's economic objectives (as happens, for example, in Germany and other countries) so that there is wider understanding of the consequences of unrealistic bargaining and industrial action.

Pay bargaining in the private sector should be left to the companies and workers concerned. At the end of the day, no one should or can protect them from the results of the agreements they make.

Different considerations apply to some extent to the public sector, of whose seven million workers the Government directly employs only a minority. In the great public corporations, pay bargaining should be governed, as in private ones, by what each can afford. There can be no question of subsidising excessive pay deals.

Pay bargaining in central and local government, and other services such as health and education, must take place within the limits of what the taxpayer and ratepayer can afford. It is conducted under a variety of arrangements, some of long standing, such as pay research. In consultation with the unions, we will reconcile these with the cash limits used to control public spending, and seek to conclude no-strike agreements in a few essential services. Bargaining must also be put on a sounder economic footing, so that public sector wage settlements take full account of supply and demand and differences between regions, manning levels, job security and pension arrangements.

A MORE PROSPEROUS COUNTRY

Labour have gone to great lengths to try to conceal the damage they have done to the economy and to our prospects of economic expansion. Even in the depression of the 1930s the British economy progressed more than it has under this Labour government. Their favourite but totally false excuse is that their appalling record is all due to the oil crisis and the world-wide economic depression. Yet since the oil crisis, despite our coal, and gas and oil from the North Sea, prices and unemployment in Britain have risen by more than in almost any other major industrial country. And output has risen by less. With much poorer energy supplies than Britain, the others have nonetheless done much better because they have not had a Labour government or suffered from Labour's mistakes.

To become more prosperous, Britain must become more productive and the British people must be given more incentive.

Cutting income tax

We shall cut income tax at all levels to reward hard work, responsibility and success; tackle the poverty trap; encourage saving and the wider ownership of property; simplify taxes – like VAT; and reduce tax bureaucracy.

It is especially important to cut the absurdly high marginal rates of tax both at the bottom and top of the income scale. It must pay a man or woman significantly more to be in, rather than out of, work. Raising tax thresholds will let the low-paid out of the tax net altogether, and unemployment and short-term sickness benefit must be brought into the computation of annual income.

The top rate of income tax should be cut to the European average and the higher tax bands widened. To encourage saving we will reduce the burden of the investment income surcharge. This will greatly help those pensioners who pay this additional tax on the income from their life-time savings, and who suffer so badly by comparison with members of occupational or inflation-proofed pension schemes.

Growing North Sea oil revenues and reductions in Labour's public spending plans will not be enough to pay for the income tax cuts the country needs. We must therefore be prepared to switch to some extent from taxes on earnings to taxes on spending. Value Added Tax does not apply, and will not be extended, to necessities like food, fuel, housing and transport. Moreover the levels of State pensions and other benefits take price rises into account.

Labour's extravagance and incompetence have once again imposed a heavy burden on ratepayers this year. But cutting income tax must take priority for the time being over abolition of the domestic rating system.

A property-owning democracy

Unlike Labour, we want more people to have the security and satisfaction of owning property.

We reject Labour's plan for a Wealth Tax. We shall deal with the most damaging features of the Capital Transfer and Capital Gains Taxes, and propose a simpler and less oppressive system of capital taxation in the longer term. We will expand and build on existing schemes for encouraging employee share-ownership and our tax policies generally will provide incentive to save and build up capital.

Industry, commerce and jobs

Lower taxes on earnings and savings will encourage economic growth. But on their own they will not be enough to secure it.

Profits are the foundation of a free enterprise economy. In Britain profits are still dangerously low. Price controls can prevent them from reaching a level adequate for the investment we need. In order to ensure effective competition and fair pricing policies, we will review the working of the Monopolies Commission, the Office of Fair Trading and the Price Commission, with the legislation which governs their activities.

Too much emphasis has been placed on attempts to preserve existing jobs. We need to concentrate more on the creation of conditions in which new, more modern, more secure, better paid jobs come into existence. This is the best way of helping the unemployed and those threatened with the loss of their jobs in the future.

Government strategies and plans cannot produce revival, nor can subsidies. Where it is in the national interest to help a firm in difficulties, such help must be temporary and tapered. We all hope that those firms which are at present being helped by the taxpayer will soon be able to succeed by themselves; but success or failure lies in their own hands.

Of course, government can help to ease industrial change in those regions dependent on older, declining industries. We do not propose sudden, sharp changes in the measures now in force. However, there is a strong case for relating government assistance to projects more closely to the number of jobs they create.

Nationalisation

The British people strongly oppose Labour's plans to nationalise yet more firms and industries such as building, banking, insurance, pharmaceuticals and road haulage. More nationalisation would further impoverish us and further undermine our freedom. We will offer to sell back to private ownership the recently nationalised aerospace and shipbuilding concerns, giving their employees the opportunity to purchase shares.

We aim to sell shares in the National Freight Corporation to the general public in order to achieve substantial private investment in it. We will also relax the Traffic Commissioner licensing regulations to enable new bus and other services to develop – particularly in rural areas – and we will encourage new private operators.

Even where Labour have not nationalised they interfere too much. We shall therefore amend the 1975 Industry Act and restrict the powers of the National Enterprise Board solely to the administration of the Government's temporary shareholdings, to be sold off as circumstances permit. We want to see those industries that remain nationalised running more successfully and we will therefore interfere less with their management and set them a clearer financial discipline in which to work.

High productivity is the key to the future of industries like British Rail, where improvements would benefit both the work-force and passengers who have faced unprecedented fare increases over the last five years.

Fair trade

Just as we reject nationalisation, so we are opposed to the other Socialist panacea-import controls. They would restrict consumer choice, raise prices and invite damaging retaliation against British goods overseas. We will vigorously oppose all kinds of dumping and other unfair foreign trade practices that undermine jobs at home.

We fully support the renegotiated Multi-fibre Arrangement for textiles and will insist that it is monitored effectively and speedily. We also believe in a revised 'safeguard' clause under GATT, to give us a better defence against sudden and massive surges of imports that destroy jobs.

Small businesses

The creation of new jobs depends to a great extent on the success of smaller businesses. They have been especially hard hit under Labour. Our cuts in direct and capital taxation, the simplification of VAT and our general economic and industrial relations policies are the key to their future. We shall make planning restraints less rigid; reduce the number of official forms and make them simpler; provide safeguards against unfair competition from direct labour; review the new 714 Certificate system for sub-contractors and review with representatives of the self-employed their National Insurance and pension position. We shall amend laws such as the Employment Protection Act where they damage smaller businesses – and larger ones too – and actually prevent the creation of jobs.

We shall also undertake a thorough review of the enforcement procedures of Customs and Excise and the Inland Revenue, and introduce an easier regime for small firms in respect of company law and the disclosure of their affairs.

Energy

The development of our energy resources provides a challenge for both our nationalised industries and the private sector. Nowhere has private enterprise been more successful in creating jobs and wealth for the nation than in bringing North Sea oil and gas ashore. These benefits will be short-lived unless we pursue a vigorous policy for energy saving. Labour's interference has discouraged investment and could cost Britain billions of pounds in lost revenue. We shall undertake a complete review of all the activities of the British National Oil Corporation as soon as we take office. We shall ensure that our oil tax and licensing policies encourage new production.

We believe that a competitive and efficient coal industry has an important role in meeting energy demand, together with a proper contribution from nuclear power. All energy developments raise important environmental issues, and we shall ensure the fullest public participation in major new decisions.

Agriculture

Our agricultural and food industries are as important and as efficient as any that we have. They make an immense contribution to our balance of payments; they provide jobs for millions of people and they sustain the economy of the countryside. Labour have seriously undermined the profitability of these industries, without protecting consumers against rising food prices which have more than doubled during their term of office. We must ensure that these industries have the means to keep abreast of those in other countries.

We believe that radical changes in the operation of the Common Agricultural Policy (CAP) are necessary. We would, in particular, aim to devalue the Green Pound within the normal lifetime of a Parliament to a point which would enable our producers to compete on level terms with those in the rest of the Community. We will insist on a freeze in CAP prices for products in structural surplus. This should be maintained until the surpluses are eliminated. We could not entertain discriminatory proposals such as those which the Commission recently put forward for milk production.

The Uplands are an important part of our agriculture. Those who live and work there should enjoy a reasonable standard of life.

Fishing

The Government's failure to negotiate with our Community partners proper arrangements for fishing has left the industry in a state of uncertainty. The general adoption of 200-mile limits has fundamentally altered the situation which existed when the Treaty of Accession was negotiated. We would work for an agreement which recognised: first, that United Kingdom waters contained more fish than those of the rest of the Community countries put together; secondly, the loss of fishing opportunities experienced by our fishermen; thirdly, the rights of inshore fishermen; last, and perhaps most important of all, the need for effective measures to conserve fish stocks which would be policed by individual coastal states. In the absence of agreement, we would not hesitate to take the necessary measures on our own, but of course on a non-discriminatory basis.

Animal welfare

The welfare of animals is an issue that concerns us all. There are problems in certain areas and we will act immediately where it is necessary. More specifically, we will give full support to the EEC proposals on the transportation of animals. We shall update the Brambell Report, the codes of welfare for farm animals, and the legislation on experiments on live animals. We shall also re-examine the rules and enforcement applying to the export of live animals and shall halt the export of cows and ewes recently calved and lambed.

THE RULE OF LAW

The most disturbing threat to our freedom and security is the growing disrespect for the rule of law. In government as in opposition, Labour have undermined it. Yet respect for the rule of law is the basis of a free and civilised life. We will restore it, re-establishing the supremacy of Parliament and giving the right priority to the fight against crime.

The fight against crime

The number of crimes in England and Wales is nearly half as much again as it was in 1973. The next Conservative government will spend more on fighting crime even while we economise elsewhere.

Britain needs strong, efficient police forces with high morale. Improved pay and conditions will help Chief Constables to recruit up to necessary establishment levels. We will therefore implement in full the recommendations of the Edmund Davies Committee. The police need more time to detect crime. So we will ease the weight of traffic supervision duties and review cumbersome court procedures which waste police time. We will also review the traffic laws, including the totting-up procedure.

Deterring the criminal

Surer detection means surer deterrence. We also need better crime prevention measures and more flexible, more effective sentencing. For violent criminals and thugs really tough sentences are essential. But in other cases long prison terms are not always the best deterrent. So we want to see a wider variety of sentences available to the courts. We will therefore amend the 1961 Criminal Justice Act which limits prison sentences on young adult offenders, and revise the Children and Young Persons Act 1969 to give magistrates the power to make residential and secure care orders on juveniles.

We need more compulsory attendance centres for hooligans at junior and senior levels. In certain detention centres we will experiment with a tougher regime as a short, sharp shock for young criminals. For certain types of offenders, we also support the greater use of community service orders, intermediate treatment and attendance centres. Unpaid fines and compensation orders are ineffective. Fines should be assessed to punish the offender within his means and then be backed by effective sanctions for non-payment.

Many people advocate capital punishment for murder. This must remain a matter of conscience for Members of Parliament. But we will give the new House of Commons an early opportunity for a free vote on this issue.

Immigration and race relations

The rights of all British citizens legally settled here are equal before the law whatever their race, colour or creed. And their opportunities ought to be equal too. The ethnic minorities have already made a valuable contribution to the life of our nation. But firm immigration control for the future is essential if we are to achieve good community relations. It will end persistent fears about levels of immigration and will remove from those settled, and in many cases born here, the label of 'immigrant'.

- (i) We shall introduce a new British Nationality Act to define entitlement to British citizenship and to the right of abode in this country. It will not adversely affect the right of anyone now permanently settled here.
- (ii) We shall end the practice of allowing permanent settlement for those who come here for a temporary stay.
- (iii) We shall limit entry of parents, grandparents and children over 18 to a small number of urgent compassionate cases.
- (iv) We shall end the concession introduced by the Labour government in 1974 to husbands and male fiancés.
- (v) We shall severely restrict the issue of work permits.
- (vi) We shall introduce a Register of those Commonwealth wives and children entitled to entry for settlement under the 1971 Immigration Act.
- (vii) We shall then introduce a quota system, covering everyone outside the European Community, to control all entry for settlement.
- (viii) We shall take firm action against illegal immigrants and overstayers and help those immigrants who genuinely wish to leave this country – but there can be no question of compulsory repatriation.

We will encourage the improvement of language training in schools and factories and of training facilities for the young unemployed in the ethnic communities. But these measures will achieve little without the effective control of immigration. That is essential for racial harmony in Britain today.

The supremacy of Parliament

In recent years, Parliament has been weakened in two ways. First, outside groups have been allowed to usurp some of its democratic functions. Last winter, the Government permitted strike committees and pickets to take on powers and responsibilities which should have been discharged by Parliament and the police. Second, the traditional role of our legislature has suffered badly from the growth of government over the last quarter of a century.

We will see that Parliament and no other body stands at the centre of the nation's life and decisions, and we will seek to make it effective in its job of controlling the Executive.

We sympathise with the approach of the all-party parliamentary committees which put forward proposals last year for improving the way the House of Commons legislates and scrutinises public spending and the work of government departments. We will give the new House of Commons an early chance of coming to a decision on these proposals.

The public has rightly grown anxious about many constitutional matters in the last few years – partly because our opponents have proposed major constitutional changes for party political advantage. Now Labour want not merely to abolish the House of Lords but to put nothing in its place. This would be a most dangerous step. A strong Second Chamber is necessary not only to revise legislation but also to guarantee our constitution and liberties.

It is not only the future of the Second Chamber which is at issue. We are committed to discussions about the future government of Scotland, and have put forward proposals for improved parliamentary control of administration in Wales. There are other important matters, such as a possible Bill of Rights, the use of referendums, and the relationship between Members of the European Parliament and Westminster, which we shall wish to discuss with all parties.

Northern Ireland

We shall maintain the Union of Great Britain and Northern Ireland in accordance with the wish of the majority in the Province. Its future still depends on the defeat of terrorism and the restoration of law and order. We shall continue with the help of the courage, resolution and restraint of the Security Forces to give it the highest priority. There will be no amnesty for convicted terrorists.

In the absence of devolved government, we will seek to establish one or more elected regional councils with a wide range of powers over local services. We recognise that Northern Ireland's industry will continue to require government support.

HELPING THE FAMILY

Homes of our own

To most people ownership means first and foremost a home of their own. Many find it difficult today to raise the deposit for a mortgage. Our tax cuts will help them. We shall encourage shared purchase schemes which will enable people to buy a house or flat on mortgage, on the basis initially of a part-payment which they complete later when their incomes are high enough. We should like in time to improve on existing legislation with a realistic grants scheme to assist first-time buyers of cheaper homes. As it costs about three times as much to subsidise a new council house as it does to give tax relief to a home buyer, there could well be a substantial saving to the tax and ratepayer.

The prospect of very high mortgage interest rates deters some people from buying their homes and the reality can cause acute difficulties to those who have done so. Mortgage rates have risen steeply because of the Government's financial mismanagement. Our plans for cutting government spending and borrowing will lower them.

The sale of council houses

Many families who live on council estates and in new towns would like to buy their own homes but either cannot afford to or are prevented by the local authority or the Labour government. The time has come to end these restrictions. In the first session of the next Parliament we shall therefore give council and new town tenants the legal right to buy their homes, while recognising the special circumstances of rural areas and sheltered housing for the elderly. Subject to safeguards over resale, the terms we propose would allow a discount on market values reflecting the fact that council tenants effectively have security of tenure. Our discounts will range from 33 per cent after three years, rising with length of tenancy to a maximum of 50 per cent after twenty years. We shall also ensure that 100 per cent mortgages are available for the purchase of council and new town houses. We shall introduce a right for these tenants to obtain limited term options on their homes so that they know in advance the price at which they can buy, while they save the money to do so.

As far as possible, we will extend these rights to housing association tenants. At the very least, we shall give these associations the power to sell to their tenants.

Those council house tenants who do not wish to buy their homes will be given new rights and responsibilities under our Tenants' Charter.

Reviving the private rented sector

As well as giving new impetus to the movement towards home ownership, we must make better use of our existing stock of houses. Between 1973 and 1977 no fewer than 400,000 dwellings were withdrawn from private rental. There are now hundreds of thousands of empty properties in Britain which are not let because the owners are deterred by legislation. We intend to introduce a new system of shorthold tenure which will allow short fixed-term lettings of these properties free of the most discouraging conditions of the present law. This provision will not, of course, affect the position of existing tenants. There should also be more flexible arrangements covering accommodation for students. At the same time, we must try to achieve a greater take-up in rent allowances for poorer tenants.

Protecting the environment

The quality of our environment is a vital concern to all of us. The last Conservative government had a proud record of achievement in reducing pollution, and protecting our heritage and countryside. We shall continue to give these issues a proper priority. Subject to the availability of resources we shall pay particular attention to the improvement and restoration of derelict land, the disposal and recycling of dangerous and other wastes, and reducing pollution of our rivers and canals.

We attach particular importance to measures to reduce fuel consumption by improving insulation.

Standards in education

The Labour Party is still obsessed with the structure of the schools system, paying too little regard to the quality of education. As a result we have a system which in the view of many of our parents and teachers all too often fails – at a cost of over £8 billion a year – even to provide pupils with the means of communication and understanding. We must restore to every child, regardless of background, the chance to progress as far as his or her abilities allow.

We will halt the Labour government's policies which have led to the destruction of good schools; keep those of proven worth; and repeal those sections of the 1976 Education Act which compel local authorities to reorganise along comprehensive lines and restrict their freedom to take up places at independent schools.

We shall promote higher standards of achievement in basic skills. The Government's Assessment of Performance Unit will set national standards in reading, writing and arithmetic, monitored by tests worked out with teachers and others and applied locally by education authorities. The Inspectorate will be strengthened. In teacher training there must be more emphasis on practical skills and on maintaining discipline.

Much of our higher education in Britain has a world-wide reputation for its quality. We shall seek to ensure that this excellence is maintained. We are aware of the special problems associated with the need to increase the number of high-quality entrants to the engineering professions. We shall review the relationship between school, further education and training to see how better use can be made of existing resources.

We recognise the valuable work done by the Youth Service and will continue to give help to those voluntary bodies which make such a considerable contribution in this field.

Parents' rights and responsibilities

Extending parents' rights and responsibilities, including their right of choice, will also help raise standards by giving them greater influence over education. Our Parents' Charter will place a clear duty on government and local authorities to take account of parents' wishes when allocating children to schools, with a local appeals system for those dissatisfied. Schools will be required to publish prospectuses giving details of their examination and other results.

The Direct Grant schools, abolished by Labour, gave wider opportunities for bright children from modest backgrounds. The Direct Grant principle will therefore be restored with an Assisted Places Scheme. Less well-off parents will be able to claim part or all of the fees at certain schools from a special government fund.

The arts

Economic failure and Socialist policies have placed the arts under threat. Lightening the burden of tax should in time enable the private sponsor to flourish again and the reform of capital taxation will lessen the threat to our heritage. We will strengthen the existing provision whereby relief from CTT is available on assets placed in a maintenance fund for the support of heritage property. We favour the establishment of a National Heritage Fund to help preserve historic buildings and artistic treasures for the nation. We will continue to give as generous support to Britain's cultural and artistic life as the country can afford.

Sport and recreation have also been hit by inflation and high taxation. We will continue to support the Sports Councils in the encouragement of recreation and international sporting achievement.

Health and welfare

The welfare of the old, the sick, the handicapped and the deprived has also suffered under Labour. The lack of money to improve our social services and assist those in need can only be overcome by restoring the nation's prosperity. But some improvements can be made now by spending what we do have more sensibly.

In our National Health Service standards are falling; there is a crisis of morale; too often patients' needs do not come first. It is not our intention to reduce spending on the Health Service indeed, we intend to make better use of what resources are available. So we will simplify and decentralise the service and cut back bureaucracy.

When resources are so tightly stretched it is folly to turn good money away from the NHS and to discourage people from doing more for themselves. We shall therefore allow pay-beds to be provided where there is a demand for them; end Labour's vendetta against the private health sector; and restore tax relief on employer-employee medical insurance schemes. The Royal Commission on the Health Service is studying the financing of health care, and any examination of possible longer-term changes – for example, greater reliance for NHS funding on the insurance principle – must await their report.

In the community, we must do more to help people to help themselves, and families to look after their own. We must also encourage the voluntary movement and self-help groups working in partnership with the statutory services.

Making sense of social security

Our social security system is now so complicated that even some Ministry officials do not understand it. Income tax starts at such a low level that many poor people are being taxed to pay for their own benefits. All too often they are little or no better off at work than they are on social security.

This was one of our principal reasons for proposing a tax credit scheme. Child benefits are a step in the right direction. Further progress will be very difficult in the next few years, both for reasons of cost and because of technical problems involved in the switch to computers. We shall wish to move towards the fulfilment of our original tax credit objectives as and when resources become available. Meanwhile we shall do all we can to find other ways to simplify the system, restore the incentive to work, reduce the poverty trap and bring more effective help to those in greatest need.

Restoring the will to work means, above all, cutting income tax. It also involves bringing unemployment and short-term sickness benefit within the tax system, an objective fully shared by Labour Ministers. The rules about the unemployed accepting available jobs will be reinforced and we shall act more vigorously against fraud and abuse.

We welcomed the new Child Benefit as the first stage of our tax credit scheme. One-parent families face much hardship so we will maintain the special addition for them.

The elderly and the disabled

We will honour the increases in retirement pensions which were promised just before the election. However, like others, pensioners have suffered from the high taxes and catastrophic inflation of Labour's years.

It is wrong to discourage people who wish to work after retirement age, and we will phase out the 'earnings rule' during the next Parliament. The Christmas Bonus, which the last Conservative government started in 1972, will continue. We will exempt war widows' pensions from tax and provide a pension for pre-1950 widows of 'other ranks' who do not receive one at present.

Much has been done in recent years to help the disabled, but there is still a long way to go. Our aim is to provide a coherent system of cash benefits to meet the costs of disability, so that more disabled people can support themselves and live normal lives. We shall work towards this as swiftly as the strength of the economy allows.

A STRONG BRITAIN IN A FREE WORLD

Improving our defences

During the past five years the military threat to the West has grown steadily as the Communist bloc has established virtual parity in strategic nuclear weapons and a substantial superiority in conventional weapons. Yet Labour have cut down our forces, weakened our defences and reduced our contribution to NATO. And the Left are pressing for still more reductions.

We shall only be able to decide on the proper level of defence spending after consultation in government with the Chiefs of Staff and our allies. But it is already obvious that significant increases will be necessary. The SALT discussions increase the importance of ensuring the continuing effectiveness of Britain's nuclear deterrent.

In recent times our armed forces have had to deal with a wide variety of national emergencies. They have responded magnificently despite government neglect and a severe shortage of manpower and equipment. We will give our servicemen decent living conditions, bring their pay up to full comparability with their civilian counterparts immediately and keep it there. In addition, we must maintain the efficiency of our reserve forces. We will improve their equipment, too, and hope to increase their strength.

The European Community

If we wish to play our full part in shaping world events over the next few critical years, we must also work honestly and genuinely with our partners in the European Community. There is much that we can achieve together, much more than we can achieve alone.

There are some Community policies which need to be changed since they do not suit Britain's – or Europe's – best interests. But it is wrong to argue, as Labour do, that Europe has failed us. What has happened is that under Labour our country has been prevented from taking advantage of the opportunities which membership offers.

Labour's economic policies have blunted our competitive edge and made it more difficult for our companies to sell in our partners' markets. What is more, the frequently obstructive and malevolent attitude of Labour Ministers has weakened the Community as a whole and Britain's bargaining power within it.

By forfeiting the trust of our partners, Labour have made it much more difficult to persuade them to agree to the changes that are necessary in such important areas as the Common Agricultural Policy, the Community budget, and the proposed Common Fisheries Policy.

The next Conservative government will restore Britain's influence by convincing our partners of our commitment to the Community's success. This will enable us to protect British interests and to play a leading and constructive role in the Community's efforts to tackle the many problems which it faces.

We shall work for a common-sense Community which resists excessive bureaucracy and unnecessary harmonisation proposals, holding to the principles of free enterprise which inspired its original founders.

Our policies for the reform of the CAP would reduce the burden which the Community budget places upon the British taxpayer. We shall also strive to cut out waste in other Community spending programmes.

National payments into the budget should be more closely related to ability to pay. Spending from the budget should be concentrated more strictly on policies and projects on which it makes sense for the Community rather than nation states to take the lead.

We attach particular importance to the co-ordination of Member States' foreign policies. In a world dominated by the super-powers, Britain and her partners are best able to protect their international interests and to contribute to world peace and stability when they speak with a single voice.

Africa and the Middle East

In Africa and the Middle East, there is an increasing threat from the Soviet Union and its Cuban allies. That threat must be countered, not only through collaboration with our European and American allies but also by the people and governments in Africa and the Middle East whose independence is threatened.

We shall do all we can to build on the Egyptian/Israeli peace treaty, to seek a comprehensive settlement which will bring peace to the whole region.

Rhodesia

The Conservative Party will aim to achieve a lasting settlement to the Rhodesia problem based on the democratic wishes of the people of that country. If the Six Principles, which all British governments have supported for the last fifteen years, are fully satisfied following the present Rhodesian Election, the next government will have the duty to return Rhodesia to a state of legality, move to lift sanctions, and do its utmost to ensure that the new independent state gains international recognition.

Trade, aid and the Commonwealth

Like other industrial countries, Britain has a vital interest in bringing prosperity to poorer nations which provide us with a growing market and supply many of the raw materials upon which we depend. The next Conservative government will help them through national and international programmes of aid and technical co-operation and by the encouragement of voluntary work. But we also attach particular importance to the development of trade and private investment through such instruments as the European Community's Lomé Convention. In particular, we will foster all our Commonwealth links and seek to harness to greater effect the collective influence of the Commonwealth in world affairs.

A NEW BEGINNING

In this manifesto we have not sought to understate the difficulties which face us – the economic and social problems at home, the threats to the freedom of the West abroad. Yet success and security are attainable if we have the courage and confidence to seize the opportunities which are open to us.

We make no lavish promises. The repeated disappointment of rising expectations has led to a marked loss of faith in politicians' promises. Too much has gone wrong in Britain for us to hope to put it all right in a year or so. Many things will simply have to wait until the economy has been revived and we are once again creating the wealth on which so much else depends.

Most people, in their hearts, know that Britain has to come to terms with reality. They no longer have any time for politicians who try to gloss over the harsh facts of life. Most people want to be told the truth, and to be given a clear lead towards the action needed for recovery.

The years of make-believe and false optimism are over. It is time for a new beginning.

THE CONSERVATIVE MANIFESTO 1983

CONSERVATIVE PARTY GENERAL ELECTION MANIFESTO 1983

Date of Election	Thursday 9 June
Party Leader	Margaret Thatcher
Candidates	633
MPs	397
Votes	13,012,315
% of vote	42.4%

Foreword – the challenge of our times

In the last four years, Britain has recovered her confidence and self-respect. We have regained the regard and admiration of other nations. We are seen today as a people with integrity, resolve and the will to succeed.

This Manifesto describes the achievements of four years of Conservative government and sets out our plans for our second term.

The choice before the nation is stark: either to continue our present steadfast progress towards recovery, or to follow policies more extreme and more damaging than those ever put forward by any previous Opposition.

We face three challenges: the defence of our country, the employment of our people, and the prosperity of our economy.

How to defend Britain's traditional liberties and distinctive way of life is the most vital decision that faces the people at this election.

We have enjoyed peace and security for thirty-eight years – peace with freedom and justice. We dare not put that security at risk.

Every thinking man and woman wants to get rid of nuclear weapons. To do that we must negotiate patiently from a position of strength, not abandon ours in advance.

The universal problem of our time, and the most intractable, is unemployment.

The answer is not bogus social contracts and government overspending. Both, in the end, destroy jobs. The only way to a lasting reduction in unemployment is to make the right products at the right prices, supported by good services. The Government's role is to keep inflation down and offer real incentives for enterprise. As we win back customers, so we win back jobs.

We have a duty to protect the most vulnerable members of our society, many of whom contributed to the heritage we now enjoy. We are proud of the way we have shielded the pensioner and the National Health Service from the recession.

Only if we create wealth can we continue to do justice to the old and the sick and the disabled. It is economic success which will provide the surest guarantee of help for those who need it most.

Our history is the story of a free people – a great chain of people stretching back into the past and forward into the future.

All are linked by a common belief in freedom, and in Britain's greatness. All are aware of their own responsibility to contribute to both.

Our past is witness to their enduring courage, honesty and flair, and to their ability to change and create. Our future will be shaped by those same qualities.

The task we face is formidable. Together, we have achieved much over the past four years. I believe it is now right to ask for a new mandate to meet the challenge of our times.

Margaret Thatcher

The road to recovery

Britain is once more a force to be reckoned with. Formidable difficulties remain to be overcome. But after four years of Conservative government, national recovery has begun.

When we came to office in May 1979, our country was suffering both from an economic crisis and a crisis of morale. British industry was uncompetitive, over-taxed, over-regulated and over-manned. The British economy was plagued by inflation. After only a brief artificial pause, it was back into double figures. This country was drifting further and further behind its neighbours. Defeatism was in the air.

We did not disguise the fact that putting Britain right would be an extremely difficult task. The second sharp oil price increase and the deepest world recession since the 1930s have made those difficulties worse. At the same time, the Western world is passing through another transformation from the age of the smokestack to the era of the microchip. Traditional industries are being transformed by the new technologies. These changes have led to a rapid rise in unemployment in almost every Western country.

Our opponents claim that they could abolish unemployment by printing or borrowing thousands of millions of pounds. This is a cruel deceit. Their plans would immediately unleash a far more savage economic crisis than their last; a crisis which would, very soon, bring more unemployment in its wake.

The truth is that unemployment, in Britain as in other countries, can be checked and then reduced only by steadily and patiently rebuilding the economy so that it produces the goods and services which people want to buy, at prices they can afford.

What we have achieved

This is the task to which we have steadfastly applied ourselves with gradually increasing success. Prices are rising more slowly now than at any time for fifteen years. Britain is now among the low-inflation nations of the Western world. Output is rising.

- We are creating the conditions in which trade and industry can prosper. We have swept away controls on wages, prices, dividends, foreign exchange, hire purchase, and office and factory building.
- We have returned to free enterprise many state firms, in order to provide better service to the customer and save taxpayers' money.
- We have cut income tax rates and raised allowances at all levels.
- We have more than protected pensions against rising prices. We have strengthened the National Health Service. We have given council tenants the right to buy their own homes.
- We have strengthened the police and the armed forces of the Crown.
- We have done all this and more, and still kept our promise to bring public spending under control.
- We have paid off nearly half the overseas debts the Labour Party left behind. Once the IMF's biggest borrower, we are now playing a leading part in strengthening international trade and finance – to the benefit of the poorest countries on earth.
- And we have acted so that people might live in freedom and justice. The bravery, skill and determination with which Britain's task force recaptured the Falklands reverberated around the world. Many small nations gave thanks for that stand; and our allies in the North Atlantic are heartened by what Britain achieved in the South Atlantic.

Over the past four years, this country has recaptured much of her old pride. We now have five great tasks for the future. They are:

- to create an economy which provides stable prices, lasting prosperity and employment for our people;
- to build a responsible society which protects the weak but also allows the family and the individual to flourish;
- to uphold Parliamentary democracy and strengthen the rule of law;
- to improve the quality of life in our cities and countryside;
- to defend Britain's freedom, to keep faith with our allies in Europe and in NATO, and to keep the peace with justice.

These tasks will require sustained determination, imagination and effort from Government and people alike.

Jobs, prices and unions

During the years of recession, now coming to an end, even the most successful of our competitors have faced increasingly serious problems and mounting unemployment. Despite all these difficulties, the Conservative Government has been overcoming Britain's fundamental problems: restoring sound money, setting a better balance between trade unions and the rest of society, bringing efficiency to the nationalised industries, and developing effective policies to mitigate the curse of unemployment.

The foundations of recovery have been firmly laid. In the next Parliament, we shall build on this progress.

Success against inflation

Steadier prices and honest money are essential conditions for recovery. Under the last Labour government, prices doubled and inflation soared to an all-time peak – despite the existence of a battery of controls on prices, profits, dividends and pay.

Today, there are no such controls. Yet prices are rising more slowly than at any time since the 1960s. During the last year, inflation has come down faster in Britain than in any other major economy. With lower inflation, businessmen, families, savers and pensioners can now begin at last to plan and budget ahead with confidence.

In the next Parliament, we shall endeavour to bring inflation lower still. Our ultimate goal should be a society with stable prices. We shall maintain firm control of public spending and borrowing. If Government borrows too much, interest rates rise, and so do mortgage payments. Less spending by Government leaves more room to reduce taxes on families and businesses. We shall continue to set out a responsible financial strategy which will gradually reduce the growth of money in circulation – and so go on bringing inflation down.

Our opponents are once again proposing the same financial policies that led to such appalling inflation and chaos in the past. Labour's 'National Economic Assessment' is a stale repeat of the Social Contract which ended so disastrously in the Winter of Discontent. Once again, the Labour Party is committed to carry out trade union leaders' instructions in exchange for mere expressions of goodwill.

Commonsense in pay bargaining

With lower inflation. we have seen a return to commonsense in pay bargaining. Uncertainty and anxiety about rising prices have contributed to the absurdly high pay claims that destroyed so many jobs. As inflation subsides, people in work can see the prospect of real, properly-earned improvements in their living standards – which have gone up by more than 5 per cent on average over the last four years. So long as sensible government policies are matched by sensible attitudes in industry and commerce, these living standards can continue to improve.

The last four years have shown that a bureaucratic machine for controlling wages and prices is quite unnecessary. It simply stores up trouble and breeds inefficiency.

But Government remains inescapably responsible for controlling its own costs. We are committed to fair and reasonable levels of pay for those who work in the public services. We shall therefore continue to seek sensible arrangements for determining pay in the Civil Service and the National Health Service, following the Megaw Report and the resolution of the NHS pay dispute.

It is equally our duty to the nation as a whole to prevent any abuse of monopoly power or exploitation of the sick, the weak and the elderly. So we must continue to resist unreasonable pay claims in the public sector.

Trade union reforms

In the return to more sensible pay bargaining, the trade unions have an important part to play.

They can be powerful instruments for good or harm, to promote progress or hinder change, to create new jobs or to destroy existing ones. All of us have a vital interest in ensuring that this power is used democratically and responsibly.

Both trade union members and the general public have welcomed the 1980 and 1982 Employment Acts, which restrain secondary picketing, encourage secret ballots, curtail abuse of the closed shop, and restore rights of redress against trade unions responsible for committing unlawful acts.

But some trade union leaders still abuse their power against the wishes of their members and the interests of society. Our 1982 Green Paper, *Democracy in Trade Unions*, points the way to give union members control over their own unions. We shall given union members the right to:

- hold ballots for the election of governing bodies of trade unions;
- decide periodically whether their unions should have party political funds.

We shall also curb the legal immunity of unions to call strikes without the prior approval of those concerned through a fair and secret ballot.

Political levy

Consultations on the Green Paper have confirmed that there is widespread disquiet about how the right of individual trade union members not to pay the political levy operates in practice, through the system of contracting-out. We intend to invite the TUC to discuss the steps which the trade unions themselves can take to ensure that individual members are freely and effectively able to decide for themselves whether or not to pay the political levy. In the event that the trade unions are not willing to take such steps, the Government will be prepared to introduce measures to guarantee the free and effective right of choice.

Essential services

The proposal to curb immunity in the absence of pre-strike ballots will reduce the risk of strikes in essential services. In addition, we shall consult further about the need for industrial relations in specified essential services to be governed by adequate procedure agreements, breach of which would deprive industrial action of immunity. The nation is entitled to expect that the operation of essential services should not be disrupted.

Involving employees

Good employers involve their employees by consulting them and keeping them fully informed. This is vital for efficiency as well as harmony in industry. We shall continue to encourage it. Many employers have already done much in recent years to establish a long-needed sense of common purpose with their workforces. We shall resist current attempts to impose rigid systems of employer/employee relations in Britain. We will continue to encourage workers to identify with the success of the firm for which they work, by the promotion of share-ownership and profit-sharing.

In each of the last two years, largely as a result of tax changes we have introduced, about a quarter of a million employees have acquired shares in the companies that employ them.

When state industries are offered to the private sector, we have given their employees the chance to buy shares in them, and many have exercised this right.

Unemployment: coping with change

During the last four years, unemployment in the industrialised countries has risen more sharply than at any time since the 1930s. Britain has been no exception. We have long been one of the least efficient and most over-manned of industrialised nations. We raised our own pay far more, and our output far less, than most of our competitors. Inevitably, this pushed prices up and drove countless customers to buy from other countries, forcing thousands of employers out of business and hundreds of thousands of workers out of jobs.

At the same time, there has been a rapid shift of jobs from the old industries to the new, concentrated on services and the new technologies. Tragically, trade unions have often obstructed these changes. All too often this has delayed and reduced the new and better-paid jobs which could replace those that have been lost.

This Government has an impressive record in helping the unemployed who, usually through no fault of their own, are paying the price of these past errors.

We have committed over £2,000m. this year to training and special measures for the unemployed. This is supported by substantial help from the European Community's Social Fund, amounting to over £250m. in 1982. As long as unemployment remains high, we shall maintain special measures of this kind, which bring effective help to many of those who have no job.

This year, some 1,100,000 people are being trained or helped by the most comprehensive programme of its kind in Europe.

For the first time, the new Enterprise Allowance Scheme offers many thousands of unemployed people the support they need, but previously could not get, while they start their own businesses. We will maintain special help for the long-term unemployed through the Community Programme, and for the older unemployed through early retirement schemes.

Removing the barriers to jobs

We shall go on reducing the barriers which discourage employers from recruiting more staff, even when they want to. And we shall help to make the job market more flexible and efficient so that more people can work part-time if they wish, and find work more easily.

That is why we have amended the Employment Protection Act and why we shall continue to:

- minimise the legal restrictions which discourage the creation of new jobs;
- encourage moves towards greater flexibility in working practices, such as Part-Time Job Release, which makes it financially possible for people nearing retirement age to go part-time; and the Job-Splitting Scheme which helps employers to split a whole-time job into two part-time jobs;

- improve the efficiency of the employment services in identifying and filling job vacancies;
- ensure that Wages Councils do not reduce job opportunities by forcing workers to charge unrealistic pay rates, or employers to offer them.

Training

If we are to make the most of the employment opportunities that present themselves in an age of rapid change and more varied patterns of work and occupation, up-to-date training is essential.

Training for work must start with better, more relevant education at school. For school leavers, we have provided the most imaginative and far-reaching scheme in our history. The Youth Training Scheme offers every 16 year old a year of serious training for work. It should help 350,000 youngsters by the autumn of this year. From now on, no one leaving school at 16 need be unemployed in his first year out of school.

This is only a part of our wider strategy to ensure effective training for the skills and jobs of tomorrow – on a scale and of a quality to match the world's best. At its heart is our reform of industrial training and the apprenticeship system.

We are improving the scope and quality of our training for the employed and unemployed alike; tackling problems which the Labour Party has never had the courage to face.

We shall continue to provide for, and improve, the special employment and training needs of the disabled, and to reform our training agencies to meet more effectively the needs of industry and workers alike.

The nationalised industries

Reform of the nationalised industries is central to economic recovery. Most people who work in these industries work hard and have a sense of public service. Since 1979, we have gone to great lengths to improve the performance of the state sector, to appoint top-class managers and work closely with them to tackle each industry's problems.

But for all this, few people can now believe that state ownership means better service to the customer. The old illusions have melted away. Nationalisation does not improve job satisfaction, job security or labour relations – almost all the serious strikes in recent years have been in state industries and services. We have also seen how the burden of financing the state industries has kept taxes and government borrowing higher than they need have been.

A company which has to satisfy its customers and compete to survive is more likely to be efficient, alert to innovation, and genuinely accountable to the public. That is why we have transferred to private ownership, in whole or in part, Cable and Wireless, Associated British Ports, British Aerospace, Britoil, British Rail Hotels, Amersham International, and the National Freight Corporation. Many of their shares have been bought by their own employees and managers, which is the truest public ownership of all.

We shall continue our programme to expose state-owned firms to real competition. In telecommunications, we have licensed a new independent network, Mercury, and have decided to license two mobile telephone networks. We have allowed competition in commercial postal services. Already, standards of service are beginning to improve. Investment is rising. And better job opportunities are being opened up.

We shall transfer more state-owned businesses to independent ownership. Our aim is that British Telecom – where we will sell 51 per cent of the shares to the private sector Rolls Royce, British Airways and substantial parts of British Steel, of British Shipbuilders and of British Leyland, and as many as possible of Britain's airports, shall become private sector companies. We also aim to introduce substantial private capital into the National Bus Company. As before, we will offer shares to all those who work in them.

We shall also transfer to the private sector the remaining state-owned oil business – the British Gas Corporation's offshore oil interests.

We have abolished the Gas Corporation's statutory monopoly of the supply of North Sea gas to industry. Already there has been a vigorous new lease of life for gas exploration and development in the North Sea, which had ground to a complete halt under Labour. In the last Parliament, we passed a law to encourage the private generation of electricity. In the next Parliament, we shall seek other means of increasing competition in, and attracting private capital into, the gas and electricity industries.

Merely to replace state monopolies by private ones would be to waste an historic opportunity. So we will take steps to ensure that these new firms do not exploit their powerful positions to the detriment of consumers or their competitors. Those nationalised industries which cannot be privatised or organised as smaller and more efficient units will be given top-quality management and required to work to clear guidelines.

Encouraging free enterprise

We want to see an economy in which firms, large and small, have every incentive to expand by winning extra business and creating more jobs. This Conservative Government has been both giving those incentives and clearing away the obstacles to expansion: the high rates of tax on individuals and businesses; the difficulties facing the small firm trying to grow, and the self-employed man trying to set up on his own; the blockages in the planning system; the bottlenecks on our roads; the restrictions on our farmers and fishermen; and the resistance to new ideas and technologies.

In the last four years, many British firms have made splendid progress in improving their competitiveness and profitability. But there is some way to go yet before this country has regained that self-renewing capacity for growth which once made her a great economic power, and will make her great again.

Only a government which really works to promote free enterprise can provide the right conditions for that dream to come true.

Lower and simpler taxes

In the last four years, we have made great strides in reducing and simplifying taxes. We have:

- cut the basic rate of income tax; raised tax allowances above the level we inherited after allowing for price rises; brought the higher rates of income tax down to

European levels; and made big reductions in the investment income surcharge, which have particularly helped the old;

- removed many of the worst features of Capital Transfer Tax, Capital Gains Tax and Development Land Tax;
- cut business taxes, in particular the National Insurance Surcharge, Labour's tax on jobs, from 3½ per cent to 1 per cent; and improved stock relief for businesses;
- much reduced the taxes on, and increased the incentives for, gifts to charities;
- greatly reduced tax bureaucracy. Manpower in the Inland Revenue and Customs & Excise has fallen from 113,400 in April 1979 to 98,500 in April 1983, and is set to fall further.

This dramatic progress is all the more striking when compared with the vast increases in taxation which our opponents' policies would inevitably bring.

The changes to this year's Finance Act on which Labour have insisted show that they intend just this. We shall reverse those changes at the earliest opportunity.

Further improvements in allowances and lower rates of income tax remain a high priority, together with measures to reduce the poverty and unemployment traps.

We want to encourage wider ownership. This means lowering taxes on capital and savings; encouraging individuals to invest directly in company shares; and encouraging the creation of more employee share schemes.

More small firms

We have reduced the burdens on small firms, especially in employment legislation and planning, and cut many of the taxes they pay, particularly Corporation Tax. Our Loan Guarantee Scheme has already backed extra lending of over £300m. to about 10,000 small firms. The new Business Expansion Scheme, a major extension of the Business Start-up Scheme, will encourage outside investment in small companies by special tax reliefs. The construction of new premises for small businesses has more than doubled.

To help the engineering industry and the areas most dependent on it, we have introduced and now extended a very successful scheme of grants (SEFIS) to smaller firms, which help them to buy new machinery.

Thanks to these policies and over one hundred other important measures, the climate for new and smaller businesses in the UK has been transformed and is now as favourable as anywhere in the world.

Help for the new technologies

Even during the recession, our new industries and technologies made remarkable progress. Britain has more micro-computers in relation to its population than any other country. We have speeded this progress by supporting research and spreading knowledge of the technologies of tomorrow; and by increasing government support for the new technologies from £100m. in 1978–79 to over £350m. in 1983–4. But that is only the beginning. We will now:

- promote, in partnership with industry, the Alvey programme for research into advanced information technology;

- accelerate the transfer of technology from the university laboratory to the market place, especially by the encouragement of science parks;
- help firms to launch new products through pilot schemes and public purchasing;
- build on the successes of our 'Micros-in-Schools' scheme and our network of Information Technology Centres for the young unemployed so that they are equipped with tomorrow's skills;
- sanction the launch of new cable networks to bring wider choice to consumers, not just for entertainment, but for the whole new world of tele-shopping and tele-banking.

Regions, Enterprise Zones and freeports

We shall continue to maintain an effective regional policy which is essential to ease the process of change and encourage new businesses in areas which have been dependent on declining industries. We do not propose sudden changes in regional policy. But we will:

- make sure that these policies are economical and effective in creating genuine jobs;
- secure more effective co-ordination between central and local government and the European Community's Regional Development Fund to ensure that their actions offer the greatest help to communities in need;
- further develop local self-help initiatives, the 24 Enterprise Zones and, our latest innovation, duty-free trading zones, which will be established in certain experimental 'Freeports';
- diversify regional economies by encouraging the fullest use of our schemes for innovation.

Planning

In our crowded country the planning system has to strike a delicate balance. It must provide for the homes and workplaces we need. It must protect the environment in which we live.

One particular way to achieve this is by bringing back into use the thousands of acres lying derelict and unused, so much of which is in the ownership of local authorities or other public bodies. We have set up Land Registers to identify this land, and we shall now use our powers to bring it into use. The more this land can be used, the less the need to build on Green Belts and the countryside. We will also bring open-cast coalmining within normal proper planning control, and we shall establish more control over intensive livestock units near residential areas.

Energy

Britain has come from nowhere to be the world's fifth largest oil producer. The North Sea success story has been a triumph of private enterprise for the nation's benefit. We shall continue to ensure that our taxation and licensing policies encourage development in the North Sea.

In the next Parliament, the interests of the whole country require Britain's massive coal industry, on which we depend for the overwhelming bulk of our electricity generation, to return to economic viability.

We shall press ahead with the development of safe nuclear power. It is an important way of securing lower-cost electricity for the future. We shall set up an Energy Efficiency Office to co-ordinate the Government's conservation effort, so as to ensure that the taxpayer gets the best value for money.

We recognise that some energy users have special needs. This is why we have:

- ensured that standing charges no longer dominate the bills of small gas and electricity consumers;
- increased help for the needy with their fuel bills, leading to many fewer disconnections;

and

- introduced more favourable terms for the energy-intensive industries.

Better transport for industry

The national motorway and trunk road network will continue to be developed and improved to high-quality standards. This will not only make driving much safer for all, but also speed and cheapen the transport of goods. We will also seek to make rail freight more competitive.

Many of our ports have now been returned from state control to independent ownership. We intend that they should provide profitable and efficient services without the taxpayers' support.

Tourism

Our hotels, resorts and tourist attractions are important because they provide hundreds of thousands of jobs, earn valuable foreign exchange, and provide holidays for millions of our own people. We shall continue to support the Tourist Boards and tourism projects throughout the country.

Farming and fishing

British farming and horticulture have improved dramatically since 1979. Exports have leapt to £2,500m. a year. Since 1978, our self-sufficiency in food has risen by more than a sixth, from 53 per cent to 62 per cent.

In Europe, our tough negotiating stance has doubled our farmers' share of the help available under the Common Agricultural Policy. The cost of the CAP to British taxpayers doubled under Labour. Under us, it has been falling in real terms. We have reversed the Labour Government's disastrous policy for the Green Pound which harmed British farmers. At the same time, we have not neglected the consumers' interest. Food prices more than doubled under Labour and rose faster than other prices. Under the Conservatives, they have risen less than other prices. Last year they grew by less than one per cent, the smallest rise for nearly twenty years.

We have given special help to Britain's hill farmers, and agreed very worthwhile Community schemes for beef and sheepmeat. These have all brought great benefits to Wales, Scotland, Northern Ireland and the uplands of England. We have launched successfully the 'Food from Britain' campaign, which should help us sell far more of our products both at home and in the rest of the Community.

We shall help the glasshouse industry to sell more fruit and vegetables, and to make use of the best possible arrangements for heating and insulation.

We welcome the fact that, after long negotiations, the National Farmers' Union and the Country Landowners' Association have agreed on the best way to make more farm tenancies available for young people. We shall legislate on these lines at an early opportunity. We intend to make sure that British agriculture and horticulture continue to make the greatest possible contribution to our economic success.

We have successfully negotiated a Common Fishing Agreement that provides British fishermen with the greatest advantages in our waters in the industry's history. For the first time since we joined the Community, we now have effective conservation measures, and can look forward to expanding, rather than declining, stocks of fish. During the next Parliament, we shall introduce measures to restructure the fishing industry and to encourage investment and better marketing.

Responsibility and the family

Freedom and responsibility go together. The Conservative Party believes in encouraging people to take responsibility for their own decisions. We shall continue to return more choice to individuals and their families. That is the way to increase personal freedom. It is also the way to improve standards in the state services.

Conservatives believe equally strongly in the duty of Government to help those who are least able to help themselves. We have more than carried out our pledges to protect pensioners against price rises and to maintain standards in the National Health Service. This rebuts the totally unfounded charge that we want to 'dismantle the Welfare State'. We are determined that our public services should provide the best possible value both for people they seek to help and for the taxpayer who pays the bill.

A free and independent society is one in which the ownership of property is spread as widely as possible. A business which is partly or wholly owned by its workers will have more pride in performance. Already firms like the National Freight Company, where managers and workers joined together to take over the business, are thriving.

Under this Government, the property-owning democracy is growing fast. And the basic foundation of it is the family home.

Housing: towards a home-owning democracy

We have given every council and New Town tenant the legal right to buy his or her own home. Many Housing Association tenants have been granted the same right, too. This is the biggest single step towards a home-owning democracy ever taken. It is also the largest transfer of property from the State to the individual. No less than half a million council houses and flats were sold in the last Parliament to the people who live in them. By our encouragement of private housebuilding and our new range of schemes to help first-time buyers, there are a million more owner-occupiers today than four years ago.

The Labour Party has met these proposals with vicious and prolonged resistance and is still fighting a rearguard action against wider home ownership. A Labour government would take away the tenant's right to buy his council house, would prevent councils selling even voluntarily at a discount, and would force any former tenant who wanted to sell his house to sell it back to the council.

In the next Parliament, we will give many thousand more families the chance to buy their homes. For public sector tenants, the present 'Right to Buy' scheme will be improved and extended to include the right to buy houses on leasehold land and the right to buy on a shared ownership basis. The maximum discount will be increased by one per cent a year for those who have been tenants for between twenty and thirty years, taking the maximum discount to 60 per cent. We shall also help first-time buyers who are not council tenants through our various low-cost home-ownership schemes: 'homesteading', building for sale, improvement for sale, and shared ownership.

Britain needs more homes to rent, too, in the private sector as well as the public sector. For years, the blind prejudice of the Labour Party has cast a political blight on privately rented housing. But our assured tenancy scheme has encouraged builders to start building new homes to rent again, and our shorthold scheme is helping the private sector to meet the needs of those who want short-term rented accommodation.

We shall extend our Tenants' Charter to enable council tenants to get necessary repairs done themselves and be reimbursed by their councils. Housing Improvement Grants have been increased substantially in the last two years and will continue to play an important role.

We shall conduct early public consultation of proposals which would enable the building societies to play a fuller part in supporting the provision of new housing and would bring up to date the laws which govern them.

Our goal is to make Britain the best housed nation in Europe.

Protecting the pensioner

Over the last four years, the retirement pension has risen from £19.50 to £32.85 a week for a single person and from £31.20 to £52.55 for a married couple. Even after allowing for price rises, pensioners can buy more with their pension today than they could under the last Labour government. We have ended Labour's unreliable system of relying on forecasts of price rises to decide by how much to increase the pension. In five of the last seven years, those forecasts turned out to be wrong. In future, pensions will be related to actual and not estimated price increases.

In the next Parliament, we shall continue to protect retirement pensions and other linked long-term benefits against rising prices. Public sector pensioners will also continue to be protected on the basis of realistic pension contributions. In this Parliament, we raised to £57 a week the amount pensioners may earn without losing any of their pension. It remains our intention to continue raising the limit and to abolish this earnings rule as soon as we can. The Christmas Bonus, which Labour failed to pay in 1975 and 1976, will continue to be paid every year in accordance with the law we passed in 1979.

Over 11.5m people – half the working population – are now covered by occupational pension schemes. We will consider how the pension rights of 'early leavers', people who change jobs, can be better protected and how their members may be given fuller information about their pension schemes.

Social security

Supplementary benefits, too, have been raised ahead of prices. To encourage thrift, instead of penalising it, the Government has also raised the amount of savings people can keep without losing any supplementary benefit. At the same time, we have clamped down firmly on fraud and abuse of social security.

Expenditure on cash benefits to the disabled is 21 per cent higher than under Labour, even after allowing for rising prices. There has been extra help, too, for those who are least able to afford their fuel bills.

We have introduced – and extended – a widows' bereavement allowance. We have kept the war widows' pension ahead of prices and removed it from tax altogether.

Child benefit and one-parent benefit are to be raised in November to their highest-ever level in real terms. We have also improved the family income supplement scheme to help low-paid working families.

Our record shows the strength of our commitment. But our ability to help depends on the wealth which the country produces. In Britain today, over 40p in every pound of public spending is already devoted to health and social security. It is hypocritical for the Labour Party to pretend that they could raise public spending on benefits by thousands of millions of pounds without admitting the vast increases in taxation and National Insurance contributions that would be needed, or the increased inflation that would result.

The National Health Service

We have more than matched our pledge to maintain spending on the National Health Service and secure proper value for money. Even after allowing for price rises, the nation is spending substantially more on health, and getting better health care.

By last year, there were 45,000 more nurses and midwives, and over 6,500 more doctors and dentists, working for the NHS than in 1978. This has helped to make it possible to treat over two million more patients a year in our hospitals. Until last year's futile strike, waiting lists for treatment fell sharply.

We intend to continue to make sure that all patients receive the best possible value for the money that is spent on the Health Service. The treatment of the elderly, the mentally handicapped and the mentally ill will continue to make extra provision for those parts of the country in the North and the Midlands which have always been comparatively short of resources.

Unlike the last Labour government which actually cut the hospital building programme by one-third, we have committed £1,100m. to our large-scale programme for building new hospitals. There are now 140 new hospitals in that programme being designed or built. We shall continue to upgrade existing hospitals and brighten up shabby wards.

To release more money for looking after patients, we will reduce the costs of administering the Health Service. We are asking health authorities to make the maximum possible savings by putting services like laundry, catering and hospital cleaning out to competitive tender. We are tightening up, too, on management costs, and getting much firmer control of staff numbers.

Most people who are ill or frail would prefer to stay in or near their own homes, rather than live in a hospital or institution. Helping people to stay in familiar surroundings is the aim of our policy 'Care in the Community'. The Government has given extra powers and extra cash to health authorities to enable them to finance such community care for individual patients on a long-term basis.

Partnership in care

Conservatives reject Labour's contention that the State can and should do everything.

We welcome the growth in private health insurance in recent years. This has both made more health care available, and lightened the load on the NHS, particularly for non-urgent operations. We shall continue to encourage this valuable supplement to state care. We shall promote closer partnership between the State and the private sectors in the exchange of facilities and of ideas in the interests of all patients.

We also welcome the vital contribution made by voluntary organisations in the social services. We shall continue to give them strong support. The Conservative Government has already made many radical changes in law and taxation which have greatly improved the way charities and voluntary bodies are financed. The terms governing gifts under covenants have been much improved, and the liability to capital taxation has been lightened or swept away.

We shall continue to support our highly successful 'Opportunities for Volunteering' scheme. In the next Parliament, we shall develop other new ways to encourage more private giving.

Schools: the pursuit of excellence

For a long time now, parents have been worried about standards and discipline in many of our schools. This Conservative Government has responded to that worry with the Parents' Charter and the 1980 Education Act. For the first time:

- local authorities were obliged to take account of parents' choice of school for their children;
- schools were obliged to publish prospectuses, giving details of their examination results;
- parents were given the right to be represented on school governing bodies;
- the Government offered Assisted Places to enable less well-off parents to send bright children to some of the best independent schools.

Giving parents more power is one of the most effective ways of raising educational standards. We shall continue to seek ways of widening parental choice and influence over their children's schooling. We shall defend Church schools and independent schools alike against our opponents' attacks. And we shall defend the right of parents to spend their own money on educating their children.

This country is now spending more per child in school than ever before, even after allowing for price rises. As a result, the average number of children per teacher is the lowest ever. Exactly how the money is spent, and how schools are run, is up to local education authorities. But the Government can help improve standards and make sure that children are taught and trained for the world they will grow up into.

- Until now, HM Inspectors' reports have remained secret. Now we are publishing them and making sure they are followed up, too.
- We are not satisfied with the selection or the training of our teachers. Our White Paper sets out an important programme for improving teacher training colleges.
- We shall switch the emphasis in the Education Welfare Service back to school attendance, so as to reduce truancy.
- We have given special help for refresher courses for teachers, research into special schools, and play groups and nursery schools where they are most needed.
- We shall also encourage schools to keep proper records of their pupils' achievements, buy more computers, and carry out external graded tests. The public examination system will be improved, and O-level standards will be maintained.
- We are setting up fourteen pilot projects to bring better technical education to teenagers. The success of these will play a vital part in raising technical training in Britain to the level of our best overseas competitors.

Higher education

Our universities and polytechnics, too, must generate new ideas and train the skilled workforce of the next generation. We have unrivalled institutions and unrivalled inventive genius – as the number of British Nobel prize-winners shows. What matters is to bring the two closer together and make the best practical use of both.

Britain has more students in professional training than Japan, and a greater proportion of young people in higher education than France or West Germany. More of our young people are now entering full-time degree courses than under the last Labour government. And a larger proportion of them complete their courses than in most other countries.

The very large sums of public money now going to higher education must be spent in the most effective way. Within that budget, we want to see a shift towards technological, scientific and engineering courses.

- We have set aside money for 700 new posts for young lecturers over three years to bring new blood into research.
- Over the next three years, we will provide for more teaching and research on information technology, with new posts for lecturers, and 2,200 new places for students.

Sport and recreation

The Government has increased the real level of funding for the Sports Council. The Urban Aid and Derelict Land Programmes have also contributed to new sporting projects. By these means, and by offering one pound of government money for every one pound raised locally, we have begun to transform sports facilities in the inner cities. But there are still plenty of sports facilities which could be opened up to the general public. In particular, to reinforce our initiatives for better use of schools and playing fields, we shall urge every local education authority to make school and college premises available for use outside school hours and in the holidays. In all these initiatives, voluntary bodies will be enabled to play a bigger part.

We have kept up the pressure for public access to parks and reservoirs for anglers and all those who enjoy and respect the countryside.

Safety, quality and value for money

The best way to protect the consumer is to bring price rises down and keep them down, and to increase competition. We have achieved both, and so helped the housewife far more than any bureaucratic system of controls. We have also brought the state industries under the scrutiny of the Monopolies and Mergers Commission, and exposed many of them to competition to prevent them from exploiting their customers.

We shall remain vigilant in defence of the quality and safety of the products people buy. But we shall also reduce government intervention wherever it is unnecessary or harmful to the interests of the customer.

The provisions of our Data Protection Bill will meet public concern that computers pose a particular threat to privacy, and will enable us to ratify the European Convention on Data Protection.

Supporting family life

It is not for the Government to try to dictate how men and women should organise their lives. Our approach is to help people and their families fulfil their own aspirations in a rapidly changing world. As an employer, this Government is fulfilling its commitment to equal opportunities for men and women who work in the public services. We have brought forward for public discussion proposals for improving the tax treatment of married women, whether or not they go out to work.

We are reviewing the family jurisdiction of the courts, including their conciliation role, with a view to improving the administration of family law. We shall also reform the divorce laws to offer further protection to children, and to secure fairer financial arrangements when a marriage ends.

Law, democracy and the citizen

The rule of law matters deeply to every one of us. Any concession to the thief, the thug or the terrorist undermines that principle which is the foundation of all our liberties. That is why we have remained firm in the face of the threats of hijackers and hunger strikers alike. The defeat of the occupation of the Iranian Embassy is only one example of our determination to be patient but still unyielding.

Backing the crime-fighters

We recognised from the start the immense and continuing public concern about lawlessness, particularly in some of our larger cities. We acted immediately to fulfil our pledges to give the hard-pressed police every possible backing.

- The strength of the police force now stands at record levels: 9,000 extra policemen have been recruited in England and Wales alone since 1979. They are much better paid and equipped than ever before. We shall be ready to increase police establishments where necessary in the war against crime.

- Thousands more policemen are back on the beat, where the public wishes to see them, instead of being isolated in panda cars. It takes time for any reform in police training and methods to achieve its full effect, but already street crime is being reduced and public confidence improved in some of the worst inner-city areas.
- The proposals embodied in our Police and Criminal Evidence Bill will help the police to bring criminals to justice. At the same time, they will reinforce public support for the police by laying down clear rules for the proper treatment of suspects. We shall also build more courtrooms to reduce delays in trying criminal cases.
- Last year's Criminal Justice Act has given the courts tougher and more flexible sentencing powers. This Act makes parents more responsible for crimes committed by their children, and improves compensation for the victims of crime.
- Courts will also continue to impose Community Service Orders which compel offenders to make amends by doing useful work for the local community. We shall set up more compulsory attendance centres to which the courts can send young hooligans. The invaluable work of the Probation Service will continue to be supported.
- There must be enough prison places to cope with sentences imposed by the courts. We shall complete our major programme of building which will provide another 4,800 places in ten new prisons. And we are recruiting more prison officers to staff them.
- We will also respond to the increasing public concern over obscenity and offences against public decency, which often have links with serious crime. We propose to introduce specific legislation to deal with the most serious of these problems, such as the dangerous spread of violent and obscene video cassettes.
- We accept the case for an independent prosecution service, and will consider how it might best be set up.
- We intend to extend substantially the grounds that disqualify those with criminal records from serving on juries.

Dealing with crimes, civil disobedience, violent demonstrations and pornography are not matters for the police alone. It is teachers and parents – and television producers, too – who influence the moral standards of the next generation. There must be close co-operation and understanding between the police and the community they serve.

Immigration: firm and fair

We are utterly opposed to racial discrimination wherever it occurs, and we are determined to see that there is real equality of opportunity. The Conservative Party is, and always has been, strongly opposed to unfairness, harassment and persecution, whether it be inspired by racial, religious or ideological motives.

To have good community relations, we have to maintain effective immigration control. Since 1979, immigration for settlement has dropped sharply to the lowest level since control of immigration from the Commonwealth began more than twenty years ago. By passing the British Nationality Act, we have created a secure system of rights and a sound basis for control in the future; and we will continue to pursue policies which are strict but fair.

The supremacy of Parliament

The British Constitution has outlasted most of the alternatives which have been offered as replacements. It is because we stand firm for the supremacy of Parliament that we are determined to keep its rules and procedures in good repair.

We have modernised the Select Committees to improve Parliament's ability to keep a check on the actions of the Executive. We shall continue to pursue sensible, carefully considered reforms where they are of practical value.

Labour want to abolish the House of Lords. We will ensure that it has a secure and effective future. A strong Second Chamber is a vital safeguard for democracy and contributes to good government.

Northern Ireland

In Northern Ireland, building upon the courage, commitment and increasing success of our security forces, we will give the highest priority to upholding law and order. We will continue to give the support essential for the Province to overcome its economic difficulties.

The people of Northern Ireland will continue to be offered a framework for participation in local democracy and political progress through the Assembly. There will be no change in Northern Ireland's constitutional position in the United Kingdom without the consent of the majority of people there, and no devolution of powers without widespread support throughout the community. We believe that a close practical working relationship between the United Kingdom and the Government of the Republic can contribute to peace and stability in Northern Ireland without threatening in any way the position of the majority community in the Province.

The quality of government

This country is fortunate to have a Civil Service with high standards of administration and integrity. The Civil Service has loyally and effectively helped to carry through the far-reaching changes we have made to secure greater economy, efficiency and better management in Government itself. It is a tribute to this spirit of co-operation that the number of civil servants has been reduced from 732,000 to 649,000 with the minimum of redundancies and with higher standards of service to the citizen. This has saved the taxpayer about £500m. a year, and is helping us to improve Civil Service working conditions.

The efficiency 'scrutinies' launched by Lord Rayner and other money-saving techniques have now identified savings worth £400m. a year to the taxpayer. We have abolished 500 Quangos and done away with no less than 3,600 different types of government forms.

We are successfully putting out to tender more services needed by central government. We shall press on with this wherever public money can be saved and standards of service maintained or improved.

Public spending is now planned in terms of hard cash instead of so-called constant prices, and the discipline of cash limits on spending has been extended. As a result, public spending is firmly under control.

Local government: saving ratepayers' money

We have checked the relentless growth of local government spending, and manpower is now back down to the level of 1974. The achievement of many Conservative authorities in saving ratepayers' money by putting services like refuse collection out to tender has played a major part in getting better value for money and significantly reducing the level of rate increases. We shall encourage every possible saving by this policy.

There are, however, a number of grossly extravagant Labour authorities whose exorbitant rate demands have caused great distress both to businesses and domestic ratepayers. We shall legislate to curb excessive and irresponsible rate increases by high-spending councils, and to provide a general scheme for limitation of rate increases for all local authorities to be used if necessary.

In addition, for industry we will require local authorities to consult local representatives of industry and commerce before setting their rates. We shall give more businesses the right to pay by instalments. And we shall stop the rating of empty industrial property.

The Metropolitan Councils and the Greater London Council have been shown to be a wasteful and unnecessary tier of government. We shall abolish them and return most of their functions to the boroughs and districts. Services which need to be administered over a wider area – such as police and fire, and education in inner London – will be run by joint boards of borough or district representatives.

Improving our environment

The Conservative Party has a long record of practical and effective action to improve the quality of life in our cities and countryside and to preserve our heritage. Since 1979, no government in Western Europe has done more for the environment – a clumsy word for many of the things that make life worth living.

Reviving Britain's cities

We have to cure the disastrous mistakes of decades of town-hall Socialism by striking a better balance between public and private effort. Our approach to reviving the run-down areas of our great cities is to use limited public money to stimulate much larger investment by private enterprise. The £60m. we have earmarked for the Urban Development Grant this year will be matched by up to four times that sum from private firms investing in new developments. On Merseyside, Operation Groundwork has brought together landowners, local industry and local authorities to tackle the squalor and dereliction on the edge of towns. The lessons of this and many other Merseyside initiatives will now be applied in other urban areas.

We have encouraged people to move back into the inner cities. Builders are now being helped to build homes of the type that young couples in particular can afford. We shall promote this revival of our inner cities, both by new building, and by sales by local councils of some of their rundown property to homesteaders who will restore the homes themselves.

We shall encourage greater opportunity for all those who live in our inner cities, including our ethnic minorities.

- Our small business schemes are helping to bring firms back into the city centres, and the Enterprise Zones we have set up are already bringing new life to some of the hardest-hit places in industrial Britain.
- We shall continue to give priority to the areas most in need. Our programme for the reclamation of derelict land will continue. We shall increase our efforts to secure the disposal of under-used public sector land, using the powers available to us in order to require sites to be sold for homes and jobs.

Public transport

We have already taken important steps to improve the standards of public transport. We have lifted restrictions on long-distance coach services. As a result, about one hundred new express coach services have been started, fares have been substantially reduced and comfort improved. We shall further relax bus licensing to permit a wider variety of services. We shall encourage the creation of smaller units in place of the monolithic public transport organisations which we have inherited from the Socialist past, and encourage more flexible forms of public transport. City buses and underground railways will still need reasonable levels of subsidy. But greater efficiency and more private enterprise will help keep costs down.

The GLC has grossly mismanaged London Transport. We shall set up a new London Regional Transport Authority for the underground, buses and commuter trains in the London area. This will provide the opportunity to split the different types of transport into separate operating bodies, put more services out to private tender and offer the passenger better performance.

In the country, we shall ensure better use of school and special buses for local communities. Restrictions on minibuses will be cut. So will the red tape which makes it so difficult for small firms and voluntary bodies to provide better ways to get around for those without cars, particularly the very old and the disabled.

We want to see a high-quality, efficient railway service. That does not mean simply providing ever-larger subsidies from the taxpayer. Nor, on the other hand, does it mean embarking upon a programme of major route closures. There is, however, scope for substantial cost reductions in British Rail which are needed to justify investment in a modern and efficient railway.

Fewer restrictive practices and much more attention to the customer are also essential. Rail services are now facing vigorous competition from coaches and cars, and they need to respond with more innovative and more modern work methods. We shall examine ways of decentralising BR and bringing in private enterprise to serve railway customers.

To make life more agreeable in our towns and villages, we will push ahead our bypass programme, which will help to take more lorries away from them.

Rural policy and animal welfare

Conservatives understand the need for a proper balance between the strengthening of the rural economy and the preservation of the beauty and habitat of our countryside.

Economic development will be encouraged in areas where this balance can be best maintained. At the same time, we have introduced the Wildlife and Countryside Act – the most important piece of legislation yet affecting the countryside – to safeguard areas of natural beauty and sites of scientific interest.

We have taken the lead in the much acclaimed measures to save the whale from extinction and to protect seals, and we shall co-operate fully in the important international work to protect all endangered species.

Since 1979, we have been working to achieve full European agreement on the treatment of animals. We have introduced measures to improve the conditions of farm animals being transported or exported. There is now a European Convention on the Protection of Animals. We welcomed this agreement, and immediately introduced a White Paper on Animal Welfare to foreshadow changes in the law. We now propose to introduce legislation to update the Cruelty to Animals Act 1876 which will ensure more humane treatment of laboratory animals in scientific and industrial research. The sale of pet animals in street markets has been banned.

Controlling pollution

We intend to remove lead from petrol, and are taking the initiative with our European partners to achieve this at the earliest possible date. We will press ahead with our plans to reduce lead in paints, food and drinking water.

We will continue our policy to reduce river pollution – the length of polluted rivers has been halved in the last ten years, and this work will continue. We shall tighten up the controls on the disposal of hazardous waste and continue to support the movement for recycling and reclamation.

The worst problems of air pollution have been resolved. But in some areas the levels of smoke and sulphur dioxide need to be further reduced.

The peaceful application of nuclear energy, if properly controlled (as it always has been in this country), will be beneficial to the environment as well as to the economy. We intend to make sure that the safety record of the British nuclear industry continues to be second to none. The Sizewell Inquiry into Britain's first Pressurised Water Reactor is well under way. The project will go ahead only if both the independent inspector and the Government are satisfied it is safe.

Arts and the heritage

Despite the recession, this Government has strengthened its support for the best of our heritage and for the performing arts. We have created the National Heritage Memorial Fund, which fulfils the long-delayed wish to commemorate the dead of two world wars in a permanent and tangible way. We are building a new British Library. The new Commission for Ancient Monuments and Historic Buildings will both safeguard our heritage and give more people a chance to enjoy it. Under the Conservatives, Britain's opera, theatre and ballet continue to win world-wide renown. And our tax changes have helped to revive the British film industry. We shall keep up the level of government support, including a fair share for the regions. We shall also examine ways of using the tax system to encourage further growth in private support for the arts and the heritage.

Britain in the world

For nearly four decades, Europe has been at peace. The strength of the Western Alliance has kept our own freedoms secure. The possession of nuclear weapons by both sides has been an effective deterrent to another war in Europe.

The policies which our Labour opponents now propose would put at risk all this hard-won security.

The protection of peace

The invasion of Afghanistan and the suppression of dissent in Poland remind us of the true nature of the Soviet Union. It remains a threat to the liberty and security of the West. The Soviet Union maintains massive armed forces in Europe, and is extending its naval power throughout the world. Soviet nuclear strength continues to grow, despite the false assurances of their propaganda machine.

Labour's support for gestures of one-sided disarmament is reckless and naive. There is no shred of evidence to suggest that the Soviet bloc would follow such an example. Labour would give up Britain's nuclear deterrent and prevent the United States from using its bases in Britain which are part of its nuclear shield over Europe. That would shatter the NATO Alliance, and put our safety in the greatest jeopardy. We will fully support the negotiations to reduce the deployment of nuclear weapons. But we will not gamble with our defence.

The Soviet Union now has over one thousand SS20 warheads, two-thirds of which are targeted on Europe. If the Soviet Union does not recognise over the coming months the legitimate anxieties of the West by agreeing to our proposals to eliminate this class of weapons, we will start deploying Cruise missiles by the end of this year. Even after this, the West will remain entirely ready to negotiate for the removal of some or all of the missiles which we deploy, on the basis of a balanced and fair agreement with the Soviet Union.

The Western Alliance can keep the peace only if we can convince any potential aggressor that he would have to pay an unacceptable price. To do so, NATO must have strong conventional forces backed by a nuclear deterrent. And we in Britain must maintain our own independent nuclear contribution to British and European defence. At the same time, we shall continue to support all realistic efforts to reach balanced and verifiable agreements with the Soviet Union on arms control and disarmament.

We have substantially increased our defence expenditure in real terms. We have honoured our promise to give our regular and reserve forces proper pay and conditions and the equipment they need to do the job.

There could be no greater testimony to the professional dedication and the quality of equipment of the British Armed Services than the brilliant recapture of the Falkland Islands in just 74 days. We take pride in their achievement.

Civil defence

Our overriding desire and policy are to go on preserving peace. However, no responsible government can simply assume that we shall never be attacked. To plan for civil defence is a humanitarian duty – not only against the possibility of nuclear. but also of conventional attack. That is why we must take steps to provide the help that could be vital for millions. To proclaim a nuclear-free zone, as some Labour councils have, is a delusion.

The Conservative Government has accordingly carried out a thorough review of civil defence, brought forward new regulations to require local authorities to provide improved protection, strengthened the UK Warning and Monitoring Organisations, and nearly doubled spending on civil defence.

We propose to amend the Civil Defence Act 1948 to enable civil defence funds to be used in safeguarding against peacetime emergencies as well as against hostile attacks.

Britain in Europe

The creation of the European Community has been vital in cementing lasting peace in Europe and ending centuries of hostility. We came to office determined to make a success of British membership of the Community. This we have done.

Our first priority in 1979 was to cut our financial contribution to the Community Budget to a fairer level. Labour made a song and dance about renegotiating the terms, but had achieved nothing. The bill to British taxpayers soared.

We have stood up for Britain's interests, and substantially reduced our net contribution to the Community Budget. We have tenaciously sought a permanent alternative to the annual wrangles about refunds. Until we secure a lasting solution, we shall make sure of proper interim safeguards for this country. Meanwhile, with the help of Conservatives in the European Parliament, we shall continue to try to shift the Community's spending priorities away from agriculture and towards industrial, regional and other policies which help Britain more.

We shall continue both to oppose petty acts of Brussels' bureaucracy and to seek the removal of unnecessary restrictions on the free movement of goods and services between member states, with proper safeguards to guarantee fair competition.

The Labour Party wants Britain to withdraw from the Community, because it fears that Britain cannot compete inside and that it would be easier to build a Socialist siege economy if we withdrew. The Liberals and the SDP appear to want Britain to stay in but never to upset our partners by speaking up forcefully. The Conservatives reject both extreme views.

The European Community is the world's largest trading group. It is by far our most important export market. Withdrawal would be a catastrophe for this country. As many as two million jobs would be at risk. We would lose the great export advantages and the attraction to overseas investors which membership now gives us. It would be a fateful step towards isolation, at which only the Soviet Union and her allies would rejoice.

A trading nation

Our most important contribution to a healthy world economy is to manage our own affairs successfully. We shall also build on our important role in promoting international action to encourage recovery through the IMF and other international organisations. With the other leading industrial nations, we shall continue with our realistic initiatives to improve currency stability in the Western world, and assist nations with excessive debts to regain stability. Together with the Community, we are also playing a leading part in preserving an open world trading system, while safeguarding our most vulnerable industries.

While world trade declined last year, our exports and share of world trade increased, and we enjoyed a healthy balance of payments surplus, despite the pessimists who said the pound was uncompetitive. We believe in reinforcing success. This Government has given wholehearted support to British companies tendering for major overseas projects, and helped them secure many important contracts in the face of the toughest competition.

We will build on these initiatives to help our exporters, and vigorously promote the interests of British trade and industry in international negotiations – where we have already made our presence very effectively felt. We have no intention of becoming a dumping ground for the goods of other nations. We shall continue to challenge other nations' unfair barriers, whether in the shape of tariffs or trading practices.

Our wider role

In a troubled world, Britain is increasingly respected because we stand up for our own interests. But we are also respected because we stand up for the cause of freedom and the spread of prosperity throughout the world.

We resisted unprovoked aggression in the Falkland Islands, when the loyal support of our friends throughout the world reminded us of our common heritage of freedom. We will continue to uphold the principles for which we fought.

We shall continue to give our full support to the Commonwealth and to play an active and constructive part at the United Nations.

Our generous but carefully controlled aid programme is both an investment in the freedom and prosperity of the poorer countries and in a stable and expanding world economy. That programme helps us as well as those who receive it, since most of it is spent on British goods and services. More than many other nations, we direct our aid to the poorest countries, particularly in the Commonwealth.

But government aid is only a part of the total help we give the developing world. Unlike the Labour Party, we believe in permitting a free and profitable outflow of British investment. That flow to poorer countries has now grown far larger than British Government aid, bringing with it an invaluable transfer of skills and technology.

The resolute approach

This Government's approach is straightforward and resolute. We mean what we say. We face the truth, even when it is painful. And we stick to our purpose.

Most decisions worth taking are difficult. Cutting a clear path through the jungle of a modern bureaucracy is hard going. The world recession of the past four years, and the high level of unemployment throughout the industrial world, have made the going harder.

During these difficult years, we have protected the sick and the elderly. We have maintained Britain's defences and her contribution to the Western Alliance. And at the same time, we have laid the foundations for a dynamic and prosperous future. The rewards are beginning to appear. If we continue on our present course with courage and commonsense, those rewards should multiply in the next five years.

We shall never lose sight of the British traditions of fairness and tolerance. We are also determined to revive those other British qualities – a genius for invention and a spirit of enterprise.

Under Conservative government, confidence is brushing aside pessimism at home. Abroad, Britain is regarded for the first time in years as a country with a great future as well as a great past.

We mean to make that future a reality.

THE NEXT MOVES FORWARD

THE CONSERVATIVE MANIFESTO 1987

CONSERVATIVE PARTY GENERAL ELECTION MANIFESTO 1987

Date of Election	Thursday 11 June
Party Leader	Margaret Thatcher
Candidates	633
MPs	376
Votes	13,763,066
% of vote	43.4%

Foreword

In the last eight years our country has changed –changed for the better.

We have discovered a new strength and a new pride. We have fostered a new spirit of enterprise. We have risen to fresh challenges at home and abroad. Once again our economy is strong. Our industries are flourishing. Unemployment is falling.

Founded on this new prosperity, we are building a better Health Service and providing more care for those in need. Living standards are higher than ever before. Our people have the protection of a stronger defence and more police.

Britain has come right by her own efforts. We trusted in the character and talents of our people. The British instinct is for choice and independence. Given the opportunities provided by Conservative policies, many more families now enjoy the pride of ownership of homes, of shares and of pensions.

Together we are building One Nation of free, prosperous and responsible families and people. A Conservative dream is at last becoming a reality.

This Manifesto points the way forward.

Margaret Thatcher

The British revival

This manifesto sets out our vision for the Britain of the 1990s and beyond, a future based on the aspirations of millions of individuals and their families their hopes, their needs, their security. For the first time in a generation this country looks forward to an era of real prosperity and fulfilment.

A vast change separates the Britain of today from the Britain of the late 1970s. Is it really only such a short time ago that inflation rose to an annual rate of 27 per cent? That the leader of the Transport and General Workers' Union was widely seen as the most powerful man in the land? That a minority Labour Government, staggering from crisis to crisis on borrowed money, was nonetheless maintained in power by the Liberal Party in return for the paper concession of a Lib-Lab pact? And that Labour's much-vaunted pay pact with the unions collapsed in the industrial anarchy of the 'winter of discontent', in which the dead went unburied, rubbish piled up in the streets and the country was gripped by a creeping paralysis which Labour was powerless to cure?

It seems in retrospect to be the history of another country. Yet these things happened and people had to accept them as an unavoidable part of everyday life.

Reversing the decline

Remember the conventional wisdom of the day. The British people were 'ungovernable'. We were in the grip of an incurable 'British disease'. Britain was heading for 'irreversible decline'.

Well, the people were not ungovernable, the disease was not incurable, the decline has been reversed.

- Britain today is in the seventh successive year of steady economic growth. We have moved from the bottom to the top of the growth league of major European countries.
- In Britain today, inflation has reached its lowest levels for almost twenty years.
- In Britain today, the number of strikes has dropped to the lowest levels for 50 years.
- In Britain today, far from being in debt to the IMF, we have built up our net overseas assets to their highest level since the Second World War – higher than France, Germany and the United States, second only to Japan.
- In Britain today, living standards are higher than ever before in our history.

But these are bald statistics. What matters is the feel of the country – the new enthusiasm for enterprise, the new spirit that Britain can make it, that we can prosper with the best. Investment in British industry is rising strongly. Our services sector, employing almost two-thirds of our workforce, generates a vast surplus of foreign earnings. And our manufacturers are travelling the globe with a new confidence born of the knowledge that Britain is internationally competitive again.

The world stage

This national revival is not confined to increased economic strength. Britain is also playing a major part on the international stage. From the White House through Europe to the Kremlin our voice is heard on arms control, on East-West issues, on human rights, on the Middle East and on African affairs.

With the Conservative Government, Britain has played a strong and responsible role internationally. We have defended civilised values by fighting terrorism relentlessly. We have secured our national interests, as when we liberated the Falklands. We have been ready to settle long-standing issues like Hong Kong where we reached an agreement to safeguard the way of life of the people.

Time and again we have shown that we possess the essential requirements of successful diplomacy: we stand firm on principles yet are ready to negotiate and prepared to take decisive action.

Founded in strength

The ability to act internationally does not come without effort. It must be founded on a strong economy and a robust defence. This Government took the necessary steps to build up both. Success has followed.

- Prudent financial policies have made Britain one of the world's largest creditors. Today we are able to shape world efforts to sustain trade and promote international monetary co-operation.
- We gave a lead in NATO and installed Cruise missiles. Today, as a result, the Soviet Union is at last prepared to negotiate to remove its own missiles targeted against us.
- This Government is modernising our own independent deterrent. Today Britain retains an independent influence in arms control negotiations between the superpowers.

By such steadfastness, we have not only rebuilt our economy and re-established our world reputation; we have also regained our national self-respect. But restoring a country's greatness is not easy. The new Conservative policies met bitter resistance every step of the way.

Remember . . .

- The year-long coal strike, with its violence and intimidation on a massive scale. It failed and mining productivity has since soared.
- The battle we had to fight to ensure that Britain paid no more than its fair share of the European Community Budget. We now get automatic rebates – this year, over £1.3 billion.
- The doubling of the oil price which confronted the new Government with a worldwide recession – and, more recently, an equally dramatic fall in the oil price which halved government oil revenues and in earlier times would have threatened a collapse of confidence in the pound. Both these oil 'shocks' were successfully withstood by prudent policies which have produced a sustained growth of prosperity.
- And let us not forget the challenge of the Falklands War.

How many of the alternative governments on offer would have stood firm, overcome, or even survived such difficulties? Does anyone suppose that the Labour Party would have resisted, let alone defeated, the violence and intimidation in the coal strike? Or that the Liberals or the Social Democrats would have fought so hard for our rebate from the European Community? Or that any of the Opposition parties would have persevered through all these difficulties to break the back of inflation and restore honest money?

A strong and stable government

How has it been done? All these improvements in the wealth and standing of our country have only been possible because we have had a strong government with sound policies and a decisive majority in Parliament. A weak government with uncertain policies would not have known how to withstand the pressures upon it; a government without a good overall majority in Parliament would not have been allowed to do so; and a strong government with unsound policies would have been a positive force for disaster.

In this election, only the Conservative Party is offering strong, decisive and united government.

The next moves forward

The next Conservative Government will build on the achievements of the past eight years with a full programme of positive reform.

We will continue:

- to pursue policies of sound financial management, the conquest of inflation, the promotion of enterprise and the growth of employment;
- to spread the ownership of homes, shares, pensions and savings ever more widely to give families greater financial independence;
- to give people greater choice and responsibility over their own lives in important areas such as housing and education;
- to improve the well-being of the people through better health care, and to safeguard the living standards of those who have to depend on the community;
- to improve the quality of life by conserving the best of our heritage and our countryside, and by fostering provision for the arts and sport;
- to exercise strong leadership where government needs to be strong in protecting the nation against potential aggression and the citizen against lawlessness.

We intend to press on with the radical Conservative reform which we embarked upon in 1979, and which has already revived the spirit of our people and restored the reputation of our country.

Wider ownership and greater opportunity

Conservatives aim to extend as widely as possible the opportunity to own property and build up capital, to exercise real choice in education, and to develop economic independence and security.

Our goal is a capital-owning democracy of people and families who exercise power over their own lives in the most direct way. They would take the important decisions – as tenants, home-owners, parents, employees, and trade unionists rather than having them taken for them.

Of course, it is not possible to give people independence. That is something we must all achieve by our own efforts. But what this Conservative Government has done is to make it easier for people to acquire independence for themselves:

- by introducing the right to buy council houses;
- by returning nationalised industries to the people in ways that encourage the widest possible spread of ownership;
- by making it easier to buy shares in British industry through employee share schemes and Personal Equity Plans.

These opportunities – all too often introduced in the teeth of fierce resistance from the Opposition parties – have achieved spectacular results. There has been a surge of home-ownership, share-ownership and self-reliance.

And because these first-time shareholders and home-owners are more independent, they develop a more independent outlook. They are no longer content that some of the most important decisions in their lives – what school their children attend, for example, or whether or not to go on strike should be taken by officialdom or trade union bosses. People want to decide such things for themselves.

In this way the scope of individual responsibility is widened, the family is strengthened, and voluntary bodies flourish. State power is checked and opportunities are spread throughout society. Ownership and independence cease to be the privileges of a few and become the birthright of all.

In this way One Nation is finally reached not by a single people being conscripted into an organised socialist programme but by millions of people building their own lives in their own way.

Better housing for all

Home ownership

Nowhere has the spread of ownership been more significant than in housing. Buying their own home is the first step most people take towards building up capital to hand down to their children and grandchildren. It gives people a stake in society – something to conserve. It is the foundation stone of a capital-owning democracy. A home should be a source of pride and independence to the family living in it, regardless of whether it is owned or rented. We will ensure that every family in the land has the opportunity to make it so.

Home-ownership has been the great success story of housing policy in the last eight years. One million council tenants have become home-owners and another one and a half million more families have become home-owners for the first time. Two out of every three homes are now owned by the people who live in them. This is a very high proportion, one of the largest in the world. We are determined to make it larger still.

Some people are still deterred by the costs and complications of house purchase. That is why we must look for new ways to make house-buying simpler and easier. Our abolition of the conveyancing monopoly has already made it cheaper. We will keep the present system of mortgage tax relief. We will target improvement grants to where they are most needed – to the least well-off. To meet the special needs of old people, we will ensure that all local authorities have powers to give improvement grants, where necessary, for properties where elderly people move in with relatives. We will extend the 30 per cent housing association grant to help schemes for old people.

A right to rent

Most problems in housing now arise in the rented sector. Controls, although well-meant, have dramatically reduced the private rented accommodation to a mere 8 per cent of the housing market.

This restricts housing choice and hinders the economy. People looking for work cannot easily move to a different area to do so. Those who find work may not be able to find rented accommodation nearby. Those who would prefer to rent rather than buy are forced to become reluctant owner-occupiers or to swell the queue for council houses. Some may even become temporarily homeless. And it is not only these people and their families who suffer from the shortage of homes for rent. The economy as a whole is damaged when workers cannot move to fill jobs because there are no homes to rent in the neighbourhood.

This must be remedied. We have already taken some modest steps in this direction by making it easier to part-own and part-rent homes through shared ownership; by bringing in and widening the scheme for assured tenancies; by our system of shortholds; and by providing a new 30 per cent housing association grant to build hostels for young workers. We have also directly tackled the problem of homelessness through new grants to housing associations and other measures. More must now be done. The next Conservative Government, having already implemented the right to buy, will increase practical opportunities to rent.

We must attract new private investment into rented housing – both from large institutions such as building societies and housing associations as well as from small private landlords. To do this we intend, in particular, to build on two initiatives we have already taken.

First, to encourage more investment by institutions, we will extend the system of assured tenancies. This will permit new lettings in which rents and the period of lease will be freely agreed between tenants and landlords. The tenant will have security of tenure and will renegotiate the rent at the end of the lease, with provision for arbitration if necessary.

Second, to encourage new lettings by smaller landlords, we will develop the system of shorthold. The rents of landlords will be limited to a reasonable rate of return, and the tenant's security of tenure will be limited to the term of the lease, which would be not less than 6 months. This will bring back into use many of the 550,000 private dwellings which now stand empty because of controls, as well as making the provision of new rented housing a more attractive investment.

And we will revise the housing benefit system to ensure that it prevents landlords from increasing rents to unreasonable levels at the taxpayer's expense. All existing private and housing association tenants will continue to have their present protection in respect of rents and security of tenure. We will strengthen the law against harassment and unlawful eviction.

Rights for council tenants

Many council estates built in the sixties and seventies are badly designed, vulnerable to crime and vandalism and in bad repair. In many areas, rent arrears are high. In all, over 110,000 council dwellings stand empty. Yet it is often difficult for tenants to move. If they are ever to enjoy the prospect of independence, municipal monopoly must be replaced by choice in renting.

We will give groups of tenants the right to form tenant co-operatives, owning and running their management and budget for themselves. They will also have the right to ask other institutions to take over their housing. Tenants who wish to remain with the local authority will be able to do so.

We will give each council house tenant individually the right to transfer the ownership of his or her house to a housing association or other independent, approved landlord.

In some areas more may be necessary. The success of Estate Action and Housing Action Areas shows how a carefully targeted approach can transform an area of poor housing and give people there new hope. Our Urban Development Corporations have been successful in restoring derelict industrial areas. We believe that a similar approach could be adopted for housing in some places. We will take powers to create Housing Action Trusts initially as a pilot scheme to take over such housing, renovate it, and pass it on to different tenures and ownerships including housing associations, tenant co-operatives, owner-occupiers or approved private landlords.

We will reform the structure of local authority housing accounts so that public funds are directed at the problems of repair and renovation; maintenance and management are improved; resources are directed to the areas where the problems are greatest; rent arrears are reduced; and fewer houses are left empty.

Housing is the biggest single investment that most people make – whether in money or in time, skill and effort. In the last eight years, as a result of our policies, we have seen a dramatic increase in home-ownership. In the next five years, we will complement that with policies designed to improve the supply and condition of the rented housing stock.

A CAPITAL-OWNING DEMOCRACY

Share ownership

Home-ownership leads naturally to other forms of financial provision for the future – notably to pensions and share-ownership. Half of the working population are in occupational pension schemes, but in 1979 only seven per cent of the population held shares.

People were deterred by the sheer unfamiliarity of owning shares. Young people were reluctant to save for a retirement which seemed far away. And most tax incentives encouraged saving through institutions rather than directly.

With a Conservative Government, all that has been changing. We were determined to make share-ownership available to the whole nation. Just as with cars, television sets, washing machines and foreign holidays, it would no longer be a privilege of the few; it would become the expectation of the many. We achieved this historic transformation in three ways:

- First, we introduced major tax incentives for employee share-ownership. Seven out of the last eight budgets have included measures to encourage people to purchase shares in the company in which they work.
- Second, starting this year, we brought in Personal Equity Plans, which enable people to invest in British industry entirely free of tax.
- Third, we embarked on a major programme of privatisation, insisting that small investors and employees of the privatised companies should have a fair chance to join in the buying.

The results have been dramatic, and the direct consequence of government policy. Share ownership has trebled. Almost one in five of the adult population now own shares directly. And the figure will continue to rise. Of this total, the majority are first-time shareholders and most of them own shares in either privatised companies or the TSB group. One-and-a-half million people hold shares in the companies where they work.

After eight years of Conservative Government, Britain is now at the forefront of a world-wide revolution in extending ownership. One in every five British adults now owns shares compared to one in ten Frenchmen and one in twenty Japanese. Only the Americans, where a quarter of the people are shareholders, remain ahead – and the gap is narrowing.

This is the first stage of a profound and progressive social transformation – popular capitalism. Owning a direct stake in industry not only enhances personal independence; it also gives a heightened sense of involvement and pride in British business. More realistic attitudes to profit and investment take root. And the foundations of British economic achievement are further strengthened.

We will press on with the encouragement of popular capitalism. In the next Parliament:

- We will continue to extend share-ownership as we have done with home-ownership.
- We will reintroduce our proposed tax incentives for profit-related pay.
- We will privatise more state industries in ways that increase share-ownership, both for the employees and for the public at large.

RAISING STANDARDS IN EDUCATION

Parents want schools to provide their children with the knowledge, training and character that will fit them for today's world. They want them to be taught basic educational skills, They want schools that will encourage moral values: honesty, hard work and responsibility. And they should have the right to choose those schools which do these things for their children.

Raising standards in our schools

How can all this best be done? Resources obviously matter. This Government has provided more resources for pupils than ever before.

With the Conservatives:

- Spending per primary pupil has risen by 17 per cent after allowing for inflation and per secondary pupil by 20 per cent under our Government.
- There are more teachers in proportion to pupils than ever before.
- British schools are world leaders in the use of computers in the classroom.

But money alone is not enough. Increased resources have not produced uniformly higher standards. Parents and employers are rightly concerned that not enough children master the basic skills, that some of what is taught seems irrelevant to a good education and that standards of personal discipline and aspirations are too low. In certain cases education is used for political indoctrination and sexual propaganda. The time has now come for school reform.

Four major reforms

First, we will establish a National Core Curriculum. It is vital to ensure that all pupils between the ages of 5 to 16 study a basic range of subjects – including maths, English and science. In each of these basic subjects syllabuses will be published and attainment levels set so that the progress of pupils can be assessed at around ages 7, 11 and 14, and in preparation for the GCSE at 16. Parents, teachers and pupils will then know how well each child is doing. We will consult widely among those concerned in establishing the curriculum.

Second, within five years governing bodies and head teachers of all secondary schools and many primary schools will be given control over their own budgets. They know best the needs of their school. With this independence they will manage their resources and decide their priorities, covering the cost of books, equipment, maintenance and staff. Several pilot schemes for financial devolution to schools have already proved their worth, such as those in Cambridgeshire and Solihull.

Third, we will increase parental choice. The most consistent pressure for high standard in schools comes from parents. They have a powerful incentive to ensure that their children receive a good education. We have already done much through the 1980 and 1986 Education Acts so that parents can make their voice heard. But parents still need better opportunities to send their children to the school of their choice. That would be the best guarantee of higher standards. To achieve this: we will ensure that Local Education Authorities (LEAs) set school budgets in line with the number of pupils who will be attending each school. Schools will be required to enrol children up to the school's physical capacity instead of artificially restricting pupil numbers, as can happen today. Popular schools, which have earned parental support by offering good education, will then be able to expand beyond present pupil numbers.

These steps will compel schools to respond to the views of parents. But there must also be variety of educational provision so that parents can better compare one school with another. We will therefore support the co-existence of a variety of schools – comprehensive, grammar, secondary modern, voluntary controlled and aided, independent, sixth form and tertiary colleges as well as the reasonable rights of schools to retain their sixth forms, all of which will give parents greater choice and lead to higher standards. We will establish a pilot network of City Technology Colleges. Already two have been announced and support for more has been pledged by industrial sponsors. We will expand the Assisted Places Scheme to 35,000. This highly successful scheme has enabled 25,000 talented children from less-well-off backgrounds to gain places at the 230 independent schools currently in the scheme. We will continue to defend the right to independent education as part of a free society. It is under threat from all the other parties.

Fourth, we will allow state schools to opt out of LEA control. If, in a particular school, parents and governing bodies wish to become independent of the LEA, they will be given the choice to do so. Those schools which opt out of LEA control will receive a full grant direct from the Department of Education and Science. They would become independent charitable trusts.

In the area covered by the Inner London Education Authority, where entire borough councils wish to become independent of the LEA, they will be able to submit proposals to the Secretary of State requesting permission to take over the provision of education within their boundaries.

Village schools

We recognise the important contribution made by small rural primary schools to education and to the community life of our villages. We will ensure, therefore, that the future of these schools is judged by wider factors than merely the number of pupils attending them.

Pre-school education

Eighty per cent of all three- and four-year-olds in this country attend nursery classes, reception classes or playgroups. Formal nursery education is not necessarily the most appropriate experience for children. Diversity of provision is desirable. LEAs should look to support the voluntary sector alongside their own provision.

A better career for teachers

We recognise the importance of teachers and wish to enhance their professional status. The Government has provided a record amount of money to increase their pay by an average 16.4 per cent this year, 25 per cent over 18 months. Our new pay award will encourage able young people to enter the career of teaching and reward the many good teachers already in the profession.

The Burnham negotiating machinery finally broke down and has been temporarily replaced by an Interim Advisory Committee. The Government wants an effective and permanent machinery for settling teachers' pay, in which the interests of all parties will be recognised.

The Government will produce a Green Paper setting out the various alternatives and will enter into wide consultations with a view to establishing a new and effective machinery.

Higher and further education

The British system of higher education is among the best in the world. It ranges from universities to further education colleges providing skills and qualifications. We recognise the value of research and scholarship for their own sake. At the same time we must meet the nation's demand for highly qualified manpower to compete in international markets.

Building on our achievements since 1979 – 157,000 more full-time and part-time students – we want to expand higher education opportunities still further. By 1990, we plan to increase student numbers by a further 50,000, and to raise the proportion of 18-year-olds in higher education.

We will replace the University Grants Committee with an independent statutory body on the lines recommended by the Croham Committee. The new body will be called the Universities Funding Council (UFC) and will have broadly equal numbers of academic and non-academic members with a chairman who has substantial experience outside the academic world. The primary responsibility of the UFC will be the allocation of funds to individual universities under new contractual arrangements.

Polytechnics are today strong, successful and mature institutions. They are complementary to the universities. Their present structure, under local authorities, is inappropriate for an expanding national role. As part of our policy to delegate power and responsibility, we will legislate to convert the polytechnics and other mainly higher education colleges in England to free-standing corporate bodies under boards of governors. We will set up a new Polytechnics and Colleges Funding Council independent of central Government, in place of local authority control.

As part of our aim to widen access to higher education we have begun a review of student support which is the most generous in the western world. We need to modernise this system which has not changed for 25 years. The purpose of the review is to improve the overall prospects of students so that more are encouraged to enter higher education. No final conclusions have been reached, but we believe that top-up loans to supplement grants are one way, among others, of bringing in new finance to help students and relieve pressure on their parents.

We will take care to ensure that the best aspects of the present system are retained in any new proposals which we bring forward.

Trade unions

It is not only in relation to government, however, that people's right to choice and independence must be safeguarded and extended. Great social institutions can sometimes become too powerful and cease to represent their members, denying them any control over the decisions taken in their name and even forcing them to act against their own interests. That was the case with trade unions before 1979.

Since then, Conservative reforms have redressed the balance between the individual and his union, preventing coercion of the majority by activists and militants. These highly successful and popular measures have encouraged democracy within the unions, restrained the abuses of secondary action and picketing, reversed the growth of closed shops, restored the rights of redress against unions acting unlawfully and removed the immunity of unions that call a strike without a fair ballot.

The result has been a transformation of shopfloor relations, allowing management and workforce to co-operate to improve working practices and introduce new technology to mutual gain. In the next Parliament we will protect the rights of individual trade union members.

We will introduce legislation to:

- empower individual members to stop their unions calling them out on strike without first holding a secret ballot of members;
- protect individual members from disciplinary action if they refuse to join a strike they disagree with;

- ensure that all members of trade union governing bodies are elected by secret ballot at least once every five years;
- make independently supervised postal ballots compulsory for such elections;
- limit further the abuse of the closed shop by providing protection against unfair dismissal for all non-union employees, and removing any legal immunity from industrial action to establish or enforce a closed shop;
- provide new safeguards on the use of union funds;
- establish a new trade union commissioner with the power to help individual trade unionists to enforce their fundamental rights.

Building prosperity and employment

Since this Government took office in 1979, we have restored honest money and established a stable economic framework in which business can flourish. We have been careful not to spend money before we earned it. We have brought the nation back to living within its means. We have massively rebuilt our international assets. We have refused to be drawn into an auction of pledges for higher spending that the country simply could not afford. We have balanced the books. We have paid our way.

The results have been dramatic.

- Despite the coal strike and the collapse of the oil price, Britain has moved from being bottom to the top of the growth league of major European countries.
- Inflation has reached its lowest levels for almost 20 years.
- The basic rate of income tax has been cut from 33p to 27p, four taxes have been abolished, and almost a million and a half people have been taken out of income tax altogether.
- Over a million extra jobs have been created since 1983; more than in the rest of the European Community put together.
- Unemployment, a problem throughout Europe, is now firmly on a downward trend – with youth unemployment in this country below the European average.
- We have rebuilt our net overseas assets to some £110 billion from a mere £12 billion when we first took office. This will provide substantial foreign earnings in the years ahead and a cushion, should oil revenues fall.

While the Opposition parties cling to the failed policies of the past, our strategy has become widely accepted abroad. Socialist Spain as well as Christian Democratic Germany, Social Democratic Sweden as well as France, Labour New Zealand and Conservative Canada, all accept that governments must reduce their borrowing, curb state spending, reduce taxation, privatise state firms and do away with unnecessary controls. What we began in 1979 is today common international practice.

Stable prices

Our greatest economic challenge on entering office was to defeat inflation. Rampant inflation under the Labour Government, when money lost a quarter of its value in a single year, had reduced our economy to 'the sick man of Europe'.

Nothing erodes a country's competitive edge faster than inflation. Nothing so undermines personal thrift and independence as to see the value of a lifetime's savings eaten away in retirement through spiralling prices. And nothing threatens the social fabric of a nation more than the conflicts and divisiveness which inflation creates.

Our success in the battle against inflation has been the key to Britain's economic revival. It required firm control of public expenditure, a substantial reduction in government borrowing, curbing the growth of money in circulation, maintaining financial discipline, stimulating competition and moderating trade union power.

The Opposition parties opposed nearly every aspect of this strategy. If even some of their policies were implemented today, higher borrowing and higher spending would once again unleash inflation.

There is no better yardstick of a party's fitness to govern that its attitude to inflation. Nothing is so politically immoral as a party that ignores that yardstick.

The Conservative Government will continue to put the conquest of inflation as our first objective. We will not be content until we have stable prices, with inflation eradicated altogether.

Lower taxes

We are the only Party that believes in lower taxation. As the Party determined to achieve growing prosperity we recognise that it is people who create wealth, not governments. Lower taxation coupled with lower inflation makes everyone better off. It encourages people to work harder, to be inventive and to take risks. It promotes a climate of enterprise and initiative.

Lower tax on earnings enables people to build up savings to give them financial security in later life. Lower taxation, by increasing take-home pay without adding to industry's costs, improves competitiveness and helps with jobs. And tax relief for charitable donations encourages more people to give and to give more generously.

There is a strong moral case for reducing taxation. High taxes deprive people of their independence and make their choices for them. The desire to do better for one's family is one of the strongest motives in human nature. As a party committed to the family and opposed to the over-powerful State, we want people to keep more of what they earn, and to have more freedom of choice about what they do for themselves, their families and for others less fortunate.

Governments should trust people to spend their own money sensibly and decently; high taxation prevents them doing so. That is why we have:

- cut the basic rate of tax from 33p to 27p in the £, and increased the personal allowances (the starting point for paying tax) by 22 per cent more than inflation. If Labour's tax regime were still in force, the family man on average earnings would today be paying more than £500 per year in extra income tax: a headmaster married to a nurse would be paying more than £1,300 extra;
- reduced sharply the absurd top rates of tax inherited from Labour which were causing so many of our most talented people to work abroad;
- increased greatly the tax relief for charitable donations. Giving to charities has doubled since we first took office;
- abolished four taxes completely: the National Insurance surcharge – the tax which

Labour put on jobs – the investment income surcharge, the development land tax and the lifetime gifts tax;

- reformed and simplified corporation tax, and cut its rate to the lowest of any major industrial country;
- cut the small business corporation tax rate by more than a third, and extended it to many more small businesses;
- reformed and reduced capital taxes as well as slashing stamp duty.

In every case where taxes have been reformed and reduced there has been an increase in the amount of tax collected.

Labour totally fail to understand the benefits this brings to everyone. Today they openly threaten to raise taxation. To fulfil their plans, they would have to raise taxes substantially. Indeed, all the Opposition parties – Labour, Liberals and SDP – would raise taxation. We believe that it is precisely the wrong thing to do.

It will be our aim to do the opposite.

In the next Parliament:

- We aim to reduce the burden of taxation.
- In particular, we will continue the process of tax reform.

Spending we can afford

Over the past eight years we have managed the nation's finances with care. Even allowing for inflation, this has enabled us to spend substantially more on the Health Service (up by 31 per cent), defence (up by 23 per cent), roads (up by 17 per cent), education per pupil (up by 18 per cent), the police and the battle against crime (up by 47 per cent), the disabled and long-term sick (up by 72 per cent), and government training schemes (up by 120 per cent).

How have we been able to do this without running into the financial crises which Labour's spending policies invariably set off? First, we have been prudent with the nation's money. We have slashed public borrowing and sought savings in government expenditure wherever they could sensibly be found. Second, we are engaged in steadily reducing the share of the nation's income taken by the State. This means that more will be left for families and for business to invest – the only safe route to higher growth in the economy. Third, we have constantly improved the efficiency of the public services, ensuring that we get more value for every pound spent.

For the next Parliament:

- Our aim is to ensure that public expenditure takes a steadily smaller share of our national income.
- Within that objective, we will continue to spend more on our priorities. We have set out our plans for further increased spending in these areas over the next three years.

Creating new jobs

High unemployment is one of the most intractable problems facing all Western industrialised countries.

We understand the anxiety and stress which unemployment can cause. For almost a year unemployment in the United Kingdom has fallen faster than among any of our major competitors in Europe, and faster than at any time since 1973. It is falling because of the growth and enterprise we have achieved, assisted by the employment and training programmes we have developed.

Since we were last re-elected in 1983, the number of jobs has risen by over 1 million more than in the rest of the European Community put together. This Government has established the conditions in which business can prosper and create new jobs. This has not just been achieved through the revitalisation of traditional industries. We have encouraged growth in those crucial areas of new enterprise which provide the foundation for the jobs of the future – self-employment, small firms, the creation of new enterprise, the expanding service sector – particularly tourism and leisure – and new technology.

Self-employment is the seedcorn of the new enterprises of tomorrow. Without sufficient people to start new businesses, the future of our whole economy is in jeopardy. Today we have the highest number of self-employed for over 60 years. One worker in ten is now his own boss – or her own boss, since a quarter of the self-employed are women. Indeed, the eighties have seen almost three-quarters of a million people become self-employed. More and more of our young people today seek self-employment as a worthwhile career. It is particularly encouraging that almost half the growth in self-employment since 1983 has been in the northern part of our country.

Small firms, along with all businesses, have benefited from our management of the economy. Since this Government took office, the number of registered businesses has shown a net increase of more than 500 a week – and the number has increased in every region of the country.

Helping unemployed people into jobs

As well as creating a climate in which business could employ more people, we have developed programmes to help those out of work.

The Youth Training Scheme (YTS) caters for school-leavers aged 16 and 17 who wish to participate in training and work experience. Every trainee is given the opportunity of working towards a recognised qualification.

The new Job Training Scheme (JTS), which started in April this year, will offer a chance to any person over 18 who has been unemployed for six months or more, who wants to work and train with an employer for a recognised qualification. This year it will help nearly a quarter of a million people.

Under our Community Programme, each year over 300,000 people who have been out of work for some time gain valuable experience working on community projects. They have a reference to show potential employers. We will improve the Community Programme to make it full-time and better able to help those with families. We shall pay those working on the programme an allowance giving a premium over and above their social security payments.

Under the Enterprise Allowance Scheme, 230,000 unemployed people have started to work for themselves. Many of them have now become employers themselves. JobClubs were first opened in 1985 to help the unemployed help themselves back into jobs. Over 1,000 have been established. At present two-thirds of those leaving JobClubs go into employment. The JobClubs programme has been a great success. We aim to expand it. Our economic success means that we can now do more to help those out of work.

Although youth unemployment has declined in the last year it still remains a problem. Far too many of our youngsters leave school with an education that has failed to prepare them for the world of work. At the same time, by maintaining high starting wages comparable to those of fully trained craftsmen, trade unions have kept many of them out of work.

In 1983 we introduced the first Youth Training Scheme. It is now a national two-year programme aimed at giving young people qualifications for work.

The first guarantee

We will now guarantee a place on the Youth Training Scheme to every school-leaver under 18 who is not going directly into a job. As a result, none of these school-leavers need be unemployed. They can remain at school, move to college, get a job, or receive a guaranteed training. YTS will serve as a bridge between school and work. We will take steps to ensure that those under 18 who deliberately choose to remain unemployed are not eligible for benefit. We will of course continue to protect other young people, such as those who suffer from disabilities.

The second guarantee

There are still too many young people without the right qualifications for employment in today's world.

Within a year we aim to guarantee a place, either on the Job Training Scheme or on the Enterprise Allowance Scheme or in a JobClub, for everyone aged between 18 and 25 years who has been unemployed for between six and twelve months.

The third guarantee

In addition to these major programmes we have taken one further important step. Restart is a programme we have set up for interviewing and counselling the long-term unemployed to help them into a job or training. Everyone who has been unemployed for more than one year has already been given an interview. We will guarantee to provide the Restart service in the future at six-monthly intervals, to all those who have been unemployed for more than six months.

Over the next five years we will aim, through the Restart interviews, to offer everyone who is under 50, and who has been unemployed for more than two years, a place in the Job Training Scheme or in the new Community Programme, in a JobClub or in the Enterprise Allowance Scheme.

Regional assistance

Money spent on earlier programmes attracting firms to regions has sometimes created very few jobs. Our new system of regional assistance, introduced in 1984, ensures that aid is directly targeted towards the creation of new jobs. New activities in the service sector from which so many of the new jobs come have also been made eligible for assistance. Under the new policy, offers of assistance have already been made which should secure almost 300,000 jobs. We will continue to ensure that assistance is directed where it is most needed.

The Employment and Training Services

We will take further steps to provide a comprehensive service to the unemployed. We will consult the Manpower Services Commission about transferring JobCentres to the Department of Employment so that they can work more closely with Unemployment Benefit Offices. The Manpower Services Commission would then become primarily a training agency. It is employers who are best equipped to assess their training needs. We will increase employer representation on the Commission and its advisory bodies.

More jobs are being created by business and industry. Nothing would destroy whole industries more effectively than a return to the overmanning and restrictive practices of the 1970s. Our policies form a practical and realistic approach to help people back into work. We will build on prosperity to create more employment.

A framework for business and industry

British business is in a healthier state than it has been for a generation. Output has been rising steadily for six years. Productivity has increased at a rate second only to Japan. Company profitability is at its highest for over twenty years. Industry has a confidence in the future that would have been unthinkable seven years ago.

Moreover, setting new records has not been confined to the private sector. Since 1983 productivity in the coal industry has risen by over 50 per cent. British Steel has more than doubled its productivity since 1979 and made a profit last year for the first time in over ten years. British Rail will cost the taxpayer 25 per cent less in subsidy this year than in 1983 and without any major route closures.

The Conservative Government has created a framework in which once again enterprise can flourish – by cutting red tape, by denationalising state-owned companies, by removing unnecessary restrictions, by abolishing exchange control, by enabling the City of London to become the foremost financial centre in the world, by keeping down prices through extending competition, and by ensuring access to open trade so that British exporters and consumers can both benefit.

Privatisation

Over a third of the companies and industries which used to be owned by the State have been returned to free enterprise. Productivity and profitability have soared in the newly privatised companies.

- In 1980 Jaguar made 14,000 cars a year, losing well over £3,000 on each car sold. Now the company is hard put to keep up with overseas demand and last year sold over 40,000 cars, making a pre-tax profit of over £120m.
- Since the National Freight Consortium was sold to management and staff in 1982, pre-tax profits have increased sevenfold.
- British Aerospace, Cable & Wireless, Amersham International and Associated British Ports have all strikingly increased their profits.

It is no mystery why privatisation has succeeded. The overwhelming majority of employees have become shareholders in the newly privatised companies. They want their companies to succeed. Their companies have been released from the detailed controls of Whitehall and given more freedom to manage their own affairs. And they have been exposed to the full commercial disciplines of the customer. Even former monopolies now face increased competition.

We will continue the successful programme of privatisation. In particular, after the privatisation of the British Airports Authority we will return to the public the Water Authorities, leaving certain functions to a new National Rivers Authority.

Following the success of gas privatisation, with the benefits it brought to employees and millions of consumers, we will bring forward proposals for privatising the electricity industry subject to proper regulation.

Competition

Competition forces the economy to respond to the needs of the consumer. It promotes efficiency, holds down costs, drives companies to innovate and ensures that customers get the best possible value for money.

Accordingly, this Government has:

- deregulated long-distance coach services creating over 700 new services with improved quality and lower fares;
- removed the monopoly on conveyancing of houses in England and Wales;
- removed the opticians' monopoly, making it easier and cheaper to buy spectacles;
- relaxed advertising controls on accountants, solicitors, stockbrokers and vets, and permitted greater fee competition for architects and surveyors;
- increased competition on air routes within the UK and between certain European countries, which has resulted in cheaper fares, a more responsive service and greater choice of carriers for the passenger;
- deregulated telecommunications, so that customers can now choose between suppliers when buying telephones and private exchanges, and business can choose between two alternative telecommunications networks;
- suspended the Post Office monopoly of time-sensitive and valuable mail, stimulating a dramatic increase in the number of private courier companies.

We will continue this approach.

But competition must be supplemented by legal protection for consumers. Those who make their living from their ideas and creations also require protection against theft. We will introduce further measures to impose tighter controls on pyramid selling.

We will introduce measures to reform the law on copyright, design and performance protection.

The City

The City of London is the world's leading market place in foreign exchange, international bank lending and international insurance, It is a major source of funds for British companies. The financial services sector as a whole accounts for nearly 6 per cent of our national income, generates a net £7 billion per year to our balance of payments, and employs over one million people.

Like other sections of British industry, however, the City was held back by restrictive practices until they were swept away in last year's 'big bang'. This has brought nearer the day when shares can be bought and sold over the counter in every high street. We have also given building societies greater freedom to make a wider range of financial services available to the average family.

At the same time, the Conservative Government has introduced a legal framework to protect investors and consumers:

- The Companies Acts of 1980 and 1981 strengthened the powers of investigators and increased the courts' power to disqualify directors for misconduct in the City as elsewhere.
- The Insolvency Act of 1985 made it easier to disqualify directors who had been guilty of unlawful trading.
- And now the Financial Services Act of 1986 provides the first comprehensive system of investor protection we have had in this country. It also contains stringent new powers to investigate insider dealing which was first made a criminal offence by the Conservative Government in 1980.

The Conservative Party is the party of law and order. That applies just as much to City fraud as to street crime.

Parliament has just approved our proposals for establishing a Serious Fraud Office to improve the work of investigating and prosecuting the worst cases of fraud and for streamlining court procedure. After the election we will reintroduce our proposals to reform the outdated rules on evidence, as recommended by the Roskill Committee.

Trade

Britain exports 30 per cent of all that it produces. If this country is to remain a key trading nation, industry must remain competitive. That is one reason why the Conservative Government attaches great value to maintaining an open multinational trading system. Another is that increased trade is a major way of encouraging growth and prosperity in the Third World. There is little point in demanding more aid for these countries and then refusing them the opportunity to trade.

We will continue to fight for free and fair trade in international negotiations and resist the growth of protectionism. We will press for international rules of fair trading to be extended to international investment, trade in services and the protection of intellectual property such as patents, trademarks and copyright. We will continue to exert pressure on countries such as Japan to open up their markets and provide the same freedom to trade for our exporters as they expect us to provide for theirs. As well as creating the commercial and legal framework in which industry can flourish, the Government must also ensure that the practical services on which industry and the citizen rely – transport, energy, research and development, and an efficient civil service – are provided to a high standard.

Efficient transport

The Conservative Government is proud of a record that has:

- modernised the transport system by investing over £10 billion in the nation's motorways, roads, airports, seaports and railways;
- since 1979 completed over 680 miles of motorway and trunk roads and 67 bypasses;
- secured greater efficiency by privatising British Airways, the National Freight Corporation, Sealink and Associated British Ports;
- increased competition by deregulating long-distance coach services and abolishing local bus licensing.

These measures have laid the foundations of an efficient and more flexible transport system. We will develop it further along these lines. We are now returning the nationalised bus companies to the private sector in many cases to management buy-outs. We are also privatising the former British Airports Authority, the world's leading international airports group.

We are committed to a major capital investment programme through:

- new investment to build an extra 450 miles of motorway and trunk roads to 1989/90;
- British Rail's plans to invest £500m a year over the next 3 years;
- private sector financing, construction and operation of the Dartford Bridge and the Channel tunnel.

Energy

Britain is the only major Western industrial country that is a net exporter of energy. This owes much to North Sea oil so successfully developed by free enterprise. But it is an advantage that will not last indefinitely.

Coal will continue to meet much of the steadily rising demand for electricity. Renewable sources of energy can make some contribution to the nation's energy needs, which is why government-sponsored research has been increased. Nevertheless, to reject, as our opponents do, the contribution of nuclear energy to supplying reliable, low-cost electricity, and to depend on coal alone, would be short-sighted and irresponsible.

The world's resources of fossil fuels will come under increasing strain during the 21st century; so may the global environment if the build-up of carbon dioxide – the so-called 'greenhouse effect' – significantly raises temperatures and changes climates.

After the most careful and painstaking independent assessment of the safety case for a new pressurised water reactor at Sizewell, therefore, the Government has decided to proceed with the next phase of our nuclear programme. It is vital that we continue to give the highest priority to safety. Our nuclear industry has a record of safety and technical excellence second to none.

We intend to go on playing a leading role in the task of developing abundant, low-cost supplies of nuclear electricity, and managing the associated waste products.

Science and R&D

Government support for research and development amounts to more than £4½ billion per year. It is larger as a share of our national income than that of the United States, Japan or Germany. A country of our size cannot afford to do everything. These resources need to be better targeted. The task of government is to support basic research and to contribute where business cannot realistically be expected to carry all the risks.

We will ensure that government spending is firmly directed towards areas of high national priority, by extending the role of the Advisory Council on Applied Research and Development, drawing on the full range of advice from the academic community and from business.

The Civil Service

We have long had in this country a professional and dedicated public service which is the envy of the world. We are now building on those traditional qualities which can too easily be taken for granted with new strengths and skills: a greater readiness to adapt efficiently to change, including technological change, to manage the public service more effectively, and to see that the taxpayer gets value for money. The size of the Civil Service at under 600,000 people today is the smallest since the war. This is already saving the taxpayer £1 billion a year.

We will press on with long-term management reforms in order to improve public services and reduce their cost.

Agriculture and the rural economy

Farming

Britain's farmers serve the nation well. They produce 80 per cent of the food we grow compared with 60 per cent only 10 years ago. They have made us into the world's sixth largest exporter of cereals when we had been a net importer for decades before. They look after 80 per cent of the British countryside. And consumer food prices have risen less than the cost of living, unlike the Labour years.

But farmers world-wide are under pressure because of rising surpluses and the huge costs of disposing of them. It is just as much in the farmers' interest as in the consumers' and taxpayers' that this over-production be stopped and a radical overhaul of the Common Agricultural Policy achieved. Farmers need a more sustainable environment in which to plan ahead.

We will continue:

- to play a leading part in European Community negotiations to reform the CAP;

- to strive for even-handed and fair treatment between Member States and between the different regions of the UK;
- to work for an early devaluation of the Green Pound, especially in relation to beef;
- to uphold the interests of the efficient family farm;
- to reduce costs and tackle surpluses, by bringing supply and demand in the Community into better balance by a combination of measures including price restraint;
- to reduce the role for intervention;

At home we will continue:

- to promote competitiveness and innovation in British farming and horticulture;
- to give particular assistance to farmers in the Less Favoured Areas, recently extended, where farming is difficult;
- to encourage better marketing of agricultural and horticultural products and to ensure that the consumer has as much information about the contents of food as is necessary to make sensible choices.

We will not introduce rating on agricultural land and will oppose two-tier pricing in the CAP, which would greatly disadvantage our farmers and benefit their competitors.

The rural economy

Farming is, and will remain, the major industry in the countryside and food production will continue to be the farmer's basic purpose. The higher production resulting from greater efficiency and modern techniques initially means more land coming out of agriculture. A new balance of policies has to be struck, with less support for expanding production of commodities already in over-supply and more support for diversifying into other activities.

We have recognised the new needs of the countryside and rural economies in two ways. First, we now place more emphasis on support for the environment and the beauty of the countryside; we now give grants to plant hedgerows, not dig them up. Second, we encourage alternative uses of land and more diverse job opportunities to maintain thriving communities in the rural economy.

We will therefore:

- emphasise environmental protection and promotion of non-farming rural businesses in the planning system;
- continue to support the Development Commission in developing rural enterprises;
- extend the Environmentally Sensitive Areas scheme which makes conservation a more integral part of farming;
- introduce new schemes to assist diversification of new enterprises on farms;
- introduce a new Farm Woodland Scheme to assist alternative land use.

The UK fishing industry

Our fishing industry supplies two-thirds of the fish we eat. It is an important source of jobs and income in many areas. The Government's success in further improving the

Common Fisheries Policy has meant that international policing has been made more effective; and increasingly stringent conservation measures have secured the future for our fleets. We will introduce legislation to ensure that UK quotas are reserved for UK fishermen. We are pledged to measures to enable our fishermen to take full advantage of all their opportunities and to improve and modernise their boats.

Animal welfare

The Conservatives have a proud record over the years of promoting animal welfare. Most of the legislation was either initiated by Conservative governments or introduced as Private Members' measures by Conservative MPs when the Conservatives were in office.

Since 1979 we have:

- set up the Farm Animal Welfare Council which advises the Government on the welfare of farm animals. We will continue to care for them with the advice and guidance of the Farm Animal Welfare Council;
- honoured our commitment to replace the 1876 legislation with the Animals (Scientific Procedures) Act 1986 – the most effective in Europe. It imposes tight new controls on the use of animals for experiments. The number of experiments has declined in each of the last nine years, and we expect that decline to continue.

Better health, better care

Achievements in health

The health of the British people is steadily improving. Quite simply, we live longer. Life expectancy has increased and infant mortality has declined.

Over the last eight years the Government has spent more on the Health Service than any previous government, Labour or Conservative. In 1979, the outgoing Labour Government planned to spend less than £8 billion on the nation's health. This year, the Conservative Government will spend nearly £21 billion. After allowing for inflation, that is an increase of almost a third. This extra money has been spent wisely and well. The Health Service today is treating more patients than ever before in its history.

Money is important, but the success of the NHS depends still more on the dedication of the people working in it. There are over 75,000 more doctors, dentists and nurses than in 1978. These extra staff have enabled the NHS to treat 6 million more patient cases – in-patients, day cases, out-patients – than when we took office. Sometimes they work in very difficult conditions. That is why the Government has reduced nurses' basic hours from 40 to 37½ hours per week and increased their pay by 30 per cent after allowing for inflation.

We will continue to improve the Health Service.

Future tasks for the Health Service

Our policies rest on six principles. First, we will give greater emphasis to the prevention of avoidable illness and the promotion of good health to make the NHS more truly a health service and not merely a sickness service.

Much progress has been made in the past eight years.

- The improvement of the maternity services has helped to reduce by a third the death rate among babies in the weeks around birth.
- The expansion of vaccination and immunisation has prevented illness and death among children.
- Screening for cervical cancer has been improved and death rates from the disease have fallen by almost 10 per cent in the past decade.
- We have already embarked on a major campaign to tackle the problem of coronary heart disease.
- To fight AIDS, the Government has undertaken the biggest health education campaign ever seen in this country, one much admired abroad, and is fully supporting the Medical Research Council in a special programme of research into treatments and vaccines.

These are welcome advances. In the next Parliament, we will build on this work by:

- completing the network of computerised 'call and recall' systems for cervical cancer screening and extending them to younger women;
- developing a national programme for breast cancer screening;
- backing the newly established and powerful Health Education Authority.

Second, we will continue to show our support for the million people working in the NHS, of whom half are nurses.

Nurses wanted the assurance that, without recourse to strike action, they would receive fair treatment over pay. That is why we set up the independent Nurses' Pay Review Body. After the latest award, we will have increased nurses' pay by 30 per cent since 1979, after allowing for inflation. That compares to the severe reduction of more than 20 per cent, which they suffered under the last Labour Government.

Nurses also want a training and career structure which reinforces their professionalism, rewards experience, and offers opportunities for managerial responsibility without being removed to a distant desk. We share those views, and will seek to further them. We are particularly keen to attract experienced nurses back into the profession, and to encourage others to take up nursing as a new career.

Hospital doctors and consultants, too, are a vital part of the Health Service. We have already increased the number of consultant posts and we will continue to work for improvements in the medical career structure.

The NHS could not function without ancillary services. Some of these – cleaning, catering, and laundry – have been put out to competitive tender to enable health authorities to select the best and most effective way of providing these services. Savings are now approaching £100 million a year and they have gone directly and immediately into better patient care.

We have undertaken consultation on the improvement of primary care. Our aim is to develop the strength and flexibility of the services provided by GPs, dentists, pharmacists, opticians and nurses who work in the community.

There are particular problems affecting health care in inner cities. Doctors and nurses there take on a particularly tough and difficult job. We shall continue to look for new ways of helping them and improving health care, especially primary care in the inner cities.

Our third principle is to modernise the whole framework of the health service – its hospitals, its clinics, its equipment. In the face of economic collapse, the last Labour Government cut the hospital building programme by a third. This Government has embarked on the biggest building programme ever. It will cost £3 billion. In seven years we have already carried through over 200 major building projects from start to finish. We will complete some 125 further major new building schemes in the next three years, and get many more under way.

New hospitals, too, are being built in areas lacking the provision they need. Old and inefficient Victorian buildings are being replaced with purpose-built modern hospitals. Much modern medicine and surgery is better carried out in the new larger hospitals, equipped with new medical technology. Wherever possible, however, small old hospitals have found a new role as community hospitals staffed by local GPs.

Fourth, elderly, disabled, mentally ill and mentally handicapped people, should be cared for within the community whenever this is right for them. In the past some people who should have been cared for in other ways have remained in hospitals, sometimes for years. That is changing. The number of children in long-stay hospitals for the mentally handicapped has fallen by almost three-quarters. The number of adults in long-stay mental handicap and mental illness hospitals has fallen by around 11,000.

This changing pattern has already brought a better life to many thousands of people. It has the potential to do so for many thousands more. But we need to examine carefully various alternatives to discover what is now best for patients. We have set in hand the first ever full-scale review of community care. We will develop our policies in the light of its findings.

Our fifth principle is to strengthen management. The NHS is a large and complex organisation. It needs good management. It is not a business, but it must be run in a business-like way.

The reduction of waste and inefficiency has released hundreds of millions of pounds for better patient care. The sale of property which the NHS no longer needs – for example, because of new hospital developments – is currently raising £200 million a year for better health care. We will continue to ensure that the Health Service is as efficient as possible. But good management is not just a matter of efficiency. We value enterprise in the public service just as much as in the private sector. We will continue to encourage district and regional managers to devise new ways of providing better patient care.

Finally, the ultimate purpose of the Health Service is to serve the patient: that principle is at the heart of the Government's policy. The time some patients have to wait for treatment is the most widespread concern in the NHS. The Government has given priority to reducing waiting lists and times. We have set up a special £50 million two-year programme. This year it will give treatment to over 100,000 people who are waiting for operations. We have set targets for more hip operations for old people, and more bone marrow transplants for children.

Putting patients first was the theme of our consultative document on primary care. We want the patient to have more information about services available from family doctors so that they can make a more informed choice.

Social security – a fair deal for those in need

We are spending about £46 billion this year on social security benefits – over £800 a year for every man, woman and child in the country. Expenditure on pensions and other benefits has risen by £13 billion on top of inflation, since we came into office. Most of this, an extra £9 billion, has gone to provide better standards of help and support to more elderly people, families with children, disabled people and those suffering long-term illness. The other £4 billion has gone to help the unemployed. But we have done more than provide extra resources, massive as the increase has been.

For the first time for 40 years the Government has undertaken an overall review of the social security system. The review showed a social security system which was too complex and which too often did not provide help for those most in need. The 1986 Social Security Act tackled these problems and reformed the position so that the system is simpler to understand and to run. It will be fairer in the way it directs help to those who need it most. And it will be a system in which people can look forward to independence and security in retirement.

Our policies for social security have four main aims.

First, to ensure that those in retirement have a secure standard of living through state provision and their own pensions and savings. This Government has honoured its pledges to the pensioner and more than maintained the buying power of the state pension. Total spending on state pensions and benefits for elderly people has risen by 29 per cent after allowing for inflation. We will continue to maintain the value of the state retirement pension.

But retired people value their independence. They do not want to rely on the State alone for their income nor, increasingly, are they doing so. We share Beveridge's original goal of a good basic pension from the State, together with a second income from occupational and personal pensions and savings.

Pensioners have benefited from our success against inflation. Almost three-quarters of all pensioners have savings. Their income from these has grown by over 7 per cent on average every year since 1979. Income from savings fell by 3.5 per cent every year under the last Labour Government, eaten away by inflation.

Occupational pensions, pensioners' savings, social security benefits and the state retirement pension have all increased. The total increase in income for the average pensioner is more than double that achieved during the last Labour Government.

We are now offering new opportunities for people to obtain additional pensions from their jobs or their own savings. We have already improved the treatment of those now retiring early and of the pension rights of people changing jobs.

We wish to encourage the 10 million employees who do not yet have their own occupational pension scheme to have a pension of their own. Every employee should have the right to take out a personal pension, fully portable from job to job. That is why we are extending favourable tax treatment from employers' schemes to personal pensions.

As a result of these reforms, millions more people will have the opportunity to take out additional pensions of their own.

In the next Parliament: we will reintroduce measures to give substantial tax incentives to personal pensions, and to enable members of occupational schemes to make additional voluntary contributions to a pension plan that is completely separate from their employers' schemes. These measures will further increase choice for millions of employees.

Second, to bring more help to low income families, child benefit will continue to be paid as now, and direct to the mother. Families on income support which replaces supplementary benefit will benefit from the new family premium. In addition, we will introduce the new family credit which will benefit twice as many low income families in work as family income supplement. The new system will also help tackle both the unemployment and the poverty traps.

Third, to improve the framework of benefits for disabled people, spending on benefits for disabled people and those suffering long-term sickness has been increased by 72 per cent after inflation to £6 billion. The amount spent on mobility allowances has been doubled, invalid care allowance extended, the new severe disablement allowance introduced and the invalidity trap abolished. The introduction of the new disablement premiums will bring an extra £50 million per year to disabled people.

We are carrying out a major new survey of the needs of disabled people. This will be completed next year.

Fourth, to reform the tangled web of income-related benefits which has grown up piecemeal over forty years, for the first time all the income-related benefits will be calculated in the same way. Where people are working, the amount of benefit they get will depend on their pay after tax and National Insurance contributions. Thus people will not be made worse off by taking a job and will not lose money when their gross pay rises.

The new rules, which come into effect in April next year, will be easier for claimants to understand and staff to run. In addition, our programme of computerisation – the biggest programme ever in this country will help staff to deliver benefits to all who are entitled to them quickly, accurately and courteously.

Success in social policy depends on growth in national prosperity. Labour's economic failure led to damaging cuts in health care and benefits. Our increasing economic strength means that resources for care have grown and are growing – with programmes better managed, better adapted to changing demands, and better directed to those most in need.

Freedom, law and responsibility

Conservatives have always believed that a fundamental purpose of government is to protect the security of the citizen under the rule of law. There can be no half-heartedness, no opting out, in the fight against crime and violence: all of us, not just the Government or the police, share a responsibility to make safer our streets and homes.

The fight against crime

We do not underrate the challenge. Crime has been rising steadily over the years; not just in Britain but in most other countries, too. The origins of crime lie deep in society: in families where parents do not support or control their children; in schools where discipline is poor; and in the wider world where violence is glamorised and traditional values are under attack.

Government alone cannot tackle such deep-rooted problems easily or quickly. But Government must give a lead: by backing, not attacking the police; by providing a tough legal framework for sentencing; by building the prisons in which to place those who pose a threat to society – and by keeping out of prison those who do not; and by encouraging local communities to prevent crime and to help the police detect it. All this we have done; and we will intensify these efforts.

- The manpower available to the police has been increased by 16,500 since 1979.
- We have given the police more powers to avert public disorder.
- We have encouraged tougher sentences for violent criminals. The maximum penalties for trafficking in hard drugs and for attempted rape have been raised to life imprisonment. The courts have been empowered to strip drug traffickers of their profits.
- We have brought forward a number of reforms to help tackle child abuse and make it more likely that offenders will be successfully prosecuted.
- We have embarked on the biggest prison building and modernisation programme this century and increased staff numbers by almost a fifth.

Care for the innocent

At the same time we have extended protection for innocent people and for the victims of crime.

- We have strengthened the safeguards against any abuse of police power by setting up an independent police Complaints Authority, providing for the tape-recording of police interviews and setting down clear rules on the proper treatment of the individual citizen.
- We have given special priority to helping the victims of crime. Police treatment of rape victims has been made more sensitive. More criminals now pay compensation to their victims. We are providing more money to help local Victim Support Schemes.
- We have launched a determined drive to improve the administration of justice by providing for time limits by which the cases of those held in custody must be heard. 58 more Circuit Judges have been appointed and 43 court building projects have been completed.

Better justice

The challenge before us remains great; but much has been done. The great majority of those who commit serious crimes of violence are brought to book. There are more police, better equipped to fight crime. Those who commit serious crimes can now expect much tougher punishment.

Early in the new Parliament the Criminal Justice Bill will have to be reintroduced. It will:

- enable child victims of physical and sexual abuse to give evidence by a live video link in order to reduce the anguish which they would otherwise face;

- raise to life imprisonment the penalty for carrying firearms while committing a crime;
- tackle, by providing for reference to the Court of Appeal, the problem of lenient sentences which undermine public confidence in the criminal justice system;
- give victims of crime a statutory right to compensation under the Criminal Injuries Compensation Scheme;
- build on our previous measures stripping drug traffickers of the proceeds of their crimes and extend the same approach to other serious crimes.

We have already signed an extradition treaty with the United States which will make it more difficult for terrorists to escape British justice: now we will reform our own law on extradition so as to make still more effective the international war against crime.

Building on strength

We will continue to put a high priority on the fight against crime, so that the citizen can feel safe on the street or in his home.

We will:

- increase the number of police further to ensure a stronger police presence on our streets, to combat crime and to protect the public;
- strengthen the law dealing with the sale and possession of offensive weapons;
- maintain the operational independence of the police and resist pressure from the Opposition parties to politicise the police by letting local authorities decide policing priorities;
- continue our present prison building programme and achieve more professional and efficient working practices in the prison service;
- institute a thorough review of the workings of the parole system.

Our approach in all these cases is strongly supported by the general public. We will go further in drawing on that support by promoting crime prevention. Already more than 29,000 Neighbourhood Watch Schemes have sprung up since the last Election. We are committed to the success of this popular anti-crime movement.

We will build on the support of the public by establishing a national organisation to promote the best practices in local crime prevention initiatives.

We will seek ways to strengthen the special constabulary.

Tackling drug abuse

We have taken the battle against drugs into every corner of the globe where production or trafficking flourishes. We have more than doubled the number of customs specialist drug investigators. We have strengthened the effectiveness of the police in the fight against drug abuse. Traffickers can now be sentenced to life imprisonment. They also stand to lose all the wealth generated by their evil trade under the most far-reaching asset seizure provisions anywhere in the world.

We have funded about 200 new drug treatment facilities. Our prevention campaign, targeted on youngsters at risk, is encouraging a strong resistance to hard drugs amongst teenagers. The battle against drugs can and must be won. Already there are some signs that the heroin problem may have passed its peak. The cocaine explosion has never happened. It need never happen. We will continue to make the defeat of the drug trade a key priority.

Immigration and race relations

Immigration for settlement is now at its lowest level since control of Commonwealth immigration first began in 1962. Firm but fair immigration controls are essential for harmonious and improving community relations. We will tighten the existing law to ensure that the control over settlement becomes even more effective.

We now require visas for visitors from the Indian sub-continent, Nigeria and Ghana, both to protect genuine travellers and to guard against bogus visitors seeking to settle here illegally. We are tackling the problem of those who fraudulently pose as refugees and who seek to exploit Britain's long tradition of giving refuge to the victims of persecution.

We want to see members of the ethnic minorities assuming positions of leadership alongside their fellow citizens and accepting their full share of responsibility. Racial discrimination is an injustice and can have no place in a tolerant and civilised society. We are particularly concerned about racial attacks. They require effective and sympathetic attention from the police and we have ensured that increasingly they receive it.

Progress towards better community relations must be on a basis of equality. Reverse discrimination is itself an injustice and if it were to be introduced it would undermine the achievement and example of those who had risen on their merits.

Immigrant communities have already shown that it is possible to play an active and influential role in the mainstream of British life without losing one's distinctive cultural traditions. We also want to see all ethnic minorities participating fully in British culture. They will suffer permanent disadvantage if they remain in linguistic and cultural ghettos.

Reforming the law

Since the last election the Government has made a number of important reforms of family law. These cover the law of maintenance and distribution of property following divorce, measures to prevent the abduction of children and the law of illegitimacy.

Particular laws which are not enforced or which are full of obvious anomalies risk bringing the law itself into disrepute. Changing tastes also require the reform of outdated laws which govern personal habits and behaviour: such reform should, where possible, be on the basis of a wide consensus.

The present laws on Sunday trading and licensing contain innumerable anomalies. They are frequently flouted. We will therefore look for an acceptable way forward to bring sense and consistency to the law on Sunday trading. And we will liberalise the laws on liquor licensing hours so as to increase consumer choice, but we will also keep a sensible limit on late-night opening.

We have already extended absent voting rights to new categories of electors. In particular we have enfranchised British citizens who have lived abroad for less than 5 years. We propose to extend this eligibility.

Northern Ireland

The British people have shown their commitment to the people of Northern Ireland in the common fight against terrorism, and in helping improve the economic and social situation in the Province. We resolutely support the security forces in their outstanding service to the whole community.

We are determined that terrorism will not succeed; that the vital principles of democracy will be upheld; and that the people of Northern Ireland themselves should determine their constitutional position. We will maintain, against Socialist opposition, for as long as is necessary the special powers which the police need throughout the UK to prevent terrorism and bring terrorists to justice. There will be no change in the present status of Northern Ireland as part of the United Kingdom unless the people of Northern Ireland so wish it.

That is at the heart of the Anglo-Irish Agreement which was signed with the Republic of Ireland in 1985. The Agreement offers reassurance to both sides of the community that their identities and interests will be respected, and that any change in the status of Northern Ireland would only come about with the consent of a majority of the people of the Province. It commits both governments to work together in the fight against terrorism.

We will continue to work within the Province for a devolved government in which both communities can have confidence and will feel able to participate.

Local government and inner cities

The Conservative view of local government is that local people should look after the interests of the local community which they were elected to serve, maintaining and improving essential services at a price people can afford. That is an honourable tradition of public service, still upheld by councillors in most local authorities.

But the abuses of left-wing Labour councils have shocked the nation. The Labour Party leadership pretends that this is a problem in only a few London boroughs. The truth is that the far Left control town halls in many of our cities.

The extremists have gained power in these areas partly because too few ratepayers have an interest in voting for responsible councillors pursuing sensible policies. Many people benefit from local services yet make little or no contribution towards them: this throws too heavy a burden on too few shoulders.

There is much else wrong with the present system of domestic rates. They seem unfair and arbitrary. And companies are left with little protection against huge rate rises levied by councils controlled by Labour, Liberals and Social Democrats, which drive them out of business and destroy jobs.

We have acted to protect ratepayers' interests in a number of ways. The wasteful and unnecessary tier of the GLC and metropolitan counties has been eliminated – to the substantial benefit of ratepayers. Our rate-capping legislation so bitterly opposed by the Labour, SDP and Liberal parties in Parliament has protected ratepayers from huge rate increases. This year alone, twenty councils will be rate-capped – nineteen of them

Labour and one controlled by the Liberals and the SDP – saving ratepayers several hundred million pounds.

We will now tackle the roots of the problem. We will reform local government finance to strengthen local democracy and accountability. Local electors must be able to decide the level of service they want and how much they are prepared to pay for it. We will legislate in the first Session of the new Parliament to abolish the unfair domestic rating system and replace rates with a fairer Community Charge. This will be a fixed rate charge for local services paid by those over the age of 18, except the mentally ill and elderly people living in homes and hospitals. The less-well-off and students will not have to pay the full charge but everyone will be aware of the costs as well as the benefits of local services. This should encourage people to take a greater interest in the policies of their local council and in getting value for money. Business ratepayers will pay a Unified Business Rate at a standard rate pegged to inflation.

We will require local authorities to put out to tender a range of services, including refuse collection, the cleaning of streets and buildings, vehicle maintenance, catering and ground maintenance. Ratepayers expect councils to provide their services as efficiently as possible. Yet some local authorities steadfastly oppose private sector companies tendering for services even though they could provide them more cheaply and effectively. The independent Audit Commission has estimated that some £500 million a year could be saved if all councils followed the practices of the best sums which could be used to lower rates or improve services.

The Widdicombe Report into the conduct of local authority business painted a disturbing picture of the breakdown of democratic processes in a number of councils. We will take action to strengthen democratic processes in local authorities.

Inner cities

The regeneration of the inner cities must be tackled. The growth in our national prosperity in recent years has been founded on a rebirth of enterprise. But in many of our inner cities the conditions for enterprise and pride of ownership have been systematically extinguished by Socialist councils. For the sake of those living in our inner cities we must remove the barriers against private investment, jobs and prosperity which such councils have erected.

We are setting up five new Urban Development Corporations which will have the powers, resources and management structure to reclaim and redevelop great tracts of derelict land: these new Corporations will follow the model successfully applied in London Docklands and on Merseyside.

Our Unified Business Rate will ensure that companies and jobs are not driven out of inner city areas by the high rates of profligate councils.

We have roughly doubled the resources to reclaim derelict land. We will improve procedures to accelerate the process of bringing vacant and under-used public sector land back into productive use.

We will build on the experience of Urban Development Corporations by creating new mini-UDCs. These will operate on a smaller scale in areas where there is clear economic potential but where the local authorities are failing to tackle the problem. Our Urban Programme provides a range of grants to help industry and local councils undertake projects that will improve the environment and encourage new investment.

We are helping to lead local action through our five City Action Teams, sixteen Inner City Task Forces and the Inner City Partnerships. All of them draw on government assistance and work with local business and local people to promote enterprise, employment and training.

Great cities are built on the enterprise and vitality of the individuals who live there. Our aim is to create a climate which encourages and harnesses that energy in the interests of all.

A better society

Planning and the environment

Conservatives are by instinct conservationists – committed to preserve all that is best of our country's past. We are determined to maintain our national heritage of countryside and architecture. Since taking office we have:

- more than doubled the area of specially protected Green Belt: we will continue to defend it against unsuitable development;
- established new arrangements, backed with public funds, to make farming more sensitive to wildlife and to conservation;
- completed the work of listing pre-war buildings which receive legal protection and extended such protection to the best post-war buildings;
- established a new, powerful Pollution Inspectorate;
- passed new laws on the control of pesticides and implemented new controls on the pollution of water;
- put in hand plans for cleaning up Britain's beaches, costing over £300 million over the next four years;
- more than doubled spending after allowing for inflation on countryside and nature conservation since 1979;
- set in hand the establishment of the new Norfolk Broads Authority – a major environmental initiative;
- established a huge programme, costing over £4,000 million, to clean up the environment of the Mersey Basin by the early years of the next century.

We are determined to maintain the Green Belt. We will protect the countryside for its own sake and conserve its wildlife, while allowing for those small-scale and well planned developments which are needed to provide jobs and keep country areas thriving.

Wherever possible we want to encourage large-scale developments to take place on unused and neglected land in our towns and cities rather than in the countryside. We want to improve on our performance in 1986 when nearly half of all new development took place on reused land.

A practical agenda

Only the Conservatives have a serious costed agenda for further environmental action for another five years of Government. We will:

- continue our £600 million programme of modifying power stations, to combat acid rain;
- adopt improved standards, in concert with Europe, for reducing pollution from cars. We have already reduced tax on lead-free petrol and will encourage its wider use;
- introduce new laws on air pollution and dangerous wastes;
- double the funding for Environmentally Sensitive Areas;
- introduce new laws giving extra protection to the landscape of our National Parks;
- encourage more small woodlands in lowland areas through new grants;
- legislate to safeguard common land on the basis of the Common Land Forum, and continue to protect public access to the countryside through footpaths;
- support scientifically justified, international action to protect the atmosphere and the sea from damage from pollutants;
- establish a National Rivers Authority to take over responsibilities for ensuring strict safeguards against the pollution of rivers and water courses and to pursue sound conservation policies. The water supply and sewage functions of the water authorities will be transferred to the private sector;
- set up safe facilities for disposing of radioactive waste from power stations, hospitals and other sources: we have asked UK NIREX to come forward with proposals for deep disposal.

The arts

Our international reputation in the arts has never been higher. Tourists flock to this country to enjoy the highest standards of theatre, music, artistic excellence and our museums. Art centres have nearly doubled in number since 1979. Attendances at theatres, concerts, cinemas and historic houses have all risen significantly.

Under the Conservatives, spending on the arts has risen by 15 per cent since 1979 after allowing for inflation. Over the same period, the Arts Council grant has risen from £61 million to nearly £139 million. And schemes like the Business Sponsorship Incentive Scheme have pushed the value of such sponsorship from £72 million to £25 million over the last decade.

In future years:

- We will maintain government support for the arts and continue to encourage private support.
- We will make it a major objective to ensure that excellence in the arts is available in all parts of the country.
- We will continue to safeguard our heritage, particularly through the National Heritage Memorial Fund, created by this Government in 1980 to assist the preservation, maintenance and acquisition of items of outstanding merit which might otherwise be lost to the nation.
- We will encourage our great national museums and galleries to make the national treasures which they house more widely accessible.

Sport

We have increased funding for the Sports Council from £15 million in 1978/79 to £37 million in 1987/88. We will continue to work with the Council and, through our funding of the Sports Council National Centres, we will encourage the pursuit of excellence in our sports. We want to encourage competitive sports through schools and clubs and we strongly oppose any attempts to ban competitive sports in schools. We will continue to encourage schools and colleges to open their facilities for community use wherever possible to co-operate with other owners to achieve public access to sport premises.

Football hooliganism has tarnished the good name of British sportsmanship. We have acted to control the sale of alcohol at sports grounds. We have enhanced police powers to stop and search at football grounds and we have encouraged tougher sentencing of hooligans.

Broadcasting

Our objectives for broadcasting are to provide consumers with a wider range of programmes, to encourage independent producers, and to preserve the high standards which we have traditionally enjoyed in British broadcasting.

Vital decisions will need to be made in the next Parliament. We have already published proposals for a less regulated and more diverse radio system. We shall follow a policy of more competition, variety and innovation in our domestic networks and encourage the export of British programmes to international audiences and markets. The development of the broadcasting industry will be allowed to occur, wherever possible, commercially.

We will therefore introduce a major new Broadcasting Bill in the new Parliament. It will enable the broadcasters to take full advantage of the opportunities presented by technological advances and to broaden the choice of viewing and listening. The broadcasters owe it to the lively talent in the independent sector to take more programmes from them. We will ensure that at least 25 per cent of programmes broadcast on both ITV and BBC will be supplied by independent producers as soon as possible.

The responsibility for enforcing broadcasting standards must rest with the broadcasting authorities. The present Broadcasting Complaints Commission has a relatively narrow remit. But there is deep public concern over the display of sex and violence on television. We will therefore bring forward proposals for stronger and more effective arrangements to reflect that concern.

We will remove the current exemption enjoyed by broadcasters under the Obscene Publications Act 1959.

Britain and the world

Britain is once again giving a lead in world affairs. We are forthright in support of freedom and justice. We stand up vigorously for Britain's interests abroad. Our voice is heard with respect on the crucial issues of war and peace, of finance and trade.

Defending the nation

The first duty of government is the defence of the realm and the preservation of peace. Nuclear weapons are vital to that task. In the 40 years since 1945, more than 10 million people have died in wars around the globe. But there has been peace in Europe.

Conventional weapons did not succeed in deterring war. But nuclear weapons have prevented, not only nuclear war, but conventional war in Europe as well. A strong defence policy has proved to be the most effective peace policy.

Labour's policy is to give up Britain's independent nuclear deterrent without asking anything in return. The Labour Party would require the United States to withdraw its nuclear weapons from our soil and to close down NATO nuclear bases in Britain. It would remove Britain altogether from the protection of the United States' nuclear umbrella.

That policy would abandon the defence policy followed by every British government, Labour or Conservative, since the Second World War. It would expose us to nuclear blackmail from the vast Soviet armoury, to which we would have no reply. It would inflict damage, perhaps fatal damage, on the Atlantic Alliance on which we and Western Europe depend for our security. It would strike at our relations with our most important ally, weakening the American commitment to Europe's defences. It would, in short, be the biggest victory for the Soviet Union in 40 years.

The defence policy of the Liberals and Social Democrats is muddled and confused. They would cancel Trident and they have no clear idea of what to put in its place. Their suggested replacements are much more expensive than Trident, which costs only 3p in every £ of defence spending. None would be available in time. None would provide equal security.

The Liberal and SDP defence policy would be one-sided disarmament by default or inadvertence. The only difference between it and Labour policy is a matter of timing. Labour would scrap Britain's deterrent immediately upon entering office. The Liberals and Social Democrats would allow it to wither on the vine.

Only the Conservative Party stands by the defence policy which every post-war government has seen to be necessary and which has kept the peace of Europe for more than a generation. We are not prepared to take risks with Britain's security:

- We will stand fully by our obligations to our European and American allies in NATO.
- We will retain our independent nuclear deterrent and modernise it with Trident. Because of improvements in Soviet defences we need the greater capability of Trident to retain the necessary deterrence which Polaris gives. No amount of money spent on conventional defence would ever buy us the same degree of deterrence.
- We will continue to increase the effectiveness of our conventional forces, to provide them with the most modern equipment and to obtain better value for money from the defence budget. We have already increased defence spending by more than 20 per cent in real terms since 1979 and restored the pay and conditions of our servicemen.

But we also want to see a world in which there are fewer nuclear weapons. That is why Britain is at the forefront of arms control negotiations.

We strive with our allies to achieve balanced and verifiable agreements for:

- the elimination of medium-range nuclear missiles in Europe and preferably world-wide;
- agreed constraints on shorter-range missiles;
- a 50 per cent cut in strategic nuclear missiles;
- a world-wide ban on chemical weapons.

Western strength and resolution are essential to achieve these aims. That is why the Conservative Government deployed Cruise missiles. All the Opposition parties – Labour, Liberals and SDP – voted against deployment in the House of Commons. Yet it was the deployment of Cruise and Pershing missiles which brought the Soviet Union back to the negotiating table. We can look forward to an agreement this year which will, for the first time, reduce the numbers of nuclear weapons.

With the Conservatives Britain is also taking the lead in working towards greater trust and confidence between East and West, and to encourage changes in the East, where disillusion with totalitarian Socialism grows inexorably. The Prime Minister's historic visit to Moscow was a major contribution to this. We shall welcome any move by the Soviet Union towards respect for basic human rights. But we must not lower our guard. Strong defence is still the surest foundation for building peace.

Europe grows in strength

This Government has taken Britain from the sidelines into the mainstream of Europe. But being good Europeans does not prevent us from standing up for British interests. The agreement we negotiated on the Community Budget has saved Britain £4,500 million since 1984. We will continue to work for strict controls on the Community Budget.

Britain has led the way in establishing a genuine common market, with more trade and services moving freely across national boundaries. We will campaign for the opening of the market in financial and other services and the extension of cheaper air fares in Europe. We will also continue to work with our European partners to defend our own trading interests and press for freer trade among all nations. All of this will help safeguard existing jobs and create new ones.

We will continue to play a responsible leading role in the development of the Community, while safeguarding our essential national interests.

Firm against terrorism and aggression

Britain has stood at the forefront in the fight against international terrorism. No democracy has a better record than Britain in standing up to the terrorists, who threaten the most basic values of civilised life.

We will seek the support of other democratic nations for the provisions of the European Convention on the Suppression of Terrorism.

We stood up to aggression in the Falklands and would do so again, if necessary. We want normal relations with Argentina. We have made numerous proposals to that end. But we stand by our pledges to the Islanders. We will not negotiate on the sovereignty of the Falklands.

The wider world

When other countries are prepared to act in good faith, the Conservative Government has shown the will and the diplomatic skill to find solutions to age-old conflicts and misunderstandings. Our record of tackling long-standing problems in Hong Kong, Zimbabwe and Gibraltar demonstrates our determination to seek peaceful and imaginative settlements of difficult international disputes. We have played a prominent part in bringing Israel and the moderate Arab states closer to peace negotiations in the framework of an international conference.

We believe that the issues of Southern Africa, too, will be tackled best by dialogue, not violence. We want to see an end to apartheid in South Africa. But trade and economic sanctions would only serve to entrench apartheid, increase the risk of bloodshed and inflict severe hardship on black South Africans without bringing a settlement any nearer. Negotiations between the leaders of the South African people are the best way to resolve the problems of that unhappy country.

Overseas aid

We have the sixth largest aid programme in the western world, and the third largest in Europe, spending about £1,300 million each year. Britain pioneered the reform of Europe's food aid policy, to make it more rapid and effective. We have substantially increased our support for the disaster, famine and refugee relief activities of voluntary agencies, as well as for their long-term development work. We have led the way in giving help to the people of Ethiopia, ravaged by famine. Our 'Aid and Trade Provision' funds have helped win good development contracts for British firms worth over £2 billion since 1979.

We will maintain our substantial aid programme and direct it ever more effectively. We will bring more young people from Commonwealth and other countries to train and study in Britain. We ourselves have made positive and practical proposals for international action to help some of the poorest and most indebted countries of sub-Saharan Africa.

Labour's proposal of selective import controls would damage developing countries, open the door to protectionism and harm those poorest countries which most need our help. It would also be bad for Britain. The best contribution Britain can make to developing countries is to champion open trade and free enterprise abroad and to practise them at home.

A fateful choice

For decades there was basic agreement between political parties on defence and foreign policy. That agreement was firmly in the national interest. It has been torn up by our opponents. Labour's policy would mean not a secure Britain, but a neutralist Britain. And eventually, for there can be no trifling with Soviet power, a frightened and fellow-travelling Britain. The Liberals and Social Democrats would take us more slowly down that same disastrous road. This election matters more for our safety and freedom than any election since the Second World War.

Conclusion: the way forward

The proposals outlined in this manifesto are the extension of policies which have already proved outstandingly successful.

Today Britain is a stable and well-governed country which exercises great influence in the world.

We seek the support of the British people to make this achievement truly secure, to build upon it and to extend its benefits to all.

No previous government with eight years of office to its credit has ever presented the electorate with such a full programme of radical reform.

No other party, presenting its manifesto proposals to the nation, has been able to support them with such a solid record of achievement.

We commend them with confidence to the British people.

THE BEST FUTURE FOR BRITAIN

THE CONSERVATIVE MANIFESTO 1992

CONSERVATIVE PARTY GENERAL ELECTION MANIFESTO 1992

The best future for Britain

Date of Election	Thursday 9 April
Party Leader	John Major
Candidates	645
MPs	336
Votes	14,092,891
% of vote	42.3%

Foreword

At the end of this Parliament a new Millennium will be in view. We must raise our sights high. This Manifesto is about making our country respected and secure, and helping you achieve a better, safer and more prosperous future. For I believe – strongly – that you, and not the Government, should be in charge of your life. That's what Conservatism stands for. That principle underlies all the policies in this Manifesto.

I believe in a responsible society. Government's duties are clear: to protect Britain in a dangerous world; to look after those who cannot look after themselves; to protect law-abiding people from crime and disorder; and to protect the value of our currency – without which all spending pledges are worthless and all savings at risk.

But I believe also in a society in which government doesn't try to take responsibility away from people. Politicians must never make the mistake of thinking the state always knows best, or that it is entitled to the lion's share of people's money. I believe in low taxes not just because they ignite enterprise – the spark of economic growth – but because they put power and choice where it belongs: in your hands.

So when you compare what the politicians are saying in this election, ask yourself these questions. Whom do you trust to take responsibility for Britain's defence; to keep us safe and strengthen our influence for good? And who, at the same time, wants to give you the opportunity to do your best for yourself and your family?

Who will give you the power to choose – to say for yourself what you want? And who will give you the personal prosperity that comes from low taxes – from your own savings, your own pension, your own home? Who will let you build up your own stake in Britain's success – and pass it on to your children?

Only Conservatives can truly claim to be the party of opportunity; choice; ownership and responsibility. Socialists like to keep people under the government's thumb. Conservatives want to give them independence. But we also want to put government at your service, giving you what you've paid for – good public services, responsible to you.

I do not believe the answer to every problem is simply for government to dig deeper in your pocket. I believe it often lies in changing the way government works; in making it respond to you. Government should look outwards. It should listen. It should put you in the know, not keep you in the dark.

We have made quite a start, under the seal of the Citizen's Charter. People in schools, hospitals, public offices of all kinds are rising to the challenge. I knew they would. They just needed encouragement, incentive and a system that is outward-looking too.

It is all part of a revolution in quality in Britain. British goods are once more winning in the toughest markets abroad. There is new vigour in the businesses liberated from state ownership; better management and better industrial relations. These are the firm foundations of economic recovery

We are raising the quality of our education and training. We are raising the standard of our housing, as more people own and improve their own homes. We are concerned for the quality of our environment. And in government, we are leading a drive for quality throughout our public services.

That, I believe, is the way we all want to live – a decent life in a civilised community. That is the way we can live: celebrating our achievements, not nurturing old grudges; enjoying our successes, not talking Britain down. We can be free of old prejudices and class bafflers. We can encourage diversity, not division; achievement, not antagonism. We can all make our own contribution to the success of the United Kingdom; and we must keep that kingdom united.

You know I believe in choice. And in this election, as always, there is another choice. You can vote for our opponents, and watch them take Britain back to the 1970s. Back to socialism. Back to strikes. Back to strife. Back to the world's pity, or worse still, contempt. I don't believe Britain wants that. I know the world doesn't want that for Britain.

I hope you will choose a different path – to go forward, not back; to go for the best, knowing that Britain can be the best and do it best. My belief is clear. Only the best is good enough for Britain.

John Major

Taking responsibility for Britain

The world has been transformed in recent years. Communism has collapsed in Eastern Europe, and the Soviet Union has fallen apart. Everywhere Socialism is in retreat and democracy, human rights and market economics are advancing. The authority of the UN has been bolstered and Iraqi aggression seen off. Talks are under way in the Middle East and South Africa. It is a time of great opportunity, but also of new dangers.

Britain needs firm leadership at this time. We must be represented by a team of quality and experience. A team which can help shape the world for the next century. A Conservative team.

Under the Conservatives, Britain has regained her rightful influence in the world. We have stood up for the values our country has always represented. We have defended Britain's interests with vigour and with success.

The respect with which Britain is regarded in the world has rarely been higher. We play a central part in world affairs as a member of the European Community, NATO, the Commonwealth and the Group of 7 leading industrial countries, and as a Permanent Member of the UN Security Council. No other country holds all these positions.

We are taking a leading role in recasting all the main international institutions to which we belong: the United Nations, the European Community, NATO, and the Commonwealth. The Prime Minister convened the first ever meeting of the UN Security Council at Heads of Government level. Between now and the end of 1992 there will be seven Summits where issues of critical importance to our future will be determined: two EC Councils, at Lisbon and Edinburgh, the G7 Summit, the CSCE Summit, EC Summits with the US and Japan, and the Earth Summit at Rio de Janeiro. Britain will be at the centre of these negotiations.

The need for leadership

The end of the Cold War has enabled the UN to act with new unity and authority. Under the authority of the UN, British forces played a leading and courageous part in the Gulf War and the liberation of Kuwait. At the Prime Minister's instigation, the UN also backed the operation to protect the Kurds.

Britain has led the world in helping the reforms in the former Soviet Union. The Prime Minister gave full and immediate support to President Yeltsin in the August coup attempt, and was the first Western leader to visit Moscow after the coup failed. Britain has led the way in building up relations with the republics of the new Commonwealth of Independent States. We have provided valuable economic and humanitarian aid to ease the transition to a market economy.

- We will support an enhanced role for the UN in peace-keeping and combating state-sponsored terrorism.
- We are determined that Iraq should comply with the terms of the Gulf War cease-fire agreement, and in particular that it should co-operate with the UN in dismantling its weapons of mass destruction.
- We support early Russian membership of the IMF and World Bank, as well as a stabilisation fund for the rouble.
- We are co-operating with our partners to provide urgent help to the former Soviet Union and Eastern Europe to upgrade the safety of their nuclear power stations.
- We strongly support the peace process in the Middle East. The outcome of the talks must safeguard the security of Israel and achieve self-determination for the people of the occupied territories.
- We will safeguard the prosperity of Hong Kong, nurture democratic institutions and work with the Chinese Government within the terms of the Joint Declaration.
- We seek a solution to the dispute which has divided Cyprus since 1974. A settlement must recognise that Cyprus is indivisible and that the rights of both communities must be assured. We will support the UN's efforts to secure a fair and lasting solution.
- The problems of Kashmir cannot be resolved by violence. We urge both India and Pakistan to address and resolve the issue, and we stand ready to help.

Our influence for good

All over the world countries are turning to democracy and free markets. Last October in Harare, the Commonwealth took on a new role as a promoter of democracy, the rule of law, and respect for individual freedoms. Already the Commonwealth is monitoring elections to ensure that they are free and fair. Britain is taking the lead in encouraging these trends.

We give substantial aid to the relief of poverty and to help the struggling economies of the developing world. Our aid programme next year (excluding aid to Eastern Europe and the CIS) will reach £1,800 million. Britain also makes more direct private investment in the developing world than any other EC country – some £2,400 million in 1989. We are urging the international community to take decisive action on debt relief, the liberalisation of world trade and support for good government.

We continue to accept the long-term UN target for aid of 0.7 per cent of GNP, although we cannot set a timetable for its achievement. The quality of Britain's overseas aid programme is second to none. It is well targeted and highly effective. Eighty per cent of our bilateral aid goes to the poorest countries. New aid to the poorest is given as grants, not loans.

We are supporting projects designed to build efficient institutions and accountable government. We are helping to improve public administration and the legal system in a number of countries.

The English language is one of our nation's greatest assets – culturally, politically and commercially. The BBC World Service has unrivalled standing around the globe. The British Council acts as a cultural ambassador for Britain and for the English language.

- We will use overseas aid to promote good government, sensible economic policies, the rooting out of corruption, and – crucially – respect for human rights and the rule of law.
- We will press creditor countries to accept the Prime Minister's proposal – the 'Trinidad Terms' – for a two-thirds reduction in the official debt of the poorest countries.
- We will promote the development of multi-party systems through the new Westminster Foundation for Democracy.
- We will promote the English language by strengthening both the British Council and the BBC World Service. We will encourage both to become more entrepreneurial in order to finance their activities in developing markets.

The risks we face now

The collapse of the old Soviet Union has dramatically vindicated Conservative defence policy. We have always put the security of our country first. We have kept the peace by staying strong. Today the threat of a massive surprise attack from Eastern Europe has gone. But we still face grave risks to our security. We cannot drop our guard. Under the Conservatives, Britain will never do so.

Within the former Soviet Union there remains a huge military force. Democracy and the rule of law are yet to be firmly established. Control over these armed forces and the massive nuclear capability is uncertain. The events in Yugoslavia show what can happen when Communism collapses in disorder.

Increasingly threats come from outside Europe – as we saw so clearly in the Gulf. Many more countries are acquiring large stocks of modern arms. Some are trying to obtain nuclear, biological and chemical weapons. Britain must be able to respond to any unexpected danger.

The Conservatives are the only party who recognise both the opportunities and the threats of the new world.

For over forty years, our security has been based firmly on NATO, the most successful defensive alliance ever. We will work with our allies to ensure that NATO remains the cornerstone of our defence. Britain will command a new NATO Rapid Reaction Corps ready to deploy quickly to counter any sudden threat. As Europeans we must accept a greater role in safeguarding the peace in our continent.

We will promote arms control and reduction initiatives. On Britain's initiative, the UN is establishing a register of arms transfers in order to monitor any dangerous arsenals of weapons.

Britain has always been strongly opposed to nuclear proliferation. We will back an enhanced role for the International Atomic Energy Agency in inspecting nuclear sites and for the UN Security Council in acting against those nations which break their non-proliferation obligations.

- We will work to strengthen the Western European Union as the European pillar of NATO. We will press for a European reaction force.
- We will intensify the co-ordination of security policies within the Twelve.
- We will work through the CSCE to safeguard the security of Europe.
- We will support a comprehensive and verifiable ban on chemical weapons, and further controls on the export of items which could be used in making biological weapons.
- We will help Russia in her efforts to dismantle nuclear weapons.

Our armed forces

Only the Conservatives can be trusted to maintain the quality and capability of our Armed Forces. We are proud of the skill, courage and professionalism which they displayed in the Gulf and which they show daily in Northern Ireland.

We are the only party unambiguously committed to the preservation and modernisation of our independent nuclear deterrent. Our defence would be unsafe in the hands of the opposition parties. Labour have opposed our defence policies at every turn. They have twisted and turned in their attitude to our nuclear deterrent. They would devastate our conventional forces by cuts of at least 27 per cent, which would lead to huge job losses in the defence industries.

The Liberal Democrats would cause even more damage to Britain's defences. Their aim is to cut our defence spending by half by the end of the decade. We insist that our forces have the modern, effective equipment that they need. The Gulf War showed that the Services must have the latest technology to give them maximum flexibility and mobility. That is why we have ordered the new Challenger II tank for the Army, the

Merlin helicopter for the Navy, the ASRAAM air defence missile for the RAF and a wide range of other new equipment for our Forces.

Our reappraisal of Britain's defence needs will result an a major restructuring of our Armed Forces to take account of the changing world situation. In future our Forces will be smaller, but better equipped. Our Services deserve the excellent pay and conditions which we have secured for them and will maintain.

- We will complete the deployment of the next generation of Britain's minimum nuclear deterrent. We will order and complete the fourth Trident submarine.
- We will ensure the Forces have the best and most modern equipment.
- We will improve the quality and management of service housing and help those in the Forces save towards buying a home of their own.
- The Reserves will play an even more important role and we will introduce legislation to allow their more flexible use.

The European Community

The Conservatives have been the party of Britain in Europe for 30 years. We have argued when argument was necessary; but we have not wavered nor changed our views. We have ensured that Britain is at the heart of Europe; a strong and respected partner.

We have played a decisive part in the development of the Community over the past decade. It was a British initiative which launched the Single Market programme and our insistence which reformed the Community's finances. Britain has promoted co-operation on foreign policy and in combating terrorism. Britain has also persuaded our partners to welcome new countries who apply for Community membership.

The Maastricht Treaty was a success both for Britain and for the rest of Europe. British proposals helped to shape the key provisions of the Treaty including those strengthening the enforcement of Community law defence, subsidiarity and law and order. But Britain refused to accept the damaging Social Chapter proposed by other Europeans, and it was excluded from the Maastricht Treaty.

All Member States must live up to their obligations under Community law. At Maastricht, we secured agreement that the European Court will be able to fine any Member State which fails to do so.

- We will work closely with our partners in foreign policy and in the war on international crime.
- We will continue to resist changes to the Treaty of Rome that would damage British business.
- We will resist Commission initiatives which run counter to the principle that issues should be dealt with on a national basis wherever possible.
- Britain is a great trading nation. We prosper through the maintenance of an open trading system. We will work for a successful outcome to the GATT negotiations.
- We will redouble our efforts to reform the Common Agricultural Policy and will stoutly defend the interests of British farmers and consumers.
- We will insist on more effective control over Community spending and will resist pressure to extend Community competence to new areas.
- We will work to strengthen the external frontiers of the Community whilst main-

taining the checks needed at our own borders against illegal immigration, drugs, terrorism and disease.

The British Presidency

In the second half of 1992 Britain will take the Chair of the Council of Ministers. The British Presidency comes at a turning point in the Community's history. It gives us the opportunity to shape the direction of the Community and to establish its priorities. We shall use it to promote our vision of an outward-looking Community based on free enterprise.

Our Presidency will reach its climax at the Edinburgh meeting of the European Council, which we will hold in the historic palace of Holyrood House. While the attention of Europe is focused on Edinburgh, the strength of our Union will be visible to all.

Our priorities will be:

- To start negotiations with those EFTA countries who want to join the Community so that they can join by 1995.
- To build on the EC's Association Agreements with Czechoslovakia, Hungary and Poland so that we can welcome them to full membership by the year 2000.
- To conclude EC trade and co-operation agreements with the main republics of the former Soviet Union.
- To complete the single market and extend it to the seven countries of EFTA. Over half our trade is with the rest of the Community. The single market will create an open market of 350 million customers for British goods and services. To complete the single market we shall aim to:
    - open up the market for life insurance to free competition;
    - liberalise air travel to bring down air fares in Europe closer to those in America;
    - free up the shipping and road transport markets so that British operators can carry freely within the EC;
    - increase competition in the European energy sector.
- We will provide guidance and help to any British company encountering a trade barrier illegal under European law.
- We will press for progress on the environment, including the Fifth Environment Action Programme.
- We will chair the negotiations on the future spending priorities of the Community to ensure value for money. We will safeguard the abatement negotiated by Mrs Thatcher which has so far brought some £12,000 million in budget rebates to Britain.

Wealth and ownership

The 1990s present a great economic opportunity for Britain. We have got the scourge of inflation under control. We have cut direct tax rates. And a stable currency gives industry a chance to realise the potential released by the reforms of the 1980s.

We have extended ownership more widely – of homes, savings and shares – with millions more sharing directly in Britain's success. We will promote enterprise through low taxes, sound money and a stable currency.

When the Exchange Rate Mechanism was being created, during the final days of the last Labour Government, the then Prime Minister decided Britain could not take part. It was easy to see why the economy was too weak. Inflation was too high. In 1974–79, the inflation rate averaged over 15 per cent. It peaked at 27 per cent. Public borrowing rose to nearly 10 per cent of national income – equivalent to £55,000 million today Penal taxes blunted enterprise. Britain was a byword for strikes.

The Conservatives have changed all that. Since 1979, our inflation rate has averaged 7½ per cent. Now it is only just over 4 per cent – below the average for the European Community In the 1960s and 1970s, Britain had the slowest growth rate in the European Community. But in the 1980s, we grew faster than either France or Germany Industrial disputes became rare events. And in 1990, a Conservative Government joined the ERM.

Penal taxes have been abolished. A man on average earnings, with a wife and two children, has an income today which after tax and inflation is 39 per cent higher than it was in Labour's last year. That great advance in the standard of living is at risk in this election.

Since the war, living standards have always risen faster under Conservative Governments than under Labour. Now we are pledged to cut tax rates again – and have made a start on the road to 20p Income Tax.

Corporate tax rates have been cut, too. Our business investment has increased more rapidly than in any other major economy except Japan. Britain attracts by far the biggest share of Japanese and American investment in Europe. That, too, is at risk in this election.

Britain's opportunity

We are now members of:

- The biggest free market in the world. British industry is again respected in Europe.
- A zone of low inflation, in which we can compete with the best.

Britain must not throw this opportunity away by electing a Labour government. The world recession has been tough for all of us, at home and abroad. Unemployment has risen. But in Britain we have laid the foundations for recovery. What is needed to trigger confidence and growth is a Conservative victory with a decisive majority. What would postpone recovery, and turn this promise of growth into the certainty of hard times, is the election of our opponents whose policies would mean higher taxes, higher inflation, higher interest rates, more bureaucratic regulation and more strikes.

In the 1990s, the Government's task will be to provide an economic environment which encourages enterprise – the mainspring of prosperity. Our aims must be:

- To achieve price stability.
- To keep firm control over public spending.
- To continue to reduce taxes as fast as we prudently can.
- To make sure that market mechanisms and incentives are allowed to do their job.

Price stability does not mean a frozen economy in which no price ever moves. But we must drive inflation down so low that it no longer affects the decisions made by ordinary people, businesses and government.

When inflation rises, so do bankruptcies. When inflation falls, industry can plan again for a profitable future. Inflation creates strife, as different groups in society struggle to restore their living standards. It destroys jobs. It erodes savings and social benefits and threatens our currency.

Inflation and Europe

Membership of the ERM is now central to our counter-inflation discipline. But the ERM is not a magic wand. It would not protect Labour; it would merely expose the folly of Labour policies. Some Labour politicians know that all too well – others simply don't. They – and some of the unions – would put irresistible spending pressure on a Labour government.

Some members of the European Community are anxious to hurry on from the ERM to Economic and Monetary Union. Others have doubts. Quite apart from the constitutional issues, they do not want to take risks with what is being achieved in the ERM.

The Treaty negotiated at Maastricht laid down the process under which the Community can, if its members meet certain economic conditions, create a monetary union with a single currency for some or all of them. Together with Germany we fought for tough criteria. We believe a monetary union would collapse, with damaging consequences, if it were imposed on economies that were too diverse.

A union will only come about by 1997 if a substantial majority of Community members agree it should. It would only include those members who were judged to have met specified conditions. And it would only come about if a majority of members were judged to have done so.

But the Treaty goes on to say that monetary union will come about automatically in 1999, for all who meet the conditions. We did not want to exclude ourselves from membership; but we could not accept such an automatic commitment. By the end of this decade the EC's membership will have changed; the economic performance of many of its members may have changed. We cannot tell who the members of such a union might be.

We therefore secured the freedom to make a proper judgement on events. We are as free to join if we wish as any other member. We would have to meet the same conditions – no more, no less. We will play our full part in the discussions of the monetary institutions Europe may create in the 1990s. But we are not obliged to join in a single currency if we do not want to.

- In due course, we will move to the narrow bands of the ERM.
- We will play our full part in the design and discussion of monetary institutions for Europe.
- When or if other members of the EC move to a monetary union with a single currency, we will take our own unfettered decision on whether to join. That decision will be taken by the United Kingdom Parliament.

The route to lower taxes

Economic growth is created by people's hard work, ingenuity, thrift and willingness to take risks. An enterprise economy rewards the industrious and thrifty. We believe that government should not gobble up all the proceeds of growth, and that those who create prosperity should enjoy it, through lower taxes and more opportunity to build up personal wealth.

Our policy is therefore to reduce the share of national income taken by the public sector. In the mid-1970s, public spending peaked at over 49 per cent of our gross national product. In the early 1980s, it peaked at over 47 per cent. In this recession, it is peaking at only 43 per cent. We aim to reduce this steadily as the recovery gets under way.

Keeping control of public spending will enable us to cut taxes while bringing the Government's Budget back towards balance in the years ahead. Excessive government borrowing can lead to inflation. Government should always be on guard against that danger. However, when demand in the economy is weak, public borrowing will tend to rise.

Because companies pay taxes according to how well they did the previous year, the deficit tends to be deepest just as we come out of recession. We must make sure that as the economy grows, borrowing slows.

By bringing tax and spending decisions together in a unified Budget from next year, we will make the choices clearer. But lower taxes and a prudent approach to borrowing do not mean public spending must fall; quite the reverse. A lightly-taxed economy generates more economic growth, and more revenue. High taxes kill the goose that lays the golden eggs. In the course of its last five years in office, Labour was forced to cut public spending, in real terms. By contrast, the Conservatives have been able to raise public spending by nearly a quarter in real terms.

Higher tax rates do not always bring in more money. In practice, they can bring in less. The Conservative Government has more than halved the top rate of tax. Yet top rate taxpayers today provide a bigger share of our tax revenues than they did before. Lower taxes have encouraged more people to work harder – not to spend their time working out how to avoid penal taxes.

During the past 13 years we have cut, simplified or abolished a whole range of direct taxes.

- We have cut the basic rate of Income Tax from 33p to 25p, and the top rate from 83p to 40p.
- We have now announced a new starting Income Tax rate of 20p.
- We have raised the basic single person's tax allowance by 27 per cent more than would be needed to keep pace with inflation.
- We have simplified and reduced the burden of taxation on capital.
- We have cut Corporation Tax from 52 per cent to 33 per cent (and from 42 per cent to 25 per cent for small companies).
- We have reduced the burden of National Insurance on low earners.
- We have introduced independent taxation of husbands and wives, giving married women full eligibility for tax allowances.
- We have introduced new tax incentives for savings.

- We have abolished several taxes completely including the surcharge on income from savings, the National Insurance Surcharge, Development Land Tax, and Capital Transfer Tax.

We are the only party that understands the need for low taxation. Labour and the Liberals openly advocate increased taxation. Yet lower taxes clearly create a more productive economy. They also achieve another prime objective of Conservative Governments, which is to transfer power from the state to the people.

Labour would:

- Reverse our cut in the starting rate of Income Tax to 20p.
- Raise the top rate.
- Abolish the National Insurance ceiling.
- Introduce a new savings surcharge.

We announced in the Budget an important first step towards a basic Income Tax rate of 20p. By applying a 20p rate to the first £2,000 of taxable income, we have cut taxes for all 25 million taxpayers, and taken the four million on lowest incomes out of 25p tax altogether. We will make further progress towards a basic Income Tax rate of 20p. We will reduce the share of national income taken by the public sector. We will see the budget return towards balance as the economy recovers.

The right to own

Since 1979, wealth has been spread more widely through the community. Home ownership, share ownership and the build-up of personal pensions have all contributed. Over two-thirds of people live in homes that they own, 10 million people own shares, 6 million of them in newly-privatised industries. About 2.5 million have benefited from tax incentives to encourage employee share schemes. And over 4½ million people are now building up their own personal pensions. But these freedoms are at risk.

Labour would:

- Halt the privatisation programme and threaten the value of shares in privatised industries with renationalisation and new Government controls.
- Bring back credit rationing, leading to mortgage queues.
- Turn the pensions market on its head, making pension provision costly and difficult.

These changes would drive savings overseas and make wealth again the prerogative of the few.

By contrast, we want to do more to encourage the wider distribution of wealth throughout society. Sustaining not just a home-owning but a capital owning democracy is crucial to our vision for the 1990s. We intend to spread the ownership of shares, homes, pensions and savings. We will do so through future privatisations, help for would-be home owners in council tenancies and further encouragement for the spread of personal pensions. We intend to lighten the burden of capital taxes and reform the taxation of savings.

We believe Inheritance Tax is particularly inequitable. It falls only on those who do not dispose of their assets seven years or more before their death. It is inevitably the case that these tend to be people who are not rich enough to engage in high-powered tax planning, or who, for lack of knowledge or advice, fail to take the necessary precautionary action. In the Budget, we announced that we would take most family businesses out of Inheritance Tax altogether. During the new Parliament, we will aim to lessen the burden on families to whom home ownership has brought the threat of this erratic tax.

- As detailed later in this Manifesto, we will aim to bring home ownership, share ownership and personal pensions within the reach of more families.
- We will continue to reform the taxation of savings, building on the success of PEPs and TESSAs.
- We will raise the tax threshold for Inheritance Tax so that the homes and savings of an increasing number of our citizens can pass unencumbered from one generation to another.
- Whenever possible, we will ensure that future privatisations offer opportunities to employees to secure a stake in the ownership of their business.
- We will encourage companies to make dealing in their own shares easier, especially for small shareholders, and encourage wider share ownership, through, for example, the establishment of 'Share Shops'.
- We will abolish Stamp Duty on share transactions.

Setting the economy free

Starting with the abolition of exchange controls in 1979, the Government has created new incentives for every part of our economy.

Manufacturing industry suffered particularly badly from the harm inflicted on the British economy by Labour Governments in the 1960s and 1970s. To a far greater extent than service industries, it was the victim of militant trades unionism, restrictive practices, nationalisation, state intervention, tax distortion, planning controls and over-regulation.

We believe strongly that a vigorous manufacturing sector is essential to a healthy British economy Over the past 13 years, we have steadily dismantled barriers to its growth.

The competitiveness and performance of British manufacturing have been transformed. Its impressive recovery was recognised by the Confederation of British Industry, in its report aptly titled *Competing with the World's Best*. Manufacturing productivity has risen by more than half since 1979 – faster than in any other major industrial country. Over the past 10 years, British manufactured exports have grown faster than those of France, Germany, the United States or even Japan.

The British motor industry has achieved an astonishing revival. By 1996, Britain should again be exporting more cars than we import – for the first time since 1974. We have given the industry yet more encouragement in the Budget, by halving the special tax paid on new cars.

The British Standard for Quality management has effectively become the international standard. But that is only the beginning. We have set up a team of senior business people to pursue the idea of a new British Quality Award.

The City is Europe's greatest financial centre. It contributes £11,000 million net to our balance of payments. Financial services employ 12 per cent of our workforce. London's capital markets and financial services have grown vigorously because they are innovative and highly competitive. We will continue our efforts to break down the barriers that prevent them from competing freely throughout Europe and in the wider world.

The European Bank for Reconstruction and Development is now based in London. It puts us in the forefront of encouraging investment in the developing markets of Central and Eastern Europe.

Service industries make a vital contribution to our economy and to our balance of payments. Tourism, for example, today employs 1.5 million people, 20% more than in 1980. It is an industry which boasts many famous companies – but it is also driven by the dynamism of many small firms. We will continue to help them by simplifying rules and regulations on business and through the DTI Enterprise Initiative and a range of other schemes.

- We will continue to reduce tax burdens on business, as we have done this year for the motor industry, whenever it is possible to do so.
- We will abolish unnecessary licences and reduce the need for specific approvals for product design.
- We will back British companies encountering any discrimination, trade barriers or state subsidies that should no longer exist within the Single Market.
- We will back the regulators of the financial services industry in their efforts to achieve high standards while keeping the rule books down to manageable size.

Privatisation

Competition and private ownership are the most powerful engines of economic efficiency, innovation and choice. They lead to the creation of world-class companies.

We have returned to private enterprise two-thirds of the companies once owned by the state: 46 businesses employing about 900,000 people. This programme has been the model for governments across the whole world.

The work of liberalising markets which were once monopolised goes on. In 1984 we privatised British Telecom but only Mercury was given a licence to carry services over fixed links. In 1991 we decided to end this duopoly. The UK now has one of the most open and dynamic telecommunications markets in the world.

But much greater economic efficiency is not the only gain. Employees have been able to take a direct stake in the newly privatised companies. Millions of people have been given the same chance to own a real share in the nation's assets. Companies which looked inwards to Whitehall are now listening to their customers and shareholders.

Some activities of government must always be provided in the public sector. But in central government, Next Steps Agencies and local government, management is increasingly buying-in services from the private sector. Our proposals for developing this policy have been set out in the White Papers on 'Competing for Quality' in central and local government.

- We will continue our privatisation programme. British Coal will be returned to the private sector. So will local authority bus companies. We will encourage local authorities to sell their airports. We will end British Rail's monopoly. We will sell certain rail services and franchise others. These proposals are set out later in this Manifesto.
- The Ports Act 1991 has paved the way for the privatisation of the Trust Ports by competitive tender. Tees and Hartlepool, Tilbury, Medway, Forth and Clyde have already been privatised.
- We are privatising Northern Ireland Electricity and will privatise the Northern Ireland water and sewage services. We will look for ways of bringing private sector skills into the management of Northern Ireland Railways.
- We will bring private sector enterprise into the public services by encouraging contracting out and competitive tendering throughout government.
- We will require all government departments to report annually on their plans for market-testing, and progress in achieving it, in their own services and in those of their associated agencies.
- We will maintain our programme of compulsory competitive tendering of local authority services. We will ensure that unfair terms are excluded and will discourage investment to protect in-house services when better, more cost effective services are available through the private sector.
- We will ensure that competitive tendering is extended to white collar local authority services, such as those offered by lawyers, accountants, architects and surveyors.
- We will tackle all anti-competitive and restrictive practices with vigour. We will introduce new legislation giving stronger powers to deal with cartels.

Deregulation

We are concerned that at every level of government – in Europe, in Whitehall and in local authorities – some regulations may have been adopted in answer to legitimate concerns, but without proper regard to their overall impact on businesses and individuals. A proper balance needs to be struck between essential protection for the public, and over-zealous and intrusive controls aimed at the elimination of all conceivable risk. It is wrong that new regulations, designed to deal with isolated problems, should interfere with the private arrangements of citizens or with reasonable commercial practices that have earned broad public acceptance.

- The compliance costs of new UK and EC regulations must be assessed properly. Existing regulations which are outmoded and burdensome must be simplified or removed. We will give priority to the work of the DTI Deregulation Unit in these areas.
- We will examine ways in which the uniform scope of regulation could be eased to safeguard traditional local products or practices.
- We will examine whether certain regulations affecting individual citizens within their own homes could be made advisory, rather than mandatory.

Energy

Our energy policies have brought the consumer both lower prices and better service. We have privatised British Gas and the electricity industry in a way that has opened these markets to competition. These policies are now being seized upon in Europe as essential extensions of the Single Market.

Domestic customers are now protected by a price formula, and high standards of service are enforced by the independent regulators. For instance, electricity disconnections for debt have fallen by 43 per cent since the launch of privatisation.

We have ensured that the safety of employees comes first, and have given thousands the opportunity of acquiring a stake in their industry.

The future of the coal industry depends crucially on the competitiveness of coal as a fuel for electricity generation. British Coal has made enormous progress in increasing productivity since the end of the 1985 strike – but there is still further to go. We will support the efforts of British Coal and its workforce to improve the industry's performance. The long-term future of the industry lies in the private sector.

We have invested in clean coal technology to safeguard the environment. Renewable energy projects have received unprecedented support. North Sea oil and gas are enjoying a record expansion thanks to our policies of deregulation and low taxation.

- Safety will remain our highest priority throughout the energy sector.
- We will continue to encourage competition in energy markets. We will progressively reduce British Gas' monopoly of the retail gas market, to give small users the same rights as big firms.
- We will privatise British Coal in a way that enables employees to enjoy a stake in the industry.
- We will increase our support for British Coal Enterprise which promotes economic regeneration in areas affected by the closure of mines, and has successfully assisted 76,000 people in finding new jobs.
- We will review the future of the nuclear industry in 1994. We are committed to safe and economical nuclear power. The existing strict arrangements for nuclear waste will be maintained.
- We will maintain a guaranteed market for renewable energy projects and fluid research in this area.
- We will consult on new building regulations to improve energy use. Together with British Gas and some of the Regional Electricity Companies, we will establish an independent Energy Savings Trust to promote energy efficiency. Our grants scheme for low income households will receive record funding next year.

Science and innovation

British science has an unrivalled reputation for ground-breaking research. We believe in investing in scientific research because it enriches the quality of our lives and provides the feedstock of industrial innovation. The science budget has grown by 24 per cent in real terms since 1978–9. Increasingly funding will reflect the quality of the research output so that the best centres can truly be world leaders.

The Government spends nearly £3,000 million a year on civil research and development – at least as high a proportion of national income as the Japanese or Americans. And since 1978, British industry's spending on R&D has increased by 37 per cent in real terms.

- We will continue to support our science base to maintain the excellence of our science and to ensure that we produce the skilled technical people we need.
- We will encourage the transfer of people and technology from universities to businesses and upgrade the LINK scheme, which funds joint research.
- We will encourage the establishment of centres of technological excellence linking industrial research organisations with universities and polytechnics.
- We will continue to develop new innovation schemes for small and medium-sized businesses, including the highly-regarded SPUR programme to provide help with the development of new products and processes.

Regional policies

In recent years, the United Kingdom has attracted five times as much Japanese investment as Germany or France, which powerfully demonstrates that we have created the most attractive environment in Europe for investors. Our positive policy towards inward investment will be maintained, in contrast to that of the TUC and the Labour Party.

The Government will continue to invest in a strong infrastructure, and boost technology expertise in the regions.

- We will ensure that regional policy is well targeted.
- We will continue to support all parts of the United Kingdom in their campaigns to attract inward investment.
- We will give additional emphasis to upgrading skills and technology when allocating funds.

Small businesses

Small businesses are the seedcorn of the economy Their numbers have grown by more than a third since 1979, while the number of self-employed people has grown to over 12 per cent of the workforce. We will continue to recognise the special needs of small and medium-sized companies, and to ensure that Government delivers useful services to them.

Our tax regime for small businesses is one of the most favourable in Europe. We have raised the VAT threshold every year since 1979 and reduced the small companies rate of Corporation Tax from 42 per cent to 25 per cent.

Training and Enterprise Councils (and Local Enterprise Companies in Scotland) have developed a wide range of services for business and enterprise which assist over 150,000 small companies each year. We have developed the popular Enterprise Initiative, under which 40,000 companies have been helped to buy in outside expertise offering key management skills. We now propose to develop this initiative further.

We also propose to help businesses by easing the transfer of commercial tenancies.

- We announced in the Budget new measures to help small businesses, including full relief against Inheritance Tax on most business assets, reductions in business rates and proposals to speed up the payment of outstanding bills.
- During the new Parliament, we will develop a new Enterprise Service to give small and medium-sized companies help in diagnosing their most important strategic needs. A new Consultancy Brokerage Service will supply information to small companies. We will also develop a Technology Audit which will provide small firms with a plan for change. And we will continue to support Total Quality Management consultancies.
- TECs and LECs will be closely involved in developing and implementing this new initiative.

The independent Law Commission has recommended that a commercial tenant should in general be freed from any future liability under a lease when he assigns away his interest under it. We will consider how this principle could be put into effect for new commercial leases.

Consumer affairs

Consumers want choice, quality and value for money Competition only works effectively if consumers have the information they need to make sensible decisions.

Our food safety policy promotes consumer choice and consumer safety. We introduced the 1990 Food Safety Act to ensure the highest standards of food hygiene.

- We will introduce legislation designed to give consumers confidence that what they purchase is properly described – and that adequate compensation is offered where these requirements are not met.
- We will enable the courts to override unfair terms in contracts and improve our powers to deal with rogue traders.
- We will ensure that guarantees mean what they say, and that manufacturers or importers share responsibility with the people who sell their goods.
- We will tighten up the rules on holiday brochures and contracts, and introduce a 'cooling-off' period into timeshare contracts.
- We will introduce legislation to simplify trade mark registration and extend the rights they confer.
- We will enforce science-based controls on the use of chemicals in food production, and will maintain our policy of open access to information on pesticide safety.
- We will improve standards of food labelling in close consultation with consumer representatives.

Choice and the Charter

The Citizen's Charter is the most far-reaching programme ever devised to improve quality in public services. It addresses the needs of those who use public services, extends people's rights, requires services to set clear standards – and to tell the public how far those standards are met.

The Citizen's Charter:

- widens popular choice;
- helps people to exercise that choice in a properly informed way;
- expects all public services to put the customer first;
- promotes the challenge of competition within the public sector;
- requires clear performance standards to be set and for services to be measured against them;
- insists on a proper response to complaints and on action to set right the problems behind them.

The Charter will be at the centre of government's decision-making throughout the 1990s. No one doubts the professionalism of the vast majority of public servants. But too often the system's outdated working methods and attitudes prevent them from giving their best. The Charter's commitment to modern, open services will help them to win the respect that good service deserves.

In less than a year since the White Paper, 18 detailed Charters have been published. Each sets out tough new standards and gives new information and rights to the public. Each will be revised regularly to check on progress, and raise standards higher. But, already results are clear.

- In hospitals, from April, every out-patient will have a fixed appointment time and our guarantee of maximum waiting times for operations will be steadily improved.
- On council estates every tenant will have the right to call in a private contractor if the council fails to do a minor repair.
- In schools, all parents will have the right to a report on their child's performance and details on that of the school.

Rights such as these should not have been denied to the public. The Citizen's Charter, steadily but surely, is changing all that.

Knowledge, standards, choice

The next Conservative Government will carry the Charter still further. There will be more information about standards and performance; clear standards set within public services which are still shrouded in mystery; more choice built into public services and proper complaints procedures introduced. Many of these are outlined later in the Manifesto under Education, Health, Local Government and Transport. Here are a few examples from the programme for the next two years:

- The Audit Commission will be able to publish league tables of performance including each local council and health authority so that people can compare the quality of service.
- We will ensure that inspection reports are published and widely available. All councils will have to respond in public to criticism from auditors.
- We will introduce a new 'Charterline' that people with questions or problems with a public service will be able to ring.
- We will require British Rail to tighten its targets for reliability and punctuality

on all lines, and report monthly to passengers on how it is doing. London Underground will publish its own Charter.

- We will expect Post Offices and Job Centres to set out standards of service and levels of achievement.
- A new Charter Mark award will give recognition to those parts of the public service that best meet Charter standards.
- British Rail and London Underground are introducing compensation systems for travellers.
- We will review the powers of the Local Government Ombudsman to ensure that findings of maladministration are properly dealt with by all local authorities. We will consult on a new Lay Adjudicators scheme to help the public resolve difficulties and disputes.

We will extend competition and accountability in public services. Those who provide public services will have to prove they can give the right quality at the right cost.

- We will extend compulsory competitive tendering to local authority housing management, and examine how to apply it to white-collar services. We will act to ensure that private firms bidding to improve local authority public services are not obstructed by unscrupulous practices in councils or by unfair contracts. We will pursue more competitive tendering for central government services.
- We will encourage the wider use of performance pay inside the Civil Service and in other parts of the public service. A link between a person's effort and his or her pay is a powerful means of improving performance.
- Civil servants dealing with the public will normally identify themselves by name.
- We will toughen inspection of key public services where choice and competition must inevitably be limited. We will introduce, for the first time, regular independent inspection of all schools.
- We will act to ensure that the inspectorates of police, fire, probation, and social services, together with any new inspectorates that are established, will be truly independent of the service which they inspect.
- We will ensure that the reports from these systematic regular inspections are published. More lay inspectors, drawn from other professions and from the general public, will bring fresh insights into service improvement.
- We will publish later this year new proposals for the inspection of social work in England, setting up arrangements for systematic independent inspection of all care services and every local authority social services department.
- Inspections of local authority homes will be carried out by teams that contain lay inspectors and are independent of the influence of the management of the homes.

All of the privatised utilities have a specialist regulator who is responsible for promoting competition, reviewing prices and protecting the public interest. We have introduced legislation to increase the powers of these regulators to the level of the strongest.

- We are ensuring that the regulators have the powers they need to promote competition and safeguard the interests of the customer by controlling price increases. We will increase competition in the gas and water markets.

- We are giving the regulators powers to set standards of service, covering such matters as fixed appointment times for service calls.

The Post Office

The Post Office is among the best in Europe for speed and reliability of its letter services. Traffic has grown by 50 per cent in a decade in which it has operated without a subsidy. Last year the first-class letter service achieved record improvements in reliability. The local post office is a vital and valued feature of the rural community.

In 1981 we introduced private competition for deliveries costing over £1. This led to the rapid growth of the private courier industry with substantial benefits to business users. We believe that further benefits to consumers would flow from additional competition.

- We are committed to maintaining a nation-wide letter service with delivery to every address in the United Kingdom, within a uniform structure of prices, and with a nation-wide network of post offices.
- We will legislate to set up a new independent regulator to advise on issues affecting Post Office customers, and on the progressive introduction of competition.
- We will set performance targets for the Post Office and ensure they are published in all offices, together with results achieved.
- We will ensure there is effective redress for customers where services fail.
- We will lower the limit on the Post Office monopoly much closer to the level of the first class stamp.
- We will provide improved scope for contractors to carry mail to final delivery offices.
- We will consider requests to license limited specialist services to compete within the Post Office monopoly.

Whitehall and Westminster

Whitehall must move with the times. It is over a decade since the last major restructuring of the departments of government. Since then:

- Two-thirds of the state industrial sector has been privatised, transferring about 900,000 jobs to the private sector.
- Government has reduced the burden of regulation and the need for central bureaucracy.
- Civil Service manpower has been reduced by almost a quarter.
- Many of the functions of government have been devolved from Whitehall.
- The Citizen's Charter programme is bringing new quality to public services.

We will continue to reorganise central government in tune with its modern role, while devolving and contracting out executive functions. We want to ensure that the drive to save money to reduce bureaucracy and raise quality is powerfully led from the centre of government.

- We will give a Cabinet Minister responsibility for the Citizen's Charter programme and reforming the Civil Service, taking charge of the Citizen's Charter Unit, Efficiency Unit, the programme for creating Agencies and the Public Competition and Purchasing Unit. This will make it easier to raise quality and efficiency in government and see that contracting-out and market-testing are energetically pursued.

- We intend to create a new department, under a Cabinet Minister, with responsibility for broadcasting, arts, sport, tourism, the national heritage and the film industry. This department will aim to encourage private sector enterprise in all these fields. The National Lottery and the Millennium Fund (detailed later in this Manifesto) will also bring new responsibilities to government in these areas.
- We will transfer the core responsibilities of the Department of Energy to the Department of Trade and Industry and responsibilities for energy efficiency to the Department of the Environment, ending the need for a separate department
- Small businesses are the seedcorn of our future prosperity We believe the Department of Trade and Industry should take over responsibility for them. We also want to strengthen the links between the DTI and the highly successful Training and Enterprise Councils.
- Responsibility for overseeing all financial services will be brought together in the Treasury, in line with the practice adopted in most other advanced countries.
- New programmes for regenerating our inner cities are outlined in this Manifesto. Responsibilities will be brought together in the Department of the Environment.
- We are determined to ensure that women in the work-force realise their full potential. We will transfer from the Home Office to the Department of Employment the lead responsibility for co-ordinating government policy on issues of particular concern to women.

Open government

Government has traditionally been far too reluctant to provide information. This secrecy extends from the processes of Cabinet Government to schools which refuse to release exam results. Under the Citizen's Charter, a great deal more information is now being made available on the services provided by government.

We have also:

- replaced the catch-all provisions of the 1911 Official Secrets Act with narrower offences depending on specific tests of the harm likely to be caused by disclosure, while giving special protection to vital information relating to our national security;
- introduced rights to check certain personal records held on computer, and supported new rights of access to a range of government records;
- committed ourselves to a public right of access to information about the environment, including water supply, air quality, dumping at sea and radioactive substances;
- made available more reports on matters of public concern such as food safety and industrial risks.

We intend to carry forward this move towards greater openness.

- We will review the 80 or so statutory restrictions which exist on the disclosure of information – retaining only those needed to protect privacy and essential confidentiality.
- We will seek to provide greater access to personal records held by government.
- We will be less secretive about the workings of government. For example, when the Committees of the Cabinet are reconstituted after the election we will, for the first time, set out their names and membership. We will update and – for the first time – publish the guidance for Ministers on procedure.

The workings of Parliament

It is not just Whitehall that must change. Parliament, too, has to keep its working methods under review to make sure it attracts the best people to the service of their country and uses their talents to best effect.

- We will propose appropriate Parliamentary reforms to ensure that the House of Commons conducts its business more efficiently and effectively, taking into account the benefits of modern technology, the increasing constituency demands upon Members of Parliament and the need to attract more women to stand for election.

Opportunity for all

Conservatives believe that high standards in education and training are the key to personal opportunity and national success. We believe in partnership with parents, choice in schools and a good grounding in the basic skills all children need to make a success of their lives. We are committed to widening opportunities without compromising academic standards. We will continue to expand higher education and training. We will reinforce the rights of the individual in the world of work, and break down artificial barriers to advancement. By extending opportunity and arming people with the power to choose, we will give valuable freedoms and a powerful spur to achievement.

Schools, pupils and parents

We are now seeing real improvements in our education system. One in four young people goes on to higher education; at the beginning of the 1980s, it was only one in eight. Sixty per cent of 16 year-olds stay on in full-time education, up from only 40 per cent in 1979. And we have embarked on the most important and wide-ranging reforms since the 1940s.

For the first time in our history, we will soon have a National Curriculum which will require all the main school subjects to be covered thoroughly. The testing of 7 year-olds is well under way and tests for older children are now being developed. Starting this September, GCSE courses will be steadily integrated with the National Curriculum.

Under the Parent's Charter, all schools will have to provide at least one written report on the progress of each child each year. Information on the performance of all local schools will be given to parents, enabling them to exercise choice more effectively

We believe all parents have the right to choice in education – not only those who can afford school fees. Young people differ in their interests and aptitudes, and we need a range of schools to offer them the best opportunities. We have always fought to maintain diversity in education, protecting the right of local people to preserve their grammar schools, and defending independent schools against mindless Labour attacks. And we have always valued the important contribution made by the churches to our children's education.

We have further increased diversity by:

- Giving schools control over their own budgets and encouraging new types of school.
- Allowing schools to become independent of local councils, by applying for Grant-Maintained status if the parents involved so wish. By mid-1992, over 200 GM schools will be up and running.
- Creating a number of highly popular City Technology Colleges.
- Launching the highly successful initiative under which schools are able to bid directly for the resources to become Technology Schools.

We intend to take all these initiatives further and offer parents more choice in the new Parliament. Popular schools will be allowed to expand, and more schools will be able to apply for technology funding. We will make it easier for small schools to enjoy the benefits of GM status by grouping together.

- We will complete the introduction of the National Curriculum offering 10 subjects at a nationally-defined standard – English, Mathematics, Science, History, Geography, Technology, Art, Music, PE and, in secondary schools, a foreign language.
- Regular and straightforward tests will be in place for all 7, 11 and 14 year-olds by 1994.
- GCSE at age 16 will be integrated into the National Curriculum, with a new A+ grade to test the most able. The majority of marks will come from a written exam.
- We will continue to encourage the creation of nursery places. For the first time, over 50 per cent of three and four year-olds have places either in nursery or primary schools.
- Full information will be published annually about the performance of all local schools in each area.
- Independent inspection of schools will provide parents with straightforward reports on their child's school, together with an action plan from governors to remedy any weaknesses.
- Popular schools which are over-subscribed will be given the resources to expand.
- GM schools will be able to change their character if that is what parents clearly want and the change fits in with the wider needs of the local area.
- The Technology Schools Initiative will be expanded across the country.
- Existing schools which opt for GM status will be able to emulate City Technology Colleges and attract private technology sponsorship.
- We will maintain the Assisted Places scheme, which gives access to independent education to many families who could not otherwise afford it.
- We will ensure that the partnership between the state and the churches in education is maintained and strengthened.

- We will enable small schools to apply for GM status in groups.
- We will pay particular attention to raising educational standards in areas of deprivation in our cities.

Teaching

We are determined to reinforce the professionalism of teachers and the esteem in which they are held. We have created an independent Teachers' Pay Review Body. We accepted in full its first recommendations; nearly half of all teachers are now earning over £20,000 a year. We will press ahead with regular appraisal of teachers to encourage high standards and develop professional skills.

As a first step in the reform of teacher training, postgraduate students will spend much more time in school classrooms, learning their skills under the practised eye of senior teachers.

It is vital that the education system should attract back women who have taken a career break to raise a family Through grants to local authorities, we are financing schemes to introduce more flexible working practices – such as job-sharing.

- We will undertake reform of the teacher training system to make it more effective in developing classroom skills.
- We will develop measures to encourage women with family responsibilities to enter or return to teaching.

After 16

We believe that young people should be free to choose between college, work-based training and sixth form studies. We are giving further education colleges and sixth form colleges in England and Wales autonomy, free from council control. We also value our school sixth forms, and will ensure they retain their place in the new system. And we will allow them to attract older students as well. FE colleges will continue to receive support for adult education, while local authorities will retain the resources to respond to local demand for leisure courses.

We will defend the well-respected A-level examinations, which Labour would destroy. We will continue to encourage participation in AS examinations. We will also continue to develop new high-quality National Vocational Qualifications, and introduce a new post-16 diploma which recognises achievement in both vocational and academic courses.

- We will develop an Advanced Diploma which can be earned by students pursuing either academic or vocational courses, and a new General National Vocational Qualification.
- We intend to allow school sixth forms to open their doors if they wish to older students, and to accept training credits or fees from them.
- From April next year, further education and sixth form colleges will be independent of local government control.
- Mature students will enjoy a wider choice of courses.

Higher education

Britain maintains the best university system in Europe. We have also developed a thriving network of polytechnics, whose student numbers have increased nearly sixfold since the end of the 1960s.

By the year 2000, one in three young people will follow full-time higher education courses. Meanwhile, the number of mature entrants to higher education has risen by 65 per cent since 1979. And our universities are attracting increasing numbers of foreign students.

Despite this huge expansion, our students enjoy one of the most generous support systems in the world. The introduction of student loans has given students 30 per cent more money for their living costs than the former system of grants alone. The new system will steadily reduce the proportion of students' living costs that their parents are expected to meet.

- We will continue to expand the number of students in higher education. We are abolishing the artificial 'binary line' between universities and polytechnics.
- We are putting in place new mechanisms to ensure that academic standards are maintained in higher education.
- We will continue to provide generous support for students and to expand our student loans commitment.

The training revolution

A training revolution is under way in Britain. The Government's job is to create a framework within which men and women of all ages can develop skills, gain qualifications and shape their own futures.

We have already brought the world of work and the world of school into closer harmony. Government and industry are working together. Employers already spend over £20,000 million a year on training. Government spending on training has increased 2½ times in real terms since 1979, to £2,800 million. The Government's effort is being channelled through the 82 new Training and Enterprise Councils (and the Local Enterprise Companies in Scotland) – the most significant peacetime partnership between government and industry this century.

- 'Compacts' have resulted in many young people working to goals for attainment and attendance in school. In return, they are guaranteed a job with training – or training leading to a job.
- This year, two million students will participate in the Technical and Vocational Education Initiative.
- Investors in People is the new national standard for companies making a commitment to training. TECs play an important role in helping companies attain it.
- Employer-led TECs and LECs are delivering Government-funded training programmes which reflect industry's understanding of local needs.
- Industry is working closely with the National Council for Vocational Qualifications.

- The CBI's training targets for Britain's workforce demonstrate a new partnership between business and education.

75 per cent of 16 year-olds stay on in full-time education or Youth Training schemes, up from 46 per cent in 1979. Since 1983, over 3 million young people have taken up Youth Training places. And 82 per cent go into jobs or further education when they complete YT. Now we are offering young people aged 16 and 17 vouchers they can use to buy approved courses of education or training, and which will put the power of choice in their hands.

In 1988, we launched Employment Training, the largest programme of its kind in Europe, which has since helped 1.2 million people. While local programmes are the responsibility of the TECs, the Government guarantees the offer of help to particular groups of unemployed.

Last year, we launched the new Employment Action programme, which will help more than 61,000 people in a full year. This is a new addition to a range of measures which include Jobclubs, the Job Interview Guarantee Scheme and other tested methods of helping unemployed people back to work.

We are also supporting individual training effort. Since 1988, when we launched Career Development Loans (interest-free for up to 15 months), over 25,000 people have benefited. Last year's Budget gave tax relief on training fees – a boost to the 250,000 people a year who finance their own training. Now, with the TECs, we intend to introduce new financial help for career and training guidance.

- By the end of the new Parliament, the new system of National Vocational Qualifications should cover virtually every occupation in the economy. The CBI's training targets envisage 80 per cent of young people reaching NVQ level 2 by the end of the Parliament.
- We intend to make training credits available to all 16 year-olds and 17 year-olds within the lifetime of the new Parliament. The TECs will continue to be responsible for the YT programme for this age group.
- We will continue to finance training programmes for the long-term unemployed and those who face particular difficulties. We will launch with the TECs a new initiative, giving people a voucher with which they can buy a 'skill check', providing assessment and guidance on how to make the most of their working lives.

Workers and unions

Over the past 13 years, we have legislated to lift regulatory burdens from the shoulders of those who create jobs in Britain. To industry's relief, we shunned the job-destroying European Social Charter. And we reject Labour's job-destroying notion of a national minimum wage.

We have also legislated five times to transform industrial relations, returning power from militants to ordinary union members. As a result, the number of days lost each year through strikes has fallen from an average 12.9 million in the 1970s to less than a million last year – the lowest figure since records began a century ago.

Labour would disrupt industrial peace by weakening the power of management and the courts. They propose to take away the courts' most important sanction – the power to take over a union's assets. Sympathy strikes would be legalised by Labour, and employers would be prevented from dismissing strikers who broke their contracts. The workers' rights we believe in are those which enhance individuals' status and opportunities. We believe people should be informed and consulted by employers about issues which affect their work. No one should be allowed to deduct trade union fees automatically from an employee's pay without written authorisation. Individuals must be given greater rights to belong to the union of their choice. We also believe strongly that employers, employees and customers should not have their lives and businesses disrupted by wildcat strikes. In the new Parliament, we will legislate to enforce and enhance these rights.

- We will require employers to give everyone who works for them for more than eight hours a week a clear written statement of their terms and conditions of employment.
- We will make automatic deduction of union membership dues without written authorisation unlawful.
- We will take measures to give individuals greater freedom in choosing a union.
- We will legislate to require that all pre-strike ballots are postal and subject to independent scrutiny, and that at least seven days' notice of a strike is given after a ballot.
- People who use public services will have the right to restrain the disruption of those services by unlawful industrial action.

A share in the future

We also believe that people at work should be helped to build security for themselves and their families. Employees should be given every opportunity to acquire a stake in the business for which they work. We have ruled that executive share option schemes may grant options at a discount only if the employer also runs an all-employee scheme.

Saving for a pension reduces reliance on the state. We welcome the provision of occupational schemes covering over 11 million workers. There are already important safeguards, which we have improved, for the rights of members in such schemes. But we believe that a full review of the arrangements is now needed. We also believe that new freedoms for scheme members will strengthen accountability and benefit investors.

- We will establish a review of the framework of law and regulation within which occupational schemes operate.
- We will give every member of an occupational scheme the right to an annual statement of the value of their savings.
- In addition we will examine ways of giving those who retire with lump sum payments more choice as to how their savings are invested.

Women and opportunity

A higher proportion of women go out to work in Britain than in any other EC country except Denmark. Many women choose to work part-time, and our policies have encouraged the development of part-time work within a framework which safeguards employees from exploitation.

Throughout Europe, the UK is recognised to have the most comprehensive legislation to combat sex discrimination. We are also committed to breaking down artificial barriers to women's advancement based on prejudice or lack of imagination. As an employer, government must continue to set an example.

The tax relief we have introduced on training fees is constructed to ensure that non-tax payers – who include many married women – will be able to benefit, too. Many Training and Enterprise Councils already have specific plans to help women trainees. We will involve them further in helping employers to help with childcare.

We believe mothers should be treated equally by government, whether they work outside the home or not. We are fully committed to maintaining the real value of child benefit. And we will act where a push by government is needed to stimulate the provision of childcare.

All employers who meet childcare costs can set these off against their liability for corporation tax. In addition, we have relieved employees from paying income tax on the benefit of workplace nurseries.

After-school childcare is an area of particular importance to many working mothers. We will introduce a new initiative to encourage the provision of after-school facilities by schools, employers and voluntary groups across the country.

- The Government will amend the law relating to the employment rights of pregnant women to give effect to the EC Directive on Pregnant Workers. This addition to our already extensive legal provision will give a right to at least 14 weeks' maternity leave and protection against dismissal on grounds of pregnancy.
- We will take forward our public appointments initiative. Departments will publish plans for between a quarter and a half of public appointments to be held by women by 1996.
- We will ensure that all parts of government adopt a strategic approach to the employment and development of women staff. We will encourage them to participate in the Opportunity 2000 initiative.
- We will continue to oppose EC measures which would discourage part-time employment, valued by so many women.
- We will encourage all TECs to adopt plans to help women trainees have equal access to training opportunities.
- We will introduce a new grant, paid through TECs, to help employers, voluntary groups or schools to set up after-school care and holiday arrangements. We will ensure that schools are free to participate.

Freedom under the law

The Conservative Party has always stood for the protection of the citizen and the defence of the rule of law. Society is entitled to a sense of security; individuals to peace of mind; the guardians of that peace to our whole-hearted support. Our policies on law and order, and the rights of individuals, are designed to protect the people of this country and their way of life.

Britain experiences less violent crime than many comparable countries. But crime has continued to rise in Britain. And the challenge for the 1990s is to step up the fight against lawlessness and violence, so that our citizens can live free from fear.

We must continue to ensure that the sentence fits the crime – with long sentences for dangerous criminals, and fines and a tougher regime for punishment outside prison available as an alternative for less serious crime. And we must maintain confidence in our legal system.

We must tackle crime at its roots. Two-thirds of the offences dealt with by our courts are committed by only seven per cent of those convicted. Most of these constant offenders started down the path of crime while still of school age.

We have launched a reform of our prisons, improving the prospect that those who serve custodial sentences will not return to crime.

But above all we must remember that it is our policemen and women who are in the front line of the battle. To combat crime effectively the police need the full support of the Government and the public.

Police and the community

We Conservatives can be proud of our record in supporting the police. Since 1979 we have increased spending on the police by 74 per cent in real terms. Uniformed manpower has increased by 16,000 and civilian manpower by 12,000. We have launched a campaign to recruit 10,000 Special Constables. Over the next few years we want to see a major reform which will help provide what the public wants and needs: a visible, local police presence.

We will be encouraging police forces to develop local Community Policing, to link the police more closely with the communities they protect. The Metropolitan Police will be reorganised on this basis by the spring of 1993. Two-thirds of English and Welsh forces are already preparing similar plans. Pilot schemes suggest they can add greatly to the citizen's sense of security and build support for the police.

Community Policing will involve local residents, listen to their views and engage their help in the fight against crime. It will mean:

- smaller police units with officers serving the same area for longer. That way, people can really get to know their local police officers;
- each police force devolving its management and operational control to local units, and streamlining its chain of command;
- getting police back on the beat, and in close contact with the neighbourhoods under their care.

It will be supported by an extension of Neighbourhood Watch schemes, which are vital in deterring theft and burglaries.

Public confidence in the police is enhanced when people know what they can expect from their local police force, and when outsiders are let into the process of inspecting how they work. At least five police forces are already leading the way with charters setting out their targets.

- We are continuing to increase police numbers. There will be 1,000 extra police officers this year.
- We will continue to give the police the support and resources they need to carry out their duties effectively and efficiently.

- We will be seeking the nation-wide introduction of Community Policing.
- We will encourage civilianisation as a means of freeing police officers for operational duties.
- We will encourage the extension of Neighbourhood Watch to more residential areas.
- We will continue to increase the Special Constabulary, which has seen a rise in recruitment this year of 10 per cent.
- We want each police force to produce a charter telling local people, for example, how quickly the police will aim to respond to emergency calls.
- We will introduce lay inspectors with management experience into the police inspectorate.

Protectors and victims

We look to the police to protect us. They risk their lives to do so. Police officers are entitled to the protection of the community they serve. Those who indulge in the shameful practice of 'ambushing', or seeking to frustrate the work of the emergency services, deserve to face severe penalties. We welcome the findings of a study by the Home Office and Crown Prosecution Service which shows that assaults on policemen attract consistently heavier penalties. But we will examine ways of introducing further protection for the police.

We must also pay special attention to the needs of the victims of crime, in the courts and in rebuilding their lives. We have increased funding for Victim Support.

The number of people directly affected by violent and sexual crime remains relatively small. But fear of crime can have a devastating effect on people's lives, and particularly on women's lives. We are determined to reduce this fear.

- We will set up a working party to examine what more can be done to protect the police and members of other emergency services from assault.
- We will encourage victims to report sexual offences by giving them statutory anonymity.
- Under our Safer Cities programme, there are 124 schemes to improve street lighting, which has been shown to reduce the fear of crime significantly.
- Women-only taxi services are being encouraged under the same Safer Cities programme.

Penalties and prevention

Our armoury of criminal law and penalties requires constant review. We have just introduced a new law specifically aimed at the so-called 'joy-rider'. This places the responsibility for dangerous driving, damage, injury or death following from the taking of a vehicle squarely on the shoulders of those in it. Even where 'joy-riding' is not involved, causing death through dangerous or drink driving is a very serious offence. We believe that the maximum sentence for such a crime should reflect its gravity.

Squatting is nothing less than the seizure of another's property without consent. Having consulted widely on the subject, we have decided to extend the criminal law dealing with squatting. Illegal camping by gypsies or other travellers can affect the lives of whole communities. We believe that this problem must be tackled.

We are concerned about the small but persistent minority, particularly of young people, who re-offend while already on bail. We have announced new measures to deter them from repeated crime. Young people who find themselves on probation for shoplifting, vandalism or petty thuggery should be shown where the path of crime may lead. They should be given a brief personal experience of the nature of prison life.

- 'Joy-riders' will now face prison sentences of up to 5 years, unlimited fines and unlimited driving bans.
- We will extend the maximum sentence for causing death through dangerous or drink driving.
- We will create a new criminal offence of squatting, to give greater protection to the owners and occupants of shops, commercial premises, houses and flats.
- The 1968 Caravan Sites Act will be reviewed with the aim of reducing the nuisance of illegal encampments.
- As part of a community sentence, young offenders will be taken to see what life is really like inside one of our prisons – a sobering experience for them.
- We will introduce a new police power to make an arrest for breach of police bail.
- We will give the courts the statutory power to increase sentences for those who offend while on bail.
- We will increase the number of bail hostel places, to enable closer supervision of those on bail.
- We will mount a drive against school truancy, and set up a Task Force to find the best ways of co-ordinating the work of local agencies helping young people at risk of becoming offenders.

Reforming our prisons

Prisons should be places which are austere but decent, providing a busy and positive regime which prepares prisoners for their ultimate release. We have been reversing the Labour Party's neglect of the prison service in the 1970s. Since 1985, 14 new prisons have been opened; 7 more will open over the next two years. The end of overcrowding is now in sight. We have already taken steps to implement the key recommendations of the Woolf report on the future of our prisons. We will bring private sector skills in to enhance efficiency and increase value for money. We have put out to tender the contract for prison escort services, an approach which has worked well in other countries. The first contract for a privately managed remand centre has been awarded.

- We will sustain our massive prison reform and building programme.
- A reconstruction programme will end the degrading need for 'slopping out' by the end of 1994.
- We will reorganise prisoners' education, training and work opportunities.
- We will establish the Prison Service as a separate agency, whose director will have the clear responsibility for day-to-day operations. The Home Secretary will remain ministerially accountable to Parliament for prison policy.
- We will increase the use of private sector management skills.

Our legal system

As a free society we must have a justice system that is fair, accessible and responsive to the citizen.

We have introduced new powers for the Court of Appeal to increase sentences for crime. And in response to public concern about a small but significant number of miscarriages of justice, we have appointed a Royal Commission to review aspects of the criminal justice system, including the conduct of investigations, the handling of forensic evidence, and the powers of the Court of Appeal.

We have already reduced the opportunity for abuse by our introduction of tape-recorded interviews of suspects by the police. At the same time, we are concerned that police investigations should not be made more difficult by the misuse of certain rights.

We have already introduced a wide range of reforms following our Civil Justice Review. Extending the jurisdiction of the County Courts has helped speed up justice. The success of the small claims system in these courts has shown that simplified procedures can enable people to conduct their own cases or rely on a lay adviser. We have also introduced a reform which will give people more choice as to who represents them legally in court.

We are committed to enabling people with limited means to have access to legal services. We are determined to ensure that these services are delivered efficiently, in a way which provides the best value for money.

The principles of the Citizen's Charter are being applied to our legal system. We will shortly be publishing a Courts Charter.

We are overhauling the way in which family matters are handled in our courts. The new family code will be applied by magistrates and judges especially trained in family law.

Our Sunday Trading laws have come into question as a result of a possible conflict with Article 30 of the Treaty of Rome. This matter is now before the European Court of Justice, and we are awaiting a judgement. The Government brought forward proposals in 1986 to reform the shopping laws, but Parliament was not able to agree a conclusion. Parliament will be given the opportunity to consider this issue again.

- We will introduce a major Criminal Justice Bill in the lifetime of the new Parliament.
- We will extend the types of cases which can be handled by the County Courts in a simplified way.
- We will consult on a Lay Adjudicators scheme to make it easier for citizens to settle disputes with service providers.
- We will provide a code of family law that will continue to underpin the institution of marriage, give priority to the welfare of the child, and emphasise the primary responsibility of parents for the welfare of children and the family.
- We will bring forward proposals for reform of the Sunday Trading laws once the legal position has been made clear by the European Court of Justice.

Pornography, privacy, libel

We have the toughest anti-pornography laws in Western Europe, and we will keep them that way.

Every year, about 300,000 people – mostly women – request advice and assistance in dealing with obscene or malicious phone calls. We intend to do more to deter this harassment, in conjunction with the telecommunications industry.

The Press Complaints Commission is now in operation, and we will monitor its work carefully to see if self-regulation succeeds. The public's dislike of unprincipled press behaviour has sometimes been expressed in the award of erratically large libel damages. While this is understandable, it has led to an inordinate number of successful appeals. We therefore propose to simplify the law relating to libel in the light of the recommendations of the Neill Committee.

- British domestic controls on pornography will remain in place even after the completion of the Single European Market.
- We will increase the maximum penalties for making obscene or malicious phone calls.
- We propose to allow judges to settle the level of damages in libel cases where the defendant offers to pay to make amends.

Community relations

Racial harmony demands restraint on all sides, and a tolerant understanding of the legitimate views of others.

Everybody, regardless of ethnic background, religious or personal belief, has the right to go about his or her life free from the threat of intimidation and assault. We are determined that everyone lawfully settled in this country should enjoy the full range of opportunities in our society. That requires openness on the part of the majority and, on the part of the ethnic minorities themselves, a determination to participate fully in the life of the wider community.

The Home Office invests £129 million in grants designed to encourage those running public services to ensure that people from ethnic minorities can enjoy the full range of public services – such as health, housing and social services. We believe that these grants would be more effective if responsibility was transferred to those Departments which can make best use of the money.

- Racial and sexual discrimination have no place in our society. We have given the police stronger powers to deal with racial hatred. We will continue to ensure that the full force of the law is used to deal with racial attacks.
- We will transfer the education share of the Home Office's 'Section 11' money to the Department of Education, to focus help on those from ethnic minority backgrounds who need additional English language teaching.

Immigration and refugees

Good community relations in this country depend upon a clear structure of immigration controls which are fair, understandable and properly enforced. We are determined to maintain our present system of immigration controls unless we have evidence that other arrangements would be equally satisfactory and cost-effective.

But an increasing number of would-be immigrants from Eastern Europe and other parts of the world seek to abuse our openness to genuine refugees. The number of people seeking refugee status has risen from 5,000 a year to 45,000 over the past four years.

We will continue to honour our commitment to the 1951 UN Convention, and give refuge to those who reach our shores with a well-founded fear of persecution.

- In the new Parliament we must therefore reintroduce the Asylum Bill, opposed by Labour and the Liberal Democrats, to create a faster and more effective system of determining who are genuine political refugees, and who are not.
- We will provide a fair and expeditious system for examining claims for refugee status. This will include a workable appeal system for applicants under which those with manifestly unfounded claims will be returned quickly to their own country or to the country they came from.
- Finger-printing will be introduced for asylum applicants, to prevent multiple applications and fraudulent benefit claims.

The danger of drugs

Illegal drug abuse poses a major threat to the fabric of our society. It can destroy the health and lives of young people in particular. We will tackle this problem with vigour.

We have already taken action on a wide front:

- we have set up co-ordinators in every local education authority to train teachers about the harm drugs can do, and to bring the fight against drug abuse into the classroom;
- we have set up 16 local drug prevention teams in inner cities to tackle particular problem areas;
- we have created the National Drugs Intelligence Unit at New Scotland Yard;
- we have taken the lead in Europe in pressing for the establishment of a Europe-wide Drugs Unit, as a first step towards the creation of Europol;
- we have set up a network of 31 drug liaison officers, in 19 different countries, tracking the international drugs traffickers who threaten Britain with their trade.

We now have the toughest sanctions in Western Europe against drug traffickers.

A number of public services and voluntary bodies are engaged in fighting drug misuse at local level. Such efforts need co-ordination to ensure that local effort and dedication are directed to best effect.

- We will not legalise any banned drugs.

- We will bring forward proposals to ensure that the control of drug misuse is co-ordinated effectively.
- We intend to strengthen our confiscatory powers still further. And we will ensure that our controls against drug-trafficking are not weakened by any changes in Europe.
- We will make it an offence to supply anabolic steroids to minors.

The threat of terrorism

Tragic and dangerous events remind us only too frequently of the need for the special measures provided by the Prevention of Terrorism Act. While Labour proposes to weaken or dismantle them, we know that for the safety of our citizens they must be continued, and the police effort against terrorism must be reinforced.

- We have set up in New Scotland Yard arrangements to co-ordinate the activities of all our police forces in the fight against terrorism.
- We will provide the necessary measures and resources to combat terrorism, whether it comes from the IRA or other evil groups who seek to undermine our democracy.

Responsibility for others

Conservatives believe we have responsibility one for another. We will continue to care for those in need and work to establish a society that is generous, as well as prosperous. Our health, care and social security systems are fundamental to government responsibilities; and we believe strongly in fostering voluntary services too.

The NHS – present and future

The Conservative Party is totally committed to the National Health Service. The Government has set out in the Patient's Charter the principles on which the NHS is based. The most fundamental of these is that need, and not ability to pay, is and will remain the basis on which care is offered to all by the NHS. Since 1979, there have been great improvements in the health of the nation.

- life expectancy has increased by two years.
- deaths amongst babies and very young children have gone down by 40 per cent.
- hospitals are treating well over a million more people a year as in-patients.
- hospitals are treating over two million more people a year as out-patients.
- kidney transplants have more than doubled.
- hip replacements have increased by over 50 per cent.
- coronary artery by-passes have nearly tripled.

Since 1979 the Government has vastly increased the resources available to the NHS.

- We have increased overall funding for the NHS by 55 per cent after allowing for inflation. The cash increases in each of the three years up to 1992–93 have been the biggest ever.

- The number of doctors and dentists has been increased by 17,000, and the real resources committed to GP services have doubled since 1979.
- The number of nurses and midwives has gone up by 69,000.
- We have established the independent Pay Review Body which nurses had sought for so long, and increased their pay by 43 per cent. It is hard now to remember that Labour actually cut nurses' pay.
- We have restored the hospital building programme so savagely cut by Labour at the end of their last term of office.

But the Conservative Government has not simply spent more money on the NHS.

- We have reformed the organisation of the NHS to encourage those working in the service to respond to what patients want and need, and to get the most out of the increased money which the taxpayer provides.

At local level, health authorities now have the task of buying health care with their local share of the National Health budget. Hospitals can now be run by their own local team of doctors, nurses and managers. By April there will be 156 NHS Trusts whose local boards will have extra freedoms to develop local NHS services. Another 156 hospitals have applied to become trusts from April 1993.

We have acted to reduce the long hours worked by junior doctors in hospitals. For the first time limits are being set on the number of hours which may be worked continuously.

Good nursing is the essential complement to good medicine. We have introduced Project 2000 – a new approach to the professional training of nurses.

The GP has a crucial role to play in the development of health services. Under the Government's fund-holding initiative, doctors have control over their own spending on behalf of patients for the first time. Over 3,000 GPs will be fundholders by April, caring for 14 per cent of NHS patients. A further 2,500 are preparing to become fundholders in April 1993. As a result, new services are being offered at local surgeries and health centres. Many general practitioners have said that they would like to become involved in fund-holding. We have already extended the scope of the fund-holding scheme to allow general practitioners to provide services such as community nursing.

- We will, year by year, increase the level of real resources committed to the NHS. Savings made through greater efficiency will be ploughed back into the Service.
- We will develop a comprehensive research and development strategy for the NHS.
- We will continue to develop the NHS Trust movement which places responsibility for managing hospitals and other services with local teams who are closest to patients.
- We will continue to encourage the involvement of doctors and other medical staff in the management of services.
- We will introduce powers for nurses to prescribe where appropriate.
- We will complete the implementation of Project 2000 training for nurses.
- We will set goals for the employment of women in professional and managerial posts in the NHS.

- We will ensure that, following maternity leave or a career break, all women working in the NHS, including those returning to nursing on a part-time or job-sharing basis, are able to return to work of a similar status or level to that which they left.
- We will ensure that the benefits of fund-holding arrangements are available to any GP who wishes to apply, and we will be ready to extend the scope of the scheme further as it develops.

The Patient's Charter

No one questions the dedication of those who work in the NHS. But before the Government's reforms, the system did not always allow that dedication to produce the service which people should be able to expect.

The Patient's Charter sets out clearly what is now expected from the NHS. We have already pledged that in future no one will wait more than two years for treatment on the NHS. In many parts of the country for most treatments, the waiting time is much shorter than this; and we will seek further progress in reducing waiting times.

- Binding guarantees will be set locally for in-patient waiting times, starting with the operations where waiting causes most distress. To ensure that progress on waiting times continues, we intend that from 31 March 1993, no one should have to wait more than 18 months for a hip or knee replacement, or a cataract operation. We are sure that, as now, many hospitals will be able to do better than this.
- We will move to a system under which a named nurse or midwife will be responsible for your care while you are in hospital.
- We will set specific targets for out-patient waiting times.
- We will make it easier for patients to find out what services are available from the NHS via a new national NHS information service.
- We will ensure that comparative information about the health standards achieved by health authorities is available to the public.
- Simple systems will be set up to allow complaints to be registered and responses given if things go wrong.

Strategy for health

This Government has embarked on the first ever strategy for health. Good health requires more than good NHS care when people are sick. A variety of factors – including preventive medicine, diet, exercise, sensible drinking and not smoking – can contribute substantially to improving health across the whole population.

- We will set health objectives to be achieved by the end of the century, including reductions in illness and death from heart disease and cancers.
- We will add new health objectives as the strategy develops.

Care services

Care services for children, the elderly and the handicapped are provided by local government, health authorities, the private sector and voluntary groups, not directly by central government. But government is indirectly involved as the provider of taxpayers money and through its duty to set standards for publicly and privately provided care.

As the number of elderly people in the population grows, there will be more frail and vulnerable citizens who need support. Many of them will want to be cared for at home. Others will need residential or nursing home care. It is vital that people should have choice in the type of care available. In all cases people must be able to rely on the quality of care. As we move towards implementation of 'Caring for People' in April 1993:

- We will take steps to ensure that individuals who need residential or nursing care continue to have a choice of homes, including independent homes. Money transferred from the Social Security budget to local social services departments will be used for this purpose.
- We will ensure that all local authorities publish information about the social services that are available, including information on standards and complaints procedures.
- We will provide choice in domiciliary and day care.
- We will provide further funding for voluntary organisations to play their vital part in the development of community care services.
- We will support the organisations which help those who care for friends and relatives at home.

Children

This Government introduced the Children Act, a landmark in legislation to protect children. The Act requires childcare facilities to be registered to ensure that standards are maintained throughout the country

We believe that the diversity of childcare provision in the UK is one of its strengths. It offers parents real choice. Over 90 per cent of 3–4 year-olds are engaged in some form of group activity. We shall continue to encourage the development of childcare arrangements in the voluntary and independent sectors.

- Each local authority will be asked to produce a Local Childcare Plan setting out the provision available in their area.
- We will ensure that the standards implemented through the Children Act are applied sensibly, and do not discourage private or voluntary arrangements which are often best suited to the needs of children and parents.
- We will carry forward a family support initiative, encouraging the voluntary sector to work in partnership with families and local authorities.

Social security

Our aim is to improve further and modernise Britain's social security system. We are providing more support than ever before, £14 for every £10 spent in 1979, after allowing for inflation. More importantly, this extra help is more clearly focused on those groups with the greatest needs – less well-off pensioners, disabled people and low income families.

We have also sought to provide those on social security with better incentives to earn, and gain independence. All too often the old system created barriers to work and penalised the thrifty.

The benefit structure is now more flexible and easier to understand. The new Benefits Agency is simplifying forms and widening choice in methods of payment. We will complete the massive investment in new technology – Europe's biggest computerisation project – that has made it possible to raise the quality of service to the public. And we will extend 'Helplines' and other means of assistance with individual difficulties.

- We will continue to simplify social security forms wherever possible.
- We will set up a new Family Credit telephone advice service to support working families.
- We will establish a new agency to carry out all social security war pensions work with the aim of providing a better, more efficient service to war pensioners and war widows.

Security in retirement

Britain's pensioners recognise the security that Conservative government brings – low inflation, savings that grow, firmness in the face of crime, public services that put the customer first. Those who have dedicated their lives to the service of the community deserve that stability.

We will continue to give the fight against inflation our first priority. The basic state retirement pension will remain the foundation for retirement. We will continue to protect its value against price rises, as we have for the last 13 years.

We also recognise that some pensioners, who have no savings or pensions from their jobs, need extra help. So we will increase the additional support, already up by over £300 million a year since 1989, available to less well-off pensioners.

The number of those over pensionable age will be far higher in the next century than it is today. If we do not make provision now, the burden we will place on our children will be too great. That is why we must encourage people to build up savings, investments, and occupational and personal pensions.

But Labour policy is hostile to such personal effort; Labour wants pensioners to depend on the State. Failure to control inflation meant that pensioners' incomes from savings were cut under the last Labour Government.

About eight in ten pensioners have some sort of second income to top up their state pension. By abolishing the hated earnings rule we have enabled pensioners to keep their retirement pension, even if they take a job in retirement. And we have increased the level of savings that is disregarded in working out entitlement to benefits for pensioners. Personal pensions have brought real choice into retirement provision. Over 4½ million people have set up their own pensions since 1988. We want to see both occupational and personal provision expand much further in the course of the 1990s. (See 'Opportunity for all – A share in the future' for our proposals on occupational pensions.)

- As evidence of our continuing commitment to poorer pensioners, we have announced in the Budget an increase of £2 a week for single people, £3 a week for couples, in income support for pensioners. Combined with the increases this April, this measure will provide less well-off pensioners with between £5.73 and £10.70 a week extra.

- We will continue to pay, from April 1993, a rebate at the level recommended by the Government Actuary for all those who contract out of the State Earnings Related Pension Scheme.
- We will legislate to provide a new 1 per cent incentive for holders of personal pensions aged 30 and over from April 1993, when the existing incentive ends.
- We will consider proposals for a new system of rebates to come into effect from April 1996 with the aim of ensuring that personal pensions remain attractive across the age range.
- We are firmly committed to equal treatment for men and women in pensions. Following assessment of the responses to our discussion paper, we will bring forward legislation to achieve this.

Supporting families

Our reforms have cut away the barriers that meant many breadwinners lost money if they went to work. Family Credit has transformed the prospects of 350,000 low-income families. As a result of improvements since 1988, we have made available an extra £600 million a year in real terms to low-income families with children.

But we also recognise that all families face extra costs in bringing up children. So we have raised Child Benefit. For a two-child family the increases we are making will, by April 1992, have raised the total value of Child Benefit by almost £3 in a single year, to £17.45 a week.

Our new Child Support Agency will make sure that absent parents make a proper contribution – and that far more lone parents and their children get the maintenance that is theirs by right. And benefit changes make it easier for more families – including single parents – to combine work and family responsibilities.

- Child Benefit will remain the cornerstone of our policy for all families with children. Its value will increase each year in line with prices.
- Child Benefit will continue to be paid to all families, normally to the mother, and in respect of all children.

Help for disabled people

Under the Conservatives, more disabled people than ever before are getting the help they need and deserve. Since 1979, the number receiving Attendance Allowance has more than trebled; the number receiving Mobility Allowance has risen sixfold; the number receiving Invalid Care Allowance has risen 25-fold. Today we spend some £12,000 million a year on benefits for long-term sick and disabled people. Even after allowing for inflation, that is 2½ times as much as Labour spent in the 1970s.

Disability Living Allowance will bring together the existing Attendance and Mobility Allowance, providing new help to many disabled people who at present get no such help. Disability Working Allowance will make it easier for disabled people to take up a job.

We are introducing new disability benefits which will, in the next Parliament, bring extra help to at least 300,000 people. By 1993–94 these and other improvements will mean that we will be directing an extra £300 million a year to long-term sick and disabled people.

The Independent Living Fund has proved a great success in giving severely disabled people an opportunity to live in the community. We are committed to maintaining a fund which supports the most severely disabled people.

The voluntary sector

Charities and voluntary groups play a vital role in our national life. Britain is rich in its citizens' willingness to give time, effort and money to helping others. We have a great tradition of voluntary work at home and overseas. There are now about 350,000 voluntary groups in Britain – and personal donations to charities now amount to some £5,000 million a year.

We have done much to boost charitable giving.

- Under the Payroll Giving Scheme, employees can now contribute up to £50 a month tax-free.
- Gifts and bequests have been exempted from Inheritance Tax.
- The Gift Aid scheme allows charities to claim tax relief on one-off gifts of more than £400 – a change just announced in the Budget.
- The maximum limit on single charitable gifts qualifying for Income and Corporation Tax relief has been abolished.

The new Charities legislation will ensure that charities are better managed and properly regulated. We believe this will enhance public confidence in charities and further boost charitable giving.

The Government gives some £2,500 million a year to support the activities of the voluntary sector (including housing associations). Industry has been generous with its sponsorship and with technical support. But money is not the only contribution that government and business can make. Businesses have become much more practically involved in work in the community And government could do more to encourage new forms of volunteering, to encourage the most effective use of the money it gives, and to bring together voluntary effort at the local and national level.

- We will continue to support the work of the voluntary sector and promote volunteering.
- We will work with voluntary agencies to develop, over the life of the next Parliament, a national bank of information on opportunities for volunteering.
- We will encourage efforts to improve the co-ordination and promote the growth of local volunteer support, building on the success of Neighbourhood Watch to develop a network of voluntary help in local communities.

Animal welfare

We are leading the European Community in our achievements in improving animal welfare. We have also taken action at home and abroad to improve conservation, and will continue to do so.

English Nature, which advises the Government on wildlife issues, has embarked on an ambitious programme to restore endangered species. The Wildlife and Countryside Act 1981 provides special protection for 304 species of birds and animals, as well as protecting our heritage of wild plants.

We are firmly opposed to international trade in rare and protected species such as rhinoceroses, cheetahs, leopards, and bears. We have pushed successfully for an EC ban on large-scale drift nets that threatened dolphins, and we support the UN resolution calling for a moratorium on their use. We support the extension of the moratorium on commercial whaling and have co-sponsored resolutions against 'scientific' hunting of whales. We have successfully pressed for an EC ban on the importation of baby seal products and of furs from those countries which permit leghold traps.

We have set up the Farm Animal Welfare Council and have brought in welfare codes covering livestock on farms and in transit. We are establishing an ethical committee to look at the effects of advanced techniques in animal breeding. We have banned the use of veal crates, and taken action to ensure humane slaughter. We insisted that we should retain our power to stop the export of live horses. At Maastricht we secured a landmark in animal welfare: our partners' agreement to a declaration that the welfare of animals should be taken into account in the framing of EC legislation.

We now have the toughest set of controls on animal experimentation in Europe, and the number of animals used in experiments has fallen steadily We have supported stronger laws to protect badgers and stop cruel tethering, and have increased the penalties for organising animal fights and for cruelty.

- We will introduce a Wildlife Enhancement Scheme and expand the Species Recovery Scheme, both to be run by English Nature.
- We have tightened controls on the import of wild birds and will press the EC to do the same.
- We oppose resumption of the trade in ivory or elephant products, and will provide additional support for elephant conservation projects in Africa.
- We will urge our EC partners to bring animal welfare standards up to UK levels, for example by banning veal crates and stalls and tethers for pigs. We will press them to put into practice the principles of the Maastricht declaration.
- We will use our EC Presidency to toughen up EC regulations and improve EC compliance with rules governing animal experiments.
- We will press for higher EC standards for the keeping of battery hens and for the care of animals in transit.
- We will not accept any weakening of our rabies prevention safeguards.

A brighter Britain

Making Britain a brighter and better place in which to live requires a high quality physical environment – including housing, transport and reinvigorated urban areas. The Conservative commitment is both to the re-creation of our civic pride and also to the preservation and integrity of our rural heritage, founded on the core industry of agriculture. Our aim is to enhance the quality of life for the British people.

Home ownership

The opportunity to own a home and pass it on is one of the most important rights an individual has in a free society. Conservatives have extended that right. It lies at the heart of our philosophy. We want to see wealth and security being passed down from generation to generation. Some 4 million more householders own their own homes compared with 1979. The number of former council tenants who have bought their homes has risen to 1.4 million.

We now need to make it easier for those council tenants living in high-cost areas or on low incomes to move gradually into home ownership, without taking on too heavy a financial burden at any one time. This will bring the benefits of home ownership within the reach of more people and introduce more diversity in local authority estates. We also want to help more leaseholders to own and control the management of their property.

But we recognise that not everyone can, or will want to, buy his or her home. So we are determined to encourage a strong private rented sector while continuing to safeguard the rights of existing regulated tenants. Bringing empty private sector dwellings back into use will extend choice, make it easier for people to move jobs, and help tackle homelessness.

- We will maintain mortgage tax relief.
- We will continue 'Right to Buy' discounts, and ensure that local authorities respond reasonably and rapidly to applications.
- We will introduce a new nation-wide 'Rents to Mortgages' scheme, enabling council tenants to take a part-share in their home, gradually stepping up to full ownership.
- We will put more of the Housing Corporation's £2,000 million budget into Do-It-Yourself shared ownership. This will enable first time buyers to choose a home and buy a share of it – usually 50 per cent – with a housing association paying rent on the rest until they wish to increase their stake in the property.
- We will introduce 'Commonhold' legislation, giving residential leaseholders living in blocks of flats the right to acquire the freehold of their block at the market rate. Leaseholders of higher rated houses will also be given the right to buy the freehold of their property. Leaseholders who live in a block which does not qualify will have a new right to buy an extended lease.
- We will introduce statutory time limits for answers by local authorities to standard inquiries by house-buyers, and explore the idea of a new computerised Property Data Bank bringing together information held by the Land Registry and other public bodies.
- We will extend nation-wide the scheme we have piloted to increase private renting, whereby housing associations manage properties, building trust between tenant and private sector landlord.
- As soon as possible in the new Parliament, we will introduce a new 'Rent a Room' scheme under which home-owners will be able to let rooms to lodgers without having to pay tax on the rent they receive.

Meeting housing need

We are also committed to securing a better deal for council tenants and increasing the supply of affordable housing for those in housing need. We will introduce more choice, improve management of estates and create new rights as part of the Tenant's Charter. Our aim will be to give tenants a choice of landlord wherever possible, and make management of both council and housing association stock more responsive to the needs of tenants.

We will improve the way in which council housing is managed by bringing in new private sector providers operating on contract to the local authority We will introduce more competition and choice, thereby improving services to the tenant and increasing accountability. And we intend to give council tenants new opportunities themselves to improve the flat or house in which they live.

We have already begun a process of Large-Scale Voluntary Transfer which allows local authority tenants to opt to transfer to a housing association. We wish to see this result in diversity, not local monopoly, and will therefore act to limit the size of blocks that can be transferred.

Nearly all new social housing is now being built by housing associations. Over the next three years, we are committed to spend nearly £6,000 million through the Housing Corporation to provide 153,000 homes.

We will do more to bring into use properties owned by central and local government which are standing empty for no good reason. This will enable us to house more people on the waiting list and, in some cases, to provide more opportunities for homesteading.

Through Estate Action and Housing Action Trusts we have invested £1,000 million in recent years in a concentrated attack on the country's worst housing estates. Some 360,000 dwellings have been improved as a result. As part of those programmes, on which we are committed to spend a further £1,400 million over the next three years, we are demolishing or redesigning tower blocks and deck access estates, rebuilding on a more human scale. Wherever we can, whenever tenants want it, and where resources allow, we will pull down the eyesores which have blotted our cityscapes and too often provided breeding grounds for crime and delinquency.

The Government is spending about £100 million tackling the problem of rough sleeping in our cities. As a result we have seen a sharp fall in the numbers who sleep rough on our streets. Working closely with the voluntary sector we will continue to provide help for those sleeping rough, particularly in the capital.

- We will revolutionise the management of council houses and flats. Compulsory competitive tendering will oblige local authorities to bring in managers who demonstrate their ability to deliver the best services to tenants.
- We will continue our programme of Large-Scale Voluntary Transfer of council properties to housing associations. But in order to bring management closer to tenants, we intend to reduce the limit on the number of properties transferred in a single batch.
- We will give tenants a new Right to Improve, so they can receive compensation for certain home improvements which they undertake. And we will improve the existing Right to Repair. We will continue our Estate Action and Housing Action Trust programmes which concentrate resources on the worst council estates.

- We will enable tenants to apply for Housing Action Trusts to take over and improve the worst estates.
- We will work with the Housing Corporation to establish a new Ombudsman for housing association tenants. We will also encourage the Corporation to extend opportunities for tenant involvement in the management of housing association properties.
- We will set up a Task Force – headed by an independent chairman – to help bring empty government residential properties back into use. These will either be sold or let on short-term leases to those in housing need.
- As part of Estate Action we will introduce a new pilot scheme to promote homesteading. Local authorities will be encouraged to offer those in housing need the opportunity to restore and improve council properties. In exchange, homesteaders will pay a lower rent or be able to buy at a reduced price.

Transport

Under the Conservatives, transport in Britain is being transformed. More competition on the roads and in the air has led to better services and more choice. Our successful policies of deregulation and privatisation have gone hand in hand with a sustained and growing programme of investment. Over 1,000 miles of new trunk roads and motorway have been built, more than 100 bypasses constructed, and some 750 miles of railway electrified. Airlines now operate 50 per cent more flights. More people travel further and more easily than ever before.

Over the next three years we are committed to the biggest investment in Britain's transport infrastructure in our history.

We will also seek further opportunities for the private sector to contribute, as it has for example with the Channel Tunnel, the Queen Elizabeth II Bridge at Dartford, the second Severn Bridge and the Birmingham Northern Ring Road. We intend the proposed new rail link from the Channel Tunnel to King's Cross to be taken forward by the private sector.

The railways

We believe that the railways can play a bigger part in responding to Britain's growing transport needs, and are investing accordingly. Next year alone, British Rail's external finance will top £2,000 million. The new Passenger's Charter will help to raise the quality of service. For the first time ever performance targets will be set, widely published and rigorously monitored; fare levels will reflect the standards set; and discounts will be paid to regular travellers where performance targets are not met. We believe that the best way to produce profound and lasting improvements on the railways is to end BR's state monopoly. We want to restore the pride and local commitment that died with nationalisation. We want to give the private sector the opportunity to operate existing rail services and introduce new ones, for both passengers and freight.

A significant number of companies have already said that they want to introduce new railway services as soon as the monopoly is ended. We will give them that chance.

Our plans for the railways are designed to bring better services for all passengers as rapidly as possible. We believe that franchising provides the best way of achieving that.

Long term, as performance improves and services become more commercially attractive as a result of bringing in private sector disciplines, it will make sense to consider whether some services can be sold outright.

In the next Parliament:

- By franchising, we will give the private sector the fullest opportunity to operate existing passenger railway services.
- Required standards of punctuality, reliability and quality of service will be specified by franchises; subsidy will continue to be provided where necessary; arrangements to sustain the current national network of services will be maintained; and through-ticketing will be required.
- A new Rail Regulator – who will ensure that all companies have fair access to the track – will award the franchises and make sure that the franchisees honour the terms of the contract.
- BR's accounting systems and internal structures will be reorganised. One part of BR will continue to be responsible for all track and infrastructure. The operating side of BR will continue to provide passenger services until they are franchised out to the private sector.
- The franchise areas will be decided only after technical discussions with BR. But our aim will be to franchise out services in such a way as to reflect regional and local identity and make operating sense. We want to recover a sense of pride in our railways and to recapture the spirit of the old regional companies.
- We will sell BR's freight operations outright. We will also sell its parcels business.
- We will be prepared to sell stations – which we want to be centres of activity – either to franchisees or independent companies.
- The Railway Inspectorate will be given full powers to ensure the highest standards of safety.

Roads

Nine out of every ten journeys, whether passenger or freight, are made by road. We must therefore continue to provide an efficient road network. In the years ahead we will concentrate particularly on the bypass programme.

As part of the Citizen's Charter, we will bring forward reforms which will enable the private sector to start filling the gaps in the motorway service area network and to introduce more variety Rather than large, intrusive stations at long intervals we should see smaller, more frequent service areas providing a much wider range of facilities.

We will investigate ways of speeding up, within the Department of Transport, the procedures for building new roads. We will continue our campaign to keep 'coning off' on motorways to a minimum by extending lane rental schemes, under which contractors who fall behind schedule incur financial penalties. Next year two-thirds of all motorway maintenance work will be carried out in this way.

Britain has the best road safety record in the European Community. In spite of the vastly increased volume of traffic, fewer people are now killed on our roads than at any time since 1948. Our aim is to improve on that record still further.

In spite of the benefits they bring, cars carry an environmental cost. In Britain catalytic converters will be compulsory on all new cars from the end of 1992. This will eliminate virtually all harmful exhaust gases, except for the emission of CO_2. The only certain way of cutting CO_2 emissions is to encourage fuel efficiency. Action is needed at international level and we will play our full part.

Buses have an increasingly important part to play. The deregulation of long-distance coach services has led to a major expansion in reliable and cheap services. Bus deregulation outside London has increased mileage by 16 per cent. We now propose to take deregulation and privatisation further.

We will improve road transport by:

- Investing £6,300 million in our trunk road and motorway network over the next three years, concentrating particularly on bypasses. Some 40 new ones will be opened by 1993 on trunk roads alone.
- Increasing penalties for those convicted of drink driving.
- Installing cameras at dangerous road junctions to film those who drive through red traffic lights.
- Encouraging local councils, assisted by a special budget we have set aside, to introduce pedestrian priority areas and cycle lanes.
- Privatising the remaining 39 local authority bus companies.
- Deregulating buses in London and privatising the London Buses subsidiaries. A new London Bus Executive will be responsible for bus-stops, stands and stations and for contracting out socially necessary services. The concessionary fares scheme in London will continue.
- Changing the system under which motorway service areas are provided.
- Encouraging action internationally, and within our own motor industry, to promote more fuel-efficient vehicles.

Aviation and shipping

More competition in aviation means more choice, better services and lower fares. That is why we have been pressing within the EC for full liberalisation of services. We also want to see more transatlantic flights, particularly to regional airports. People in the regions should not have to travel to London in order to fly to the United States. Direct flights would boost local economies and apply downward pressure on fares. The key regional airports are still in local authority ownership. They should be well placed to benefit from an increase in the number of direct point-to-point flights. But if they are really to grow and prosper, they need access to private capital, freed from the constraints of public ownership.

Air safety cannot be compromised. Over the next five years the Civil Aviation Authority will invest £750 million in modernising its systems.

More can be done to cut some of the regulatory burdens our shipping industry faces. We will ensure that the recommendations of the Government Industry Joint Working Party are put into effect as rapidly as possible.

- We will further liberalise transatlantic air services and encourage more international flights to and from regional airports.
- We will encourage local authorities to sell their airports.

- We will reduce airport congestion by increasing the capacity of our air traffic control.
- We will continue to campaign within the EC for further liberalisation, particularly of cabotage, so that there are more commercial opportunities for British companies.

London's transport

A major programme of renewal and modernisation is transforming public transport in London – including the biggest expansion of London's rail network since the 1930s. The £750 million upgrading of the Central Line is already under way, to be followed by a similar programme on the Northern Line; the Jubilee Line extension and Crossrail will follow.

London Underground is planning to invest £3,500 million over the next three years. It has introduced an ambitious Company Plan which will lead to better service, cleaner trains and more staff at stations and on platforms. Their new Charter will be published shortly.

Responsibility for the Docklands Light Railway has been transferred to the London Docklands Development Corporation. As its performance continues to improve, we expect to see growing private sector interest in purchasing it outright.

- We will seek to privatise the Docklands Light Railway during the lifetime of the next Parliament.
- The new Jubilee Line is being extended to Docklands and South East London and will be followed by the East-West Crossrail, linking Paddington to Liverpool Street. The Docklands Light Railway is being extended at an eventual cost of £800 million.
- London Underground's Charter will set out tougher new standards and what it will do to compensate passengers should it fail to meet those standards.

Local government

Local councillors – some 25,000 men and women throughout Britain – are responsible for some of our most important public services. Since 1979 we have sought to create an accountable local government system capable of delivering high quality local services at a price that local people are prepared to pay.

Conservatives councils in shires, districts and cities have been at the forefront of these reforms. In a responsive and efficient manner, they have demonstrated how to deliver good services at an affordable price.

Over the past 13 years, we have:

- held down unjustified rises in the cost of local government;
- abolished the power of local councils to shift the burden of taxation on to local business, for the first time limiting the overall rise in business rates to no more than the rate of inflation;
- abolished an expensive and bureaucratic layer of government in London and other big cities;

- developed the local authority role from direct provider to effective enabler, encouraging many tenants to buy their own homes, allowing schools the freedom to manage their own affairs and improving the quality of local services by allowing private business to compete for contracts.

Labour threaten all these reforms. They would 'uncap' local spending, leading to higher local and national taxes. They would 'uncap' business rates, threatening a return to the 1980s when the English rate poundage rose 37 per cent more than inflation. They would abolish the requirement on local authorities to seek value for money through competitive tendering. They would remove the freedom of local communities to preserve their grammar schools. They would introduce a new expensive layer of government bureaucracy at regional level. They would return local government finance to the bad old days of domestic rates, with unrestrained power for local councils to charge householders as much as they like. And they would abolish the Audit Commission, which not only maintains the probity of local government accounting, but also pioneered the drive for better quality of service and value for money in local government.

We now propose further reforms in the structure, finance and accountability of local government. In the meantime, we have transferred a further share of the burden of financing local services to central government. Today, local community chargepayers bear only a small proportion of the cost of local councils.

- We will set up a commission to examine, area by area, the appropriate local government arrangements in England. Local communities will be fully consulted and their loyalties and interests will be central to the commission's task in deciding whether in any area a single tier of local government could provide better accountability and greater efficiency.
- We are looking at ways in which the internal management of local authorities might become more effective.
- We are applying the principles of the Citizen's Charter to local government, requiring the publication of more information which will enable local people to judge the efficiency of their councils in providing services.
- We will continue to 'cap' local spending where necessary.
- As we announced in the Budget, no one's Uniform Business Rate will go up this year by more than the rate of inflation, 4.1 per cent. And we have speeded up the benefits of revaluation for those businesses who gain from it.
- In future years, we will maintain our pledge to prevent UBR poundage rising by more than inflation.
- We will replace the Community Charge with a new Council Tax in April 1993. The Council Tax will be simple and straightforward to administer. It will be fair and will rightly reflect both the value of the property and the number of adults who live in it.
- Single householders, who suffered under the rates, will receive a 25 per cent discount. By grouping properties into a limited number of bands, the Council Tax also avoids the punitive bills which would be imposed by an unfettered rating system of the kind proposed by Labour. Students and people on low incomes will not have to pay.

Cities

We take pride in our cities. Right across Britain they have been given a new lease of life. From London to Glasgow; from Cardiff to Newcastle, historic buildings have been restored and areas which had been run down have been transformed. The £4,000 million Action for Cities programme underlines the Conservative commitment to our inner cities and the people who live there. It highlights our determination to spread opportunity as widely as possible. We want all our people to share in growing prosperity and to have a stake in the country's future. Much has been achieved in recent years. The Urban Development Corporations and the wide range of central government grants have helped to regenerate many of our inner city areas. But more remains to be done.

The best way to restore the spirit of enterprise which first made our cities great is for local people, the private sector, the voluntary sector and local and central government, to work together in partnership. That is the principle which lies behind City Challenge. Its new approach of competitive bidding has already galvanized towns and cities into bringing forward imaginative proposals for regeneration. It has improved co-ordination, secured better value for money and encouraged programmes which tackle problems on a number of fronts.

- We will continue to extend City Challenge and allocate a greater proportion of resources by competitive bidding.
- We will support Urban Development Corporations in their critical task of urban regeneration.
- We will bring together resources targeted on inner city programmes into a single budget. This will mean that funding will go where it is most needed locally rather than according to a set of priorities determined in Whitehall.
- We will strengthen the machinery for co-ordination in the regions. New, integrated regional offices of the appropriate Whitehall departments will be established so that business and local government will have only one port of call.
- We will establish a new Urban Regeneration Agency to pull together our efforts to clear up and develop derelict land, helping to bring it back into commercial use and provide new opportunities for local people.

Working in the urban areas, the URA will administer much of the Urban programme of the Department of the Environment. It will have a dual function. First, outside the existing UDC areas, it will reclaim derelict land, assembling suitable sites for redevelopment using vesting or compulsory purchase powers where necessary. Second, it will itself be able to develop land in partnership with the private sector. This represents a major step forward in unlocking the commercial potential of our inner cities and of breathing new life into areas which may have been derelict for many years.

But our focus is not just on physical regeneration. We want to see more opportunities for training, more encouragement to enterprise, better education and more measures to tackle drugs and crime.

Encouraging enterprise, improving the environment and providing new opportunities for the unemployed are central to our inner city policies. Remotivating individuals and providing the right conditions for business are the only ways to make lasting change.

- We will offer the Loan Guarantee Scheme for small firms on more generous terms in inner city areas. The scheme will be extended from Task Force areas to include successful City Challenge bidders.
- We will make more people eligible for our successful Job Interview Guarantee Scheme, which links unemployed people with local jobs.
- We will carry out pilot projects for the 'foyer' concept, whereby young people are given a place in a hostel if in exchange they give a commitment to train and look for work.
- We will pilot a number of 'back to work' bonus schemes in inner city areas for the long-term unemployed.
- We will extend customised training under the Job Link programme to include City Challenge areas.
- We will make inner city Task Force and City Challenge areas eligible for regional innovation grants.

We are also determined to raise standards in our inner city schools, to crack down on truancy, and to help prepare young people for the world of work.

The City Technology Colleges show what can be done. They are overwhelmingly popular with parents and pupils and are doing much to raise standards for children of all abilities in the inner cities.

Under the Citizen's Charter, we shall soon be able to identify much more precisely than ever before those schools which are delivering unacceptably low standards. So will parents. We will publish test results, exam results and truancy rates and ensure that there is regular independent inspection. This will enable us to put the spotlight on those inner city LEAs and schools which are failing their pupils.

- We will continue to seek opportunities to open new CTCs in deprived inner city areas.
- We will ensure that more schools, especially in the inner cities, have the opportunity to develop their technological expertise.

Tackling crime and the fear of crime forms a vital part of the strategy to make our inner cities better places to live and work. The Safer Cities initiative, launched in 1988, has successfully brought together local groups and agencies to tackle crime in some of our worst affected urban areas. Twenty schemes are already in operation.

We will double the number of Safer Cities Schemes to cover 40 urban areas.

London

London is a magnet to visitors and business from across the world. Since 1979 we have invested heavily to secure that status. Billions of pounds have gone into improving air, rail and underground links. We will continue that programme of modernisation. We are determined to sustain into the next century London's special position as one of the world's leading capital cities. We reject Labour's plan to recreate a bureaucratic and wasteful GLC. Instead, as part of our Millennium programme, we will launch a London 2000 initiative. The Secretary of State for the Environment will convene a new private sector forum to promote London internationally as a business, tourist and cultural centre. The Secretary of State will also chair a new Cabinet sub-committee to bring together Ministers from all key departments and co-ordinate policy for the further improvement of London. A single Minister will be given responsibility for co-ordinating London's transport services. London's place as a world centre for financial and insurance services is pre-eminent; we intend to keep it that way And we will support the vigorous cultural life of the capital, which has seen new galleries, theatres and museums opening over the last decade.

- We will launch a London 2000 initiative.
- We will convene a new private sector forum to promote London's position internationally.
- We will establish a new Cabinet sub-committee to co-ordinate policy on London.
- We will give a single Transport Minister responsibility for services in London. He will chair a new Transport Working Group which will bring together public transport operators from both public and private sectors – to discuss transport issues in London.

The countryside

We have always cared for the countryside. We support its major industries and way of life, while recognising the place it holds in the hearts of those who live in towns. We want to protect our most beautiful landscapes, conserve the abundance and variety of our wildlife and habitats, promote access and public enjoyment of the countryside, and encourage public participation in caring for the countryside.

But the countryside is more than just a pretty picture. It is a place where people live and work, as they have done in the past and will do in the future. In providing our public services, we will continue to recognise the particular needs of people who live in the countryside.

We will continue to promote a diverse rural economy, balancing the need for jobs, housing and services in rural areas with protection of the rural environment.

Agriculture

Centuries of farming have shaped our countryside. Now farming is at a crossroads, both here and in the rest of the European Community. World-wide pressure to reduce protectionist measures, and the need to contain the cost of the Common Agricultural Policy, mean that farmers will face reduced support and increased competition. We believe that farming in the UK can meet these challenges. But many farmers will need help to adapt to the new conditions, and we will continue to provide assistance.

It will become increasingly important for farmers to obtain a greater proportion of their income from the market. We will encourage farmers, retailers and manufacturers to work together to increase our share of the European food market.

We are committed to reducing the burden of regulation on business in general, and farming in particular. We will not accept UK farmers being put at a disadvantage by EC laws being applied differently in other countries.

Responsible farmers have always combined efficient farming with care for the countryside. We will continue to encourage this approach through schemes to protect landscape and habitats of special importance. We will also maintain direct support for farming in the Less Favoured Areas in ways which encourage good environmental practice

- We will seek a reform of the CAP which brings agriculture closer to the market; reduces the costs to taxpayers and consumers; is implemented at a pace which the industry can bear; affects all Community farmers equitably, regardless of size or location; and recognises the importance of environmental protection.
- We will build on the producer marketing initiatives which we have already launched, including the Group Marketing Grant.
- We will assist the Milk Marketing Board's move to a new structure which will be better able to protect the interests of producers and consumers in the Single Market.
- We will publish target response times for grant and licence applications made to the Ministry of Agriculture.
- We will take forward proposals for radical liberalisation of the agricultural tenancy laws in order to make more land available for rent, especially for new entrants.
- We will enforce effective pollution control regulations while helping farmers to meet the high standards required.
- We will press for an agreement in the EC's Agricultural Council which will allow us to provide financial encouragement for organic agriculture.

Forestry

Forestry is a traditional rural industry, which also affects the landscape, and gives pleasure to millions of people. The needs of a successful industry, landscape conservation, and public access must all be accommodated; and we will reorganise the Forestry Commission to reflect these objectives more effectively.

- We will plant a new national forest in the Midlands and community forests elsewhere.
- We will review the effectiveness of the current incentives for forestry investment.
- We will produce guidance on the preparation of local Indicative Forestry Strategies designed to encourage new woodlands, while steering planting away from sensitive areas.

Fishing

Fishing is a vital industry in many parts of our islands. Many fishermen have done well in recent years but they now face great pressure on the fish stocks. This means that fishing quotas are likely to fall in coming years in order to preserve the long-term future of the fisheries. We will continue to work for the profitable and sustainable future of our fishing fleet.

- We are determined to see that the renegotiation of the Common Fisheries Policy protects the interests of UK fishermen and retains our share of the Community's fishing opportunities.

- We will introduce a balanced package of measures, including decommissioning and controls on fishing activity, to conserve fish and safeguard the future of the industry.

Rural jobs and services

Changes in agriculture and other traditional industries will affect employment opportunities in the countryside. We will continue to target help through the Rural Development Commission, and ask the RDC to review the Rural Development Areas to ensure that its efforts are targeted on the areas of most need. We are committed to developing tourism in ways which provide all-year-round jobs and bring benefit to less well-known parts of our countryside, without damaging the environment. We have recently published new planning policy guidance which makes it clear how the countryside can benefit from new businesses and jobs, if the location and design of development are handled with sensitivity.

In local government, many of our shire counties and districts have led the way in raising the quality of public service. Local post offices, local transport and local schools all have an important role to play in sustaining rural life.

- We will consult on our recently published draft planning policy guidance designed to provide a clear framework for decisions on developments to aid tourism.
- We will widen the availability of the Rural Development Commission's successful Redundant Buildings Grant Scheme, and strengthen other RDC programmes.
- We will maintain our special programmes to promote affordable homes in rural areas.
- We are fully committed to maintaining a national network of post offices.
- We will continue to assist local authorities who want to subsidise rural transport.
- We will enable village schools that wish to apply for Grant-Maintained status to do so in small groups, thus enabling them to share management tasks while still enjoying the benefits of independence.
- The expansion of GP fund-holding will bring particular benefits to rural areas because of the convenience of different services – such as physiotherapy and consultant appointments – being offered in the GP's surgery.

Caring for the countryside

Some of our finest landscapes are designated as National Parks. All National Park authorities will become independent Boards, which will make it easier for them to carry out their tasks effectively. The New Forest will be given a statutory status which will give it as great a level of protection as any National Park.

Last summer the Government launched an experiment in Countryside Stewardship. This aims to conserve, enhance and re-create fine landscapes so that they may be enjoyed and appreciated by the public. The response from farmers, landowners and environmental bodies has been very positive. We therefore propose to expand the scheme and to introduce a new scheme to preserve hedgerows – a much valued feature of the English landscape, and a haven for wildlife.

The Government endorsed and supported the Countryside Commission's target designed to bring 120,000 miles of rights of way into good order by the end of the century.

At parish level, individuals can work together either to safeguard the character of their local village, or to improve its appearance. Local action can also preserve local wildlife and habitats. Under the Rural Environmental Action Scheme, grants of up to £2,000 per project will be available to support local environmental action.

The Government is keen to promote the fullest possible use of inland waterways for leisure, recreation and amenity, in the regeneration of inner cities and for freight transport where appropriate. But we recognise that the various uses of canals and rivers must be properly managed to protect the character and environment of the waterways.

- We will expand the Countryside Stewardship Scheme to cover the conservation of historic landscapes, meadows, pasture and hedgerows. Public access to qualifying schemes will be encouraged.
- We will introduce a Hedgerow Incentive Scheme to help preserve hedgerows of particular historic, landscape or wildlife importance.
- We will contribute to the Countryside Commission's new Parish Path Partnership designed to stimulate local maintenance and improvement schemes.
- We will continue to support the development and redevelopment of our canals, as well as enhancing the environmental standards of our waterways.

The environment

The Conservative Party's commitment to the environment is beyond doubt. Other parties promise the earth. We have taken action – both nationally and internationally – to preserve it.

Environmental protection can impose financial costs on producers, consumers and taxpayers, so we must make sure the threat of damage is a real one. But we also accept the precautionary principle – the need to act, where there is significant risk of damage, before the scientific evidence is conclusive. And we recognise that higher environmental standards can offer new opportunities for business.

We published the first comprehensive White Paper on the Environment in 1990. It covered everything from the stratosphere to the street corner. We will continue to publish annual progress reports.

This Conservative Government has taken a lead in working to protect the ozone layer. We will strive to accelerate the eradication of ozone depleting substances.

One of the most important issues facing all countries is the threat of global warming. Effective action to combat global warming must be international action. Again we have taken a lead. The Prime Minister was the first world leader to announce his intention to attend the Earth Summit in Rio de Janeiro this June. We have said that we will consider stabilising our CO_2 emissions earlier than our existing conditional target of 2005. We have promised to provide new and additional resources to help the developing countries to tackle their environmental problems.

Within Britain, and ahead of other European countries, we have introduced the concept of integrated pollution control.

We have set up, for the first time, powerful co-ordinating machinery within Whitehall to ensure that environmental considerations are given due weight in all decision-making.

We are committed to openness on environmental matters. We support the establishment of a European Environment Agency to provide a Europe-wide environmental database. We believe that the public should have access to information held by the pollution control authorities. Public registers are now provided by bodies such as the National Rivers Authority and Her Majesty's Inspectorate of Pollution.

- We will establish a new Environment Agency which will bring together the functions of the National Rivers Authority, Her Majesty's Inspectorate of Pollution and the waste regulation functions of local authorities.
- The new EA will have a statutory duty to publish an annual State of the Environment report.
- Within the European Community we will press for the introduction of integrated pollution control on the UK model.

Towards the millennium

A more prosperous Britain can afford to be ambitious. We can aspire to excellence in the arts, broadcasting and sport. We can use our increased leisure time, energy and money, to improve life for ourselves and our families. The National Lottery we propose to introduce can be used to restore our heritage and promote projects which will become a source of national pride.

National Lotteries have been found useful at several times in our history. The British Museum was founded out of the proceeds of such a lottery. Fourteen years ago, a Royal Commission recommended the creation of a National Lottery in Britain to provide extra money for deserving causes. The case has become even stronger as British people gain more opportunities to participate in foreign lotteries – thus increasing the risk that funds which we could put to good use in Britain will be diverted abroad.

We believe a well-run, carefully controlled form of national lottery would be popular, while raising money for many good causes.

We will canvass views on how such a lottery should be run and controlled, and how it would fit within the pattern of charitable fund-raising in Britain.

We believe that the funds generated by a National Lottery should be used to enhance the life of our nation. People who enjoy the arts, sport, Britain's heritage and fine countryside could all benefit from the proceeds from a National Lottery. Charities, right across the country and covering such areas as medical research, will also be potential beneficiaries.

The Millennium Fund

We will be consulting widely on the best way to distribute the proceeds of a lottery. But we have decided that part of the proceeds should be put aside, year by year, into a Millennium Fund specifically dedicated to projects which will commemorate the start of the twenty-first century and will be enjoyed by future generations.

We therefore propose to introduce a National Lottery from 1994, which would help provide funds for a number of good causes in the artistic, sporting, heritage and charitable fields – and from which some funds would be put aside for a Millennium Fund.

The Millennium Fund could be used, for example:

- To restore the fabric of our nation: our great inheritance of buildings which symbolise and enrich our national life.
- To help endow our cities and regions with facilities to enhance the celebration of United Kingdom 2000, such as the sporting facilities Manchester would need to host the 2000 Olympics.
- To help another major city – chosen by competition – to hold an international trade fair designed to be a showcase of British innovation for the twenty-first century.
- To enable voluntary groups and local communities to bid for funding for their own Millennium projects for local restoration schemes, or for improving the amenities of canals and rivers, as a source of enjoyment for local people and a habitat for wildlife.
- To provide Millennium bursaries for young people (and newly retired people) offering their time, energy and commitment to schemes designed to change the face of the United Kingdom by the year 2000.

The arts

Britain has a great artistic heritage and a lively contemporary arts scene. The arts have flourished in recent years, with growing attendance at theatre, opera, dance and arts festivals.

We have supported this by increasing the public funding of the arts, by 60 per cent in real terms since 1979, and introducing new incentives to personal giving. The arts have also forged new partnerships with local authorities, businesses and private patrons. Business sponsorship in particular has expanded hugely.

- We have set up new Regional Arts Boards and supported the Scottish and Welsh Arts Councils in order to diversify and enrich cultural life throughout the country.
- We have financed the European Arts Festival to be held throughout Britain during our Presidency of the Community in the second half of this year, as well as the first National Music Day in June.

In this year's Budget, we announced further tax relief on film-making in this country. Our aim is to make the performing arts, museums and our heritage accessible to all. We will encourage the young to become involved and will facilitate access for the disabled.

- The National Lottery will provide a new source of finance for the arts.
- We will maintain support for the arts and continue to develop schemes for greater sponsorship in co-operation with business and private individuals.
- We will re-examine the role of the Arts Council, as many of its functions are now carried out regionally.

- We will continue our support of libraries as educational, cultural and community centres, and urge local authorities to keep up standards. We will complete the new British Library building for which we have provided £450 million.

Sport

Success in sport is a source of national pride. Enjoyment of sport can enrich every life. We have given strong support to the Sports Council and its efforts to raise participation in sport. We actively support Manchester's bid to bring the Olympic Games to Britain.

We want to restore the good image of football. Tough action has cut down football hooliganism. We have helped to establish the Football Trust, which now devotes £20 million a year to improving the safety of grounds.

Under the National Curriculum all primary and secondary age pupils will follow a course of PE. All pupils will be taught to swim by the age of 11.

We will continue to encourage private sector sponsorship of sport. We will encourage more effective use of local sport and leisure facilities through compulsory competitive tendering. We want to see more dual use of school playing fields and halls and will give schools more freedom in their management.

We are asking Local Education Authorities not to make sales of school playing fields in future unless there is no evidence of long-term need.

- Sport, too, will benefit from the resources generated by the National Lottery.
- We will actively support Britain's bid to host the 2000 Olympic Games in Manchester. We will provide £55 million towards the preparation of the site and key facilities in the first stage of the bid, and we will ensure that the project, whether successful or not, contributes to the effective regeneration of East Manchester.
- We will set up a new Business Sponsorship for Sport scheme. This is expected to raise £6 million in its first year to support local and youth sport.

Our heritage

Public interest and involvement in Britain's heritage have never been greater. We have created in the past decade English Heritage and the National Heritage Memorial Fund to give greater focus and drive to the Government's policies. The National Trust and private owners take a leading part in preserving our almost unrivalled heritage. Government will work in partnership to secure our heritage for the benefit of future generations.

Our cathedrals are among our national glories. We therefore launched the Cathedral Repair Grant Scheme in April 1991, providing £11.5 million over three years.

We have increased, to £12 million, the grant to the NHMF for the purchase of historic properties, objects and collections. The Government also provides help to private owners through English Heritage repair grants, and tax relief in return for commitments on upkeep and public access.

We want to preserve the special character of our old town and city centres. We will encourage councils to ensure that new developments are in character with the past; to maintain buildings of importance to the character of towns and cities; to limit unnecessary street furniture and signs; and to plant trees and preserve historic patterns and open spaces.

- The National Lottery will also provide funds for the preservation of our heritage.
- We will continue to provide substantial financial assistance for the protection and preservation of the heritage.
- Together with the heritage agencies, we will work to make heritage sites accessible to the public.

Broadcasting

We are proud of our record of extending choice, encouraging new producers and maintaining high standards in broadcasting. We opened the way to the setting-up of Channel 4, independent radio, satellite television and multi-channel cable TV networks. The 1990 Broadcasting Act means that three new independent radio services and a fifth television channel will be set up during the next Parliament.

Over two million homes already receive satellite TV. We have now licensed well over a hundred cable TV networks and this new industry expects to invest £3,000 million over the next five years. In coming years, British viewers will have an increasing choice of channels and programmes. The new and sophisticated cable networks will open the way not only to new telecommunication services, but also to the spread of emerging technologies such as high definition television.

We attach great importance to the work of the Broadcasting Standards Council, which we set up under the 1990 Act. All television and radio companies accept the need to maintain standards of taste and decency in their treatment of sex and violence and their use of bad language.

The European Community regulates standards in satellite broadcasts originating from each Member State. We were one of the first countries to ratify a new Council of Europe convention applying similar rules to all its Member States. We also, in the Broadcasting Act, brought in sanctions against the transmission of offensive satellite broadcasts from abroad, and made it an offence for advertisers and equipment suppliers to support such programmes.

Independent television producers are benefiting from the requirement put on the BBC and ITV to commission a quarter of all their programmes, excluding the news, from outsiders. There are now great opportunities for independent producers to sell their programmes to new television channels and international markets, and there is much greater choice for viewers as a result.

In 1996, the BBC's Charter comes up for renewal. This will be considered against the background of the much more varied and competitive broadcasting environment which our policies have created. It is important that there should be a wide public debate about the future direction the BBC should take.

- We will back the work of the Broadcasting Standards Council and remain vigilant about ensuring high standards in satellite broadcasts from abroad.
- We will publish a discussion paper on the future of the BBC, recognising its special responsibilities for providing public service broadcasting.

A United Kingdom

The United Kingdom is far greater than the sum of its parts. Over many centuries its nations have worked, and frequently fought, side by side. Together, we have made a unique mark on history Together, we hold a special place in international affairs. To break up the Union now would diminish our influence for good in the world, just at the time when it is most needed.

Nationalist plans for independence are a recipe for weakness and isolation. Higher taxes and political uncertainty would deter investment and destroy jobs. The costly Labour and Liberal devolution proposals for Scotland and Wales have the same drawbacks. They do not intend to bring about separation, but run that risk. They could feed, but not resolve, grievances that arise in different parts of Britain. They would deprive Scotland and Wales of their rightful seats in the United Kingdom Cabinet, seats the Conservatives are determined to preserve. We believe strongly that we should go on working together in full partnership in a Union that has served every part of the United Kingdom well.

The plans for devolution put forward by the other parties would have a grave impact not just on Scotland and Wales, but also on England. They propose new and costly regional assemblies in England, for which there is no demand. We will oppose all such unnecessary layers of government.

The Union has brought us strength both economically and politically. Yet it has preserved the historic and cultural diversity of our islands. Our constitution is flexible, fair and tolerant. It has made this country one of the best places in which to live, work and bring up our children. These benefits cannot be tossed away lightly We will fight to preserve the Union, a promise which only the Conservatives can give at this election.

Scotland

Scotland has achieved an economic and cultural regeneration over the past 13 years. The Scottish economy has responded vigorously to the policies we have introduced to liberate enterprise, and many more people are now saving, investing and owning their homes. The public services are better funded and more efficient. There has been a flowering of Scottish culture.

Scotland enjoys a rich and distinct tradition and her own institutions, which we have preserved and strengthened. Scotland has its own framework for the encouragement of enterprise, investment and training; its own education system which continues to excel, with more pupils leaving school better qualified and more going on to further and higher education; its own health budgets which deliver high standards of care; and its own glorious inheritance of buildings and countryside.

A separate Manifesto for Scotland sets out our record in detail and our proposals for building on these achievements. In this document, therefore, we list only a selection.

- Business in Scotland has received a boost from our creation of Scottish Enterprise and the Local Enterprise Companies. We have formed Scottish Trade International to help our exporters, as Locate in Scotland does for inward investors. To assist business further, we will complete the harmonisation of business rates in Scotland with those in the rest of the country.

- The massive bureaucracies and layers of local government have few supporters in Scotland. We will continue to press local authorities to provide the value for money and the quality of services that people expect. We will press ahead with the reform of the current burdensome system of local government by introducing single tier councils throughout Scotland.
- We will continue to strengthen Scotland's education system for the benefit of parents, pupils and teachers. We will respond to the proposals of the Howie Committee to ensure that upper secondary education matches the best in Europe. We will continue to increase the number of places in higher and further education and will complete our reforms of the system.
- We will extend our reforms to improve NHS patient care in Scotland. Scotland has led the way in setting limits to waiting-times for operations and will now be reducing these further.
- We are creating a new body, Scottish Natural Heritage, with overall responsibility for conserving the natural environment. We will go further, and will create a Scottish Environmental Protection Agency to bring together powers to ensure the quality of our air, rivers and bathing waters.

Wales

Since 1979, the economy of Wales has changed spectacularly With only 5 per cent of the United Kingdom's population, Wales has consistently enjoyed 20 per cent of its inward investment. New industries have sprung up. Self-employment has risen by two-thirds. Welsh manufacturing now has the highest productivity of any part in the United Kingdom.

Land made derelict by old industries has been reclaimed on a massive scale. The Cardiff Bay development and the Ebbw Vale Garden Festival are outstanding examples, together with the Programme for the Valleys.

Since 1979, we have spent more than £3,000 million on roads in Wales. Spending on health has increased by 60 per cent in real terms since 1979. We have spent more than £5 million on our radical Waiting Times Initiative, leading to the treatment of 35,000 extra patients. In school we are spending nearly half as much again, in real terms per pupil, as in 1979. And there has been an enormous expansion in the training budget.

More Welsh homes – 72 per cent – are owned by those who live in them than in the United Kingdom as a whole. Since the 'Right to Buy' was introduced in 1980, we have enabled almost 90,000 council and housing association tenants to buy their own homes.

A separate Manifesto, in both English and Welsh, sets out our full programme for building on these achievements for Wales.

- We will set up a Welsh Economic Council to bring together the various bodies with interests in inward investment, tourism and small business to advise the Secretary of State.
- We aim to remove all significant dereliction from Wales by the end of the new Parliament.
- We will promote the work of the Countryside Council for Wales, in order to protect the countryside and those who earn their livelihood there.

- We will give further resources to our Rural Initiative. And we will continue to support hill farmers through the Hill Livestock Compensatory Allowances.
- We will continue to invest heavily in road improvements, including the second Severn Bridge, completing the M4 in South Wales and the M5 in North Wales.
- We will continue with our record hospital building programme.
- We will continue to offer generous funding for Housing for Wales and concentrate our efforts on the special needs of rural Wales. All major publicly funded housing developments will make adequate provision for the less well off.
- We will introduce a new Welsh Language Act.
- We will publish a White Paper on local government reform this autumn with a view to establishing unitary authorities, based on the historic counties and county boroughs. We will ensure a full role for Community Councils under these arrangements.

Northern Ireland

We have upheld our pledge that Northern Ireland will remain an integral part of the United Kingdom in accordance with the democratically expressed wishes of the majority of the people who live there. It is a pledge that only the Conservative and Unionist Party can give. Conservative candidates are standing in our name and in that cause.

Our overriding objective in Northern Ireland is to eliminate the evil of terrorism. This requires progress in four areas: security, economic, social and political. The security forces in Northern Ireland perform their duties with courage and professionalism. They are entitled to expect all the necessary encouragement, and legal and material support from the Government. Under the Conservatives, the strength of the RUC has been increased, while the Emergency Provisions Act 1991 contains new powers to combat terrorist funding.

Northern Ireland is sharing in the economic transformation of the United Kingdom as a result of Conservative policies. Belfast is attracting significant new private investment. Harland and Wolff and Shorts have been successfully privatised. Major work is also under way to regenerate Londonderry and many of Ulster's smaller towns. We will continue to pursue policies to encourage enterprise and bring new jobs – by contrast with Labour, whose plan for a national minimum wage would hit the Province particularly hard.

In the new Parliament we will continue to seek to re-establish stable institutions of Government in Northern Ireland, so that powers currently exercised by Ministers in the Northern Ireland Office can be returned to locally-elected politicians.

- We will always give the security forces our full backing within the rule of the law, and – against Labour opposition – ensure that they have the special powers they need to protect the whole community from violence.
- We will complete the privatisation of Northern Ireland Electricity, transfer the water and sewage services to the private sector, and examine ways of bringing private sector skills into the management of Northern Ireland Railways.
- We will continue to pursue policies designed to alleviate social needs, to promote

equity of treatment and to widen the sense of common purpose which is growing in the Province.

- We will build on the close security co-operation that has been established with the Republic of Ireland under the Anglo-Irish Agreement.
- We will continue to work strenuously for a political agreement which is acceptable to all the parties involved in the talks which the Secretary of State has had during the past year with the main constitutional parties in Northern Ireland and the Government of the Republic of Ireland. They have provided a firm basis for political progress in Ulster, and for building new relationships both between Northern Ireland and the Republic, and in these islands as a whole.

Your choice at this election

This Election is about the future. Your future. Britain's future. Our future role in the world. This is a time to go forward with conviction and confidence, not to go back to the failure and bitter controversies of the past.

It is difficult to remember the Britain we were elected to transform in 1979. The country we did transform. It was a depressed and divided country, accustomed to failure and suspicious of change.

During the succeeding Parliaments, we have curbed inflation, reformed trade union law; encouraged enterprise, cut taxes, modernised our education and training, improved the management of our health service, given more help to the needy, extended ownership, helped through our vigilance to end the Cold War, widened our influence in Europe, and earned the respect of the world.

A decade of success ended with the problems of recession – a world recession. We know how tough it has been for many but we are poised to move forward again, lacking only the spark of confidence with which a Conservative victory would ignite recovery.

The challenge ahead

The challenges of the 1990s demand a responsible and sure-footed government which understands the nature of the achievements of the 1980s and is ready to build successfully on them. A government committed to the principles of choice, ownership, responsibility and opportunity; committed to low inflation and low taxes; committed to better quality and value in our public services; committed to strong defences. Labour cannot provide that leadership. They lack experience, principle and vision.

With Socialism everywhere in rout or retreat, it is unclear what the Labour Party stands for. For public consumption, Labour leaders purport to have jettisoned the principles of a life-time. But how much can they be trusted? How genuine is the conversion and what do they actually believe?

It is clear only that Labour would threaten our achievements, undo our reforms and hamstring Britain. They would turn the clock back to policies that impoverished and divided our country. Socialism here and abroad is the regret of yesterday not the hope of tomorrow.

Only the best for Britain

We believe that only the best is good enough for Britain, and that the best will only be accomplished if we give the British people the freedom and the opportunity they need to succeed.

We have a new leader, proven in office, and a new agenda – yet a tried set of principles. Those principles reflect our conviction that Britain has done best when the people of Britain have been given the personal incentive to succeed. National success has not been primarily the result of accidents of geography, landscape and natural resources. Nor has it been the result of government action and state control. Success has been won when we have given our people their head: when their natural skills, talents, energy; thrift and inventiveness have been released, not suppressed. That was true when this century began; it is still true as this century draws to its close.

Britain should approach the Millennium with head and spirits high, with a strong economy, with a high standard of living, with generously endowed and well managed public services, and with secure defences. We want Britain to be an example to the world of how a free people can make the very best of their destiny. That prospect is within the grasp of us all. We must now make it happen.

The prize is great, the hope invigorating, the dream attainable. We want, with you, to make the dream a reality. A Conservative Government will help you to achieve the very best. The very best future for Britain.

YOU CAN ONLY BE SURE WITH THE CONSERVATIVES

THE CONSERVATIVE MANIFESTO 1997

CONSERVATIVE PARTY GENERAL ELECTION MANIFESTO 1997

You can only be sure with the Conservatives

Date of Election	Thursday 1 May
Party Leader	John Major
Candidates	650
MPs	165
Votes	9,600,943
% of vote	30.7%

Foreword

The Conservative administrations elected since 1979 are among the most successful in British peacetime history. A country once the sick man of Europe, has become its most successful economy. A country once brought to its knees by overmighty powerful trade unions, now has industrial peace. Abroad, the cold war has been won; at home, the rule of law has been restored. The enterprising virtues of the British people have been liberated from the dead hand of the state. There can be no doubt that we have created a better Britain.

Why, then, do we still need a Conservative Government? Because resting on what we have achieved is not enough. To stand still is to fall back. Our goal must be for Britain to be the best place in the world to live. We live in a tougher, more uncertain world. A fast-moving global free market is emerging. New economic powers are rising in the East. Family life and social attitudes are changing. Europe is adjusting to the end of communism. The European social model is failing. The nation state is under threat. We must respond to these challenges. We have turned around our economic fortunes. We have fewer people out of work and more in work than any other major European economy. British people now have the opportunity of a prosperous future. But that prosperity cannot be taken for granted. We have to compete to win. That means a constant fight to keep tight control over public spending and enable Britain to remain the lowest taxed major economy in Europe. It means a continuing fight to keep burdens off business, maintaining our opt-out of the European Social Chapter. If we relax for one moment, our hard won success will slip away again.

We have strengthened choice and personal ownership for families, and rolled back the state from areas where it was interfering unnecessarily in our lives. But we now have the opportunity to achieve a massive expansion in wealth and ownership so that more families can enjoy the self-respect and independence that come with being self-sufficient from the state. Our far-reaching proposals for personal pension funds are central to achieving this – so too are our plans to increase support for the family in our tax system.

Our aim is to spread opportunity for all to succeed, whoever they are and wherever they come from, provided they are prepared to work hard. To turn the 'have nots' into the 'haves'. To support the family in providing security and stability. We have modernised and reformed many of the areas where the state still has a vital role. But we now have to build on these reforms to deliver even better services. We must continue providing the resources to invest in our modernised health service. We can now provide parents with a hard-edged guarantee of standards in schools. We need also to widen choice in areas where state bureaucracy has constrained it. We have pioneered new ways of building partnerships that engage the private sector in areas previously dependent on the public purse. We now need to capture private sector investment on a massive scale to regenerate our cities, transform our crumbling local authority housing estates and modernise other public assets.

The only way to secure this future of opportunity is to stick with the Conservative programme of continuing reform. Now would be the worst possible moment to abandon the pathway to prosperity on which we are set. We must keep up the momentum. At the same time we must maintain the security that a stable nation provides in an uncertain, fast-changing world. We must protect our constitution and unity as a nation from those who threaten it with unnecessary and dangerous change. And we must stand up for our interests in shaping a free-market Europe of sovereign nation states.

There is, of course, an alternative on offer: to load costs on business while calling it 'stakeholding'; to increase the role of the state, while calling it 'the community'; to succumb to a centralised Europe while calling it 'not being isolated'; to break up our country while calling it 'devolution'. To risk this alternative would be a disaster for our country. We have come a very long way. We must be sure that we do not throw away what we have gained, or lose the opportunities we have earned. You can only be sure with the Conservatives.

John Major

Our vision for Britain: the Enterprise Centre of Europe

A choice of two futures: the Enterprise Centre of Europe

Our record – enterprise

- The UK is on course to grow faster than both France and Germany for the sixth successive year in 1998 – a post-war record.
- Inflation has now been below 4% for well over 4 years, the longest period of low inflation for over half a century.
- Mortgage rates are at their lowest levels for 30 years.
- Unemployment has fallen to its lowest level for 6 years. We now have a lower unemployment rate than any other major European economy. Youth unemployment in Britain has fallen to less than 15% whereas by contrast, in France it has risen to 27% and in Italy to 33%.
- A higher proportion of our people are in work than in any other major European economy – 68% against a Continental average of 57%.

- The UK is the favourite location for inward investment into Europe, attracting around one third of inward investment into the European Union.
- We have the lowest tax burden of any major European economy, with the government taking almost 8% less of national income than the European average.
- Public borrowing has averaged 3.4% of GDP since 1979 compared with 6.8% (and a peak of 9.5%) under the last Labour Government. Our level of public debt is now one of the lowest in the European Union – whereas it was one of the highest in 1979.
- In 1994 the UK lost 300,000 working days through strikes, the lowest figure ever recorded; in 1979 the figure was 29,500,000: nearly 100 times that figure.
- Britain ranks fifth in the world in international trade, and exports more per head than America or Japan. Exports account for 28% of GDP as against 9% for Japan, 11% for USA and 24% for Germany and France. Britain's current account is broadly in balance, reflecting our increased competitiveness and improved trading.

1. Doubling living standards

The free market is winning the battle of ideas the world over. From Russia to Vietnam, from China to Romania, people are realising that the socialist model has failed. This is not just an economic triumph. It is a triumph for human freedom. Britain helped to secure it. We should take pride in it. The spread of the free market heralds a new age of global competition. That means new markets for British goods and services, but new competitors for British companies as well. If we try to protect ourselves from these challenges with more regulations, public subsidies and a cosy dependence on government then Britain will fail. But if we boldly embrace these new opportunities by pushing forward the economic revolution we began in 1979, then we will enter the next millennium with boundless prospects for growth and prosperity. That choice – between stagnation and dynamism – is the choice which faces Britain at this election.

It is a stark choice between the British way – of trusting the people and unleashing enterprise – and the failing social model, practised on the continent, which the Labour Party wants to impose on us here under the guise of 'stakeholding'. Hard economic evidence shows how great is the divide between these two strategies. Britain is now in its fifth year of growing faster than France or Germany. Unemployment in Britain has fallen to less than two million, while it rises across Europe. Britain attracts nearly forty per cent of all the American and Japanese investment in Europe. Our aim now is to safeguard these achievements and build on them, so Britain becomes the unrivalled Enterprise Centre of Europe.

A low tax economy

For enterprise to flourish, the state must get out of the way of the wealth creators. We are the only party that can cut taxes because we are the only party which is serious about controlling public spending.

The choice between the two economic philosophies is clear. In the years before 1979, public spending in Britain kept pace with the average for Europe as a whole. Since then, it has continued rising on the Continent, while we have restrained public spending here. Now, public spending takes about 40% of our national income as against an average of 50% on the continent. We have broken free from a trend in which the rest of

Europe is still trapped. Conservative government will keep public spending under tight control and ensure that it grows by less than the economy as a whole over the economic cycle. At the same time we will continue to spend more on the services which matter most to people – hospitals, schools and the police.

Over the next parliament, we will achieve our goal for the government to spend less than 40% of our national income. That means we can reduce the amount government borrows too, and meet our aim of moving towards a balanced budget in the medium term. Our plans show how we can virtually eliminate public borrowing by the year 2000.

Thanks to our success in controlling public spending, Britain is now Europe's low tax economy. This is one of the reasons why we are becoming the Enterprise Centre of Europe. Our aim is to ensure Britain keeps the lowest tax burden of any major European economy. In the election manifesto of 1992, we promised that 'We will make further progress towards a basic income tax rate of 20p'. Since then, we have cut the basic rate of income tax from 25p to 23p, and extended the 20p band so that over a quarter of all taxpayers now only pay income tax at the 20p rate.

Achieving our public expenditure goals will mean we can sustain permanently low tax levels. Over the next parliament, our aim will be to achieve our target of a 20p basic rate of income tax, while maintaining a maximum tax rate of no more than 40p.

Stable Prices

Inflation has to be kept firmly under control for an economy to thrive. Britain is now enjoying the longest period of stable prices for almost fifty years. We are on target to reach our goal of 2½% inflation this year. Low inflation has delivered lower interest rates whilst preserving the value of people's savings. Homeowners are now enjoying mortgage rates at the lowest levels for 30 years. It has taken tough decisions to break free from our reputation as a high inflation economy. No Conservative government will jeopardise this achievement. During the next parliament, we will maintain an inflation target of 2½% or less.

Rising living standards

The only secure base for rising living standards is a strongly growing economy, low levels of public spending and taxation, and stable prices. That is exactly what Britain is achieving. People are reaping the rewards of their hard work as their take home pay increases. Between 1974 and 1979, the take home pay for a family on average earnings rose, in real terms, by just £1 a week in today's prices. Since 1979 it has increased by £100 a week and; this year alone it will increase by £7 a week.

The goal which we set ourselves in 1995 is to double living standards over 25 years. We are on course to achieve our goal.

2. Jobs and business

Our priority is to create jobs. This is not just an economic priority, but also a social and moral one. Jobs and enterprise are the best ways of tackling poverty and deprivation. Britain is succeeding. 900,000 jobs have been created over the past 4 years. By contrast the European social model is stifling job creation on the continent by imposing regulations and burdens on business. In the United Kingdom unemployment is much lower than in the rest of Europe and falling, whereas in Germany, France, and Italy it has risen to its highest level for a generation. This is no accident. It is because we have pursued very different policies from those on the Continent.

Curbing the power of trade unions, opening up markets and cutting red tape, have given us a low strike, low cost economy: and as a result we are the number one location for foreign investment in Europe. Never have such policies been so important. For the first time this century we face a world full of capitalist competition. The only way Britain will be able to compete and win in world markets is by sticking to the Conservative policies that are delivering success. We can earn prosperity as one of the world's most successful global trading nations. We should not risk this progress by adopting the very policies that have made the Continent uncompetitive and have increased unemployment in Europe by 4.5 million over the past 5 years.

Small businesses – Britain's risk-takers

Governments do not create jobs. Businesses do. The source of tomorrow's jobs will be small businesses, the seedcorn of Britain's prosperity. Over the last 15 years, small businesses have created over 2 million jobs. By the year 2000, over half the workforce should be working in companies which employ fewer than 50 people. Back in 1979 only a third of the workforce did.

Entrepreneurs often risk everything when they set up their own business. We have already helped them: raising the VAT threshold, cutting employer's National Insurance contributions, simplifying audit requirements and much more besides. Now we intend to go further, tackling the remaining problems they face.

High taxes and rates deter enterprise. Our low tax structure has been crucial to our industrial revival. We already have the lowest corporation tax of any major industrialised country. As we want small businesses to flourish, we will go even further. We will cut the small companies rate of corporation tax in line with personal taxation as we move towards a 20p basic rate. Investment and enterprise are deterred if the tax man takes too much of the capital that is built up by a successful business. Capital is ever more mobile, flying around the world to places where the tax on it is low: Britain must be one of those places. We will continue to reduce the burden of capital gains tax and inheritance tax as it is prudent to do so.

One of the heaviest burdens small businesses face is business rates. At the moment, this bears more heavily upon small businesses than large ones. In the next parliament, we will reform business rates to reduce the cost that falls upon small businesses. No businessman has time to fill out reams of forms. We will continue to simplify the administration of NICs and PAYE for small firms, allowing them to concentrate on satisfying customers not bureaucrats. We are also tackling a problem that hits small businesses particularly hard – the late payment of bills. On top of our programme to ensure government departments and local authorities pay on time we have legislated to require companies to publish their payment policy and to report their record on how quickly they pay their bills to small businesses. We have already abolished over a thousand regulations. New regulations must only be introduced if it is clear that their benefits exceed their costs and they do not place an undue burden on a small firm. We will introduce 'sunset' requirements into new regulations whenever it is suitable so that they are automatically reviewed or dropped after a specific period.

Many businessmen suffer regulatory burdens imposed by local government and quangos. We will therefore insist that the whole of the public sector adopts the same stringent rules that we require of central government in justifying the benefits of new regulations against their costs.

Reducing the burden on companies

Jobs depend on British firms winning orders: the difference between success or failure can be wafer thin. Any extra burden on business will destroy jobs. Britain is enjoying more jobs and record investment, thanks to the competitive edge we have over other European countries. We are a low cost economy. But that does not mean we are a low pay economy.

Our competitive advantage comes from the lower costs facing our businesses. It can be measured by the social costs an employer has to pay on top of every £100 of wages: in Germany it is £31, in France £41, but in Britain, it is only £15.

Many countries in Europe have tried to cocoon themselves from global competition behind layers of red tape and regulation – such as the Social Chapter and a national minimum wage. This provides a false sense of security, playing a cruel trick on working people. It also excludes the unemployed from work. As companies in the rest of Europe have grown more uncompetitive, employers have found it too expensive to employ new workers, investment has gone elsewhere, and the dole queues have lengthened. The European social model is not social and not a model for us to follow. But if Britain signed up to the Social Chapter it would be used to impose that model on us – destroying British jobs. No Conservative government will sign up to the Social Chapter or introduce a national minimum wage. We will insist at the Intergovernmental Conference in Amsterdam that our opt out is honoured and that Britain is exempted from the Working Time Directive: if old agreements are broken, we do not see how new ones can be made.

We will resist the imposition of other social burdens on the work place through a new European employment chapter.

Welfare into work

Although governments cannot create jobs, they can help people train and find work. We now have in place a battery of schemes working with Training and Enterprise Councils to provide targeted help and training, including remedial education in literacy and numeracy. We are also developing new incentives, alongside Family Credit, to help people move off benefit into work. We will always help those in genuine need: in return, the unemployed have a responsibility to look for work and accept a reasonable offer. That belief underpins our new Jobseekers Allowance which ensures that no-one can refuse reasonable work opportunities and remain on benefit.

As unemployment falls, we want to focus on those who have been unemployed for some time. At present, Project Work is helping 100,000 people who have been unemployed for more than 2 years in cities around Britain. They are first given help in finding a job – which includes giving employers incentives to take them on. Those who do not find jobs are then required to work for a specific period on a community project.

This helps them regain work habits and ensures they are available for work. As Project Work succeeds and demonstrates that its costs can be met by the savings from getting people into work, we will extend the programme to cover the long-term unemployed nationwide. We will also develop an innovative 'Britain Works' scheme which uses the experience and ingenuity of private and voluntary sectors to get people off welfare into work.

Britain has one of the most mobile economies in Europe. People move on and up, into better paid jobs more easily than on the Continent.

The information society

Britain is at the forefront of creating tomorrow's information society. Already we have exposed domestic telecommunications to competition and stimulated investment in cable and satellite entertainment systems. And by opening up international telecommunications we will continue to encourage companies worldwide to base their global operations here.

- We will make sure that the digital revolution comes to Britain first.
- We are launching an ambitious programme with industry to spread 'IT for All', giving every adult the opportunity to try out and learn about new IT services.
- We will work with industry to ensure that all schools are connected to the information superhighway.
- We will use the Millennium Lottery Fund to transform the computer facilities and information links available in schools, libraries, museums, voluntary organisations and other public places after the turn of the century. This will give the public much wider access to information services in the years ahead.
- We will also take advantage of information technology to transform the way government provides services to the public.
- We will keep Britain in the vanguard of new mobile service development – including mobile telephone and information services – by introducing a pricing system for the radio spectrum to achieve more efficient allocation of radio frequencies.
- We will maintain a strong, free and competitive broadcasting and press environment at both national and local level, while continuing to be vigilant in monitoring whether action is needed to curb breaches of standards, and prevent unacceptable press intrusion.

Science

British science enjoys a worldwide reputation for excellence and cost-effectiveness, which makes Britain an attractive base for many domestic and overseas companies.

We will continue to invest in science and target funds at basic research, which would not otherwise be funded by industry. At the same time we will provide an enterprising environment which encourages firms to invest with confidence in applied science.

2020 Vision

There is no part of the globe which has not been reached by British enterprise and British culture. We have always looked out beyond these shores, beyond this Continent.

Our language, our heritage of international trading links, our foreign investments – second only to America's – are historic strengths which mean we are ideally placed to seize the opportunities of the global economy.

Thanks to Conservative policies of liberalisation and privatisation we are strong in industries of the future such as telecommunications, financial services, and information technology. These are the industries that will benefit from opening up trade around the world. We will push for completion of the European Single Market and continue to pursue the objective of transatlantic free trade against the background of world trade liberalisation. Our aim is nothing less than tariff-free trade across the globe by the year 2020.

Free competition is important for free markets. Companies should not make agreements that restrict competition and hence result in poor value for consumers. We have set out proposals to give companies greater protection against price fixing, dumping, and other restrictive practices by larger competitors. We will introduce a Competition Bill to take forward these proposals in the first session of the next parliament. We are committed to pushing forward our competitiveness agenda which is making Britain the Enterprise Centre of Europe.

OPPORTUNITY AND OWNERSHIP FOR INDIVIDUALS AND FAMILIES

Our record: opportunity

- The right to buy has allowed 1.5 million council tenants to become homeowners. There are over 4 million more homeowners today than in 1979.
- The Government has spent £6 billion through housing associations to provide homes for rent. Between 1992 and 1995 housing associations provided 178,000 new lettings – 25,000 more than promised in the 1992 Manifesto.
- There are now around 10 million private shareholders, up from about 3 million at the time of the last Labour government. 2.5 million people now have tax-free savings in PEP accounts, and 4.5 million in TESSAs.
- Since 1979, the success of private pension provision has raised the average income of pensioners by 60% more than inflation. Almost 90% of recently retired pensioners now have incomes over and above state benefits.
- Savings in private pension funds have increased to £650 billion – more than 4 times the level in 1979. Their value is greater than the pension funds in all other EU countries added together.
- Over the period 1979 to 1995, education spending per pupil rose from £515 to £1,890 – an increase in real terms of 48%. Real spending on books and equipment per pupil rose 56%. Teachers' real pay rose 57%: from £270 per week in 1979 to £420 in 1995.
- In 1979, 40% of three and four year olds attended nursery school; in 1995 the figure was 59%. Our nursery vouchers now give this opportunity to every child.
- The proportion of sixteen year olds staying on in full-time education rose from 4 out of 10 in 1979 to 7 out of 10 in 1995.
- Almost 1 in 3 young people now go to university, compared with 1 in 8 in 1979.
- The proportion of adults with no academic qualifications has halved since 1979

and the proportion of adults with a degree or equivalent has more than doubled rising from 5% to 12%.

3. Choice and security for families

The family is the most important institution in our lives. It offers security and stability in a fast-changing world. But the family is undermined if governments take decisions which families ought to take for themselves. Self-reliance underpins freedom and choice. Families are stronger if they have the money to look after themselves: that is why we are shifting power and wealth back to working families and away from the state.

We have already achieved much – the average family's disposable income has gone up by 40% since 1979. But we want to go further. The next Conservative government intends to reform the tax system so that it gives substantially more help to families. We also want to encourage people to save so they have the security and self-respect that comes from being able to rely on their own resources rather than immediately turning to the state. We have already made much progress here too with widening ownership of homes, pensions, and the new PEPs and TESSAs. We now propose further radical measures for more saving for retirement.

Families and tax

We believe families should be left with as much of their own money as possible. They know better than politicians how to spend it. We have already cut the basic rate of income tax from 33p to 23p, and our aim is to get it down to 20p, benefiting 18 million taxpayers. We intend to do even more to help families in particular. At the moment, if one spouse does not take paid work in order to look after children or dependent relatives, they not only give up earnings but may also be unable to benefit from their personal tax allowance. Yet this is the time at which their income is often most stretched. We believe our tax system should recognise and support the crucial role of families in their caring responsibilities. We will give them that support. We will give priority to future reductions in personal taxation that help families looking after dependent children or relatives by allowing one partner's unused personal allowance to be transferred to a working spouse where they have these responsibilities. This will provide a targeted reduction in the tax bill to those families who need it most. Around 2 million one taxpayer couples with dependent children, or looking after elderly relatives and others needing care, would gain up to £17.50 a week – around £900 a year.

Family savings

In the old days people just depended on the weekly pay packet or money from the state. But no job can be secure and the state cannot provide for every eventuality. It is ownership which brings true security and genuine independence from the state. That is why Conservatives have long dreamed of a property-owning democracy. Now we are delivering it in practice. Home ownership is up by 4.7 million. 10 million people own a direct personal stake in our economy. 16 million are gaining shares in their building societies thanks to our deregulation of them. We intend to carry forward our vision of a people's share. This is a significant increase in personal security. It is the Conservative vision of security through personal savings – not a socialist vision of security through the state.

We want people to enjoy Britain's success – especially by owning shares in the companies for which they work. We have already introduced a number of schemes to encourage employee share ownership. To encourage a further expansion of worker shares, our new Share Match Scheme will allow employees to be rewarded with additional free shares if they acquire a stake in their company. Our goal is that by 2000, more than half of the employees of Britain's larger companies will own shares in those companies.

4½ million people now benefit from tax-free TESSAs and 2.5 million from PEP schemes to encourage the accumulation of long-term saving. We will continue to build on this success by exploring ways in which existing tax exemptions for savings can be developed – allowing individuals to secure their futures and protect their families against unexpected contingencies. We will continue to raise the threshold for inheritance tax as it prudent to do so.

People are not just saving for themselves but for their children and grand-children. These savings should not be penalised by the tax system. For many people their biggest asset is their pension. Thanks to the steps we have already taken to encourage occupational and personal pensions, we now have £650 billion invested in private pensions – more than the rest of the European Union put together. We now plan to build further on this achievement. We will make it easier for small employers to set up personal pension plans for groups of employees. We will create more flexibility for people who save in personal pension plans to continue investing in those schemes if they subsequently move to jobs with company pension schemes. We will also create flexibility for employees with savings in Additional Voluntary Contributions (AVC) schemes to take part of that pension earlier or later than their main company pension. But we believe the time has now come to plan for another important step in improving Britain's pension provision. Britain is already much better placed than many other countries to afford state pensions in the future, but we want even more people to be able to look forward to a properly funded pension that grows with the economy and is free from dependence on taxes paid by future generations.

We now propose a practical way of achieving a gradual transformation of the state pension scheme. At the start of the next parliament we will set out proposals to provide all young people entering the workforce with a personal pension fund paid for through a rebate on their National Insurance contributions. At retirement they would be entitled to the full pension earned by this accumulated investment. This could give them a pension significantly higher than they would currently receive from the state. But they would be guaranteed a pension at least equal to the current basic state pension, increased in line with inflation. This will be one of the most significant improvements in the state pension system since it was introduced. Older people currently in the workforce would be unaffected – they will continue to contribute as now and receive the normal state pension when they retire. This policy would come into effect early in the new millennium. Gradual phasing in of the new system over 40 years will make the impact on public finances affordable. Even at its peak, the net revenue forgone will be only a fraction of the savings from the recent Pensions Act. And eventually, the new policy will produce massive public expenditure savings. This far-sighted idea is in the best Conservative tradition. The growing wealth of the nation will provide for the next generation through private funding, underpinned by a state guarantee. British people will be able to look forward to retirement with even greater confidence. And our young people will have a pensions opportunity unrivalled in the world.

Support for families

Conservatives believe that a healthy society encourages people to accept responsibility for their own lives. A heavy-handed and intrusive state can do enormous damage. Some families need help to cope with their responsibilities. For them, Social Services play a vital role. They help with children where parental care has failed. They deliver an ever wider range of services to people with learning difficulties or who are mentally ill. Our community care reforms have given them a central role ensuring that elderly people get care of the highest quality: and in their own homes where possible. We need to ensure that role is properly fulfilled.

Early in the next Parliament we will introduce a Social Services Reform Bill which will create a new statutory framework for social services. The Bill will provide for greater openness and accountability in social services. We will provide new guidance to ensure social workers properly reflect the values of the community – focusing their efforts on those families who most need support, and minimising unnecessary interference. Social workers working with children will receive special training to cope with the often heart-rending cases they face. We will raise standards through a new regulatory framework which will apply the same standards in both the public and private sector. We will also remove the power of local authorities to operate care homes where this is in the best interests of the people for whom they are responsible.

We believe that families who use social services should be able to exercise choice wherever practicable. We have given cash payments to disabled people to purchase the services they need directly. We also want new ways of reinforcing individual choice where possible. We will therefore ensure no barriers stand in the way of local authorities wanting to issue their users with vouchers to buy certain services. We will review the direct payment scheme, and provided it has been cost effective, we will extend it to other users of social services. Above all, we want to help families to help themselves.

Caring for older – or disabled – relatives is one of the most natural human instincts. We recognise the crucial – and often demanding – role carers play, and will help them more. We will introduce a Respite Care Programme. This will enable family members with heavy responsibilities caring for a relative to take a much needed break. We will also offer more practical advice for carers who want to go back to paid work. But in some cases, elderly people need more care than their friends or relatives can provide. Financing long-term care worries many families. We will create an imaginative, fair partnership between individuals and the public sector to resolve this problem. In the first session of the next Parliament we will implement our partnership scheme for long-term care, making it easier for people to afford the cost of care in old age without giving up their lifetime savings.

Good preparation for marriage can be an important aid to a successful family, while timely help in meeting difficulties can often avoid family breakdown. These are matters for voluntary effort, not the state, but we will continue to support such effort. We need to make sure efforts to help struggling families do not turn into unnecessary meddling. When the state goes too far, it is often the children who suffer. They become victims of the worst sort of political correctness. We will introduce legislation to remove unnecessary barriers to adoption and introduce new rules to make adoption from abroad more straightforward. We will also monitor the workings of the Children Act, and act if necessary to ensure it maintains a proper balance between the rights of children and the responsibilities of adults.

Social Services departments are now the fourth arm of the welfare state. Most people will need them at some point in their lives. We will ensure that the Conservative revolution in public services now reaches Social Services.

Disabled people

We have quadrupled real spending on long-term sick and disabled people since 1979, to £22 billion. We have introduced the Disability Discrimination Act. This is the first legislation of its kind anywhere in Europe and it provides positive proof of our commitment to disabled people. We will monitor it to ensure it continues to meet its objectives. We are also providing a continuing fund to support the most severely disabled people to stay in their homes.

Security in retirement

Pensioners continue to make a positive contribution to society in retirement. They give more of their time in charitable work than any other age group. They lift some of the pressures on their own families. They help keep our nation's history and traditions alive. They have paid their National Insurance contributions and taxes and rightly expect us to continue to protect the value of the basic state pension against price rises. We will do so. We will also ensure that less well off pensioners continue to get extra help on top of the basic pension. At the same time as protecting the state pension, our encouragement of private pensions is already transforming the living standards of pensioners. The average net income of pensioners has risen by 60% since 1979. This has been achieved by our encouragement of saving for retirement. The tax system must help pensioners who have saved. Our new lower 20p rate on income from savings directly helps 1.7 million pensioners and the special age allowances raise the point at which pensioners start to pay income tax.

A better Social Security system

People in need can rely on our continuing support. And to ensure that taxpayers are willing to go on paying for that support, we have shaped a social security system we can afford, taking a steadily declining share of our national income. We are doing this by focusing benefits on those most in need, helping people off welfare and into work, and curbing welfare fraud. These policies are underpinned by our measures to help families help themselves. Social Security must be there to help families, pensioners and people in need. We will protect the value of Child Benefit and Family Credit which help with the cost of bringing up children. This is our Family Benefits Guarantee.

- We will bring the structure of benefits for lone parents into line with that for two-parent families.

- We will continue to help lone parents obtain maintenance, and assist with childcare in work: both these measures help lone parents obtain work.
- We will pilot our 'Parent Plus' Scheme that gives special help to lone parents who want to work, and extend it as it proves successful.
- Social Security fraud must be stamped out.
- We will intensify our current initiatives of inspections and checks including more home visits, to crack down further on benefit cheats.
- We will introduce benefit cards across the country.
- We will establish a Benefit Fraud Inspectorate to monitor local authorities' performance.
- We will also improve the sharing of information between government departments to catch more fraudulent claims.
- To ensure as much of the Social Security budget as possible goes into benefits, we will continue to improve the efficiency of administration, using the best mix of public and private sector operations.

Housing

Owning one's own home is an aim shared by millions of people. Over the last 18 years, the number of homeowners has increased by 4.7 million – including 1.7 million who have bought their home under the right to buy scheme. Over the next 10 years, we expect to see about one and a half million people buying their own homes – some 3,000 every week. To meet that demand, we will continue to allow local authority and housing association tenants to buy their homes or move to houses which they buy. We will also carry through our draft Bill, creating the option for those buying flats to choose a new form of commonhold ownership.

For those who wish to rent their home, we are encouraging a thriving private rental market, building on the success of housing investment trusts and protecting assured tenancies. Easier renting will help us meet our target of reducing the proportion of empty homes below 3%.

The number of empty houses has fallen in each of the last 3 years. But nothing is more frustrating for people who need social housing than the sight of a suitable property owned by the public sector lying boarded up and empty. We will stop that. Public landlords will have to sell houses which are available for occupation yet have been left empty without a good reason for more than 12 months. Housing associations and housing companies will continue to receive help in building new homes, and we will encourage more public–private partnerships. Together, these policies will help meet the demand for new public housing and make sure that there are decent homes for those in need.

Opportunities for women

Women are succeeding in Britain. More women have jobs in Britain than in almost any other European country. Women have a better education, more financial independence and more opportunities than at any other time in Britain's history. This success reflects the efforts and determination of many women. Government's role has been simpler – to level up the playing field, whether in education, where girls are now doing better than boys, or in the workplace, where opportunities for women are the best in Europe.

But we know our job is not yet done. Some women still face barriers to doing well. Some still do not have the financial security they deserve. And crime, and the fear of crime, often affect women more than men.

We will ensure women have equal opportunities in education and the workplace. This can best be achieved by keeping our economy buoyant and our labour markets flexible. And our proposals to bring crime rates down further will help women especially. But many women – and some men – face a particular problem: how to juggle job and family. For those who need or want to work, we will seek further ways to minimise the barriers to affordable, high quality childcare. For those who wish to be full-time parents, our proposals to enable them to transfer their unused personal allowance to their spouse will be worth up to an extra £17.50 a week.

We also want to give women more financial independence, particularly when they retire. We propose, as explained elsewhere, to improve flexibility in saving for retirement and to allow courts to split pensions on divorce.

Looking outwards

The spread of share ownership, the transformation of pension provision, and the sale of council houses are revolutionising our nation. Personal prosperity and property ownership are not selfish or inward-looking. People who are secure at home can look out for others in their community. Over two thirds of adults engage in some form of voluntary activity. By the end of 1997 all young people aged between 15 and 25 who want to volunteer will be helped to find an opportunity to do so. We will encourage voluntary work by others living on benefit while continuing to insist that those who are capable of work should actively seek employment. We will also develop accreditation for voluntary work to encourage employers to see it as preparation for a paid job. We will make it easier for those receiving incapacity benefit to volunteer by removing the 16-hour weekly limit on their voluntary work. It is wrong to imagine that compassion must be nationalised and that we can only help our fellow man through state action.

4. Education and opportunity

All children dream of what they might do when they grow up. Our task is to help them turn those dreams into reality whatever their background may be.

It is an exciting world, full of new opportunities for inquiring minds: it should be open to every child. Their future – and Britain's prosperity – depend on the quality of their education.

Our education guarantee

A good education is the birthright of every child. Literacy is the building block of all future learning: English is the global language of commerce and, much more, a thing of beauty. Without basic science and mathematics, the modern world is incomprehensible. Every child therefore must be taught to read, write and add up from an early age. Years of mistaken, progressive education in the 1960s and 1970s denied these precious skills to too many children. We have worked ceaselessly since 1979 to put that right. Our decision to test children and publish the results has allowed standards to be measured and exposed. We have reformed the curriculum, toughened inspections, and given more information and power to parents. Our many excellent teachers now know what is expected of them, and already standards in schools are rising. But they are still not good enough. We must do more.

Building on what we have done, we can now offer a new pledge to parents – a guarantee of education standards.

- First, we will set national targets for school performance that reflect our objective of ensuring that Britain is in the top league of international standards across the whole spectrum of education.
- Second, we will require every school to plan how to improve its performance, and to set targets which relate to similar schools and national standards.
- Third, we will give all parents full information on the performance of their child's school.
- Fourth, to underwrite our pledge, we will ensure action is taken to bring any underperforming school up to the mark. We will meet this pledge by using the full set of levers for improved standards that we have put in place.

We are revising and simplifying the National Curriculum in primary schools to emphasise high standards in the basic skills. Parents and teachers must have an overview of not just how much a child has learnt while at school, but how the school performs against others. Poor schooling must not be protected by a veil of secrecy. Parent power is a vital force for higher standards. Regular tests and exams are essential if teachers are to discover how much their pupils have learnt, and parents are to know how much progress their children are making against national standards. That is why children are already being tested at 7, 11 and 14.

- We will publish all school test results, including the results of tests of 7 and 14 year olds.
- We propose also to assess every child at five. This will give teachers and parents a benchmark against which they can measure future progress. To give a better measure of pupils' performance, marks out of 100 will be made available to parents as well as the broad-brush levels.
- We will also introduce a new test for 14-year-old children that covers the whole National Curriculum – assessing progress before they choose subjects for GCSE.

Tests and exams need to be rigorous and demanding. We will insist that they establish children's command of spelling, punctuation, and grammar in English tests. Children will sit arithmetic tests without calculators. We will not allow such extensive use of open books in tests and in GCSE exams. We will establish an English Language GCSE. We will continue to uphold the gold standard of A levels, and ensure that the great classics of our literature are studied at A level. At the same time students should have the chance to study more subjects in the sixth form. Rigorous tests show how individual children and schools are performing and expose schools that are not giving children the education they deserve. To underwrite our guarantee, we will then take action to improve standards. We cannot tolerate schools that fail their pupils. By this summer every secondary school in the country will have been inspected by independent inspectors, and by summer 1998, every primary school will have been inspected as well. We have the power to take over failing schools directly and close them if necessary. We will now go further and require every school to set and publish regular targets and plans for improving their academic results. Independent inspectors will monitor the results of weaker schools and their plans for improvement at regular intervals.

Sometimes, though, schools are failing because the local education authority which runs them is failing. The authorities with the worst GCSE results and the worst results at Key Stage 2 (11 year olds) are run by Labour. Those children need our help. We will allow for an independent inspection of education authorities and intervene directly to raise standards where education authorities are letting children down. Failing authorities will be required to set out their plans to raise standards, and work with education teams – directed by independent inspectors – to implement those plans.

The vast majority of teachers do an outstanding job. They have played a key part in implementing the reforms that we have introduced. A few, though, fail their pupils. We will establish a more rigorous and effective system of appraising teachers, which reflects how well their pupils perform in tests and exams: this will identify which teachers need more help and, where necessary, which teachers need to be replaced. Many feel that the professional standing of teachers would be strengthened by the creation of a single body which could speak with authority on professional standards. We will consult with teachers and other interested parties about the possible role of such a body.

The school should be a place of stability and stimulation for children, especially if they come from a hostile or turbulent environment. To improve standards in future our new teacher training curriculum will stress traditional teaching methods – including whole class teaching and learning to read by the sounds of letters. We will also encourage more teachers to enter the profession through practical training schemes focused on classroom experience such as the Graduate Teacher Scheme.

A child is likely to learn more in a well-ordered school. Teachers must have the powers they need to maintain discipline. We will give teachers greater power to set detentions to exclude disruptive pupils and to use reasonable physical restraint where necessary. Schools also have an important role to play in spiritual and moral education. We will take steps to ensure that every school fulfils its role of providing religious education and collective worship.

Choice and diversity

When we came to power in 1979 the schools system was totally dominated by one type of school – the monolithic comprehensive. The system failed our children. It treated every child the same. It told parents where to send their children. It did not give schools the freedom to run their own affairs. Since 1979 we have created a rich diversity of schools, to serve the varied talents of all children and give parents choice within that diversity, because we believe that parents know what is best for their children. That is why we – and only we – are committed to giving the parent of every four-year-old child a voucher for nursery education so they can choose the pre-school education they want for their child, whether in a play-group, a reception class, or a nursery school in the private or state sector.

We will give more talented children, from less well-off backgrounds, the opportunity to go to fee-paying schools by expanding the Assisted Places Scheme to cover all ages of compulsory education, in line with our current spending plans. We propose to develop it further into a wider scholarship scheme covering additional educational opportunities.

The freedoms and status of fee-paying schools will be protected. Grant-maintained schools have been popular with parents across the country – whatever their politics. We will encourage more schools to become grant-maintained and will allow new grant-maintained schools to be set up where there is sufficient local demand. We will give all grant-maintained schools greater freedoms to expand and to select their pupils. Grant-maintained schools are leading the way.

Local authority schools are also benefiting from our policy of local management of schools. Our ultimate objective is that all schools should take full responsibility for the management of their own affairs. In the next parliament we will take another step towards giving them that freedom.

- We will extend the benefits of greater self-governance to all LEA schools.
- We will require local authorities to delegate more of schools' budgets to the schools themselves.
- We will give them more freedom over the employment of their staff and over admissions.
- And, where they want it, we will allow them to take over ownership of their assets, so they can make best use of the resources.

Local authorities will continue to be responsible for their schools' standards. They will provide funds, and compete with other organisations to provide services to schools. We would expect the increased responsibility of head-teachers, and their role in achieving efficiency-savings, to be recognised by their pay review body.

Schools are stronger and more effective where head-teachers and governors can shape their own distinctive character. Sometimes that means developing a speciality in some subjects. Sometimes it means selecting children by their aptitudes: where parents want this we should not stand in their way. Special abilities should be recognised and encouraged.

- We will continue to encourage the establishment of more specialist schools in technology, arts, languages and sport. We aim to help one in five schools become specialist schools by 2001.
- We will allow all schools to select some of their pupils.
- We will help schools to become grammar schools in every major town where parents want that choice.

The high standards, real choice and genuine diversity which we have introduced will produce the best results for all our children.

Lifetime learning

Lifetime learning is a reality in Britain today. Over a half of all students in universities, and seventy per cent of those in further education colleges, are adults who have returned to education later in life. We will continue to create new opportunities for more people to participate.

There has been a revolution in further and higher education. Three and a half million people are in further education – up from just half a million in 1979. The number of young people going to university has risen from one in eight to one in three over the same period. We will ensure consistently high standards and will consult on the development of higher education when we receive the results of the Dearing Review. We have world class research in British universities which we will continue to support.

Every young person should have the opportunity to continue in education or training. We will give students between 14 and 21 a learning credit which will enable them to choose suitable education or training leading to recognised qualifications up to A levels or their equivalents. We will also introduce National Traineeships and encourage employers to offer more work-based Modern Apprenticeships to young people. Objective external assessments of a proper syllabus will be made a part of all National Vocational Qualifications. We will continue to support the network of Training and Enterprise Councils, which have created a valuable partnership between business and government. We will encourage more employers to become involved in 'Investors in People', with the public sector matching the performance of the private sector. Competitive markets demand high skills. If Britain is to win, we need to encourage learning and give people the opportunity to go where their interests and inquiring minds take them.

WORLD CLASS HEALTH AND PUBLIC SERVICES

Our record: health and public services

- Government spending has concentrated on priorities, not wasteful bureaucracy and overmanning. Despite tough overall spending plans, real spending on the NHS has risen nearly 75% since 1979, on schools by 50% and on the police by more than 100%.
- The Health Service is treating over 1 million more patients each year than before our reforms.
- The number of people waiting over 12 months for hospital treatment has fallen from over 200,000 in 1990 to 22,000 last year. The average wait has fallen from nearly 9 months to 4 months.
- The Government has set up the Citizen's Charter to provide first-class public services for all citizens. Nearly 650 organisations have received a Charter Mark for meeting demanding standards of performance, customer satisfaction and value for money.
- There are now 55,000 more nurses and midwives and 22,500 more doctors and dentists than in 1979. For every senior NHS manager, 77 people are providing direct patient care.
- Nurses' average earnings have grown 70% in real terms: from £68 a week in 1979 to £325 in 1995. Doctor's pay has risen by a third. Under Labour both were cut.
- Infant mortality has fallen from 13.2 to 6.2 per thousand over the last 18 years.
- Deaths through road accidents are now the lowest since records began in 1926. Since 1979 road deaths have fallen by 43% and serious casualties have fallen by 43% despite an 85% increase in motor traffic.

- The government has invested record amounts on transport – more than £26 billion since 1979 in investment on motorways and trunk roads; £16 billion on railways; and over £8 billion on London Transport.
- Privatisation is delivering better services at lower costs. BT's main prices are down by more than 40% in real terms. Average household bills for gas and electricity have also fallen in real terms since 1990.

5. Security in health

We have been the guardians of the NHS for most of its life, improving its services and securing its funding. The benefits can be seen in our rising standards of health. 1993 was for example the first year in which no child in this country died of measles. Between 1979 and 1995 life expectancy at birth in England has increased from 70.4 years to 74.3 years for men and from 76.4 years to 79.6 years for women. We are getting healthier and we are better looked after when we are sick.

Growing resources for a modern health service

This progress has been possible because we have increased spending since 1979 by 70% more than inflation, to nearly £43 billion. And we are not stopping there. The next Conservative Government will honour a unique guarantee to the NHS. We will continue, year by year, to increase the real resources committed to the NHS, so NHS spending will continue to share in a growing economy. Under Labour there have been years when resources for the NHS actually shrank – something that would be inconceivable with the Conservatives. Money is only really a means to an end: better patient care. Now we are treating 9.2 million hospital in-patients and day cases as against 6.9 million in 1992 and 5.1 million in 1979.

Investing in skilled staff

We are committed to expanding the medical staff of the NHS. We shall therefore increase medical school intakes to 5,000 a year by the year 2000 and are ahead of schedule in reaching the target. Good nursing is the bedrock of the NHS. In particular we will increase the number of nurses with specialist qualifications in paediatric intensive care, emergency care, and cancer care. The number of nurses qualifying each year will increase in each of the next 5 years as we continue to expand Project 2000 training.

Higher standards of service

We are tackling the problem of long waiting times which can cause so much worry, distress, and pain. We have set tough targets under the Patient's Charter and as a result average waiting times for in-patient hospital treatments have fallen from more than 6 months 5 years ago to 4 months last year.

Patients no longer put up with being kept in ignorance. They want to know more. We will publish more information on how successfully hospitals are treating patients so that they and their GPs can make more informed choices between services in different hospitals and help stimulate better performance.

Better primary care

Our vision of the NHS is one in which hospitals and family doctors gain greater power to run their own affairs. That is why we will continue to encourage the spread of fundholding among GPs. Labour by contrast would destroy the new freedoms that fundholding doctors enjoy by imposing a new layer of bureaucracy on top of them. However, we do not want the benefits of better healthcare to be confined to patients of GP fundholders. Our proposals to shift more healthcare towards family doctors are open to all. We shall implement the new Primary Care Act which will enable all family doctors to provide a broader range of patient services within their surgeries. This will include 'super surgeries' and practice-based cottage hospitals that can offer faster and more local treatment. We expect to see the number of nurses working in GP practices continue to grow, as will the number of GPs. We will extend nationwide our plans to enable more nurses to prescribe a wider range of drugs for patients, recognising their contribution to primary care.

Mental health

The last decade has also seen major changes to the care of mentally ill people. We will continue to develop a full range of services – including 24-hour nursed hostels and secure units – that can care for them in a way which is most appropriate to them and the interests of the wider community. We will not close any long-stay mental hospitals unless it can be shown that adequate care services exist in the community. We will strengthen co-operation between health and social services in the delivery of mental health services. Our recent Green Paper showed how this can be done. And we will monitor the progress of Health Authorities in developing proper mental health care plans.

Health of the nation

A modern health service is not just about treating illness, it is also about keeping people healthy. This is why we launched the Health of the Nation strategy in 1992 – the first time England has had a strategy for health. Its aim is to reduce illness and premature death by identifying common causes of ill health, like excessive smoking and obesity. Different groups in and outside the health service then work together to tackle the problems. We are already seeing progress.

Between 1990 and 1994, deaths from coronary heart disease among the over-65s, the suicide rate, and the number of teenage pregnancies fell substantially. And last year we announced that environmental targets would be added to Health of the Nation. Improved general health means fewer people requiring attention in hospitals and GP surgeries – and more resources to be spent on helping patients. Our Health of the Nation strategy is a vital part of our vision of creating a health service fit for the 21st century.

A modern health service

Healthcare is changing fast. Modern technology is constantly increasing the range of treatments which are available. Conservatives believe that the benefits of these advances should be made available to patients on the basis of their clinical need, without regard to their ability to pay. Furthermore we also believe that the NHS must have access to sufficient resources to allow it to invest in the facilities required to deliver up-to-date healthcare.

Since 1979 capital investment in the NHS has proceeded at an unprecedented rate. In the future we believe these requirements will be best met in a partnership with the private sector which allows the private sector to improve the facilities in which NHS healthcare is delivered. We will promote the Private Finance Initiative which will unleash a new flow of investment funds into the modernisation of the NHS. The NHS is a British success story. It commands universal support in Britain. It is widely admired all over the world. Conservatives are proud of the part we playing in improving it still further.

6. Better public services

The public sector is being transformed the world over. Britain is in the vanguard. Everyone else wants to learn from our vision of a smaller state doing fewer things and doing them better. Old-style public services were centrally planned with little information or choice for the public who used the service. Our reforms have made these services more responsive to the public by breaking up cumbersome bureaucratic structures and shifting power to small responsive local institutions and the people who work in them. The schools, hospitals and police have all been transformed in this way. We support the people who do, not the people who plan.

In order to get better standards we are liberating services from centralised control over capital. We will push forward our Private Finance Initiative to break down these old barriers. We have made public services genuinely accountable, with useful information and real choices for the people who use them. We set tough standards and they will get tougher.

The Citizen's Charter has raised standards of customer service. When these high standards are reached we recognise and reward excellence through our Charter Mark initiative. There are now 647 Chartermarks and we will aim for more than 2000 Chartermarks by the year 2000. We will require all government agencies to apply for Chartermarks.

The days of the bureaucratic paperchase are behind us. The future is 'government direct'. We will harness the latest information technology to place the public sector directly at the service of the citizen. People will be able to use simple computer terminals to enter information directly. This will transform time-consuming transactions like completing a tax return or registering a new business.

Privatisation and competition

In 20 years, privatisation has gone from the dream of a few Conservative visionaries to the big idea which is transforming decaying public sector industries in almost every country in the world. Britain has led the way with this new industrial revolution: we can be proud of what we have achieved.

In 1979 the Government inherited a range of businesses which had come into the public sector for different reasons. Many were known for their poor standards of service, and most were making large losses. Over the past eighteen years that situation has changed substantially. Privatisation has enhanced productivity, improved customer services, raised safety and environmental standards and substantially reduced prices. Telephone, gas and electricity bills to the customer have fallen as never before. Telephone waiting lists are unknown, and water, gas and electricity disconnections have fallen dramatically. Nearly £40 billion in private sector funding has been committed to a major investment programme to meet higher quality water standards. We can now look forward to water prices falling over the years ahead.

Service standards have improved substantially. Before privatisation published service standards did not exist. Now industry regulators monitor legal requirements to provide quality services in a competitive environment. Refunds may be made when performance standards are not met. Privatisation has benefited – and will continue to benefit – consumers, shareholders, employees, and taxpayers. In 1979 the then-nationalised industries required a £50 million per week subsidy from the taxpayer. In 1996 those now privatised companies paid taxes of £60 million per week.

- We will ensure private ownership, competition and regulation continue to deliver lower prices and better services for consumers.
- We will extend competition for domestic gas users, and introduce competition in the water industry, starting with large users.
- The Post Office occupies an important part in national life. It comprises Counter Services, the Royal Mail and Parcelforce. The network of sub-post offices is vital and most are already run as private businesses. The Royal Mail provides a universal service at a standard price in every part of the United Kingdom. No one can imagine a stamp that does not bear the Queen's head. These characteristics must continue, but reforms are needed to allow the services to develop. The Royal Mail must face up to the challenges and opportunities that are arising from increasing competition and the international liberalisation of services.
- We will guarantee to preserve the national identity, universal service and distinctive characteristics of the Royal Mail, while considering options – including different forms of privatisation – to introduce private capital and management skills into its operations.
- We will transfer Parcelforce to the private sector whilst ensuring that every Post Office in the land continues to provide a full parcel service at an economical price. Privatisation works.

We will therefore continue to pass government activities into private ownership where this can bring benefits to consumers and taxpayers.

Local government

We are developing a new vision for local government. We believe local government should take a lead in the planning and development of their communities. To achieve that, we have encouraged them to work in partnership with central government, with private enterprise, and other organisations in their community. The impact of local government is multiplied when they work in this way. To encourage this partnership, we have developed the new approach of Challenge Funding. We set up a fund to meet a particular objective and then invite competing bids for the money. Those who form effective partnerships are far more likely to win those bids. The Single Regeneration

Budget Fund, for example, has stimulated many working partnerships that are bringing new life to their communities. This innovation has the potential to transform the financing of the public sector.

- We will push Challenge Funding further to reward effective local government. In addition, we are encouraging higher standards and more cost-effective provision of local services. Local authorities can enable things to happen rather than necessarily running themselves. They must look after the interests of users of their services – and that is often best done by being a purchaser, not an employer. Standards of service are rising in many local authorities. There are, however, still great disparities between the best and worst performers, as the Audit Commission shows in their thought-provoking reports.
- We will keep up the pressure for higher standards and improved value for money by insisting on compulsory competitive tendering. The development of Challenge Funding and the shift in the role of local authorities from direct employers to purchasers of services will transform local authorities over the coming years. In the meantime we will, for so long as is necessary, retain the power to cap local authorities to protect taxpayers.

Strikes in essential services

Industrial relations in this country have been transformed. Insofar as there is a still a problem it is concentrated in a few essential services where the public has no easy alternative and strikers are able to impose massive costs and inconvenience out of all proportion to the issues at stake. We will protect ordinary members of the public from this abuse of power.

- We will legislate to remove legal immunity from industrial action which has disproportionate or excessive effect. Members of the public and employers will be able to seek injunctions to prevent industrial action in these circumstances. Any strike action will also have to approved by a majority of all members eligible to vote and ballots will have to be repeated at regular intervals if negotiations are extended.

Transport

Our railways are already improving now they have been liberated into the private sector. Passenger numbers are up: more people are using the railways every day. Investment is up: Railtrack plans to spend £4 million each day on improving stations and maintaining and renewing the network. The new train operators are committed to investing £1.5 billion in new and refurbished rolling stock. And key fares are falling in real terms for the first time in a generation, with guaranteed price controls keeping fare increases below the level of inflation until at least 2003. We intend to build on this growing success story to create a thriving railway network for the new century.

- We will complete the successful transfer of British Rail into the commercial sector.
- We now want to draw in private investment to modernise London Underground and improve services to passengers. We will bring forward plans to privatise London Underground. Proceeds from privatisation will be recycled in order to modernise

the network within 5 years – creating an underground system to serve the capital in the 21st century. We will regulate fares so they rise by no more than inflation for at least 4 years after privatisation. We will also protect services – including the Travel Card and concessionary fares. After completing the modernisation of the network, the majority of the remaining surplus from privatisation will be channelled into additional support for transport investment in London and elsewhere in the country.

We will continue to encourage public transport. In particular, we will use the existing funding for local authorities to promote developments which make it easier to transfer from rail to bus. We recognise the needs of road users, and will continue to work with the private sector to sustain our road building and maintenance programme. Already under the Private Finance Initiative the private sector is contributing some £1 billion to investment in roads and achieving significant savings in construction costs. We will also tackle road congestion by introducing new regional traffic control centres, by extending the use of variable speed limits, and by ensuring that local authorities have the necessary powers to act.

- We will promote a cleaner environment by supporting a Europe-wide reduction in vehicle emissions, and encouraging the manufacture of more fuel-efficient vehicles. We will continue to build on our record of improving safety on roll-on roll-off ferries and cargo ships through higher standards of survivability and the measures in the Merchant Shipping Act.
- We will continue to make it easier for people to travel by air. Already over the last 5 years opening up the market in Europe has led to more services and lower fares. We will build on that success in negotiations with the United States and other countries. We will also continue to encourage the development of regional airports offering new direct services to the rest of the world in the same way that we have already opened up new regional links with Europe and the United States. We will privatise the National Air Traffic System because it will be run better in the private sector. Competition and enterprise are the best way to improve our transport system.

A SAFE AND CIVIL SOCIETY

Our record: a safe and civil society

- Spending on the police has doubled since 1979 after allowing for inflation. There are now about 16,000 more police officers than when we took office. 2,360 more constables have been recruited since the last election and the Government is giving Chief Officers the resources to recruit 5,000 extra police constables over the next 3 years.
- Recorded crime has dropped in each of the last 4 years. It is now over 10% down on 1992 levels – more than half a million fewer offences – the biggest drop since records were first kept.
- There are now 153,000 neighbourhood watch schemes in England and Wales – 38,000 more than in 1992 – covering 5.5 million homes. We have helped fund over 4,000 Closed Circuit TV schemes over the last 2 years for additional security.

- Our national DNA database – the first in the world – now has over 112,000 samples on it. 3,300 matches have so far been made between suspects and crime stains.
- The Government has increased the maximum penalty for taking a gun to a crime and for attempted rape to life imprisonment. Since 1985 the average sentence for violence against the person has risen by a third and for sexual offences by nearly 40%.
- The number of cars stolen has fallen by nearly 20% in the last four years – that is about 100,000 fewer cars stolen.
- We have built 22 new prisons since 1980. Slopping out has ended. No prisoners now sleep three to a cell designed for one. Prison escapes have fallen by 80% since the last election.
- Mandatory drug testing has been introduced throughout the Prison Service. Home leave has been cut back – down by half in two years.
- We have made witness intimidation a crime. 500 people were charged with that offence in 1995 alone.
- We have stepped up the fight against drugs and organised crime, giving the Security Service powers to support the police and Customs and Excise in tracking down the serious criminals.

7. Law, order and security

People have a right to sleep safely in their homes and walk safely on the streets. Governments have a duty to maintain that security. Our reforms are aimed at ensuring that crime does not pay. And they are working – the pessimists and the scoffers are wrong. Recorded crime has fallen every year for the last 4 years. It is now 10% lower than it was in 1992. That is over half a million fewer crimes – the biggest drop since records were first kept in the middle of the 19th century. But crime is still too high. We must do more. Our aim is to keep crime falling over the lifetime of the next Parliament. This is what we will do.

Safer communities

Anti-social behaviour and petty crime disrupt communities and spread human misery. The police are rightly now vigorously tackling problems such as graffiti, vandalism and drunkenness. Where such behaviour goes unchecked more serious crimes will follow.

We will support chief constables who develop local schemes to crack down on petty crime and improve public order. Closed circuit television has proved enormously successful in increasing public safety.

We will fulfil the Prime Minister's pledge to support the installation of 10,000 CCTV cameras in town centres and public places in the 3 years to 1999. We will provide £75 million over the lifetime of the next Parliament to continue extending CCTV to town centres, villages and housing estates up and down the country that want to bid for support. We will also continue to take other steps to improve the safety of our streets and communities. In this Parliament we have given the police power to seize alcohol from under-18s caught drinking in public. The police have been given the power to stop and search in a specified area for up to 48 hours if they reasonably believe people to be carrying knives. Identity Cards can also make a contribution to safer communities.

We will introduce a voluntary identity card scheme based on the new photographic driving licence. It will, for example, enable retailers to identify youngsters trying to buy alcohol and cigarettes or rent classified videos when they are under age.

Tackling juvenile crime

A fifth of all crime is committed by under-18s. We are encouraging schools to reduce truancy through the publication of league tables and by supporting local projects to tackle the problem. We are developing a network of local teams to identify children who are at risk of turning to crime and to take early steps to address the factors which put them at risk. We will encourage these local child crime teams to refer children from primary school age upwards who are at risk of, or actually, offending to programmes to tackle their behaviour and fully involve their parents.

The courts would be able to impose an order – a Parental Control Order – on the parents of children whom they believed could keep control of their children but were refusing to do so. Courts will be given the power to attach conditions to Parental Control Orders. Conditions might include a requirement to keep their children in at night, taking their children to and from school, attending a drug rehabilitation clinic or going to sessions to improve their skills as parents. Parents who breached these conditions – in defiance of the court – would face a range of possible sanctions.

Appearing before a youth court should be a daunting experience for the juvenile concerned. All too often it is not. At the moment about a third of all juveniles appearing before the youth courts are discharged without any punishment at all. This sends all the wrong signals to youngsters – particularly first time offenders – who then feel they can get away with crime. We will give the courts the power to impose speedy sanctions on youngsters, involving wherever possible an element of reparation to the victim. The probation service – rather than social services – will be responsible for enforcing community punishments for under-16s.

Persistent juvenile offenders need to be properly punished. We are piloting a tough new regime, with a heavy emphasis on discipline, at a young offender institution and at the military prison in Colchester. In 1994 we doubled the maximum sentence for 15–17 year olds to 2 years detention in a young offenders institution. We have given the courts the freedom to allow the publication of the names of convicted juveniles. We will give the courts the power to detain persistent 12–14-year-old offenders in secure training centres once the places become available. We have given the courts the power to impose electronically monitored curfews on 10 to 15-year-old offenders. We will introduce pilots to test their effectiveness. If successful we will consider extending them nationwide.

Catching, convicting and punishing

We back the police every inch of the way. There are now about 16,000 more police officers – and over 18,000 more civilians helping them – than when we took office. We are providing chief constables with the resources to recruit 5,000 extra police constables in the three years to 1999. We support police initiatives to target the hard core of persistent criminals. Intelligence is crucial for this.

We will establish a national crime squad to provide an improved nationally coordinated approach to organised crime. Once caught, criminals must be convicted and then properly punished. The public need to be protected. We have reformed the right to silence, despite opposition from Labour. The number of suspects refusing to answer police questions has nearly halved as a result. We have piloted curfew orders for adult offenders. They have been shown to keep criminals indoors – curbing their freedom as a punishment – and keeping them out of trouble in the meantime.

We will extend electronically monitored curfew orders nationwide for those aged 16 and over. Persistent offenders account for a high proportion of all crime. Prison works – not only as a deterrent, but in keeping criminals off the street. Those sent to prison are less likely to re-offend on release than those given a community punishment. We will provide another 8,500 prison places by the year 2000. We will introduce minimum sentences for violent and persistent criminals to help protect the public more effectively, reversing Labour's wrecking amendments to our tough Crime Bill.

Anyone convicted of a second serious sexual or violent crime, like rape or armed robbery, will get an automatic life sentence. Persistent house burglars and dealers in hard drugs will receive mandatory minimum prison sentences of 3 and 7 years, respectively.

We will restore honesty in sentencing by ensuring that criminals serve the sentence intended without automatic early release.

Support for victims

Concern for the victim must be at the heart of our entire approach to the criminal justice system. We will continue to give strong backing to Victim Support. We will give courts in all cases the discretion to allow witnesses to give evidence anonymously if they believe them to be at risk from reprisal. We will also take action to allow a judge to stop a defendant from personally questioning the victim in rape cases and other cases where the victim is particularly vulnerable. Conservatives are on the side of the victims not the criminal.

Strengthening the fight against City crime

Crime that takes place through manipulation of financial accounts and markets is as serious as crime on the street. The City's unchallenged position as Europe's most dynamic and successful financial centre owes a great deal to its reputation for honesty and fair dealing. We will help ensure that this reputation is maintained.

We will bring forward in the next Parliament a package of measures designed to modernise the current systems for dealing with City fraud. This will include legislation to allow the Inland Revenue to pass confidential information to the police, the Serious Fraud Office and the financial regulators to assist in the investigation of cases involving serious financial fraud. We will also remove the remaining legal obstacles to the controlled exchange of confidential information between the police and the regulators in this kind of case.

Faster justice

Justice delayed is justice denied. It is wrong that people who are innocent should face an excessive wait before the start of their trial. The guilty need to be held to account for their actions promptly. And victims should be given the chance to draw a line under their experience as quickly as possible. We are determined to speed up justice without diminishing the genuine rights of every citizen to a fair trial.

Last October the government set up a review of delays in the criminal justice system. It made a series of detailed recommendations. We see merit in those recommendations and will seek the views of interested parties. We believe that taken together they could dramatically speed up the prosecution process, bringing the guilty to justice and acquitting the innocent more quickly. All defendants would appear in court the next working day after they were charged. At least half of them would be convicted the next day compared with just 3 per cent at the moment. And the time taken to bring juveniles to court would be cut from 10 weeks to a matter of days.

Civil justice

The civil justice system of this country is a vital part of its competitive economy and has a high international reputation. The commercial courts attract substantial litigation from all over the world, generating significant foreign earnings. We will seek to maintain the high standing of these courts. We have greatly improved the service the civil courts provide for the aggrieved citizen.

The simple procedure for small claims has been extended to claims up to £3,000. For large claims the county court now provides an efficient local service with specialised courts in many locations around the country, leaving the High Court to deal with the more complex and difficult issues. We will push ahead with the major reforms now under way which will greatly speed up the process and improve the delivery of justice without imposing additional burdens on the taxpayer.

The legal profession

We will ensure that the framework in which the legal profession operates is responsive to the changing needs of our people and is one in which unjustified restrictions have no place. We have, for example, given most solicitors rights of audience in the higher courts under appropriate conditions.

Legal aid

People are rightly concerned about the rising costs of legal aid. We have taken many steps to control the burden and to deny access to legal aid to the 'apparently wealthy' – those who qualified technically, but whose lifestyles suggested they should not. But more is required.

We will change the structure of legal aid to ensure that it, like other vital public services, functions within defined cash limits. This will enable us to identify priorities and serve them much more efficiently than the present system.

Drugs

Drugs are a menace to the very fabric of our society. They ruin the life of addicts and their families. They can destroy whole neighbourhoods. The promising youth of today can too easily become the sad dropouts of tomorrow, turning to crime and violence. The Conservative Government has a comprehensive strategy, launched in 1995, committed to fighting drugs in communities and in schools. It is tough on criminals and vigilant at our ports. It is respected throughout the world. We spend over £500m every year in tackling all aspects of drug problems.

We will continue the fight against drugs through a coordinated approach: being tough on pushers; reducing demand by educating young people; tackling drug abuse at local level through Drug Action Teams; saying 'No' to legalising drugs; and working with international agencies and foreign governments to resist the menace spreading. This pernicious evil has to be fought by all of us.

A CONFIDENT, UNITED AND SOVEREIGN NATION

Our record: the nation

- Many of our old cities have been rejuvenated through a partnership of public and private investment.
- The area of green belt has doubled since 1979.
- Water and air quality in the UK have improved significantly.
- We are one of only a few nations on course to meet our commitment to return emissions of all greenhouse gases to 1990 levels by 2000.
- The Lottery has been established as the most successful in the world – raising £3 billion for good causes in a little over 2 years.
- More support is now given to arts and heritage than at any time in our nation's history. We now provide nearly 20% more for the arts than the last Labour Government, over and above inflation.
- British talent was this year nominated for 30 Oscars. British music is again receiving international acclaim. The industry is worth £2.5 billion, more than shipbuilding or electric components: one in 5 CDs and records sold anywhere has a British connection.
- There is record investment in our sports facilities. Already the Lottery has provided £480 million for sport, including the planned British Academy of Sport, English National Stadium and for the first time direct funding for British athletes.
- We have continued to stand up for British interests in Europe, protecting our opt-out of the Social Chapter, maintaining our border controls, and preserving our budget rebate – worth £18 billion since it was introduced.
- We have the most professional armed forces in the world. We have modernised our nuclear deterrent by replacing Polaris with Trident.

8. The best place in the world to live

Britain is admired the world over. Every year, millions of tourists travel here to enjoy our heritage and culture, our cities and countryside, our way of life. Our nation's history is an anchor in a sea of change. We need to protect, cherish and build upon what is great about our country, so our children grow up in a better Britain. We also must make sure that everyone, wherever they live, has the support of a strong, tolerant and civilised community.

Our aim is for this generation and future generations to take pride in Britain as the best place in the world to live.

Britain's cities

London is one of the world's greatest cities. It is livelier than ever. Our vision of its future is set out in a separate manifesto. Many of our cities have undergone a complete transformation over the last decade. We have promoted partnerships – through schemes such as Urban Development Corporation, the Single Regeneration Budget and City Pride to attract private enterprise and investment back to inner cities. These initiatives are bringing hope, opportunity, and prosperity to what were once wastelands of urban decline.

As the country thrives and becomes more prosperous, one of our central tasks is to apply the same approach to transform the legacy of soulless, decaying public housing estates. They are places that suffer from the very worst kind of poverty – poverty of aspiration. We have already made a start – spending over £2bn over the last 10 years on improving 500 of the worst estates. And we have shown how it is possible to tackle the economic and social problems alongside new investment in buildings – where possible, bringing in a greater mix of public tenants and private housing to recreate a more balanced community. Now we will extend this approach, focusing the Single Regeneration Budget to launch a combined attack on crime, unemployment and under-achievement, and developing the government's partnership with the private sector to help fund the massive investment that will be required.

Over the next decade, we aim to raise some £25bn of new private investment in housing estates by encouraging tenants in more than half of the remaining public sector housing stock to opt for transferring their homes to new landlords. These transfers will only occur where tenants choose this route to improve their estates.

We will use this approach to regenerate the worst housing estates and transform the lives of those who live on them – targeting support for programmes to improve education standards, employment and crime prevention alongside new private sector investment. As well as this attack on poor housing, we will continue to help the homeless. We will carry through our planned extension of the Rough Sleeper Initiative from London to other big cities.

We will provide sufficient hostel places to ensure that no-one needs sleep out on the streets.

Rural communities

Britain is blessed with some of the most beautiful countryside in Europe. We need to protect the best of countryside whilst ensuring good jobs, and living conditions for people who live there. We have to strike a balance: our rural communities must not become rural museums, but remain vibrant places to live and work. We will make sure government departments work together to ensure that balance is kept. We will continue to protect the green belt from development making sure that derelict and under-used urban land is developed in preference to greenfield sites.

We will use the planning system to ensure that more new homes are built on reclaimed sites in our towns and cities. We will aim for more than 60 per cent of all new homes to be built on derelict sites. This will reduce the pressure to build in our countryside and expand choice where it is needed most. We will support our rural communities, by giving special rate support to small village shops and post offices. The planning system can do more to help too.

We will introduce a new Rural Business Use Class to encourage job creation in the countryside.

We will increase support for schemes which promote care for the countryside – like Countryside Stewardship. We believe participation in traditional country pursuits, including fishing, is a matter for individuals. A Conservative Government will not introduce legislation that interferes with the rights of people to take part in these activities. We will also encourage managed public access to private land – in agreement with farmers and landowners – but strongly resist a general right to roam, which would damage the countryside and violate the right to private property. We aim to double Britain's forest cover over the next fifty years. We will continue to encourage tree planting by targeting grants, encouraging investment in wood processing, and using new freedoms with the reform of the Common Agricultural Policy.

Agriculture and fisheries

We will continue to provide robust support to the British beef industry through the BSE crisis until its long-term strength is restored. We will vigorously pursue the eradication of BSE in the United Kingdom, as we have been doing successfully for the last eight years. We will spare no efforts in our fight against the unwarranted ban on British beef exports. Public health and food safety have been the government's top priorities throughout the BSE crises.

We will tighten up control over food safety by appointing a powerful and independent Chief Food Safety Adviser and Food Safety Council to advise government. We will continue to push for fundamental reform of the Common Agricultural Policy, moving away from production support to measures that will give our farmers the opportunity to compete while safeguarding the rural environment. We will ensure that no change to the Common Agriculture Policy unfairly disadvantages British farmers.

Fishing is a vital industry in many parts of coastal Britain. We will continue our fight to secure a prosperous long-term future for the industry and sustainable management of our fish stocks.

We will insist at the IGC and elsewhere on measures to stop quota hopping and prevent the vessels of other countries from using UK fishing quotas. The integrity of our 6- and 12-mile fishing limits is not negotiable. We reject any idea of a single European fishing fleet. We believe that fishermen should have more say in decisions affecting their industry. We will press the European Commission to establish regional committees to give fishermen a direct influence in fishing policy. We will use these committees to develop new ways of managing quota and regulating fisheries which are more sensitive to the industry's needs.

Animal welfare

A civilised society respects its animals. Britain will continue to take the lead in improving standards of animal welfare in Europe. In 1995 we secured a major breakthrough in the treatment of animals in transport; in 1996 we won victory in our campaign to ban veal crates throughout the EU. We are determined that standards should continue to rise and that all EU countries should have to meet them.

We will seek to ensure that all European countries have to raise animal welfare standards. We are not going to take any risks with rabies. There may, however, be ways other than quarantine which maintain or increase protection for public health, while improving the welfare of pets and reducing the costs to travellers.

We will publish a Green Paper on rabies protection, setting out all the options including the existing controls, early in the new Parliament.

Britain's environment

Britain has an enviable track record in protecting our environment. Our rivers, beaches and water are cleaner and we are using our energy more efficiently. We are leading the world in reducing the level of the 'greenhouse gases' that cause global warming and pressing for policies that will enable the world to sustain development without long-term damage to the environment.

Our Green Manifesto is published separately. We have clear objectives to build on this record. We will set tough, but affordable targets, with published environmental strategies to improve air quality and banish city smog – with tighter standards on vehicle emissions and pollution crackdowns around the country. We aim for sustained improvements in water quality, at a pace which industry and consumers can afford. We will develop labelling of products that gives consumers information to show the environmental impact of how they were made. In addition, we will continue to use the tax system and other incentives to encourage the use of vehicles and fuel which do not pollute the environment. And, we will continue to explore policies based on the principle of polluter pays: those who contaminate land, pollute the environment or produce harmful waste should be made responsible for their actions and pay for the consequences.

Britain – a tolerant country

Tolerance, civility and respect have always been hallmarks of our nation. It is thanks to them that we have an excellent record on race relations. Everybody, regardless of colour or creed, has the right to go about his or her life free from the threat of intimidation. We are taking tough action to tackle harassment. Under proposals in the Protection from Harassment Act 1997, it will be a crime to behave in a way which causes someone else to be harassed. The maximum penalty will be 6 months in prison. Firm, but fair, immigration controls underpin good race relations. We will ensure that, while genuine asylum seekers are treated sympathetically, people do not abuse these provisions to avoid normal immigration controls.

A world leader of sports, arts and culture

Britain is enjoying a cultural renaissance. British music, films, television, fashion, art and food are winning plaudits the world over. They add excitement, fun and enjoyment to our lives. Our success brings pride to everyone. The National Lottery, which John Major set up, will pump billions of pounds into Britain's good causes. Its proceeds will weave a new, rich thread of opportunity and charity into the tapestry of British life. In addition to benefiting major national institutions, about half of the awards are for amounts under £25,000 – benefiting local communities up and down the country. We will encourage new ways of distributing awards to support the performing arts – through support for amateur productions and community events, providing more musical instruments, and helping productions tour round the country.

The National Lottery will also help us train and promote British sporting talent. The English National Stadium and British Academy of Sport, funded by the Lottery, will be new focal points for sporting events and excellence. We will encourage more young people to play sport, by ensuring every school plays a minimum level of sport, including competitive sports, and developing a network of Sporting Ambassadors – sporting celebrities who will visit schools to inspire young people. We also encourage the Sports Council to use Lottery money to employ over 1000 additional community sports coaches to assist in Primary Schools. The development of young talent is important in all fields.

We will encourage the use of Lottery money to train young athletes and artists, with revenue funding for bursaries, concessionary tickets to professional performances and support for young people's organisations and productions. The Lottery will also fund our Millennium celebrations. They will be inspirational as well as enjoyable. We want these be a showcase of British excellence. Britain will be able to look back on past achievements with pride, and look forward with confidence.

9. Europe and the world

Britain is a world leader as well as a European nation. Our economic strength, our history and our language make us a global trading nation with links right around the world. Only the United Kingdom is a member of the European Union, the United Nations Security Council, the Commonwealth, NATO and the Group of Seven leading industrial nations. In the Gulf, Bosnia, Cyprus and Northern Iraq, John Major has shown how our nation can contribute to world peace. We will continue to work with international partners to secure peace and stability in areas of tension such as former Yugoslavia; in Kashmir; in Cyprus; and in the Middle East. We will promote reform of the United Nations to make it a more effective organisation for securing international stability. Britain will continue to deploy our outstanding Armed Forces as peacekeepers under the United Nations. And we will support the aspirations of the Poles, Czechs, Hungarians and others to join the European Union and NATO.

After the transfer of Hong Kong, we will work under the terms of the Joint Declaration to help sustain the prosperity and way of life of the people of Hong Kong and build on the substantial British interests that will remain. We will continue to support the Commonwealth, our unique global network, to encourage the spread of democracy, as set out in the Harare Declaration.

We will focus our aid programme to encourage sustainable development in countries that are growing towards self-sufficiency under democratic government. We have taken the lead in alleviating the burden of debt for the world's poorest countries. We also have significant flows of private investment to developing economies. We are more than achieving the long-term UN target of 1% of GDP for the transfer of wealth to less developed countries. We will continue to maintain a significant bilateral and multilateral aid programme reflecting the aspiration of meeting the UN's target of 0.7% of GDP for aid as a long-term objective. We will also continue to provide leadership in Europe and internationally on environmental issues, building on the Rio Conference to encourage sustainable development – meeting our commitment to reduce carbon dioxide (CO_2) emissions by 10% on 1990 levels by 2010 to prevent climate change. The Prime Minister has committed himself to attending the next UN Environmental Conference in June.

Britain and the European Union

We believe that in an uncertain, competitive world, the nation state is a rock of security. A nation's common heritage, culture, values and outlook are a precious source of stability. Nationhood gives people a sense of belonging. The government has a positive vision for the European Union as a partnership of nations. We want to be in Europe but not run by Europe. We have much to gain from our membership of the European Union – in trade, in co-operation between governments, and in preserving European peace. We benefit from the huge trade opportunities that have opened up since Britain led the way in developing Europe's single market. We want to see the rest of Europe follow the same deregulated, enterprise policies that have transformed our economic prospects in Britain. However, in June, the nations of the European Union will gather in Amsterdam to negotiate possible amendments to the Treaty of Rome. It is a moment of truth, setting the direction in which the European Union will go. It will also be crucial in ensuring that we have a relationship with the rest of Europe with which we can be comfortable.

A Conservative Government will seek a partnership of nation states. Some others would like to build a federal Europe. A British Conservative Government will not allow Britain to be part of a Federal European State. The diversity of Europe's nations is its strength. As more nations join the European Union, it needs to become flexible not more rigid. We must also ensure that any developments which only include some Members do not work to the disadvantage of others. Our priorities for Europe's development will be enlargement of the Community, completion of the single market, reform of the European Court of Justice, and further strengthening of the role of national parliaments. We will seek more co-operation between national governments on areas of common interest – defence, foreign policy and the fight against international crime and drugs. We also believe the European Union itself should do less, but do it better. So we have proposed incorporating the principle of subsidiarity – that the European Union should only do that which cannot be done by Member States acting alone – into the Treaty. This is how we are approaching the Inter-Governmental Conference.

We will argue for a flexible Europe which fully accommodates the interests and aspirations of all its Member States and where any new proposals have to be open to all and agreed by all. We will not accept other changes to the Treaty that would further centralise decision-making, reduce national sovereignty, or remove our right to permanent opt-outs.

We will retain Britain's veto and oppose further extension of qualified majority voting in order to ensure we can prevent policies that would be harmful to the national interest. We will defend the rights of national parliaments and oppose more powers being given to the European Parliament at the expense of national parliaments.

We will take whatever steps are necessary to keep our frontier controls. We will resist attempts to change the inter-governmental nature of cooperation in Justice and Home Affairs. We will not accept the development of new legal rights that extend the concept of European Citizenship. Britain's rebate has so far saved British taxpayers £18bn and we will protect it.

One of the greatest challenges Europe faces is to cut unemployment and make its businesses competitive. Here Britain is leading the way. We will continue to argue for deregulation and lower costs on Europe's businesses, the policies that have helped give Britain one of the strongest economies in Europe. We will not put that achievement at risk by signing up to the Social Chapter, which would open the door to imposing the high costs of the European Social Model on British business. Once Britain accepted the Social Chapter we could not stop many of these damaging policies being imposed on us by Qualified Majority Voting. We will insist that any new Treaty recognises that our opt-out from the Social Chapter enables Britain to be exempt from the Working Time Directive, and prevents any abuse of our opt-out. And, we will not accept a new employment chapter in any revised Treaty, which would expose British businesses to new costs.

We made it clear in the previous chapter that we will continue to work for further reform of the Common Agricultural Policy, and the lifting of the worldwide ban on British beef, and insist on measures to stop quota hopping by foreign fishing vessels. Protecting Britain's interests demands tough, experienced negotiation. John Major has proved he has these qualities – including the resolve to say no when necessary even if that means being isolated. Labour have said they would never want Britain to be isolated in Europe: they would damage Britain's success by undermining our veto, signing up to the Social Chapter and following in others' footsteps – even where they lead in the wrong direction. They support policies that would fragment the United Kingdom's influence within a Europe of Regions. The Liberal Democrats welcome the end of the nation state. Only the Conservatives can be trusted to stand up for Britain in Europe: our national interest must be protected.

A single currency: our referendum guarantee

The creation of a European single currency would be of enormous significance for all European States whether they are Members or not. We must take account of all the consequences for Britain of such a major development of policy.

John Major secured for us at Maastricht an opt-out from the commitment to enter a single currency. It is only because of this opt-out that we have the right to negotiate and then decide whether it is in Britain's interest to join. It is in our national interest to take part in the negotiations. Not to do so would be an abdication of responsibility. A single currency would affect us whether we were in or out. We need to participate in discussions in order to ensure the rules are not fixed against our interests. The national interest is not served by exercising our option – one way or the other – before we have to.

For a single currency to come into effect, European economies will have to meet crucial criteria. On the information currently available, we believe that it is very unlikely that there will be sufficient convergence of economic conditions across Europe for a single currency to proceed safely on the target date of January 1st 1999. We will not include legislation on the single currency in the first Queen's Speech. If it cannot proceed safely, we believe it would be better for Europe to delay any introduction of a single currency rather than rush ahead to meet an artificial timetable. We will argue this case in the negotiations that lie ahead. We believe it is in our national interest to keep our options open to take a decision on a single currency when all the facts are before us. If a single currency is created, without sustainable convergence, a British Conservative government will not be part of it.

If, during the course of the next Parliament, a Conservative government were to conclude that it was in our national interest to join a single currency, we have given a guarantee that no such decision would be implemented unless the British people gave their express approval in a referendum.

Defence in an unstable world

The old rivalries of the Cold War have been replaced by new tensions. Britain must be able to react rapidly to protect our security and interests around the globe. Our armed forces are the most professional in the world.

- We have cut unnecessary bureaucracy and increased efficiency, and directed money to support our services in the frontline. We have made the changes necessary to adapt our services to the threats which we might now face.
- We have set out defence plans based on stable levels of funding. There is no need for a defence review, which would raise fear and uncertainty about the future.
- We will continue to ensure the Services have the modern weapons they need to guarantee their superiority against potential aggressors.
- We will make sure we can conduct military operations throughout the world, and develop our capability to deploy the three services together and rapidly, including the ability to transport heavy equipment into an operational zone.
- We will take part in ballistic missile research so we can decide whether we should procure any such system for the United Kingdom.
- We will continue to target our efforts on recruiting for the armed forces.
- We will set up an Army Foundation College, which will provide 1,300 places for 16 and 17 year olds who want to join the Army.
- We will also enable the reserve forces to play a more active role in operations.
- We appreciate the enormous value of cadet forces, and our current plans including resources to encourage their further development.
- We will continue to support Britain's defence industry, and we will work with companies to identify the technologies of the future. NATO will remain the cornerstone of our security.
- We will resist attempts to bring the Western European Union under the control of

the European Union, and ensure that defence policy remains a matter for sovereign nations.

10. The constitution

Alone in Europe, the history of the United Kingdom has been one of stability and security. We owe much of that to the strength and stability of our constitution – the institutions, laws and traditions that bind us together as a nation. Our constitution has been stable, but not static. It has been woven over the centuries – the product of hundreds of years of knowledge, experience and history. Radical changes that alter the whole character of our constitutional balance could unravel what generations of our predecessors have created. To preserve that stability in future – and the freedoms and rights of our citizens – we need to continue a process of evolution, not revolution.

Conservatives embrace evolutionary change that solves real problems and improves the way our constitution works. In recent years we have opened up government, devolved power and accountability, and introduced reforms to make Parliament work more effectively. It is that evolutionary process that we are committed to continue.

Open, accountable government

In recent years we have taken significant steps to open up government to public scrutiny, and give individuals more information to hold government and public services to account.

- We have introduced a code on access to government information, policed by the Ombudsman.
- We have published information on the workings of government previously held secret – including the composition of Cabinet Committees, and the structure of the Security and Intelligence Services.
- We have introduced a new Civil Service Code, and reformed the process for public appointments.
- We are pledged to legislate on the commitments in our 1993 White Paper on Open Government, including a statutory right of access by citizens to personal records held about them by the government and other public authorities.
- And we have set up the Nolan Committee and have implemented its proposals to ensure that the highest standards are maintained in public life. But our reforms go even wider than that.
- We have transferred power from central bureaucracies to local organisations such as school governors and hospital trusts.
- We have introduced the Citizen's Charter.
- We have also required them to publish information on their performance – information which enables the local community to keep a check on standards and apply pressure where needed.

Wherever possible, we are widening competition and choice in public services. Regional government would be a dangerously centralising measure – taking power away from elected local authorities. We wish to go in the opposite direction, shifting power to the local neighbourhood – for example, by giving more power to parish councils.

Parliament

Parliament – alongside the Crown and our legal system – is one of the three key institutions that uphold our constitution. The supremacy of Parliament is fundamental to our democracy, and the guarantee of our freedoms. The last 17 years have seen many changes to strengthen Parliament and make it more effective – the flourishing of Select Committees, new procedures to scrutinise European legislation, reform of Parliament's working day, and a budget that brings together tax and spending. We have therefore already done much to improve the way Parliament works and will do more. We have accepted the proposal from the Public Service Select Committee and put before the House of Commons a clear new statement of the principles underlying ministerial accountability to Parliament. All these developments have made Parliament open to the citizen, and the government more accountable. In the next session of Parliament we will continue this careful reform.

To give Parliament more time to consider legislation thoroughly we will extend the Queen's Speech to cover not only legislation for the immediate year but also provisional plans for legislation in the year after that. This will mean that more draft bills will be subject to public scrutiny before they reach the floor of the House of Commons. It will give Select Committees more time to take evidence and report. And this should also mean better legislation. We do not believe there is a case for more radical reform that would undermine the House of Commons.

A new Bill of Rights, for example, would risk transferring power away from Parliament to legal courts – undermining the democratic supremacy of Parliament as representatives of the people. Whilst this may be a necessary check in other countries which depend upon more formalised written constitutions, we do not believe it is appropriate to the UK. Nor do we favour changes in the system of voting in parliamentary elections that would break the link between an individual Member of Parliament and his constituents. A system of proportional representation would be more likely to produce unstable, coalition governments that are unable to provide effective leadership – with crucial decisions being dependent on compromise deals hammered out behind closed doors. This is not the British way. We have demonstrated we are not against change where it is practical and beneficial. But fundamental changes which have not been fully thought through – such as Opposition proposals on the House of Lords – would be extremely damaging. We will oppose change for change's sake.

The Union

The Union between Scotland, Wales, Northern Ireland and England underpins our nation's stability. The Conservative commitment to the United Kingdom does not mean ignoring the distinctive individuality of the different nations. On the contrary, we have gone further in recognising that diversity than any previous government. We are publishing separate manifestos for Wales and Scotland. While preserving the role of parliament at the centre of the Union, we have given new powers to the Scottish Grand

Committee and Welsh Grand Committee – enabling Scottish and Welsh MPs to call Ministers to account and debate legislation which affects those countries – something that would be impossible with separate Assemblies.

For the first time, Welsh Members of Parliament can ask their questions to Ministers in Welsh in Wales. Most recently we have similarly extended the basic powers of the Northern Ireland Grand Committee. We believe this is the right way to go. By contrast, the development of new assemblies in Scotland and Wales would create strains which could well pull apart the Union. That would create a new layer of government, which would be hungry for power. It would risk rivalry and conflict between these parliaments or assemblies and the Parliament at Westminster. And it would raise serious questions about whether the representation of Scottish and Welsh MPs at Westminster – and their role in matters affecting English affairs – could remain unchanged. Nor do we believe it would be in the interests of the Scottish or Welsh people. A Scottish tax-raising parliament, for example, could well affect the choice of where new investment locates in the United Kingdom.

In a world where people want security, nothing would be more dangerous than to unravel a constitution that binds our nation together and the institutions that bring us stability. We will continue to fight for the strength and diversity that benefit all of us as a proud union of nations.

Northern Ireland

While we cherish the Union and Northern Ireland's place within it, we recognise that there exist within the Province special circumstances which require further action to be taken. After a quarter of a century we wish to see the unique and originally temporary system of direct rule ended and a successful restoration of local accountable democracy achieved. We want to see this brought about in a form which carries the broadest agreement possible. And we want to see the rights, traditions and interests of all parts of the community recognised within any such agreement. We will accordingly continue to pursue a policy of dialogue and negotiation with and between the democratic Northern Ireland parties. We will continue to underpin such negotiations with the guarantee that the constitutional position of Northern Ireland cannot and will not be changed without the broad consent of the people of Northern Ireland. At the same time we will continue to take whatever security measures are required to protect the people of Northern Ireland from those who seek to achieve their political goals by violent means. We seek peace. But we will never be swayed by terrorist violence nor will we ever compromise our principles with those who seek to overthrow the rule of law by force.

A choice of two futures

At this election the British people face a stark choice. A choice of two futures. They can elect to continue down the road of success and achievement. An opportunity that has been hard won by the efforts and sacrifices of the British people. An opportunity that has only come about because successive Conservative governments have been determined to face up to the long-term problems facing Britain, and take the tough steps needed to arrest our slow decline. Or they can elect to take a huge risk with that future – the future of themselves, their children, their nation – by handing over the government of the country to politicians who have fought, opposed and denigrated every step that has been taken to restore Britain's economic health and standing in the world.

Politicians whose own declared policies would burden the United Kingdom with new spending and taxation, new regulations, and new threats to the stability and sovereignty of the nation itself. You can only be sure with the Conservatives.

Our vision for Britain: 25 pledges for the nation

The Enterprise Centre of Europe

- TAX AND SPENDING. Keep tight control of public spending priorities, aiming for our target of a 20p basic rate of income tax over the next Parliament.
- PRICES AND MORTGAGES. Stick to the policies which have delivered the lowest inflation levels and mortgage rates for a generation, meeting our inflation target of 2.5 % or less.
- JOBS. Protect jobs by keeping Britain out of the European Social Chapter; build on our record of falling unemployment; and help get the long-term unemployed back to work – including by requiring those on benefit for some time to undertake work experience on a community project.
- ENTERPRISE. Support growth and investment by keeping Britain the lowest tax major economy in Europe, pursuing Britain's global trade opportunities and curbing unnecessary regulations.
- SMALL BUSINESS. Reform business rates to help small businesses.
- THE FUTURE. Keep Britain ahead in the technology of the future, encouraging new entertainment and information services, and using the Millennium Lottery Fund to give people access to new computers and information links in schools, libraries, and other public places.

Opportunity and ownership for individuals and families

- HELP FOR FAMILIES. Give priority to reducing tax bills for families looking after dependent children or relatives by allowing one partner's unused personal allowance to be transferred to a working spouse where they have these responsibilities.
- HELP FOR CARERS. Help family members with heavy responsibilities caring for a relative to take a much needed break through a new Respite Care Programme.
- OWNERSHIP. Encourage schemes that help employees build a shareholding in the company they work for, alongside tax benefits for other savings schemes.
- PENSIONS. Transform pensions by providing all young people entering the workforce with a personal pension fund paid for by a rebate on their National Insurance contributions, while maintaining a state pension guarantee.
- CARE IN OLD AGE. Make it easier for people to afford the cost of care in old age without giving up their house and savings.
- SCHOOL STANDARDS. Guarantee school standards by intervening directly to raise standards where schools or local education authorities are letting children down.

- SCHOOL CHOICE. Widen choice and diversity in schools, with more freedom for schools to develop their own character, more specialist schools, and a grammar school in every town where parents want that choice. We will also maintain our nursery voucher scheme offering a choice of places for parents of all 4 year olds.

World class health and public services

- NHS FUNDING PLEDGE. Continue, year by year, to increase the real resources committed to the NHS, so NHS spending will continue to share in a growing economy.
- FAMILY DOCTORS. Enable all family doctors to provide a wider range of services in their surgeries and in practice-based cottage hospitals – offering faster and more local treatment.
- CITIZEN'S CHARTER. Continue to improve the standards and value for money of Britain's public services, giving those who use them more information and, where possible, wider choice.
- ESSENTIAL SERVICES. Introduce measures to protect the public against strikes that cause excessive disruption to essential services.

A safe and civil society

- PUBLIC SAFETY. Support local police schemes to crack down on petty crime, and continue our funding for the installation of TV security cameras in town centres and public places that want them throughout the next Parliament.
- JUVENILE CRIME. Give the courts power to impose speedy sanctions on youngsters, including an element of reparation to the victim; and continue our war against drugs.
- PERSISTENT CRIMINALS. Ensure persistent house burglars and dealers in hard drugs receive mandatory minimum prison sentences.

A confident, united and sovereign nation

- QUALITY OF LIFE. Continue the renaissance of our towns and cities, in particular harnessing private capital to regenerate the worst public housing estates; continue to protect our countryside and heritage; and use the National Lottery to help promote British sports, arts and culture.
- THE ENVIRONMENT. Maintain our international leadership role in protecting the environment, and continue improving air and water quality at home alongside effective conservation of our wildlife.
- THE NATION. Maintain the unity of the United Kingdom and preserve the stability of the Nation through an evolutionary – rather than revolutionary – approach to constitutional change.
- EUROPE. Seek a partnership of nation states in Europe, and not allow Britain to be part of a federal European state.
- THE POUND. Guarantee that Britain will not join a single currency in the next parliament unless the British people give their express approval in a referendum.

INDEX

Printed in Great Britain
by Amazon